ARABIC   ASTRONOMY   BANKING   BEE-KEEPING   BIOLOGY
ANISATION   CALCULUS   CANASTA   CARPENTRY   CHEMISTRY
COMMERCIAL CORRESPONDENCE   COMMERCIAL TRAVELLING   TO
KING   CRICKET   DRAWING   DRESSMAKING   DUTCH   DUTTON
ELECTRICITY IN THE HOUSE   ELOCUTIONIST   EMBROIDERY
ENGLISH RENASCENCE TO THE ROMANTIC REVIVAL   ROMANTIC
EVERYDAY FRENCH   TO EXPRESS YOURSELF   FISHING   TO FLY
SE BOOK   GARDENING   GAS IN THE HOUSE   GEOGRAPHY OF
ONARY   GERMAN GRAMMAR   GERMAN PHRASE BOOK   GOLF
GOOD FARM ACCOUNTING   GOOD FARM CROPS   GOOD FARMING
IT FARMING   GOOD GRASSLAND   GOOD AND HEALTHY ANIMALS
GOOD POULTRY KEEPING   GOOD SHEEP FARMING   GOOD SOIL
LE   HINDUSTANI   HISTORY: ABRAHAM LINCOLN ALEXANDER THE
AU CONSTANTINE COOK CRANMER ERASMUS GLADSTONE AND
MILTON PERICLES PETER THE GREAT PUSHKIN RALEIGH RICHELIEU
ODROW ... EMENT
LIAN   LETTER
ENGIN   ANICS
ODERN   ORING
HILOSO   HYSICS
PLUMBI   UBLIC
RECKO   USSIAN

···· AND HE WILL BE
YET WISER *Proverbs 9.9*

: ITS N... AND PURPOSE   SOCCER   SPANISH   SPE... AND
SWA... SWEDISH   TEACHING   THINKING   TRIG... METRY
BRITISH RAILWAYS FOR BOYS   CAMPING FOR BOYS AND GIRLS
FOR GIRLS   MODELMAKING FOR BOYS   NEEDLEWORK FOR GIRLS
OYS AND GIRLS   SAILING AND SMALL BOATS FOR BOYS AND GIRLS
ORK FOR BOYS   ADVERTISING & PUBLICITY   ALGEBRA   AMATEUR
ING   BIOLOGY   BOOK-KEEPING   BRICKWORK   BRINGING UP
NTRY   CHEMISTRY   CHESS   CHINESE   COMMERCIAL ARITHMETIC
TRAVELLING   TO COMPOSE MUSIC   CONSTRUCTIONAL DETAILS
NG   DUTCH   DUTTON SPEEDWORDS   ECONOMIC GEOGRAPHY
ST   EMBROIDERY   ENGLISH GRAMMAR   LITERARY APPRECIATION
VAL   ROMANTIC REVIVAL   VICTORIAN AGE   CONTEMPORARY
FISHING   TO FLY   FREELANCE WRITING   FRENCH   FRENCH
USE   GEOGRAPHY OF LIVING THINGS   GEOLOGY   GEOMETRY
ASE BOOK   GOLF   GOOD CONTROL OF INSECT PESTS   GOOD
FARM CROPS   GOOD FARMING   GOOD FARMING BY MACHINE
D   GOOD AND HEALTHY ANIMALS   GOOD MARKET GARDENING
GOOD SHEEP FARMING   GOOD SOI... ...LISH   GREEK
ORY: ABRAHAM LINCO... ...IVAR BOTHA
RANMER ERASMUS ... ...Y V JOAN OF
AT PUSHKIN RALEIG... ...AS JEFFERSON
HOME NURSING H... ...LD DOCTOR
URNALISM   LATIN ... ...ER   MALAY
ONENTS   WORKSHO... ...MECHANICAL
MORE GERMAN   M... ...OTOR CYCLING
APHY   PHYSICAL GEOGRAPHY   PHYSICS   PHYSIOLOGY   PITMAN'S
JESE   PSYCHOLOGY   PUBLIC ADMINISTRATION   PUBLIC SPEAKING

D1252874

THE TEACH YOURSELF BOOKS
EDITED BY LEONARD CUTTS

JAPANESE

**Uniform with this volume
and in the same
series**

Teach Yourself Afrikaans
Teach Yourself Arabic
Teach Yourself Chinese
Teach Yourself Danish
Teach Yourself Dutch
Teach Yourself English Grammar
Teach Yourself Esperanto
Teach Yourself Finnish
Teach Yourself French
Teach Yourself Everyday French
Teach Yourself French Phrase Book
Teach Yourself German
Teach Yourself More German
Teach Yourself German Phrase Book
Teach Yourself German Grammar
Teach Yourself Greek
Teach Yourself Hebrew
Teach Yourself Italian
Teach Yourself Italian Phrase Book
Teach Yourself Latin
Teach Yourself Malay
Teach Yourself Norwegian
Teach Yourself Polish
Teach Yourself Portuguese
Teach Yourself Russian
Teach Yourself Russian Phrase Book
Teach Yourself Spanish
Teach Yourself Spanish Phrase Book
Teach Yourself Everyday Spanish
Teach Yourself Swahili
Teach Yourself Swedish
Teach Yourself Turkish
Teach Yourself Urdu

TEACH YOURSELF

JAPANESE

By
C. J. DUNN, B.A.
and
S. YANADA, M.Econ. (Tokyo)

Lecturers in Japanese
at the School of Oriental and African Studies
University of London

THE ENGLISH UNIVERSITIES PRESS LTD
102 NEWGATE STREET,
LONDON E.C.1

First printed 1958

©
Copyright

The English Universities Press Ltd 1958

Printed in Great Britain for the English Universities Press Limited,
by Richard Clay and Company, Ltd., Bungay, Suffolk

PREFACE

JAPAN is a country with a long cultural tradition. Her works of art are famous throughout the world. She is also one of the leading industrial and trading nations, with a population of over eighty millions increasing by a million a year. Thus many people in the world are in contact with some aspect or other of her activity; yet outside of Japan and her former Empire, and those parts of North and South America where many Japanese have settled her language is known by only a few hundred people at the most. Without a wider knowledge of her language, appreciation of her rich culture must remain restricted. Business-men, too, would find great advantage in becoming familiar with Japanese, not only in their negotiations but also in the key it provides to the way the Japanese think.

The publishers and authors have collaborated with the Linguaphone Institute Ltd., 207, Regent Street, London, W.1., in producing a course of ten gramophone records using material from this book.

The authors wish to acknowledge their debt to Mr. F. J. Daniels, Reader in Japanese in the University of London, for the helpful criticism he has given them in the course of the preparation of the book, and for allowing them to use certain materials prepared by him for teaching Japanese at the School of Oriental and African Studies.

CONTENTS

INTRODUCTION

THE object of this book is to enable you to teach yourself to speak Japanese. The vocabulary and constructions used have been chosen to provide you with the essential minimum for saying whatever you are likely to want to say without going into technicalities in any special subject, with the possibility of increasing your vocabulary as your contact with Japanese increases.

The vocabulary of Japanese is derived from three sources. First, there is native Japanese, from which come most of the declinable and conjugable words, and others, such as particles, with a mainly grammatical function. Next, there are words borrowed from or modelled on Chinese during the last fifteen centuries, which form a large part of the total vocabulary, the situation being rather similar to that of English, with its dual vocabulary of native Anglo-Saxon words and massive Latin borrowings. The third source is modern borrowing, mainly from English; this forms, however, only a small part of the whole.

The purpose of this book being the teaching of spoken Japanese, we have restricted ourselves to romanized spelling. The writing of Japanese is a complicated study in itself, and unless you can master spoken Japanese you will not make any headway with the written language. We hope before long to produce a volume which will teach you how to read and write Japanese, using, as far as possible, the vocabulary and grammar of the present book. The romanized spelling that we have used is the *kunrei-siki* (system established by government) romanization of 1937. There is one other system in common use, known as the Hepburn system, and the difference between it and our spelling is set out in the Appendix. The roman alphabet, and its use for the writing of Japanese, is now taught to all children, and its use is increasing. However, the normal method of writing the language does not use an alphabet at all, but a combination of Chinese characters and a syllabary which can be written with one or other of two sets of symbols. Thus to a Japanese the elements of pronunciation are not so much consonants and vowels as combinations of these in syllables, which normally consist of a vowel or a consonant followed by a vowel. The basic syllables can be set out in the following table:

a	ka	sa	ta	na	ha	ma	ya	ra	wa
i	ki	si	ti	ni	hi	mi		ri	
u	ku	su	tu	nu	hu	mu	yu	ru	
e	ke	se	te	ne	he	me		re	
o	ko	so	to	no	ho	mo	yo	ro	

There are other syllables that are derived from these, either by the voicing of consonants—**ga** from **ka**, **za** from **sa**, etc.—or otherwise—**ba** and **pa** from **ha**, **kya** from **ki** + **ya**, etc. The complete list of syllables will be found in the Appendix. The only consonant that can be written in isolation in the Japanese script is **n**. This is the reason for the cumbersome way of reproducing foreign names, etc., which contain consonant groups. Thus **teeburu** is the transcription of " table " and **ekisutora** that of " extra ".

The Linguaphone Institute Ltd. has produced, with the collaboration of the authors and publishers, a set of ten records * that will teach you how to acquire a good pronunciation of Japanese. This is very difficult to acquire from a book, but in the following paragraphs we shall do our best to help you.

There are five basic vowels, **a, i, u, e, o.**

- **a** has a pronunciation similar to that of the first part of the diphthong in English " bite ", or the vowel in the French *chat*.
- **i** is like the vowel in English " beet ", with a length like that of the vowel in " bit ".
- **u** is similar to the vowel in English " put ", but with the lips not rounded but left slack.
- **e** is similar to the vowel in English " bed ".
- **o** is similar to the vowel in English " cot ", but with lips slightly more rounded.

* The recorded passages are as follows: Exercises 1 (I), 2 (I), 3 (I), 4 (I), 5 (I); Conversations I, II (1–16), III (1–12), IV (1–15), V (1–16, 1st line), VI (1–16, 1st line), VII (1–16, 1st line), VIII, IX, X, XII (i), (iii–viii).

When a vowel is repeated (as in **ryokoo**) the effect is to lengthen it to almost double the length of the single vowel. It is very important that you are careful to keep the distinction between long and short vowels, otherwise confusion will arise, cf. **tori**, " bird ", **toori**, " road ".

In diphthongs the basic vowels are given their normal value, the length of a diphthong being that of a long vowel. The pronunciation of **ei**, however, is often the same as that of **ee**.

Of the consonants, the following have a constant value, regardless of following vowels and other possible modifying factors: **k, d, b, p, m, y, r, w.**

k, d, b, p, m, y are very similar to the corresponding English consonants.

r is produced with the tongue in more or less the position of English " d " or " l " but there is no actual contact between it and the gum. It is not rolled.

w is pronounced with no rounding of the lips, which are left slack.

The following change their pronunciation according to various factors: **g, s, z, t, n, h.**

g is pronounced as in English " gate " at the beginning of a word, but elsewhere, including in the particle **ga,** it is pronounced like the " ng " in " singer ".

s before **a, u, e, o** is as in English " set "; before **i** it is like the " sh " in English " ship ".

z before **a, u, e, o** it is as in English " zoo "; before **i** it is as in English " jeer ".

t before **a, e, o** it is like the " t " in English " toe ", before **i** it is like the " ch " in English " cheer "; before **u** it is like the " ts " in " cats ".

n is pronounced as in English when it forms a syllable with a following vowel. When it is an independent consonant its pronunciation is influenced by the following sound. Before **s, z, t, d, n,** it is pronounced as in English, e.g., **sansei,** " consent "; **sanzen,** " three thousand "; **nanten,** " how many marks "; **sando,** " three times "; **nan no,** " of what ". Before **b, p, m,** its sound is **m,** e.g., **sanbun** " three parts "; **sanpun**

" three minutes "; **nanmai** " how many sheets (of paper) ".   Before **k**, **g**, it is like the " ng " of " singer ", e.g., **sankagetu**, " for three months "; **sangatu**, " March ".   In all other positions, i.e., before a vowel, before **y**, **r**, **w**, and in a final position, it has an indeterminate nasal sound; thus in **arimasen**, " is not ", one makes as if to pronounce it " arimaseng " but stops just before the completion of the sound.   The effect on the vowel preceding the **n** is to make it change to a nasalized vowel during its pronunciation.   It is not always possible to distinguish from the romanized spelling whether **n** forms a syllable with a following vowel; to overcome this difficulty it is usual to place a hyphen after **n** when it is an independent consonant followed by a vowel in the next syllable.   Thus in **zyuuni**, " twelve ", it is not independent and is pronounced as in English, **ni** being a syllable, but in **Zyun-iti**, a man's name, it is independent and is pronounced as explained above.

h is pronounced as in English before **a**, **i**, **e**, **o**, but before **u** is a bilabial " f ", made by forcing the breath through the lips, which are in position for the following **u**.

Most consonants can be followed by **y**, the two components being pronounced normally except in the case of **sy**, which is pronounced like " sh " in " sham ", **ty**, like " ch " in " char ", and **zy** like " j " in " jar ".

Double consonants are given twice the length of single ones.   This causes no difficulty in the case of **s**, **sy**, **n**, **m** (**nm**), for their sounds can be prolonged indefinitely, but in the case of **k**, **h**, **t**, **ty**, the mouth is placed in the position for pronouncing the consonant and is kept there momentarily before the sound is completed.

The English " f " and " v " are not in the Japanese sound system, but they occur in certain words borrowed from English, such as **fooku**, " fork ", and **terevizyon**, " television ".

The vowels **i** and **u** are devoiced, that is whispered, when they occur between two unvoiced consonants, or at the end of a sentence after an unvoiced consonant.   The unvoiced consonants are **k**, **s**, **t**, **h**, **p**.   Thus the final **-u** of the **-MASU** form of verbs is whispered—the effect is as if one extended the **s** sound; if the **-MASU** form is followed by **ga**, the influence of the **g** gives this **-u** its full pronunciation. If two vowels between unvoiced consonants occur in adjacent syllables the second is normally voiced, as in **utukusii**, " beautiful ", where **u** in the syllable **ku** is given its full pronunciation. The devoicing of **i** after **h**, as in **hito**, " man ", results in the **h** having a pronunciation similar to the " ch " in German *ich*, in which the tongue is in the same position as it would be for " y ", but the sound is whispered, not voiced.

There is virtually no stress used in the Japanese word— all syllables are pronounced with equal force and are given equal length. There is, however, a certain amount of stress used for the sake of emphasis, and cases where it occurs are mentioned in the lessons. There is some sentence intonation. Questions with or without a final **ka** are usually spoken with the last syllable at a slightly higher pitch than the rest of the sentence. The final particles **yo** and **ne** also have a higher pitch; **nee** has a falling pitch, **ne-** being higher than, and the final **-e** returning to, the pitch of the rest of the sentence. Interrogative words have a higher pitch on the first syllable.

The book has thirty lessons, the first twenty-nine of which are accompanied by exercises to help you practise what is set out in the lesson. Care should be taken to study the examples in the lessons, and compare them with the translations given, for points which the translation explains by itself are not necessarily mentioned elsewhere. The conversation pieces 1–6 are partly revision of the first twenty-nine lessons; 7–11 are there to give you further experience in the use of the grammar and vocabulary you have learned. Words will be found in the conversations which you have not seen before; here the glossary will be of assistance. Conversation 12 shows examples of the use of respect language, women's speech, familiar speech, etc., and gives you an idea of the range of variation possible in this complex language. However, it is not expected that you will yourself use what you see there; it will give you an idea of what you must expect to hear from others.

The glossary contains what we consider is a basic

vocabulary of Japanese; some of the words included may not have been used in the various parts of the book.

You are recommended to work through the first five lessons, then, as revision, to study the first conversation. You would be wise at this point to read the notes on pronunciation again. When you feel satisfied that you have mastered the first five lessons, move on to the next five, and so on till you reach Lesson 29, when Conversation 6 will be relevant. Conversations 7–11 should then be used for general revision. Finally, read through Lesson 30 and its conversation, and you should be equipped with what you need for maintaining a conversation on any non-technical subject.

LESSON 1

VERBS in Japanese have no special forms to show whether their subjects are singular or plural, or whether they are of the 1st (" I ", " we "), 2nd (" you ") or 3rd (" he ", etc.) person. They come at the end of a main clause, sometimes being followed by a word or words adding some emotional or other flavour, and also at the end of a subordinate clause, where they are followed, if at all, by a word indicating the relationship of the clause to the rest of the sentence. The subject of the verb is not necessarily expressed (compare the English 2nd person imperative, e.g., " Go! ").

The first verb you are confronted with in this book is **arimasu,** used here with the meaning of " is ", " are " (in a place), with a non-living subject; that is to say, it is not used in statements about *what* a thing is, nor where a *living creature* is. When **arimasu** has this meaning (it has others, as we shall see later), it is almost impossible for it to have a subject of other than the 3rd person. **Arimasu** thus means " It is (somewhere) ", " They are (somewhere) ", and it can form a complete sentence if *where* the thing is is known (e.g., in answer to the question " Is the book on the table? " you may say **Arimasu,** " It is "). Note that English normally has to supply a subject, such as " it ", " they ", " some ".

Verbs have tenses, that of **arimasu** indicating a present or future or " timeless " action or state. A " timeless " action or state is expressed in English by the present tense, as in " Tables have legs ". **Arimasu** ends with **-u**, and we shall call this form the **-U** form. We shall see later that all verbs in Japanese have this **-U** form, with the same implications of tense. We shall sometimes call it the " neutral " form.

Nouns are invariable for case and for number (there *are* one or two ways of showing that a noun is plural, but their use is limited). The relations of nouns to the rest of the sentence are shown by putting after them one or two of what

we shall call particles. Two such particles are **ga** and **ni**.
Ga indicates that the noun which it follows is the subject
of the verb in the clause, e.g., **pen ga arimasu**, " a pen is
(somewhere) ". There is no definite or indefinite article,
the circumstances in which they are used in English being
either clear from the context in Japanese or are brought
out by the use of different particles. A noun plus **ga** is
sometimes best rendered by the use of the indefinite article,
e.g., **hon ga**, " a book ", " books ", " some books "; **kami
ga**, " paper ", " some paper ".

Ni has many functions, one of the most important of
which is to show a relation of position, **Tookyoo ni**, " in
Tokyo ". It is used with the pronouns of position, **koko,
soko, asoko,** to form expressions equivalent to the English
" here ", " there (by you) ", and " there (over there, away
from you and me) ". Thus **koko ni arimasu** can be translated as " it is here ". Note that **ni** is generally used only
of position at a place, and not of motion towards a place.
The difference between **soko** and **asoko** is similar to that
between the Latin *iste* and *ille* and the Spanish *eso* and
aquel. **Soko** is " that place where you are or which you
have just mentioned " and **asoko** is " that place over there,
away from you and me, by him, her, them, which he, she
has, they have, just mentioned ". In practice, of course,
soko ni and **asoko ni** are rendered as " there "; the difficulty comes when one is speaking or composing in Japanese.

We have seen that **koko ni arimasu** can be translated
as " it is here ". If we wish to include the subject of the
sentence with the particle **ga**, its usual position is after the
adverbial expression **koko ni**. **Koko ni pen ga arimasu.**
This is best translated as " There is a pen here ", for English
tends to use the idiomatic " there is " in sentences of this
type. It is unusual to say " A pen is here ".

Vocabulary

Nouns

enpitu, pencil

hon, book

inki, ink

kami, paper

nooto, exercise-book

pen, pen

pin, pin

Tookyoo, Tokyo

Pronouns	*Verb*
asoko *over there*	**arimasu** (aru ; see Lesson 5)
koko *here*	
soko *there*	*Particles*
	ga
	ni

koko ni *here*
soko ni *there by you*
asoko ni *over there*

(Note that the meanings of words explained in the lessons are not necessarily given in the Vocabularies.)

Exercise 1

I. *Translate into English:* 1. Soko ni hon ga arimasu. 2. Asoko ni pin ga arimasu. 3. Koko ni arimasu. 4. Koko ni pen ga arimasu. 5. Kami ga arimasu. 6. Koko ni nooto ga arimasu. 7. Asoko ni enpitu ga arimasu. 8. Asoko ni arimasu. 9. Soko ni inki ga arimasu. 10. Soko ni arimasu.

II. *Translate into Japanese:* 1. There is an exercise-book here. 2. It is here. 3. There are some books over there. 4. There are some pencils here. 5. There are some there (by you). 6. There is some ink over there. 7. There is a pen. 8. There are pins there (by you). 9. They are over there. 10. There is some paper there (by you).

LESSON 2

QUESTIONS are asked by putting the particle **ka** at the end of the sentence, after the final verb, e.g., " Is there a book here? " **Koko ni hon ga arimasu ka.** It is not usual to write an interrogation mark after a sentence in this form, though it *is* commonly used when writing down a question whose nature is shown only by the intonation of the sentence, without the use of **ka.** Such sentences are used only in familiar conversation and are in fact rarely written down.

The interrogative pronoun " what " is represented by **nani.** Its work in the sentence is regulated in the same way as that of nouns. Thus we say **Asoko ni nani ga arimasu ka**—" What is there there? " in the same way as we say **Asoko ni hon ga arimasu.**

Consider the answer to **Asoko ni nani ga arimasu ka.**

over there   what   is
what is there over there
what it is over there
asoko ni arimasu
it is over there

In English it might be " There is a table " (**Teeburu ga arimasu**), or we might repeat the word " there " and say, " There is a table there ", stressing the word "table ". (Of course, all these nouns, and **nani**, might be plural, i.e., " What are there there? ", " There are tables there ", but from now on the possibly plural meaning will usually be taken for granted in the explanations of the lessons.) If we wish to make this repetition in our reply in Japanese, it is usual to add the particle **wa** to the word or phrase which is repeated. In this case, then, we should say **Asoko ni wa teeburu ga arimasu**. This is one of the more easily understood uses of **wa** and may be called its " echoing " function. It follows the particle **ni** in this sentence, but when added to the subject, **wa** follows the noun immediately and replaces **ga**. For example, in reply to the question " Where is the pin? " we might say " The pin is here "— **Pin wa koko ni arimasu**, although it is not necessary in either language to repeat the word **pin**. We can say " It is here "—**Koko ni arimasu**. If we do repeat it, however, the " echoing " **wa** is required. Notice that the use of **wa** with the subject brings with it a difference in word order from what we saw when the subject had **ga**. When the ingredients of a sentence are (*a*) noun + **ga**, (*b*) verb, and (*c*) adverb phrase, the order is generally (*c*), (*a*), (*b*), but if instead of (*a*) we have (*d*) noun + **wa**, the order, more often than not, is (*d*), (*c*), (*b*). One way of stating the difference between **Hon wa koko ni arimasu** and **Koko ni (wa) hon ga arimasu** is to say that the first would be said in answer to " Where is the book? " and the second to " What is here? "

Another use of **wa** is that following the subject of sentences which are not in reply to questions, and here a translation would often require " the " before the noun—

Teeburu wa koko ni arimasu ka. Is the table here?

We may call this the " isolating " function of **wa**, for it isolates, so to speak, the person or thing we are interested in from the rest of the world so that we may say something, or ask something, about it.

A useful rule which may help you when you are in doubt whether the subject of a sentence should be followed by **wa** or **ga** is that when the subject of a sentence is an interrogative word it is always followed by **ga** (**Nani ga arimasu ka**); in the answer to such a sentence the word corresponding to the interrogative word, if it is the subject, is followed by **ga** (**Teeburu ga arimasu**); if a sentence contains an interrogative word which is not the subject, then the subject, if expressed, will be followed by **wa**.

The particle **mo** corresponds often to " also ", " too ". **Mo** replaces **wa** or **ga** after a noun, but follows some other particles—

> **Hon mo arimasu.** There is a book too.
> **Koko ni mo hon ga arimasu.** There is a book here too (as well as in some other place).

English has a tendency to ambiguity in its positioning of " too " and " also ". " There is a book here too " may mean: (*a*) " There is a book as well as something else here ", or (*b*) " There is a book here as well as somewhere else ". In Japanese, however, **mo** is placed strictly after the word to which it refers. The corresponding sentence to (*a*) is **Koko ni hon mo arimasu** and to (*b*) is **Koko ni mo hon ga arimasu.** When, in a succession of nouns or pronouns, each is followed by **mo**, a convenient translation is " Both . . . and . . ."

> **Ringo mo orenzi mo arimasu.** There are both an apple and an orange.
> **Koko ni mo soko ni mo arimasu.** There are some both here and there.

Vocabulary

Nouns

bata, butter	**pan,** bread
fooku, fork	**ringo,** apple
isu, chair	**sara,** saucer, plate, dish
mado, window	**teeburu,** table
naihu, knife	**to,** door
orenzi, orange	**tyawan,** rice- or tea-bowl

charwan

Pronoun	*Particles*

nani   **ka**
                                  mo
                                  wa

Exercise 2

I. *Translate into English:* 1. Koko ni nani ga arimasu
ka. 2. Soko ni fooku ga arimasu. 3. Tyawan wa soko ni
arimasu. 4. Koko ni mo mado ga arimasu. 5. Ringo mo
koko ni arimasu. 6. Sara mo naihu mo soko ni arimasu.
7. Asoko ni nani ga arimasu ka. 8. Pan mo bata mo
arimasu. 9. Asoko ni isu mo arimasu ka. 10. To wa koko
ni arimasu.

II. *Translate into Japanese:* 1. There is some butter
here. 2. The window is here. 3. What is there over there?
4. Over there there is a table. 5. Both the apples and
the oranges are here. 6. What is there there (by you)?
7. Here there are some chairs. 8. There is a tea-cup (rice-
bowl) over there. 9. There is a door there (by you).
10. Is there a plate here?

LESSON 3

Arimasu is, as we have seen, the verb " is ", etc., in expressions involving the position of an inanimate subject;
to show position of an animate subject, i.e., of human
beings and other members of the animal kingdom, the
appropriate verb is **imasu**—

> **Kodomo wa niwa ni imasu ka.**   Is the child in the
> garden?
> **Koko ni musi ga imasu.**   There is an insect here.

as opposed to—

> **Koko ni teeburu ga arimasu.**

We saw in the last exercise how **nani** is used. **Dare,**
corresponding to " who ", is used in the same way—

> **Uti ni dare ga imasu ka.**   Who is at home?

The use of **doko** is similar, but note that it is equivalent to a noun and should be thought of as " what place ", " which place ", though it is used, of course, to translate " where ". Thus " Where are the children? " can be translated as **Kodomo wa doko ni imasu ka**, doko requiring after it the same **ni** as in **Kodomo wa niwa ni imasu ka**. Notice again what we said in the last lesson, that if any interrogative pronoun (such as **dare, doko, nani**) is used as the subject of a sentence it is followed by **ga** and not by **wa**—

> Niwa ni dare ga imasu ka.
> Soko ni nani ga arimasu ka.

whereas if the interrogative word is not the subject, the subject is followed by **wa**—

> Kodomo wa doko ni imasu ka.

Corresponding to the demonstrative adjectives in " this book ", " that child ", are **ano, kono, sono**. As you will expect from what you have learned of **asoko, koko, soko**, the adjective **kono** equals " this ", **sono**, " that (connected with you) ", and **ano,** " that (away from both you and me) ". These words give no difficulty, for they are invariable and placed before the noun they qualify. **Kono teeburu,** " this table "; **sono kodomo,** " that child (near you) "; **ano hito,** " that person ". It is convenient to call them demonstrative adjectives in Japanese also, although they differ in their grammatical usage from other adjectives. Notice, however, that they are adjectives only, and cannot be used as pronouns. Do not be led astray by English, in which the corresponding demonstrative adjective and pronoun have the same form.

As Japanese verbs do not necessarily require their subject to be expressed, it follows that the use of personal pronouns, or what pass for personal pronouns in Japanese, as the subject of a sentence is much less frequent than in English, and the same is true of these pronouns used in other parts of the sentence, e.g., as the object. In Japanese the tendency is to use them only when it is necessary for clarity, and generally the context or the form of utterance

makes it obvious who it is one is talking about. If you
imagine a telephone conversation in which the person you
are talking to asks where you are (**Doko ni imasu ka**),
your reply could be **Uti ni imasu**—" I am at home ";
if he asked who would be at home this evening, the reply
might be **Watasi ga imasu, watasi** equalling " I ". In this
case you must obviously use the personal pronoun, or you
will not be able to answer the question.

The 2nd person pronoun is **anata,** but this is even less
used than **watasi,** for it is customary to address the person
to whom one is speaking by his name or title. (The Japanese
have two names, a family name and a given name, and use
them in that order, e.g., **Miki Santaroo,** where **Miki** is the
family name. When using English, the Japanese usually
put their names in the Western order, **Santaroo Miki,** but
they never do so in their own language. One may address
or speak of a Japanese either by his family name or his
given name, according to one's degree of acquaintance with
him, but to either the suffix **-san** must be added. This is
comparable to " Mr.", " Mrs.", or " Miss ".) However,
anata exists, and you can quite correctly say for—

Where are you?—**Anata wa doko ni imasu ka.**

" He " or " she " is **ano hito,** " that person ", with the
possibility of using **kono hito** or **sono hito** in appropriate
circumstances—

Ano hito wa doko ni imasu ka—" Where is he (she)? "

If, for example, your secretary brought in somebody's
card to you, and you wanted to ask where the person was
at the moment, you might say, looking at the card, **Kono
hito wa doko ni imasu ka ;** if the secretary announced
verbally that the person was waiting, you might ask, **Sono
hito wa doko ni imasu ka.** In the former case you might
use **kono** because the man is momentarily identified with his
card, which you hold in your hand; in the latter, **sono**
might be used because the second person (the secretary)
has just mentioned him, who thus enters, as it were, into
her orbit.

These personal pronouns (**watasi, anata, ano hito**) are
unusual in that they almost always apply to the singular

only, and have plural forms ending in **-tati** (**watasitati, anatatati, ano hitotati**).

Vocabulary

Nouns

Eikoku, Great Britain, England
heya, room
hito, person
hitotati, persons, people
inu, dog
kodomo, child
musi, insect
neko, cat
Nippon (Nihon), Japan
niwa, garden
Rondon, London
sakana, fish
tomodati, friend
tori, bird
uti, inside, home, house

Pronouns

anata
anatatati
dare
doko
watasi
watasitati

Adjectives

ano
kono
sono

Verb

imasu (iru ; see Lesson 5)

Suffixes

-san
-tati

Exercise 3

I. *Translate into English:* 1. Kodomo wa doko ni imasu ka. Uti ni imasu. 2. Ano heya ni dare ga imasu ka. Kodomo ga imasu. 3. Kono niwa ni tori mo musi mo imasu. 4. Anata wa doko ni imasu ka. 5. Watasi wa Rondon ni imasu. 6. Soko ni sakana ga imasu ka. 7. Rondon wa Eikoku ni arimasu. 8. Rondon ni tomodati ga imasu ka. Rondon ni wa Miki-san ga imasu. 9. Sono hitotati wa Tookyoo ni imasu. 10. Nippon ni mo inu mo neko mo imasu.

II. *Translate into Japanese:* 1. Are you in the garden? 2. Is he in London? 3. The children are here. 4. There is a fish here. 5. The cat is over there. 6. There is a cat there too (by you). 7. There are children in this room. 8. What is there in that room? There is a dog. 9. They are at home. 10. There are people in the garden too. 11. There are cats both in England and Japan. 12. Are there birds in London too? 13. In London there are both birds and insects. 14. Where is Mr. Miki? In England. 15. Who is (there) in Tokyo? A friend.

LESSON 4

THE particle that is used to indicate possession is **no**; thus **Ueda-san no niwa** is equivalent to " Mr. Ueda's garden " or " the garden of Mr. Ueda ". In this case, then, **no** corresponds either to the preposition " of " or to the " 's " of the genitive case. Where English uses " possessive adjectives " (" my ", " your ", etc.), Japanese uses the personal pronoun followed by **no. Watasi no teeburu,** " my table "; **anata no pen,** " your pen "; **ano hitotati no hon,** " their book ". You should pay particular attention to the order of words in such phrases, for although the position of **no** after the noun to which it refers is no different from that of other particles, there is a tendency for English students to make the mistake of reversing the order, and hence the meaning. Remember that **no** takes the same position as " 's " after the word indicating the possessor. Another point that causes difficulty is that **no** is used to connect two nouns in cases where in English a preposition of position is used. In English we can say " the chair in the garden ", but in Japanese it is necessary to use either the equivalent of " the chair which is in the garden " or **niwa no isu.** It is not possible to use the particle **ni** or any other particle denoting position, to connect two nouns.

No performs another useful function in the construction of adverbial phrases with " nouns " of position. **Ue** is the upper part of, or the space over, something; **sita** is the lower part of, or the place under, something; **naka** is the middle or interior; **mae** is the front part, or position in front; **usiro** is the back part or position behind. As these act as nouns, they have to be followed by the appropriate particle or particles to fit them into the sentence. Thus **teeburu no ue** is the top part of the table, or the space above the table; **heya no naka ni,** " in the room "; **anata no**

sita no hitotati, " people below you, under you (either in space or in rank, etc.) ". Note that **doko** can be used in similar phrases to ask whereabouts on something or some-one something is—

Hon-dana wa heya no doko ni arimasu ka. Where-abouts in the room is the bookshelf?

The verb " be " covers considerable ground in English, and we have already seen two verbs, **arimasu** and **imasu,** that are used to translate it into Japanese. There is a third which is equivalent to the verb " be " in such expressions as " this book is a novel ", where it marks the identity of something with something else. The Japanese verb used here is **desu.** A notable point with regard to this verb is that the noun preceding it needs no particle after it. Thus " this book is a novel " is **kono hon wa syoosetu desu ;** " it is a dictionary ", **zibiki desu.** It is unfortunately rarely that one is able to formulate a precise rule of Japan-ese grammar, but you can, and must, remember that the noun or noun-equivalent that comes immediately before **desu,** or a form derived from **desu,** is never followed by a particle.

You have learnt that **nani** is the interrogative pronoun equivalent to " what ". It takes the form **nan** before a word starting with **n** or **d. Nan desu ka**—" What is it "? **nan no,** " of what ", etc., but **nani ga arimasu ka.**

Corresponding to the demonstrative adjectives **kono, sono, ano,** there are demonstrative pronouns **kore, sore, are,** equivalent respectively to " this ", " that (by you) ", and " that (over there) ". Being pronouns, they have to be used with the necessary particles—

Kore wa pen desu. This is a pen.
Sore wa nan desu ka. What is that (by you)?

Vocabulary

Nouns	
atama, head	**gakkoo,** school
boosi, hat, cap	**gakusei,** student
Eigo, English (language)	**hako,** box
	hikidasi, drawer

Nouns

hon-dana, bookshelf
huku, suit, dress, clothes
mae
naka
Nihongo, Japanese (lan-
    guage)
sensei, teacher
sita
sutekki, walking-stick
syasin, photograph
syoosetu, novel
tosyokan, library
ue

usiro
zibiki, dictionary

Pronouns

are
kore
sore
nan

Verb

desu (da ; see Lesson 5)

Particle

no

Exercise 4

I. *Translate into English:* 1. Hon-dana no ue ni mo zibiki ga arimasu. 2. Are mo anata no boosi desu ka. 3. Kore wa gakkoo no tosyokan no syasin desu. 4. Hako no sita ni naihu ga arimasu. 5. Sensei mo gakusei mo heya no naka ni imasu ka. 6. Are wa dare no huku desu ka. Watasi no huku desu. 7. Mado no mae ni neko ga imasu. 8. Enpitu wa hikidasi no doko ni arimasu ka. 9. Ano hito wa nan no gakusei desu ka. Nihongo no gakusei desu. 10. Isu no usiro ni ano hito no sutekki ga arimasu. 11. Sore wa nan desu ka. Kore wa Eigo no syoosetu desu. 12. Ano hito no atama no ue ni nani ga arimasu ka. Boosi ga arimasu.

II. *Translate into Japanese:* 1. The dictionary is in front of the box. 2. Is this a Japanese novel (i.e., written in Japanese)? 3. What is that a photograph of? 4. That is a photograph of a school. 5. There is a pen under the book. 6. There is a hat on your head. 7. Is this Mr. Ueda's stick? 8. Is that a Japanese school (i.e., school of the Japanese language)? 9. Whereabouts in the room is the dictionary? 10. Whose book-shelf is that (by you)? 11. There is a table in front of the window. 12. Is my suit in the drawer? 13. This dictionary is in the school library too. 14. There is a bird behind the box. 15. Both the teacher and the student are in front of the door.

LESSON 5

Of the verbs that you have seen up to now, **arimasu** and **imasu** both end in **-masu,** and this is no coincidence, for **-masu** is an ending that can be applied to all verbs (except **desu,** which is the one exception). It is the ending used with the main verb of a sentence in normal polite conversation, as you have seen in **arimasu** and **imasu,** and **desu** may also be called an " irregular **-MASU** form ", for it is used in the same circumstances.

When you use Japanese dictionaries, you will find that verbs are not listed in their **-MASU** form, but in another, which is sometimes known as the " dictionary form ". The " dictionary " form of **arimasu** is **aru,** and that of **imasu** is **iru.** These two verbs represent the two " regular " types of verb that are found, and there are a few " irregular " verbs which you will learn as you go along; one of these is **desu,** of which the dictionary form is **da.** We shall call the two types **-U** verbs and **-RU** verbs, because these may be thought of as the removable ending of the dictionary form. Thus **aru** is a **-U** verb; to find its **-MASU** form, you cut off the final **-u** of the dictionary form and add **-imasu.** **Iru** is a **-RU** verb; to find its **-MASU** form you cut off **-ru** from the dictionary form and add **-masu.** You cannot always discover by merely looking at the dictionary form of a verb to which class it belongs, but all **-RU** verbs end in **-iru** or **-eru,** although some **-U** verbs end in **-iru** or **-eru ;** to put it another way, all verbs not ending **-iru** or **-eru** in their dictionary forms are **-U** verbs, and verbs ending in **-iru** or **-eru** may belong to either class. In the latter case you will have to rely on memory. There follow two lists which will show the formation of the **-MASU** form and at the same time increase your vocabulary.

I. *-RU verbs.*

Dictionary form	*-MASU form*
miru	mimasu
taberu	tabemasu

II. *-U verbs.*

Dictionary form	*-MASU form*
kaku	kakimasu
kagu	kagimasu
kasu	kasimasu
matu	matimasu
sinu	sinimasu
arau	araimasu
yobu	yobimasu
yomu	yomimasu
uru	urimasu

(This list of **-U** verbs includes examples of all possible sounds preceding the final **-u**, so that you now have an idea of what Japanese verbs look like.)

We have said that the **-MASU** form is used for the main verb of a sentence; in constructions where a verb occurs in the middle of a sentence, i.e., where it is a subordinate verb, what we shall call the " plain form " is used. The dictionary form is the **-U** form (or present tense) of the plain form. We shall now introduce a construction which will give you practice in these plain forms. The expression **tumori desu** at the end of a sentence can be translated by " (I) intend to . . .". It is preceded by the dictionary form of the verb. Thus if you were discussing plans for the afternoon, and you said " I intend to be at home ", the Japanese would be **Uti ni iru tumori desu.**

The particle that is used after a noun to show that it is the direct object of a verb is **o**. Like **ga**, **o** is replaced by **wa** and **mo** in appropriate sentences—

Syoosetu o yomimasu ka.   Do you read novels?
Tegami o kaku tumori desu.   I intend to write a letter.
Inu mo arau tumori desu.   I intend to wash the dog, too.
Miki-san o matu tumori desu.   I intend to wait for Mr. Miki.

Notice that whereas the verb " wait " is followed by " for " in English, the object of **matu** is followed by **o**.

On the other hand, " meet " is transitive in English, but the Japanese equivalent **aimasu** (dictionary form **au**) requires **ni** after the noun.

> **Tanaka-san ni au tumori desu ka.** Do you intend to meet Mr. Tanaka?

A further particle, **de,** has two uses that can be introduced here. The first can be called " instrumental ", and be translated as " with " or " by "—

> **Pen de kakimasu.** I write with a pen.
> **Watasi wa isya o denwa de yobimasu.** *Or* **Watasi wa denwa de isya o yobimasu.** I call a doctor by phone.

The former shows the normal sentence order, while the latter puts a little more emphasis on the fact that it is by telephone that you call a doctor. Of course, if the object of the verb has already been mentioned in the conversation, there is no necessity to express it again.

The second use of **de** is that of expressing " action in a place "—

> **Niwa de inu o araimasu.** I wash the dog in the garden.

This **de** is usually translated as " in " or " at ". Remember that verbs of being, and some similar verbs referring to a state rather than an action, require **ni** with the noun showing where the being, etc., is (**Tookyoo ni imasu**), whereas the noun showing the place where some action is performed is followed by **de.**

Vocabulary

Nouns

basu, bus
denwa, telephone
e, picture, drawing, painting
eki, station
hasi, chopstick
hude, writing-brush
isya, physician, doctor

kimono, clothes, Japanese dress
megane, spectacles
mise, shop, store
mizu, water
niku, flesh, meat
sinbun, newspaper
tegami, letter

Nouns

tumori, intention
zassi, magazine, periodical
zi, character, letter (of alphabet, etc.)

Verbs

arau, wash
au, meet
kagu, smell
kaku, write, draw
kasu, lend, let (room, etc.)
matu, wait for

miru, see, look at
sinu, die
taberu, eat
uru, sell
yobu, call, invite
yomu, read

Particles

de
o

Suffix

-masu

Exercise 5

I. *Translate into English:* 1. Kono neko wa sakana o tabemasu ka. 2. Zassi mo kasimasu. 3. Sono kimono mo urimasu ka. 4. Nani o kagu tumori desu ka. 5. Hasi mo tyawan mo mizu de araimasu. 6. Anata mo basu o matu tumori desu ka. 7. Kono megane de musi o miru tumori desu. 8. Kono hude de zi mo e mo kakimasu. 9. Sinbun mo zassi mo yomu tumori desu. 10. Mise ni iru tumori desu. 11. Isya o yobu tumori desu ka. 12. Tee-buru no ue no ringo o taberu tumori desu. 13. Eki de Tanaka-san ni aimasu. 14. Watasi wa Eikoku de sinu tumori desu. 15. Doko de niku o uru tumori desu ka.

II. *Translate into Japanese:* 1. I intend to read a book in that room. 2. Do you lend sticks too? 3. I intend to look at the picture with these glasses. 4. Who is going to smell? 5. Those students write characters. 6. He sells newspapers in that shop. 7. They eat both meat and fish with chop-sticks. 8. I intend to look at some photographs of Japan. 9. Do you intend to call your friend by telephone? 10. Where do you wash dishes? 11. Will you wait at the station too? 12. Cats die in water. 13. I shall meet the teacher at the library. 14. I intend to write letters in the garden. 15. Do you intend to wash this kimono too?

LESSON 6

HERE are more lists of verbs, giving in this case their dictionary and -MASU forms and also what we shall call their -TE form. We shall explain some of the functions of this form later in this lesson, so you should now concentrate on how to find the -TE form from the dictionary form. You will see that there is no difficulty in the case of -RU verbs, in which -te replaces -ru, but that with -U verbs the -TE form depends upon the sound which precedes the final -u; however, the list gives you examples of all types, so that, with these as models, you can find the -TE form of any verb. We have also taken the opportunity of listing some " irregular " verbs.

I. -RU verbs.

Dictionary form	-TE form	-MASU form
otiru	otite	otimasu
deru	dete	demasu

II. -U verbs.

Dictionary form	-TE form	-MASU form
aku	aite	akimasu
oyogu	oyoide	oyogimasu
kurasu	kurasite	kurasimasu
tatu	tatte	tatimasu
sinu	sinde	sinimasu
tigau	tigatte	tigaimasu
narabu	narande	narabimasu
sumu	sunde	sumimasu
huru	hutte	hurimasu

III. " Irregular " verbs

Dictionary form	-TE form	-MASU form
da	de	desu
iku	itte	ikimasu
kuru	kite	kimasu
suru	site	simasu
yuu	itte	iimasu

Before we go on to discuss the uses of the **-TE** form, it will be convenient here to introduce two more particles, commonly used with verbs of motion, **e** and **kara**. **E** can be translated by " to " in the sense of motion towards (i.e., it is not used of giving " to ", etc.)—

> **Rondon e ikimasu.**   I go to London.
> **Naka e hairimasu.**   I go inside.

Kara is " from "—

> **Ano hito wa doko kara kimasu ka.**   Where does he come from?

By adding the verb **iru** to the **-TE** form of another verb, a new tense is formed. Note that when **iru** is used in this way as an auxiliary verb, it can have any subject, animate or inanimate, as distinct from its use as a main verb, when its subject must be animate.

The **-TE IRU** form, as we shall call it, has three possible interpretations.

A. *It can describe an action or state which is going on at the time.*

> **Te o aratte imasu.**   He is washing his hands.
> **Ame ga hutte imasu.**   It is raining.   (Rain is falling.)
> **Basu o matte imasu.**   I am waiting for the bus.
> **Ano hito wa nani o site imasu ka.**   What is he doing?

B. *It can describe a state resulting from an action.*

> **Amerika e itte imasu.**   He (has gone to and) is in America.
> **Hoteru no naka e haitte imasu.**   He (has entered and) is in the hotel.
> **Hi ga dete imasu.**   The sun (has come out and) is out.
> **Pen wa hako no naka e otite imasu.**   The pen has fallen into the box (and is still there).
> **Sora wa harete imasu.**   The sky is clear.
> **Neko wa sinde imasu.**   The cat is dead.

C. *It can show habitual action.*

> **Uti no kodomo wa gakkoo e itte imasu.**

Taken out of its context, this sentence is capable of being translated in two ways (**uti no kodomo,** " the child at home ", i.e., " my (our) child ").

(a) Our child has gone to school.
(b) Our child goes to school (as a regular thing).

If the correct translation, according to the context, is (b), then **-TE IRU** is being used in accordance with C.

It is impossible to give rules about which translation any **-TE IRU** verb will require in any one sentence. The third use (C) mentioned above can apply to almost any verb, and is often used in sentences containing some such word as " every morning ", " always ", etc.

The second translation (B) is often appropriate with verbs of motion, in particular with those that imply arrival somewhere, such as **iku, kuru, hairu, deru, otiru,** and with verbs that describe a change from one state to another, such as **sinu, hareru.** The translation of this use is not always easy. In cases where it is possible to use some such expression as " is dead ", " is in ", " is out ", " is clear ", the full implication of the Japanese seems to be expressed. However, " He is in America " does not quite translate the whole of the implication of **Amerika e itte imasu** and sometimes " He has gone to America " will be more appropriate. There seems no good alternative for " It has fallen into the box " as a translation of **Hako no naka e otite imasu,** except that, once again, " It is in the box " might be enough if one knows that the object has fallen, but doesn't know where it has fallen to. (See p. 86.)

Of the verbs that you have met up to now, **otiru, deru, hairu, aku, tatu, sinu, tigau, narabu, iku, kuru** have a **-TE IRU** form which (ignoring the " habitual " meaning, which, as we have said, is applicable to any verb) describes the result of an action (B), i.e., " has fallen ", " is out ", " is in ", " is open ", " (has stood up and) is standing ", " is dead ", " is different ", " is in line ", " (has gone and) is ", " (has come and) is ", although **tigatte iru** is, as it happens, extremely rare. None of them can refer to a continuing action. All other verbs that you have seen (except **aru, iru,** which have no **-TE IRU** form) have a **-TE IRU** form (ignoring again the " habitual " meaning)

B

which can usually be translated as "is . . . ing". However, the **-TE IRU** tense of these verbs may occasionally require a translation more in line with B. Here again, the context will help you to decide which translation is to be used. In the glossary we indicate those verbs whose **-TE IRU** form is normally of type B.

The last but one of the "irregular" verbs in the list at the beginning of this lesson, **simasu,** can be used independently with a meaning like "do"—

Nani o site imasu ka. What are you doing?

Another important function is that it can be used to form verbs with many words taken into Japanese from Chinese or other sources. Thus **benkyoo** is "study", **hoosoo** is "broadcasting (by radio)", **ryokoo** is "travel", **syooti** is "consent", and the corresponding verbs are **benkyoo simasu,** "study"; **hoosoo simasu,** "broadcast"; **ryokoo simasu,** "travel"; **syooti simasu,** "agree, consent". There are both transitive and intransitive verbs of this type—

Eigo o benkyoo simasu. I study English.

Nyuusu o hoosoo site imasu. They are broadcasting the news.

Yooroppa e ryokoo site imasu. He is travelling to Europe.

The insertion of (**suru**) after a noun in the Vocabulary shows that such a verb exists, with a meaning that can easily be deduced.

Vocabulary

Nouns

ame, rain
Amerika, America
Amerikazin, an American
benkyoo (suru), study
Eikokuzin, an Englishman, the British
hi, sun, day
hoosoo (suru), broadcast
hoteru, hotel

kawa, river
Kyooto, Kyoto
nyuusu, news
ryokoo (suru), travel
sora, sky
syooti (suru), consent
te, hand
Yooroppa, Europe
yuki, snow

Verbs

aku, (become) open
deru, go out, come out
hairu, go in, come in
hareru, clear up, become clear (weather)
huru, fall (rain, etc.)
iku, go
kurasu, live
kuru, come
narabu, get in line
otiru, fall

oyogu, swim
sumu, reside
suru, do
tatu, stand (up), depart, elapse
tigau, differ
yuu, say

Particles

e
kara

Exercise 6

I. *Translate into English:* 1. Ano hito wa Tookyoo de kurasite imasu. 2. Anata wa doko ni sunde imasu ka. Kyooto ni sunde imasu. 3. Kono to mo akimasu ka. 4. Ano kawa de tomodati ga oyoide imasu. 5. Hoteru no mae ni sensei ga tatte imasu. 6. Eikoku kara kono gakkoo e gakusei ga kimasu. 7. Teeburu no sita ni anata no boosi ga otite imasu. 8. Hon-dana ni hon ga narande imasu. 9. Yamasita-san wa tosyokan e itte imasu. 10. Amerika e nyuusu o hoosoo site imasu. 11. Yuki mo hurimasu ka. 12. Mizu no naka no musi wa sinde imasu. 13. Ano hito mo Amerikazin desu ka. Ano hito wa tigaimasu; Eikokuzin desu. 14. Inu wa doko ni imasu ka. Niwa e dete imasu. 15. Amerika kara Yooroppa e ryokoo site imasu.

II. *Translate into Japanese:* 1. What are you doing? I am studying English. 2. That Englishman is travelling from England to Japan. 3. Your dictionary has fallen down (and is on the floor). 4. Students are lined up in front of the library. 5. Both the man and the dog are dead. 6. That American has gone to his friend's hotel. 7. This hat is different. 8. The teacher has consented too. 9. I broadcast the Japanese news (the news of Japan). 10. This man has come from London. 11. Do fish live in this river? 12. Is the sky clear? 13. Do you swim too? 14. The bird has gone into the room. 15. That Englishman lives in Kyoto.

LESSON 7

IN English it is not felt that there is any great difference grammatically between " This book is a novel " and " This book is red ", and at first glance they look alike in Japanese—

> **Kono hon wa syoosetu desu.**
> **Kono hon wa akai desu.**

However, one of the particularities of Japanese is that the true adjective, which ends in **-i,** as **akai** does, contains in itself a verbal idea—**akai** is equivalent to " is red ". Adjectives in Japanese can, owing to the fact that they are partly verbs, be conjugated like any other verb, and have a plain and a polite form, the latter obtained by putting **desu** after the dictionary form.

Dictionary form	*-MASU* form	Translation
akai	akai desu	is red
ookii	ookii desu	is big
samui	samui desu	is cold
siroi	siroi desu	is white

You will see that as **akai,** even in the dictionary form, is equivalent to " is red ", the **desu** following **akai** in the polite form has no other function than to put the adjective into the form used at the end of a sentence in polite conversation. Do not be led away into thinking that as the polite form is **akai desu,** the plain form is **akai da**—that form does not exist, the plain form is **akai.**

You have already met some demonstrative adjectives, **kono,** etc., and they went before the noun in a way reassuring to English speakers. The plain form of a true adjective, too, precedes the noun when used attributively, i.e., to qualify a noun without the intervention, in English, of the verb " to be ". Thus one says **akai hon,** " red book "; **samui hi,** " cold day ", and although you will normally translate them thus, it will be useful still to think, for instance, of **siroi** as " is white ", for this will give a clue to the construction which corresponds to the English relative clause, which is ushered in by a relative pronoun, such as

" who ", " which ", " that ", etc.   It will be better to call clauses of this type adjectival clauses in Japanese.   Thus **siroi inu,** " white dog ", can be thought of as " a dog that is white ", **omosiroi hito,** " interesting man ", as " a man who is interesting ", and similarly **hon o yonde iru hito** is " a man who is reading a book ".   This is the type of all adjectival clauses in Japanese—

> **Hon o yonde iru hito wa Eikokuzin desu.**   The man who is reading the book is an Englishman.
> **Te ga tiisai hito wa watasi no tomodati desu.**   The man with small hands (whose hands are small) is my friend.
> **Watasi ga yonde iru hon wa teeburu no ue ni arimasu.** The book that I am reading is on the table.

You see from these sentences that only the main verb in a sentence has to be in the polite or **-MASU** form; the rest are in the plain form.

A standardized adjectival clause is used as one of the ways of expressing the idea of " being able ".   Thus **yomu koto ga dekimasu** is equivalent to " I can read "; in other words, to add the idea of " being able " to any verb, put the plain form of the verb before the expression **koto ga dekimasu.**   Thus, to give another example, **Eigo o hanasu koto ga dekimasu ka** can be translated as " Can you speak English? "   The expression **koto ga dekimasu** is best thought of as idiomatic; **koto** is " an abstract thing " and **dekimasu,** or **dekiru,** to use the dictionary form, as we shall henceforth when referring to a verb, is a word of wide meaning, including such as " is made ", " is produced ", " is possible "; you may thus think of **yomu koto ga dekimasu** as " a reading thing is possible " or " reading is possible ", but it is probably better not to analyse the meanings of expressions such as this.   However, the construction composed of a verb followed by **koto** is a useful one, for it can be used to translate the English verbal noun ending in " -ing ".   Thus **yomu koto** is " reading ", **oyogu koto,** " swimming ", **hanasu koto,** " speaking ", e.g.,

> **Nihongo o hanasu koto wa muzukasii desu.** Speaking Japanese is difficult. *Or* It is difficult to speak Japanese.

It is worth noting too that the first component of a **suru** verb (such as **benkyoo suru,** etc., mentioned in Lesson 6) can often be used as a noun equivalent to the English verbal noun mentioned above, or to the ordinary Japanese verb followed by **koto.** Thus **ryoori** is " cooking ", **ryoori suru** is " to cook ", and one could ask a person:

> **Huransu no ryoori ga dekimasu ka.** Can you do French cooking?

To revert to the adjective—apart from the true adjective ending in **-i,** to which we referred at the beginning of this lesson, there is the **NA** adjective, so called because the form used before a noun incorporates **na,** e.g., **rippa na hon,** " a splendid book "; **hen na hito,** " a peculiar person ". This kind of adjective differs from the **-I** type in that the verbal idea has to be added; the translation of " He is peculiar " is **Ano hito wa hen desu,** the plain form of which is **Ano hito wa hen da.** The **na** used with this type of adjective when it precedes a noun is a relic of another verb " to be ", but that need not worry you. The chief thing to remember when using **na** adjectives is that they change their form, as you have seen, according to whether they occur at the end of the sentence or before the noun they qualify. Thus you must say—

> **Ame wa iya desu.** The rain is repugnant. I don't like the rain.
> **Iya na kodomo desu.** He is an unpleasant child.

There are some **-I** adjectives that have an alternative **NA** form; among them are **ookii (ooki na), tiisai (tiisa na)** and **okasii (okasi na),** being respectively " big ", " small " and " funny ", but it should be noted that these particular **NA** forms are used only before a noun. In other positions the **-I** form must be used. Another peculiarity is that **onazi,** " same ", is used before a noun—

> **Kono zassi ni mo onazi hito ga kakimasu.** The same man writes in this magazine.

but in other positions is followed by parts of the verb **da,** like a **NA** adjective—

> **Teeburu wa onazi desu (da).** The table is the same.

From **-I** and **NA** adjectives there may be formed a noun by the replacement of **-i** or **na** by **-sa**. This may be translated by adding " -ness " to the English adjective or by a noun of the same meaning, e.g., **ookisa**, " bigness ", " size "; **rippa-sa**, " splendidness ", " splendour ".

Vocabulary

Nouns

ekaki, painter, artist
hana, flower
Huransu, France
Huransugo, French (language)
Huransuzin, a Frenchman, the French
iro, colour
ki, tree
koto, (abstract) thing, fact
kutu, shoe, boot
miruku, milk
ryoori (suru), cooking
uma, horse
usi, cow, bull, ox

Adjectives

akai, red
aoi, blue
hen na, strange, peculiar, suspicious(-looking)
iya na, repugnant
kuroi, black

muzukasii, difficult
okasii (okasi na), funny, odd
omosiroi, interesting
onazi, same
ookii (ooki na), big, large
rippa na, splendid, fine
samui, cold (weather)
siroi, white
tiisai (tiisa na), small, little

Verbs

dekiru, is possible, is made, is produced
haku, wear, put on (trousers, footwear)
hanasu, speak
kaburu, wear, put on (hat, etc.)
nomu, drink
tukau, use

Particle

na

Exercise 7

I. *Translate into English:*   1. Kono kuroi usi wa ookii desu.   2. Tiisa na kodomo ga kabutte iru boosi wa aoi desu.   3. Asoko ni iru uma wa siroi desu.   4. Anata ga yonde iru Huransugo no hon wa omosiroi desu ka.   5. Muzukasii Nihongo o hanasu koto ga dekimasu.   6. Sono Huransuzin no ryoori wa rippa desu.   7. Samui heya de

benkyoo ga dekimasu ka.   8. Teeburu no ue no hana mo
onazi iro desu.   9. Akai enpitu o tukatte iru hito wa
watasitati no sensei desu.   10. Tomodati ga haite iru
kutu wa kuroi desu.   11. Ano ekaki wa okasi na boosi o
kabutte imasu.   12. Hon-dana no ue ni hen na musi ga
imasu.   13. Ame no hi ni ryokoo suru koto wa iya desu.
14. Ookii tyawan ni haitte iru miruku o nomu koto ga
dekimasu ka.   15. Ano ki no ue ni tiisai tori ga imasu.

II. *Translate into Japanese:*   1. There is a white horse
over there.   2. His hat is red.   3. I am living in a small
house.   4. The man who is drawing a picture in the garden
is a splendid artist.   5. His glasses are big.   6. Can you do
an interesting broadcast?   7. There is a peculiar insect on
the table.   8. There is the same man in this photograph.
9. Can you eat white meat too?   10. There is an unpleasant dog in front of the shop.   11. Snowy days are
cold.   12. It is difficult to write interesting novels.   13.
The black cat is drinking milk.   14. That big cow is splendid.
15. The flower which is under the small tree is blue.

LESSON 8

WHEREAS English makes a verb negative by the use of
" not " or some similar word, e.g., " I am eating ", " I am
not eating ", Japanese verbs have a special form for the
negative.   The formation of the negative of verbs in their
-MASU form (except **desu**) consists merely of substituting
-en for the final **-u.**   Thus, **tabemasu,** " I eat "—**tabemasen,**
" I do not eat ''; **tabete imasu,** " I am eating "—**tabete
imasen,** " I am not eating ".   The negative of the plain
forms of verbs, however, differs according to whether they
are **-RU** verbs or **-U** verbs.   To find the plain form of the
negative of a **-RU** verb, substitute **-nai** for the final **-ru**
of the dictionary form.

Positive	Negative	Positive	Negative
miru	**minai**	**otiru**	**otinai**
taberu	**tabenai**	**deru**	**denai**

To find the plain negative of all **-U** verbs, except **aru** and
those ending in a vowel + **-u,** substitute **-anai** for the final
-u of the dictionary form.

Positive	Negative	Positive	Negative
kaku	kakanai	kagu	kaganai
kasu	kasanai	matu	matanai
sinu	sinanai	yobu	yobanai
yomu	yomanai	uru	uranai

In the case of verbs whose dictionary forms end in a vowel + **-u,** you should substitute **-wanai** for the final **-u** of the dictionary form (this is not a real irregularity, but the representation in romanized script of the transitional [w] sound that occurs between the two vowels).

Positive	Negative	Positive	Negative
arau	arawanai	suu	suwanai

The plain present negative of **aru** is **nai,** and **desu** is first converted to **de arimasu** (from which it is thought to have derived) and has as its **-MASU** negative **de arimasen** (more idiomatically, **de wa arimasen**), from which one can consider the plain neutral negative **de nai** to have derived.

The plain neutral negative of the " irregular " verbs listed in Lesson 6 are:

Positive	Negative
iku	ikanai
kuru	konai
suru	sinai
yuu	iwanai

You will have noticed that **iku** is regular here. **Da** is mentioned above.

There is nothing requiring special mention about the use and formation of the form in **-masen;** it is used at the end of a polite sentence just like any other **-MASU** form—

Pan o tabemasen.   I don't eat bread.

However, the plain form, which is **nai** in the case of the verb **aru** or ends in **-nai,** looks like an adjective. Notice, however, that whereas the polite form of an adjective such as **akai** is **akai desu,** that of the negative of a verb is the form ending in **-masen,** the conjugation thus being—

Plain	*-MASU*	*Positive plain form*
nai	arimasen	aru
de nai	de arimasen	da
minai	mimasen	miru
yomanai	yomimasen	yomu
arawanai	araimasen	arau

The negative of **-I** adjectives is formed by adding to their -**KU** form (formed by substituting **-ku** for the **-i** of the plain form) the negative of the verb **aru**.

Plain positive	*-KU form*	*Plain negative*	*Negative -MASU*
atatakai	atatakaku	atatakaku nai	atatakaku arimasen
yasasii	yasasiku	yasasiku nai	yasasiku arimasen
karui	karuku	karuku nai	karuku arimasen
omoi	omoku	omoku nai	omoku arimasen

Note one " irregularity "—

ii	yoku	yoku nai	yoku arimasen

Tenki ga atatakaku nai tokoro ni sunde imasu. He lives in a place where the weather is not warm.

You will remember that with **NA** adjectives the form that occurs at the end of a polite sentence ends in **desu,** e.g., **ano hito wa rippa desu.** The formation of the negative of these adjectives consists merely of putting the final verb into the negative, e.g., **ano hito wa rippa de arimasen.** The negative of **NA** adjectives used before nouns ends in **de nai,** e.g., **rippa na hito, rippa de nai hito.**

In connection with the use of the plain negative of adjectives used in front of the noun they qualify, it will be convenient here to introduce another use of the verb **aru.** You will remember that it is equivalent to the verb " be " used of an inanimate thing to mark position. Another use is as " be " when it denotes mere existence, not being anywhere, but just being; in this use it can have either an animate or an inanimate subject. Once again the English idiom often requires " there is " when translating this verb. Thus—

Akai hon ga arimasu ka.   Are there any red books?
Ari o taberu hito ga arimasu ka.   Are there any people
who eat ants?

It is in utterances of this form that the negative adjective used before a noun will often occur.   Thus, if offered
a bicycle that is said to be heavy and therefore strong,
you may say:

Isn't there a bicycle that isn't heavy?   **Omoku nai
zitensya wa arimasen ka.**

The use of the plain negative of an adjective before a
noun does not, in fact, occur so very often in normal
circumstances, any more than the corresponding English
relative clause does.   The negative adjective at the end of
a sentence is more common—

Hon wa akaku arimasen.   The book is not red.

It is with negative expressions of this kind that you will
find another use of **wa.**   A typical occurrence is in instances
like the following—a person asks you if your luggage is
heavy **Nimotu wa omoi desu ka ;** you may answer " No,
it isn't "—**Omoku wa arimasen.**   This use of **wa** is found
when the idea of a contrast is present.   In **omoku wa
arimasen** there is the feeling of " contrary to what you suggest by asking if my luggage is heavy, it is in fact not
heavy ".   You will see that as many negative statements
imply the existence of a positive one that is denied, this
" contrasting " **wa** is often used in negative sentences—

Tookyoo ni wa sunde imasen.   He is not living in
Tokyo.

With the negative of **desu,** it is usual to insert this **wa**
and say **de wa arimasen.**   You will see that in many
instances this **wa** acts in a very similar way to the " echoing " **wa** we mentioned earlier.   It also occurs in conversations like the following: .

Umi ni nani ga arimasu ka.   What is there in the
sea?
Umi ni wa mizu ga arimasu.   In the sea there is water.
(" Echoing " **wa.**)

Kawa ni wa nani ga arimasu ka. What is there in a river? (" Contrasting " **wa.**)

Kawa ni mo mizu ga arimasu. There is water in rivers too.

Vocabulary

Nouns

ari, ant
asi, leg, foot
doobutu, animal
hon-bako, bookcase
inaka, the country (as opposed to town)
kome, rice
kusuri, medicine
kuuki, air
mikan, Japanese orange
nimotu, luggage
satoo, sugar
siru, juice, gravy
tenki, weather
tokei, clock, watch
tokoro, place
tyootyoo, butterfly
umi, sea
zidoosya, motor-car

zitensya, bicycle

Adjectives

amai, sweet
atatakai, warm
ii (yoi), good
karai, salty, hot (taste)
karui, light (weight)
nai, non-existent
nigai, bitter
omoi, heavy
suppai, sour
yasasii, easy, gentle, kind

Verbs

hataraku, work
suu, inhale, suck

Suffix

-nai

Exercise 8

I. *Translate into English:* 1. Inaka de wa zidoosya wa utte imasen. 2. Kono hon-bako ni wa yasasii hon ga arimasen. 3. Kome o tabenai Nihonzin ga arimasu ka. 4. Huransugo no syoosetu ga nai tosyokan wa ii tosyokan de wa arimasen. 5. Asi ga nai hito mo hataraite imasu. 6. Atatakaku nai tokoro ni mo musi ga imasu. 7. Kono niwa ni wa siroi tyootyoo ga imasen. 8. Tenki ga yoku nai hi ni wa konai hito ga arimasu. 9. Ano tokei wa hen de wa arimasen ka. 10. Kono siru wa karaku wa arimasen. 11. Amaku nai satoo ga arimasu ka. 12. Nigai kusuri o nomu koto wa iya desu. 13. Kuuki o suwanai doobutu ga arimasu ka. 14. Kono mikan no siru wa suppaku arimasen. 15. Zitensya no ue ni aru nimotu wa omoku wa arimasen; karui desu.

II. *Translate into Japanese:* 1. I don't dislike even salty gravy. 2. In this library there are no interesting books. 3. Are there any children who do not go to school? 4. There are no places where there are no cars. 5. Are there any oranges which are not sour? 6. Here there are neither ants nor butterflies. 7. This animal lives in warm places. 8. That child is drinking sweet orange juice. 9. In the country one can breathe good air. 10. There is no heavy luggage here. 11. Using a light bicycle is easy. 12. There is no clock on the top of that bookcase. 13. On days when the weather is not good we do not go to the sea. 14. I take the medicine which is not bitter. 15. He is working in a shop which sells rice.

LESSON 9

To express the past tense of a verb, the **-TA** form may be used.   The plain form of this is obtained, in all verbs except **da,** by substituting **-a** for the final **-e** of the **-TE** form.

niru	nite	nita	nimasita
kowareru	kowarete	kowareta	kowaremasita
haku	haite	haita	hakimasita
isogu	isoide	isoida	isogimasita
herasu	herasite	herasita	herasimasita
katu	katte	katta	katimasita
sinu	sinde	sinda	sinimasita
kau	katte	katta	kaimasita
erabu	erande	eranda	erabimasita
kamu	kande	kanda	kamimasita
iku	itte	itta	ikimasita
kuru	kite	kita	kimasita
suru	site	sita	simasita
yuu	itte	itta	iimasita

The one exception—

da	**de**	**datta**	**desita**

The fourth column in the above table is the **-TA** form of the **-MASU** form.

The use of the **-TA** form of the verb usually presents no great difficulty. At the end of a sentence in ordinary polite speech you will, of course, use verbs ending in **-masita,** and in the interior of a sentence, etc., the form in **-ta (-da)** will be used.

The normal translation of this form will be by the simple past tense, by the form using " did ", or the " present perfect " (with " have ", " has ")—

> **Iinkai e ikimasita ka.** Did you go to the committee meeting? *Or* Has he gone to the committee meeting?
>
> **Ano hito wa Amerika e ikimasita.** He went (has gone) to America.
>
> **Sinbun o yomimasita ka.** Have you read the paper? *Or* Did you read the paper?
>
> **Watasi ga nonda kusuri wa teeburu no ue ni arimasu.** The medicine which I took is on the table.

The difference in meaning between (*a*) **Ano hito wa Amerika e ikimasita** and (*b*) **Ano hito wa Amerika e itte imasu** is that (*a*) may refer to some past action which is now over and done with, in which case the translation will be " he went to America "—in answer, perhaps, to a question such as " Where did he go last year? " On the other hand, (*a*) may refer to a departure for America which took place relatively recently, the person concerned not having gone anywhere since, as far as you know; he may not have arrived yet even. The translation will then be, " He has gone to America." (*b*) could refer to the same action as in the second case under (*a*), but the speaker would be thinking more of the person's being in America, i.e., the result of his going. The translation " He is in America " might then be more appropriate.

There are uses of the **-TA** form that do not fit in with what we have just said, and some of them will be explained in later lessons. One, however, may be mentioned right away. Suppose, for instance, that people are waiting on a railway platform for a train; as soon as it comes into sight, those waiting for it will say, **Kimasita** (or its equivalent), which can only be translated as " Here it comes " or " The train's coming " or the like.

The negative of the **-TA** form of the **-MASU** form of verbs is obtained by adding **desita** to the **-MASEN** (" present negative ") form.

miru	mimasen	mimasen desita
iku	ikimasen	ikimasen desita
aru	arimasen	arimasen desita
da	de (wa) arimasen	de (wa) arimasen desita

The plain form of the negative of the **-TA** form is formed from the plain " present negative " by changing the final **-i** to **-katta**.

tabenai	tabenakatta
yobanai	yobanakatta
nai	nakatta

The **-TA** form of **-I** adjectives is formed in the same way as the plain negative of verbs:

atui	atukatta
yasasii	yasasikatta
atuku nai	atuku nakatta

Note, moreover, that the **-TA** form of the **-MASU** form of **-I** adjectives is obtained from the form in **-katta** with **desu** added, e.g., " it is hot ", **atui desu**; " it was hot ", **atukatta desu**.

NA adjectives use the conjugation of **desu**; rippa da, rippa datta; rippa desu, rippa desita; rippa de (wa) nai, rippa de, (wa) nakatta; rippa de (wa) arimasen, rippa de (wa) arimasen desita.

The handling of the **-TA** forms of adjectives thus appears complicated, but if you remember the fundamental difference that has already been explained between **-I** adjectives and **NA** adjectives, you will not make mistakes. To put it briefly, **atui** is equivalent to " is hot ", and **desu** in the form **atui desu** serves only to put it in the polite form. It is not surprising, then, that the polite form of **atukatta** (" was hot ") is **atukatta desu**. On the other hand, **rippa** has no verbal meaning, this being provided by **na, da, desu,** etc., according to the circumstances, and it is equally not surprising that the past tense should be **rippa desita** (**datta**) ; **da** has its full meaning, and is thus the part to be conjugated.

For the sake of convenience, a summary table of **-TA** forms follows.

	Plain		**-MASU**	
Verbs	*Positive*	*Negative*	*Positive*	*Negative*
miru	mita	minakatta	mimasita	mimasen desita
matu	matta	matanakatta	matimasita	matimasen desita
yobu	yonda	yobanakatta	yobimasita	yobimasen desita
kagu	kaida	kaganakatta	kagimasita	kagimasen desita
kuru	kita	konakatta	kimasita	kimasen desita
suru	sita	sinakatta	simasita	simasen desita
aru	atta	nakatta	arimasita	arimasen desita
Adjectives				
yasui	yasukatta	yasuku (wa) nakatta	yasukatta desu	yasuku (wa) arimasen desita
hen na (da)	hen datta	hen de (wa) nakatta	hen desita	hen de (wa) arimasen desita

Vocabulary

Nouns

doogu, tool, furniture
entotu, chimney
hanasi, story, talk, speech
hebi, snake
himo, string
huta, lid
iinkai, committee meeting
kaban, travelling bag, trunk
kago, cage, basket
kaityoo, president, chairman
kao, face
kusari, chain
mannenhitu, fountain-pen
mekata, weight
ooba, overcoat
seinen, young man
tikuonki, gramophone

Adjectives

atui, hot
takai, high, dear
tuyoi, strong
yasui, cheap

Verbs

erabu, choose
herasu, cause to diminish
isogu, hurry
kamu, bite

katu, win
kau, buy
kowareru, be smashed, broken
naku, cry, sing (bird)
niru, resemble
osieru, teach, tell
tuku, reach, arrive, become attached, accompany
tunagu, tie, link

Exercise 9

I. *Translate into English:* 1. Ano hito ga katta doogu wa rippa de wa arimasen. 2. Are ga watasi no asi o kanda hebi desu. 3. Omoi kaban no mekata o herasimasita. 4. Takai entotu ga kowaremasita. 5. Sono hitotati wa nite imasen desita. 6. Watasi ga eranda mannenhitu wa yasukatta desu. 7. Isoganakatta hito mo imasita. 8. Ano seinen wa katimasen desita. 9. Huta ga nai kago ga tukimasita. 10. Naita kodomo no kao wa atukatta desu. 11. Tuyoi himo de kusari o tunagimasita. 12. Ano gakkoo de Huransugo o osieta sensei ni aimasita. 13. Kaityoo no hanasi wa omosirokatta desu. 14. Watasi no ooba wa takaku wa arimasen desita. 15. Ano hito no tikuonki wa hen desita.

II. *Translate into Japanese:* 1. I have decreased the weight of this luggage. 2. Have you chosen your furniture? 3. He resembled you. 4. The black dog bit the white cat. 5. The trunk was not heavy. 6. Who won? 7. Where is the broken gramophone? 8. The chain was not strong. 9. The bird was singing in the cage. 10. They broadcast the chairman's speech. 11. That is the teacher who taught English. 12. I didn't hurry either. 13. I did not buy the cheap fountain-pen. 14. The lid was hot. 15. That young man did not arrive.

LESSON 10

THERE is a group of particles used to connect nouns in a similar way to some English conjunctions such as " and ", " or ". You have met **ka** as a particle at the end of a sentence to make it interrogative; placed between nouns it acts like the English " or ", or like " either . . . or ". Thus—

> **Hon ka zassi o yonde imasu.** He is reading either a book or a magazine.

The particle **to,** when used between nouns, is like " and "; thus—

> **Hon to zassi (to) o yonde imasu.** They are reading books and magazines.

Note that **to** may be, but is not necessarily, repeated after the last noun of the series, which may consist of any number of nouns—

> **Koko ni teeburu to isu to hon-bako (to) ga arimasu.** There are tables and chairs and bookcases here.

You will see from these examples that any other particle (**ga, o,** etc.) follows only the last noun of the series. **Nado** is used after a noun to indicate that that noun is taken as typical of a class of things, e.g.,

> **Pen nado (o) utte imasu.** He is selling pens and things. *Or* He is selling pens and so on.

Note that in this instance any other particle follows **nado,** but that the use of **wa, ga,** and **o** is not obligatory, and they may be omitted. When it is desired to put **nado** after more than one noun (e.g., " he is selling pens and paper and things "), i.e., when the list is not complete but the components of it are taken as typical of the sort of things intended, these other nouns should have **toka** between them. Thus the translation of the sentence just given would be **Pen toka kami nado (o) utte imasu.**

The interrogative pronouns that we have seen up to now

are **nani (nan), dare, doko.** We can now add some more to the list.

Dore, used with the meaning of " which " when more than two things are concerned, has a corresponding adjectival form **dono,** also to be translated as " which "—

> **Dore o kaimasita ka.** Which did you buy?
> **Dono hon o kaimasita ka.** Which book did you buy?

You will notice that **dore** links up with the demonstrative pronouns **are, kore, sore,** and **dono** with the adjectives **ano, kono, sono** in the same way as **doko** does with **asoko, koko, soko.** When, however, only two things are concerned, i.e., in translating " which (of two) ", the pronoun **dotira** is used. There is no adjective corresponding to this pronoun, but it forms a group with the pronouns (*a*) **atira,** (*b*) **kotira,** (*c*) **sotira,** which mean, respectively, that one of two which is (*a*) away from both of us, over there, (*b*) near me, here, (*c*) there by you, or the one you have just mentioned.

Dotira can be used either independently, e.g.,

> **Dotira o erabimasita ka.** Which did you choose?

or joined to a following noun by **no**—

> **Dotira no hon o erabimasita ka.** Which book (Which of the two books) did you choose?

It is possible to use **dono** and **dotira** of human beings, but not **dore**—

> **Dono sensei ga Nihongo o hanasimasu ka.** Which teacher speaks Japanese?
> **Dotira no sensei ga Nihongo o hanasimasu ka.** Which teacher (of two) speaks Japanese?

But—

> **Dare ga Nihongo o hanasimasu ka.** Who speaks Japanese?

or, if you are referring to a definite number of people—

> Which speaks Japanese?
> Which of you (them, etc.) speaks Japanese?

To all interrogative pronouns (but not adjectives) can be added the suffix -ka to form indefinite pronouns, which are translated by the use of " some " or " any ". Thus, if you add -ka to dare, you get dareka " somebody ", " someone ", " anyone ", " anybody "—

Dareka (ga) kimasu ka. Is someone coming?
Ano heya ni dareka (ga) imasu. There is someone in that room.
Dareka ni aimasita ka. Did you meet anybody (somebody)?

Notice that one often uses these pronouns without a following wa or ga, as indicated by the brackets in the above examples.

Other instances of this formation are:

nanika, something, anything
dokoka, somewhere, anywhere, any place, etc.
doreka, any one, etc.
dotiraka, either, one or the other
Ano hako no naka ni nanika arimasu ka. Is there anything (something) in that box?
Miki-san wa dokoka e itte imasu ka. Has Mr. Miki gone somewhere?
Koko ni aru hon no doreka o yomimasita ka. Have you read any of the books here?
Koko ni aru hon no dotiraka o yomimasita ka. Have you read one of the (two) books here?

If, instead of ka one adds mo to these pronouns, and uses them with a negative verb, the resulting expressions may be translated as pronouns of the type of " nobody ", " no one " or " not . . . anyone ". The particles ga, wa, o are not used with this form, but others (such as ni, e) are, being inserted between the pronouns and mo.

Daremo + *negative verb*

Gakusei wa daremo kite imasen. No student is here (No student has come).
Daremo mimasen desita. I did not see anybody.
Dare ni mo aimasen desita. I did not meet anybody.

Doremo + *negative verb*

Koko ni hon ga arimasu; doremo akaku arimasen.
There are some books here; none (not one) of them
is red.

Dono pen o kaimasita ka. Which pen did you buy?

Doremo kaimasen desita. I didn't buy any of them.

Dotiramo + *negative verb*

If there were only two pens referred to in the last example, it would be—

Dotira no pen o kaimasita ka. Which pen did you
buy?

Dotiramo kaimasen desita. I didn't buy either.
Or I bought neither.

Dokomo + *negative verb*

Miki-san wa dokoka e ikimasita ka. Did Mr. Miki
go somewhere?

Doko e mo ikimasen desita. He didn't go anywhere.
Or He went nowhere.

Dokoka itai desu ka. Have you a pain anywhere?

Dokomo itaku arimasen. I haven't a pain anywhere.

Nanimo + *negative verb*

Teeburu no ue ni nani ga arimasu ka. What is there
on the table?

(Teeburu no ue ni wa) nanimo arimasen. There isn't
anything (on the table).

In addition, this **mo** may be used in conjunction with
dono to form phrases such as the following:

Ooba wa dono kaban ni mo arimasen. The overcoat
isn't in any of the trunks. *Or* The overcoat is in
none of the trunks.

Dono pen mo kaimasen desita. I didn't buy any of
the pens. *Or* I bought none of the pens.

It will be convenient here to introduce an idiomatic
expression . . . **ka mo siremasen,** used at the end of a
sentence to express the idea of possibility, " It may be
that . . ." It is preceded by the plain form of verbs and

adjectives, except that when you expect the verb that occurs before it to be **da,** this is in fact usually omitted—

> **Honda-san wa Rondon ni iru ka mo siremasen.** Mr. Honda may be in London.
>
> **Ano hito wa Eikokuzin (da) ka mo siremasen.** He may be an Englishman.

Vocabulary

Nouns
biiru, beer
eda, branch
gaikoku, foreign countries
gaikokugo, foreign language
ha, leaf
kozutumi, parcel
nikuya, butcher
sima, island
tamago, egg
toori, street, road
yaoya, greengrocer

Pronouns
atira
dareka
daremo
dokoka
dokomo
dore
doreka
doremo
dotira
dotiraka
dotiramo
kotira

nanika
nanimo
sotira

Adjectives
dono
itai, painful

Verbs
aruku, walk
dekakeru, go out
hirou, pick up
kiru, cut
narau, learn
okuru, send
sireru, become known

Particles
nado
to
toka

Suffixes
-ka
-mo

Exercise 10

I. *Translate into English:* 1. Dokoka e dekakemasita ka. Doko e mo dekakemasen desita. 2. Gaikoku ni iru tomo-dati ni nanika okuru tumori desu ka. Hon toka sinbun

toka zassi nado o okuru tumori desu.   3. Doko ga atatakai
desu ka. Dokomo atatakaku arimasen.   4. Yaoya ka
nikuya de tamago o kau koto ga dekimasu ka.   5. Dono
gaikokugo o naraimasita ka.   Dono gaikokugo mo narai-
masen desita.   6. Watasitati wa kotira no zidoosya de
ikimasu.   7. Honda-san to Kimura-san ga aruite imasu.
8. Doreka kirimasita ka. Ha ga nai eda o kirimasita.
9. Dore o toori de hiroimasita ka.   10. Dotira ga hon no
kozutumi desu ka. Atira no kozutumi desu.   11. Kono
sima ni dareka sunde imasu ka.   Daremo sunde imasen.
12. E wa doremo kawanai tumori desu.   13. Anata mo
biiru o nomimasu ka. Watasi wa nanimo nomimasen.
14. Sotira no kaban mo okuru tumori desu ka.   15. Dotiraka tukau tumori desu ka.   Dotiramo tukawanai ka mo
siremasen.

II. *Translate into Japanese:* 1. Did you learn French
somewhere? 2. On the table, there are pens, ink, exercise-
books, and so on. 3. The greengrocer or the butcher may
come. 4. Which flowers did you cut?   I cut the red
flowers. 5. Do you intend to buy some of the shoes (that
are) in that shop? 6. Will you also send this parcel (i.e.,
this one of the two)? 7. Did you pick up something in the
garden? I picked up a bird's egg. 8. Did anyone drink
any beer? Nobody drunk any. 9. Which of those people
over there is Mr. Honda? 10. Will you write something?
I shall write nothing. 11. Neither of my hands hurts.
12. Which of the trunks (that are) in that room is broken?
13. I don't intend to go anywhere abroad. 14. I have
met that American and Englishman somewhere. 15. My
friend is in one of the (two) hotels over there.

LESSON 11

IN this lesson we shall study the Japanese numeral system,
which is of considerable complication and requires much
sheer memory work. The tables of numerals, and the
phonetic changes which occur when numerals combine
with each other or with other elements, are set out in the
Appendix and will not be repeated here, where you will be
concerned only with their use, but will have to be consulted
before you can do the exercises belonging to this lesson.

Notice, however, that the intention is to enable you to use the numerals in a clear and correct manner. You will no doubt find, when you come to talk to other Japanese speakers, that they will use combinations not mentioned in this book. Your knowledge of the elements that are used will enable you to understand such combinations without difficulty, but it will not be necessary for you to add them to your own speech. You will not be wrong if you restrict yourself to what you have learnt from this book.

It will be convenient first to look at expressions of time, which can be thought of as of two kinds, expressions of point of time, and those of duration.

Expressions of point of time in English are " 3 o'clock ", " 3.25 p.m.", " 1936 ", " August ", etc. Their use in Japanese presents no difficulty if you have understood what has been said about particles up to now. **Ni** is equivalent to " at ", " in ", " on "—

I was born in 1928. **1928-nen (sen kyuuhyaku nizyuuhatinen) ni umaremasita.** *Or* **Syoowa sannen ni umaremasita.**

I arrived at 6.30. **Rokuzi sanzippun ni tukimasita.**

Mr. Miki left on the 24th December, 1953. **Miki-san wa Syoowa nizyuuhatinen zyuunigatu nizyuuyokka ni dekakemasita.**

Note that when the Western system of counting years is used the word **nen** (" year ") is always added to the figure. The official system, however, uses a succession of year periods, which now correspond to the reign of the Emperor. Thus the present Emperor came to the throne in 1926, which thus became the first year of the year period **Syoowa,** this being the name by which the Emperor will be known after his death. As 1926 is the first year of the **Syoowa** period (**Syoowa gannen**), to convert any **Syoowa** year to the Western calendar, you should add to it 1925 ; similarly, to convert a Western year to its **Syoowa** equivalent, subtract 1925, e.g., 1928 was **Syoowa sannen,** and **Syoowa nizyuuhatinen** was 1953. The other two recent year periods are **Meizi** (**Meizi gannen** was 1868) and **Taisyoo** (**Taisyoo gannen** was 1912). You will have seen from the above examples that the order of presenting dates is the reverse of that in English, being year, month, day, with no intervening particles. If you wish to mention hours, minutes, seconds, they are expressed in the same order of proceeding from larger to smaller units. This order is also used on postmarks on internal mail, and in other circumstances where abbreviations are used in writing the date. Thus 25–9–30, is 30th September of the 25th year of *Syoowa* (1950).

Examples of expressions of duration of time in English are " three months ", " I waited ten minutes ". You will see from the lists that for all periods except months, weeks, and hours the same expressions as for points of time may be used; for months, you can use the expressions with **-kagetu,** for weeks, those with **-syuukan,** and for hours, those with **-zikan.** When used with a verb these expressions immediately precede it, with no particle intervening—

It takes three months. **Sankagetu kakarimasu.**
I walked for an hour. **Itizikan arukimasita.**
I waited four minutes. **Yonpun matimasita.**

They may all have the suffix **-kan** added (except, of course, **syuukan,** and **zikan,** which have it already) without any change of meaning, and if there is any possibility of it not being clear whether duration or point of time is meant, the use of **-kan** will make it certain that duration is intended—

sannen(kan) no ryokoo, a journey of three years, *or* a three years' journey

Similar in point of grammatical structure to those of duration of time are expressions of distance, and prices. The latter are measured in **en,** " yen ", and its hundredth part, the **sen,** although the *sen* has almost disappeared as a commonly used unit—

Sanzen gohyaku-en kakarimasita. It cost 3,500 yen.

Measures of distance, like those of most quantities, are officially expressed in the metric system, but older units still survive and are in everyday use. You will find lists of the usual ones in the Appendix—

Sankiro arukimasita. I walked three kilometres.

The expressions considered above give no trouble except in the learning of the forms and combinations, for in them the unit has an equivalent in English, as it also has in " two pounds of rice ", " two pairs of gloves ", but in other cases also, where English merely adds the numeral to the noun, as in " three pencils ", the Japanese requires a unit to be expressed, in the case of pencils, that appropriate to cylindrical objects, **-hon,** which is also used for trees, bottles of beer, etc. Human beings are counted with the units **-ri** or **-nin** (see Appendix), and books with **-satu.** For things which have no specific appropriate unit, you should use the forms of the numerals which end in **-tu** from one to nine (i.e., **hitotu, hutatu,** etc., to **kokonotu**); in this series numbers from 10 onwards do not have **-tu** added to them, and one says **too, zyuuiti, zyuuni,** etc. This series may be used with things like apples, eggs, oranges—

Tamago o too kowasimasita. I broke ten eggs.
Orenzi o zyuuni kaimasita. I bought twelve oranges.

Modern spoken Japanese uses far fewer of these units than there were in the older forms of the language, but there are still several which must be used.

The complete expression consists of the noun (" pencils "), the particle, which must be attached to the noun in accordance with its function in the sentence, and a combination consisting of the number and the unit. There are two constructions possible when the particle following the noun is **ga, wa, o,** or **mo.** An example of one of them is the sentence **Empitu o sanbon katte imasu**—" He is buying three pencils ", where you see that the order is noun, particle, number, and unit, with the verb following. Other examples are:

Hon ga sansatu arimasu. There are three books.
Ringo mo mittu arimasu. There are three apples too.

The other construction consists of putting the number and unit before the noun, linking them with **no,** as in **Sanbon no enpitu o katte imasu.** There is some difference of meaning between this and **Enpitu o sanbon katte imasu.** The former indicates that the three pencils form a more or less closely linked group or that there are only three pencils concerned, or that they have been mentioned before. Thus **Ano sanbon no enpitu o katte imasu** could be translated as " He is buying those three pencils ", but **Ano enpitu o sanbon katte imasu** by " He is buying three of those pencils ".

When the noun is followed by any other particle than **ga, wa, o, mo,** the more usual construction is the second one mentioned above—

> **Gohon no ki de hasi o tukurimasita.** They made a bridge with five trees.

There is no difference at all to the Japanese speaker between such units as **satu, hon,** etc., and units of measure, for their grammatical construction is the same. For instance, **syaku** is traditionally used for measuring cloth, etc.—

> **Siroi kire o hassyaku kaimasita.** She bought eight *syaku* of white cloth.

Syoo is used for rice, etc.—

> **Kome o issyoo kaimasita.** I bought one *syoo* of rice.

The official measures are, as has been said, those of the metric system, but they have not been universally adopted, and there is a bewildering variety of units of measure used with various objects. However, the construction with them all is the same.

The interrogative " how many " is expressed by the use of **nan-** with the appropriate unit, when that unit is one that is used with **iti,** etc.—

> **Hon wa nansatu arimasu ka.** How many books are there?
> **Nanri arimasu ka.** (How many *ri* are there?) How far is it (in *ri*)?

It is also used in expressions of point of time, e.g., **Nanniti,** " what day? "; **nangatu,** " what (which) month? ". With units which take **hito, huta, iku** is used with the same meaning, except that to ask " what day? " or " how many days? ", one normally uses **nanniti,** and the usual way to ask " how many people? " is **nannin.** The **-tu** of **hitotu** can be considered as a unit, and **ikutu** is thus the word to use to ask " how many . . .? " of something which has no other unit—

> **Tamago wa ikutu arimasu ka.** How many eggs are there?
>
> **Nanatu arimasu.** There are seven.
>
> **Nizyuu arimasu.** There are twenty.

You can see from these examples that if the thing you are counting or measuring is known to both parties in a conversation, it is necessary only to mention the number and unit; it is also clear that **nan** or **iku** followed by a unit is used with exactly the same construction as a numeral followed by a unit.

" How much? " is **ikura,** used for asking the price of something.

> **Tamago wa ikura desu ka.** How much are eggs?

To translate " How much does it cost ", one often uses a sentence with the verb **suru**—**Ikura simasu ka,** and likewise—

> **Kono inki wa sanzyuuen simasu.** This ink costs thirty yen.

Ikura is also used with weights, length, width, etc.

> **Kono kawa no haba wa ikura arimasu ka.** How wide is this river?

Japanese has a considerable number of exclamatory and similar expressions which give colour and variety to conversation. **Saa** at the beginning of a sentence which is a reply to a question expresses the idea that the speaker is not capable of giving an accurate answer immediately. It might correspond to " Let me see now ", " That's a teaser ", etc., or with a negative verb such as **sirimasen,** " I don't know ", it implies that the replier has thought about the matter but cannot give an answer, after all.

The words **e, ie** are used in circumstances similar to those occurring when " yes " and " no " are used in English, but they are by no means equivalent. **E** (other forms of which are **ee, hai, ha**) has two uses: (i) implying that a question has been understood and that an answer is about to come, or that an order has been understood; **hai** and **ha** are also the acknowledgement of one's name being called—

Ano budoo wa ikura desu ka. How much are those grapes?

E, zyuuen desu. Ten yen. (**e** is not translatable.)

(ii) implying " I agree ", " you are right "; this often is no different from " yes "—

Ano hito wa Rondon ni imasu ka. Is he in London?

E (Rondon ni) imasu. Yes, he is (in London).

In a reply to a negative question or statement, such as " This door is not open, is it? ", whereas in English one says " No, it isn't ", in Japanese it is **E** (I agree with you) **aite imasen.** However, in the kind of negative question that is a disguised positive request, such as " Won't you come? "—**Kimasen ka,** the answer is **E, ikimasu**—" Yes, I'll come " (notice the use of the verb **iku**), the agreement being not with the formal negative of the verb but with the speaker's intention.

Ie (other forms of which are **iya,** and, more emphatically, **iie** and **iiya**) has the opposite use to part (ii) of **e.** It means " I do not agree ", " You are wrong ". Thus to **Kimasu ka**—" Are you coming? ", one might reply **Ie, ikimasen**—" No, I'm not (coming) " and to " The door is not open is it? ", if in fact it is open, one would answer, **Ie, aite imasu**—" Yes, it is ".

Vocabulary

Nouns

budoo, grape
gannen, the first year (of year period)
haba, width

hasi, bridge
kire, piece (of cloth, etc.)
Meizi
Syoowa
Taisyoo

Verbs	*Interjections*
kakaru, cost, take (time), etc.	e (ee)
	hai (ha)
siru, get to know	ie (iie)
tukuru, make, cultivate	iya (iiya)
umareru, be born	saa

Adverbs	*Prefixes*
ikura	iku-
ikutu	nan-

Suffix

-kan

Exercise 11

I. *Translate into English:* 1. Syoowa nizyuunen sangatu tuitati ni Nippon ni tukimasita. 2. Ano hito wa nani o hanasimasita ka. Saa, sirimasen. 3. Kisya wa kuzi zyuuyonpun ni demasu. 4. Budoo mo tukurimasu ka. Ie, budoo wa tukurimasen. 5. Yamasita-san wa Meizi yonzyuusannen ni umaremasita. 6. Ano inu wa sanbon no asi de aruite imasu. 7. Taisyoo gannen wa sen kyuuhyaku zyuuninen desu. 8. Kono hasi wa itioku hassen gohyaku sitizyuuyonman sanzen gohyakuen kakarimasita. 9. Kono nimotu no mekata wa ikura arimasu ka. Ikkan roppyakumonme arimasu. 10. Sono gosatu no hon wa takakatta desu ka. E, takakatta desu.

II. *Translate into Japanese:* 1. The bus arrives at 4.23. 2. Is he American? Well now, I don't know. 3. I was born on the 3rd July, 1921. 4. The first year of Meizi was 1868. 5. That library cost 50 million yen. 6. I met three friends at the station. 7. Do you grow rice too? Yes, I do. 8. That Englishman came to Japan in 1928. 9. Were you born in August? No, I was born in September. 10. What is the width of this window (How wide is this window)? It is 5 syaku 6 sun.

III. *Translate into English, then put back into Japanese:* 1. Ku wa san no nanbai desu ka. Sanbai desu. 2. Anata no denwa wa nanban desu ka. Sanzen gozyuuhatiban desu. 3. Nakayama-san wa nanbanti ni sunde imasu ka.

Zyuurokubanti ni sunde imasu. 4. San wa kú no nanbun no ikutu desu ka. Sanbun no iti desu. 5. Gakkoo no mae ni zidoosya ga nandai narande imasu ka. Sitidai narande imasu. 6. Amerika e nando ikimasita ka Nido ikimasita. 7. Nan-en okurimasita ka. Kyuuzyuuyon-en okurimasita. 8. Nangoo no heya ni imasu ka. Rokugoo no heya ni imasu. 9. Kono tegami wa nanguramu arimasu ka. Sanzyuuguramu arimasu. 10. Nangyoo yomimasita ka. Zyuunigyoo yomimasita. 11. Biiru wa nanbai nomimasita ka. Roppai nomimasita. 12. Niwa ni inu ga nanbiki imasu ka. Nihiki imasu. 13. Mannenhitu wa nanbon erabu tumori desu ka. Sanbon erabu tumori desu. 14. Yozi nanpun ni tukimasu ka. Yozi nizyuusitihun ni tukimasu. 15. Nanpun(kan) oyogimasita ka. Zyuugo-hun(kan) oyogimasita. 16. Huransu ni nankagetu imasita ka. Yonkagetu imasita. 17. Kono hoteru wa nangai arimasu ka. Zikkai arimasu. 18. Ano doobutu wa nangan arimasu ka. Sitizikkan arimasu. 19. Sono zidoosya wa itizikan nankiro hasirimasu ka. Hyakkiro hasirimasu. 20. Kono niku wa nankiro arimasu ka. Gokiro arimasu. 21. Tegami no kami wa nanmai tukai-masita ka. Rokumai tukaimasita. 22. Kono himo wa nanmeetoru arimasu ka. Zyuumeetoru arimasu. 23. Sono inu wa niku o nanmonme tabemasu ka. Hyakumonme tabemasu. 24. Eikoku e nannen ni ikimasita ka. 1936-nen ni ikimasita. 25. Amerika ni nannen(kan) imasita ka. Sannen(kan) imasita. 26. Nanniti ni dekakemasita ka. Tooka ni dekakemasita. 27. Nanniti(kan) hatarakimasita ka. Tooka(kan) hatarakimasita. 28. Kono gakkoo ni sensei ga nannin imasu ka. Sanzyuunin imasu. 29. Nihonzin no nanpaasento ga eigo o hanasimasu ka. Zip-paasento ga hanasimasu. 30. Kono hon wa nanpeizi arimasu ka. Nihyaku sanzyuurokupeizi arimasu. 31. Anata no uti wa Tookyoo kara nanri arimasu ka. Nizyuuri arimasu. 32. Miruku wa nanrittoru arimasu ka. Itirittoru arimasu. 33. Eigo no syoosetu wa nansatu yomimasita ka. Kyuusatu yomimasita. 34. Kuroi kutu wa nansoku kaimasu ka. Nisoku kaimasu. 35. Sono sima e iku hune wa nansoo arimasu ka. Sansoo arimasu. 36. Akai kire wa nanzun kirimasu ka. Gosun kirimasu. 37. Ano entotu wa nanzyaku arimasu ka. Kyuusyaku arimasu. 38.

Anata no uti de wa itiniti ni kome o nansyoo tabemasu ka.
Issyoo tabemasu. 39. Tikuonki wa nansyurui arimasu ka.
Zyuugosyurui arimasu. 40. Ryokoo wa nansyuukan
kakarimasita ka. Sansyuukan kakarimasita. 41. Nanten
desita ka. Sitizyuugoten desita. 42. Kome wa nanto
tukimasita ka. Sito tukimasita. 43. Kono toori wa nantyoo
arimasu ka. Nizittyoo arimasu. 44. Tosyokan wa
nantyoome ni arimasu ka. Gotyoome ni arimasu. 45.
Nanzi ni hoosoo simasu ka. Gozi ni simasu. 46. Nanzikan
hoosoo simasu ka. Gozikan simasu. 47. Kono heya wa
nanzyoo arimasu ka. Hatizyoo arimasu. 48. Orenzi wa
ikuhako okurimasu ka. Tohako okurimasu. 49. Satoo wa
ikuhukuro kaimasita ka. Hutahukuro kaimasita. 50.
Hasi wa ikukumi urimasita ka. Yonzyuugokumi urimasita.
51. Kono heya ni wa mado ga ikutu arimasu ka. Hutatu
arimasu.

LESSON 12

In Lesson 7 we started the study of adjectival clauses and
dealt, if you remember, with the two following types:

> **Tegami o kaite iru hito wa ani desu.** The person who is
> writing a letter is my elder brother. (**Ani,** " elder
> brother ", is applicable only to one's own elder
> brother, or to elder brothers in general.)

> **Niisan ga yonde iru hon wa Nihongo no hon desu ka.**
> Is the book that your elder brother is reading a
> Japanese book? (**Niisan,** " elder brother " is used
> when speaking of another's elder brother, or when
> addressing your own. As a rough guide, one might
> say that one uses **niisan** for one's own elder brother
> when in English one would use his Christian name.
> The corresponding words for " elder sister " are
> **ane** and **neesan.**)

However, adjectival clauses are not restricted to instances where the noun which the clause qualifies can be
considered as the subject (as in the first example above)
or the object (second example) of the verb in the relative
clause. As in English we can say—

The man to whom we sent the book . . .
The shop in which I buy the meat . . .
The window from which the child fell . . .

so we can say in Japanese—

Hon o okutta hito . . .
Niku o kau mise . . .
Kodomo ga otita mado . . .

The method of constructing these clauses is identical
with that in the examples above, but English-speaking
students tend to be worried by the presence of the preposition connected with the relative clause in English,
and feel that there is something missing in the Japanese.
The latter, however, is content with a purely general relationship between the adjectival clause and the noun it
qualifies, more precise information being available from
the meaning of the words and from the context. Notice
that when a sentence or part of a sentence is quoted in
isolation it may be ambiguous. If you take the example
Hon o okutta hito . . . by itself, the meaning that first
comes to mind is " The man who sent the book . . .",
but in a context such as the following, " This morning I sent
off a book and a parcel. The man I sent the book to (hon
o okutta hito) is an old friend that I haven't seen for
years . . .", it would be quite clear which way the clause
was to be taken. In any case it is always possible to put
in the subject (watasi ga).

Adjectival clauses can, as in English, come within other
adjectival clauses; in fact, the adjectival clause is the
principal tool for the construction of longer sentences—

Miki-san ni okutta hon o katta mise wa toori no mukoo-
    gawa ni arimasu. The shop where (in which) I
    bought the book that I sent to Mr. Miki is on the
    other side of the street.

In this the two adjectival clauses are Miki-san ni okutta,
qualifying hon, and hon o katta, qualifying mise. If two
adjectival clauses, or an adjectival clause and an adjective,
qualify the same noun they may simply follow one after the
other—

C

Kinoo miti de atta kuroi boosi o kabutte ita hito . . .
The man I met in the street yesterday who was
wearing a black hat . . .

Miki-san ni okutta akai hon . . . The red book I sent
to Mr. Miki . . .

Note that **Akai Miki-san ni okutta hon . . .** is not impossible, but it is ambiguous, for it is not clear which is
" red ", the book or Mr. Miki, **akai** being also used in a
political sense; in conversation the ambiguity can be
avoided, even though **akai** is put first, by making a short
pause after **akai** if it is to qualify **hon,** or by not making a
pause if it is to refer to Mr. Miki. However, beginners
should play safe by putting the adjective immediately
before the noun it qualifies, as in the example given.

A rule-of-thumb method of translating an English
relative clause into Japanese will now be demonstrated.
Take the following fragments of sentences:

(a) The teacher who has gone to America . . .
(b) The parcel I sent to Japan . . .
(c) The shop the student went to . . .

The first thing to do is to dispose of the relative pronoun
and of any preposition governing it. Thus in (a) " who "
is deleted, in (b) the English has dropped it already, so
nothing has to be done about it, and in (c) the relative
pronoun is not there, but the preposition " to ", which
would have governed it if it was, persists and should be
deleted.

The next step is to translate the remainder of the relative clause, i.e., (a) " has gone to America . . .", (b) " I
sent to Japan . . .", (c) " the student went . . .", putting
the verb in the plain form, as it will not be the main verb
of the sentence—

(a) **Amerika e itte iru . . .**
(b) **Nihon e okutta . . .**
(c) **Gakusei ga itta . . .**

and put it before the noun the clause qualifies—

(a) **Amerika e itte iru sensei . . .**
(b) **Nihon e okutta kozutumi . . .**
(c) **Gakusei ga itta mise . . .**

You will soon be able to construct adjectival clauses without thinking, but until you reach that standard the above method may be of assistance.

An idiom employing an adjectival clause is used in translations of sentences like—

> Have you ever been to Paris? **Parii e itta koto ga arimasu ka.**

This is another example of **arimasu** with its meaning of " be " of simple existence (not being anywhere, but just being), that we have already seen in sentences like—

> Are there butterflies whose colour is black? **Iro ga kuroi tyootyoo ga arimasu ka.**
> Aren't there any Americans who don't own cars? **Zidoosya o motte inai Amerikazin wa arimasen ka.**

Do not forget that if an expression of place appears, **imasu** has to be used if the subject is animate—

> Are there any black butterflies on the table? **Teeburu no ue ni kuroi tyootyoo ga imasu ka.**

Let us return to the sentence—**Parii e itta koto ga arimasu ka.** In it **arimasu** is used with the meaning we have been discussing; **koto** we have already seen in the expression **koto ga dekimasu.** It is a kind of pronoun, equivalent to " thing ", and is used mainly of abstract things, facts, and so on. With a preceding adjectival clause it forms a unit often corresponding to a noun clause in English beginning with " that ", or a phrase using the *-ing* form of the verb. Thus **Parii e itta koto** would, in certain circumstances, be translated as " The fact that he went to Paris " or " His having gone to Paris "; thus **Parii e itta koto ga arimasu ka** might be thought of as meaning " Does your having gone to Paris exist? ", i.e. " Have you ever been to Paris? ". A similar expression is found in the following:

> **Parii e itta koto ga arimasen.** I have never been to Paris.
> **Parii e itta koto ga arimasu.** I have been to Paris (on at least one occasion).
> **Parii e itta koto mo arimasu.** I have also been to Paris.

You saw in Lesson 8 how to form the negative of **-I** adjectives by adding parts of the verb **aru** to the **-ku** form. This **-ku** form can be used by itself as an adverb in almost the same way as an adverb in English—

> **Atarasiku katta hon desu.** It is a book which I bought very recently. *Or* It is a newly-bought book.
>
> **Inu wa hayaku hasiru koto ga dekimasu.** Dogs can run fast.
>
> **Titi wa Eikoku no koto o omosiroku hanasimasita.** My father spoke interestingly about England.

Eikoku no koto—facts, things relating to England; . . . **no koto** is often to be translated as " about ". **Titi** is used for " father " when speaking of fathers in general, or of one's own father. The corresponding word for another's father, or used of one's own in circumstances where one would say in English " Father ", or " Dad " or the like, is **otoosan.** The corresponding words for " mother " are **haha** and **okaasan.**

To form adverbs from **NA** adjectives, you simply change **na** to **ni**—

> **Yamamoto-san wa e o zyoozu ni kakimasu.** Mr. Yamamoto paints pictures skilfully. *Or* Mr. Yamamoto is good at painting pictures.

The normal position of an adverb is immediately before the word it modifies, although it may be shifted to another position to add emphasis or for some other reason. Notice that the " numeral + unit " following the noun acts like an adverb—

> **Koko e Eikokuzin ga sannin kimasita.** Three English people came here.
>
> **Koko e Eikokuzin ga yoku kimasita.** English people often came here.

(**Yoku,** from ii, " good ", is sometimes used with the meaning of " often ", though in sentences such as the following it has its original meaning of " well "—

> **Kono isu wa yoku dekite imasu.** This chair is well made.)

The " numeral + unit " can be used without a noun—

Sannin kimasita. Three people came.

There are many other adverbs that are used without a particle. A few examples modifying verbs follow—

Rondon e wa hotondo ikimasen. I hardly ever go to London.

Kessite Rondon e wa ikimasen. I'll never go to London.

(Remember that " I have never been to London " is **Rondon e itta koto ga arimasen.**)

Kessite soo de wa arimasen. It is definitely not so.

Motiron kane o haraimasita. Of course I paid the money.

Biiru o sukosi nomimasita. I drank a little beer.

Ano hito wa taihen seikoo simasita. He was very successful.

Adverbs may modify adjectives—

Kono huku wa sukosi hen desu. This suit is a little odd.

Ano hito ga yuu koto wa hizyoo ni omosiroi desu. The things that he says (what he says) are (is) extraordinarily (very) interesting.

Some are interrogative, such as **itu**, " when ", and **doo**, " how ", " in what way "—

Nikuya wa itu sinimasita ka. When did the butcher die?

Sayoonara wa Eigo de doo iimasu ka. How do you say **sayoonara** in English?

Doo is related to the adverbs **koo**, " in this way "; **soo**, " in that way (of yours, etc.) "; **aa**, " in that way (of his, etc.) ", all translatable by " thus " or " so ".

Both **itu** and **doo** can have **ka** added to them to form an indefinite adverb. **Ituka,** " at some time ", is not remarkable for any irregularity—

Parii e ituka itta koto ga arimasu ka. Have you been to Paris at some time or another?

However, the uses of **dooka** are idiomatic and best left until later.

Itu may on occasion be followed by a particle such as **kara**—

Itu kara Nihongo o naratte imasu ka.

Literally this means " Since when are you learning Japanese? ", and the nearest equivalents in English are—

How long have you been learning Japanese? *Or* When did you begin to learn Japanese?

The answer to the question will give the point of time from which you started—

Kyonen no kugatu kara naratte imasu. I have been learning it since September last year.

Note the use of the **-TE IRU** form of the verb with **itu kara**.

Vocabulary

Nouns

ane, elder sister
ani, elder brother
asita (also adv.), tomorrow
haha, mother
kabe, wall
kane, metal, money, bell (church, etc.)
kinoo (also adv.), yesterday
kyonen (also adv.), last year
miti, road, street, way
mukoogawa, further side
neesan
niisan
okaasan
otoosan
Parii, Paris
seikoo (suru), success
titi, father

Adjectives

atarasii, new
hayai, early, quick
hizyoo na, extraordinary
zyoozu na, skilful

Verbs

harau, pay (off), wipe off
hasiru, run
kakeru, hang up, etc.
motu, hold, possess
nuu, sew
otosu, let fall
watasu, hand over

Adverbs

aa
doo
hotondo

Adverbs	sukosi
itu	taihen
ituka	
kessite	*Interjection*
koo	sayoonara (sayonara), good-
motiron	bye
soo	

Exercise 12

I. *Translate into English:* 1. Motiron titi wa zidoosya o motte imasen. 2. Ano sensei ga yuu koto wa taihen muzukasii desu. 3. Neesan ga nutta kimono wa hizyoo ni yoku dekite imasu. 4. Ano hito ni wa kessite aimasen. 5. Watasi ga miti de otosita mannenhitu o hirotta hito wa boosi o kabutte imasen desita. 6. Haha wa hotondo hasitta koto ga arimasen. 7. Kane wa itu haraimasu ka. Asita haraimasu. 8. Ane ga kozutumi o watasite iru hito wa watasi no tomodati no okaasan desu. 9. Atarasiku katta kutu wa sukosi tiisai desu. 10. Ani ga kabe ni kakete iru e wa kinoo toori no mukoogawa no mise de kaimasita. 11. Otoosan wa itu kara gaikoku e itte imasu ka. 12. Ituka seikoo sita hito no koto o hanasimasu. 13. Hude o aratte iru hito wa niisan desu ka. 14. Kessite zyoozu de wa arimasen. 15. Kyonen niwa de iro ga kuroi tyootyoo o yoku mimasita.

II. *Translate into Japanese:* 1. Was your elder brother wearing new shoes? 2. I may go abroad sometime. 3. Is that the parcel you are sending to your father? 4. Is the shop on the other side of the road very large? 5. Has he read the French book your mother lent him? 6. That horse is running very fast. 7. How long has your elder sister been teaching? She has been teaching since last year. 8. I'll never go to his home. 9. My elder brother handed over the money he picked up in the street to the person who dropped it. 10. The medicine I took yesterday was very bitter. 11. My father has hardly ever worn a hat. 12. Mr. Taguti was very successful in Tokyo. 13. My elder sister is hanging my mother's photograph on the wall. 14. What he says is a little odd. 15. Have you ever seen a bird whose colour is red?

LESSON 13

INSTEAD of **Watasi ga katta hon wa omosiroi desu**—" The book I bought is interesting ", we may say **Watasi ga katta no wa omosiroi desu**—" The one I bought is interesting ". That is to say, if the topic of conversation, here " book ", is already known, it may be replaced by the pronoun **no**, just as in English in these circumstances we can use " one ". This pronoun **no** is distinct from the particle **no**, and can refer to things abstract and concrete, time, place, persons—

> **Kinoo hanasita no wa nan desu ka.** What was it you talked about yesterday? (*Abstract thing.*)
>
> **Naihu de kitta no wa kore desu.** This is the one I cut with a knife. (*Concrete thing.*)
>
> **Parii e itta no wa kyonen desu ka.** Was it last year that you went to Paris? (*Time.*)
>
> **Sono hon o katta no wa Parii desu.** It was in Paris that I bought that book. (*Place.*)
>
> **Parii de kono hon o katta no wa anata desu ka.** Was it you that bought this book in Paris? (*Person.*)

In the above examples this **no** is preceded by an adjective clause. It may equally well be preceded by an adjective—

> **Omosiroi no wa kono hon desu ka.** Is it this book that is interesting? (Is the interesting one this book?)

Note that this **no** cannot be preceded by **kono, sono, ano, dono**; **kore, sore, are, dore** are used for " this one ", etc.

In the sentence—

> **Kore wa anata no enpitu desu ka.** Is this your pencil?

one could theoretically replace **enpitu** by **no** (**Kore wa anata no no desu ka**), but in fact the two **no** coalesce and one says—

> **Kore wa anata no desu ka.** Is this yours?

Thus we may say that the possessive pronouns (" mine ", etc.) are expressed by adding **no** to the appropriate personal pronoun—

Kore wa watasi no desu.   This is mine.
Are wa ano hitotati no desu.   That one belongs to them (is theirs).

and likewise—

Are wa otoosan no desu.   That one is your father's. *Or* That one is Father's.

Another example—

Teeburu no ue ni aru no wa anata no desu ka.   Is the one (which is) on the table yours?

Note that in the last example we may take advantage of the wide usage of the particle **no** to simplify **teeburu no ue ni aru no wa** to **teeburu no ue no wa** (" the one connected with the top of the table ", " the one on top of the table "), to **teeburu no wa** if we do not need to be precise about the position relative to the table or to **ue no wa** (" the one connected with the top ", " the one on top ") if we do not need to be precise about what it is on top of.

Another important use of the pronoun **no** is in sentences like the following :

Sinrigaku no hon o kaita no desu.

which might be translated—

It is a fact that he wrote a book on psychology.

Another way of putting it is to say that the addition of **no desu** to the plain form of what one would expect to be the main verb or adjective is a very common device, and its effect is generally to add some overtone of meaning that would not otherwise be present.   In affirmative sentences this overtone might be such as one could translate by " it is a fact that . . ." " it's because . . .", " that's why . . .", etc.   In interrogative sentences the difference is that when the sentence does not end with **no desu** the questioner is simply seeking to gain information—

Kinoo Rondon e ikimasita ka.   Did you go to London yesterday?

but when one adds **no desu**—

Kinoo Rondon e itta no desu ka.

one normally implies that for some reason or other one thinks
that the person to whom one is speaking did go to London
yesterday, and one is asking for confirmation of what one
thinks. It may perhaps be that two days ago he had said
that he might be going to London, and the day before one
had not seen him around, so one presumes that he did in
fact go, and one asks the question largely to discover
whether one thought correctly. Many forms of words can
be used in English to express this overtone, or it may be
done by variations of intonation. One turn of phrase that
often serves is, to take the present example, " You went to
London yesterday? " that is, using the affirmative construction, without inversion as in " Did you go to London
yesterday? ", but with a questioning intonation.

This overtone adding **no desu** can have the form **n' desu,**
with the dropping of the **o** of **no.** When **no** is equivalent
to " the one ", it rarely becomes **n'**—

Sinrigaku no hon o kaitan' desu.

It was said above that **no (n') desu** is added to the plain
form of the verb or adjective. There is one exception to
this; when the verb is **desu,** it changes to **na** before **no
(n') desu.** This **na** is in fact part of an old verb with the
same meaning as **desu** and is the **na** of the **NA** adjectives—

Eikokuzin desu ka. Is he an Englishman?
Eikokuzin nan' desu ka. He is English?
Ano hito no huku wa hen desu. His suit is peculiar.
Ano hito no huku wa hen nan' desu. The fact is, his
suit is peculiar.

With **naze,** " why ", and **doosite,** " how does it come
about that . . .", " why ", the construction with **no
(n') desu** is the normal one—

Naze gakkoo e ikanain' desu ka. Why don't you go to
school?

Doosite zisatu sitan' desu ka. Why did he commit
  suicide?

When a question contains an interrogative word other than
naze, doosite, the use of **no (n') desu** seems to add little
extra shade of meaning—

Nani o utte irun' desu ka.⎫
Nani o utte imasu ka.　　 ⎬ What are you selling?
Itu dekakemasu ka.　　　　⎫
Itu dekakerun' desu ka.　 ⎬ When are you leaving?

There may be a slight difference between the two sentences
of the last pair, the first being a mere request for information, and the second showing perhaps, surprise at seeing
your preparation for departure earlier than one had
thought. However, different speakers have different
speech habits, and in any case the translation would be
the same in each case, though the intonation might be
different.

There follow a few more typical examples of the construction—

Beikoku de wa waisyatu o kaun' desu. The thing to do
  in America is to buy shirts.

Otoosan wa syooti sinain' desu. The trouble is, Father
  won't say yes.

Kinoo mita kaban o kattan' desu ka. You've bought
  the case we saw yesterday? (If the case was
  in the window of a shop when you saw it with your
  friend, then, on the next day, it was gone, on meeting your friend again you might presume that he had
  bought it, and would use a sentence like this to ask
  if your presumption was correct.)

Naze Tookyoo e ikanakattan' desu ka. Why didn't
  you go to Tokyo?

Iku kane ga nakattan' desu. (It was because) I hadn't
  the money to (go).

Sono hon wa omosiroin' desu ka. Your book is
  interesting? (Implying, perhaps, that you look
  as if the book is interesting, probably from the
  absorbed way in which you are reading it.)

Vocabulary

Nouns

ana, hole
asa, morning
Beikoku, U.S.A.
densya, electric train, tram
hatake, field (cultivated but not rice)
Itarii, Italy
kaze, wind, a cold
ongaku, music
ototoi (also adv.), the day before yesterday
saki, (pointed) end, tip
sibai, play (theatre)
sigoto, work
sinrigaku, psychology
sinrui, relative(s)
waisyatu, shirt
zaisan, property, fortune
zisatu (suru), suicide

Pronoun

no

Verbs

asobu, play (not acting)
dasu, send out, take out, put out
hazimaru, begin
hikaru, shine
homeru, praise
horu, dig
huku, blow
kakusu, conceal, hide
kiku, listen, hear, ask
nakusu, lose
noru, ride on, mount, go aboard
okiru, arise, get up
sagasu, search for
simeru, shut, close
warau, laugh (at)

Adverbs

doosite
naze

Exercise 13

I. *Translate into English:* 1. Ano hito ga hometa no wa kono e desu ka. 2. Niwa de asonde iru no wa sinrui no kodomo desu. 3. Ane ga hikidasi kara dasite iru no wa haha no kimono desu. 4. Tuyoi kaze ga huita no wa ototoi desita. 5. Atarasii sibai ga hazimaru no wa itu desu ka. 6. Saki ga hikatte iru no ga anata no desu. 7. Naze hatake ni ooki na ana o hotte irun' desu ka. 8. Ano hito wa doosite kao o kakusitan' desu ka. 9. Itarii de wa ii ongaku o kikun' desu. 10. Ani wa sigoto o sagasanain' desu. 11. Naze kono densya ni noranain' desu ka. 12. Zaisan o nakusita Arita-san ga kinoo zisatu sitan' desu. 13. Ano hitotati wa nani o waratte irun' desu ka. 14. Naze asa hayaku okinain' desu ka. 15. Doosite mado o simenain' desu ka.

II. *Translate into Japanese:* 1. It is this music that I heard in Paris. 2. Is this book on psychology yours? 3. The one who is digging a hole in the garden is the child of (one of) my relatives. 4. Was it the new shirt that you took out of the drawer? 5. It was on a day when a strong wind was blowing that I lost my hat. 6. Why do you shut the door? 7. We get on the tram here? 8. The thing to do in America is to look for work. 9. When did you go to the theatre? The day before yesterday. 10. Why don't you conceal your property? 11. The thing is, we get up at five o'clock in the morning. 12. Why do you play in the field? 13. You don't praise any of the pictures? 14. Is the film which starts tomorrow an Italian one? 15. We are laughing at the one the tip of which is shining.

LESSON 14

JAPANESE has certain conjunctions which can be used to join co-ordinate main clauses. Two of these are **ga** and **keredomo,** both translatable as " but "—

> **(Niwa ni) neko wa imasu ga inu wa imasen.** (In the garden) there is a cat but no dog.
>
> **Kinoo Yokohama e ikimasita ga (keredomo) Naka-mura-san wa uti ni imasen-desita.** I went to Yokohama yesterday, but Mr. Nakamura was not at home.

The verbs in both parts of the sentence have to be in the same form, here the **-MASU** form. **Ga** may sometimes be used at the end of a sentence to suggest, for example, that a refusal is not absolute—

> **Kyoo ginkoo e ikimasu ka.** Are you going to the bank today?
>
> **Ie, kyoo wa ikimasen ga . . .** No, I'm not going to-day. (" But I am tomorrow " or " Did you want something " or some such implication is under-stood.)

or the reply might be—

> **Kinoo ittan' desu ga . . .** (The fact is) I went yester-day. (" But I'll go again today if you want to me " *or*

" It's a pity I didn't know you wanted something "
or some such deprecatory nuance is to be added.)

Two co-ordinate clauses joined by " and " in English
are often to be translated by putting the verb or adjective
in the first clause into the **-TE** form, thus—

> **Kore wa ringo de sore wa orenzi desu.** This is an
> apple, and that is an orange.
>
> **Kyooto e kite bukkyoo o benkyoo simasita.** He
> came to Kyoto and studied Buddhism.

(Note that if you translate a **-TE** form by a finite verb
it takes its tense in English from the final verb in the
sentence; thus in the first sentence above the English
uses the present tense, and, in the second, the past.)

> **Kono biiru wa kurokute tuyoi desu.** This beer is
> black and strong.

You will observe that the **-TE** form of an adjective is
formed by adding **-te** to the **-KU** form. The plain negative
has an additional form in **-naide** (e.g. **sinaide** from **suru**).

Sometimes the construction is used where " and " is
impossible in English, typically where the first clause has a
negative verb—

> **Kore wa ringo de wa nakute nasi desu.** This is a pear,
> not an apple.

One would translate the more normal " This is not an
apple, it is a pear " by **Kore wa ringo de wa arimasen;
nasi desu.**

Sometimes the **-TE** form can be translated by a form
ending in " -ing "—

> **Uta o utatte ikimasita.** We went along singing (a
> song).

Sometimes the clause ending in the **-TE** form may have a
causal or instrumental relation to the rest of the sentence—

> **Kikai o tukatte zikan o keizai simasu.** He saves time
> by using machinery.

The construction which consists of the **-TE** form of a
verb or adjective followed by the particle **mo** is generally

used to form expressions which can be translated by clauses beginning with " even if ", " even though ", etc.—

> **Denpoo o utte mo ma ni awanai ka mo siremasen.**
> Even if I sent a telegram, it might not be in time.
> (**Ma ni au**—an idiom meaning (*a*) " be in time ", (*b*) " be suitable ".)
>
> **Zitensya de itte mo, abunaku wa arimasen.** Even if you go by bicycle, it won't be dangerous
>
> **Anata wa kaburanakute mo watasi wa kaburimasu.** Even if you don't wear (your hat), I shall wear mine. (Said after hearing that you do not intend to wear a hat.)

In translating " whether . . . or (not) ", when this is connected with some such phrase as " I don't care ", or when the implication is similar, the same construction is used, reduplicated; it is not used to translate " whether . . . or " when this is a mere indirect question, after such a verb as " Do you know . . .".

> I don't care whether you stay (are) in the house or go out. **Anata ga uti ni ite mo soto e dekakete mo watasi wa kamaimasen.**
>
> Whether we finish the work early or not, I shall go to bed at nine. **Sigoto ga hayaku owatte mo owaranakute mo watasi wa kuzi ni nemasu.**

As is indicated by the translation " even if ", etc., this construction has normally a hypothetical meaning. The actions are usually only suggested, and one is not told whether they take place or not. A type of clause in English which might often be mistakenly translated by this construction is that beginning with " though ", " although ", when the action expressed really occurs or occurred. It will be simplest for you to deal with this in Japanese by the use of **ga** or **keredomo**—

> Although I often go to the City Hall, I have never met the Mayor. **Siyakusyo e wa tabitabi ikimasu ga (keredomo) sityoo ni atta koto wa arimasen.**
>
> I know what the (town) Mayor looks like, though I have never spoken to him. **Tyootyoo to hanasita koto wa arimasen keredomo, kao wa sitte imasu.**

When an interrogative word occurs in a phrase ending with **-te mo,** the meaning is like that of the English " No matter (who, etc.) ", " (who etc.) . . . ever "—

> **Dare ga kite mo, watasi wa aimasen.** No matter who comes, I shan't see him.
>
> **Ikura benkyoo site mo Nihongo o oboeru koto ga dekimasen.**
> No matter how much $\Big\}$ I study, I can't learn Japanese.
> However much

The **-TE MO** construction is very useful for translating sentences involving permission. Thus **itte mo ii desu ka** can be translated " literally " as " Even if I go it will be all right? "; in other words " May I go? "—

> **Asita doobutuen e itte mo ii desu ka.** Will it be all right to go to the Zoo tomorrow? *Or* May I go to the Zoo tomorrow?
>
> **E, itte mo ii desu.** Yes, you may.
>
> **Kono zibiki o karite mo ii desu ka.** May I borrow this dictionary?
>
> **Enpitu de kaite mo ii desu ka.** May I write it in pencil?
>
> **Eigo no bunpoo no hon ga arimasu ka.** Have you an (a book about) English grammar?
>
> **Huru-hon de mo ii desu ka.** Will a second-hand one do? (Even if it is a second-hand book will it do?)

Sometimes the affirmative pattern is used with a somewhat different meaning, applied to one's own actions—

> **Asita no kai de hanasite mo ii desu.** I don't mind speaking at the meeting tomorrow.

With a negative verb (e.g., **ikanakute mo ii desu ka**— " Even if I do not go will it be all right? ") one can express the idea of " Do you mind if I don't go? ", " Need I go? ", etc.)—

> **Konban uti ni inakute mo ii desu ka.** Will it matter if I don't stay at home this evening?
>
> **Monbusyoo e dasu tegami ni kitte o haranakute mo ii desu ka.** Will it be all right not to put a stamp on a letter to go to the Ministry of Education?

Pen de kakanakute mo ii desu ka. Will it matter if I
don't write with a pen?

Kami wa siroku nakute mo ii desu ka. Does it matter
if the paper is not white?

Huru-hon de nakute mo ii desu ka. Do you mind if it is
not a second-hand book?

Another useful construction is formed by placing the
particle **kara** after the **-TE** form; it then corresponds to the
conjunction " after "—

Issyuukan tatte kara kaerimasita. He went back after
a week (had passed).

Yuubinkyoku e itte kara nikuya e itte mo ii desu ka.
Will it be all right to go to the butcher's *after* the
Post Office?

You remember that after a noun or pronoun **kara** is to be
translated as " from "—

Doko kara kite imasu ka. Where have you come from?

There are one or two exceptions to this. In particular,
after the pronouns **are, kore, sore.** **Sore kara** is equivalent
to " next ", " after that "; **kore kara** to " after this ",
and, sometimes " immediately ", though **sugu** will always
do to translate " immediately "; **are kara,** " after that "
(referring to some time in the past) " from that time on ".

Vocabulary

Nouns	
bukkyoo, Buddhism	**konban** (also adv.), this evening
bunpoo, grammar	**kuni,** a country, one's native place
denpoo, telegram	**ma**
Doitu, Germany	**momo,** peach
doobutuen, zoo	**monbusyoo,** Ministry of Education
ginkoo, bank (financial)	**nasi,** pear
huru-hon, second-hand book	**sakura,** cherry
kai, meeting, association	**Sina,** China
keizai (suru), economy	**sityoo,** City Mayor
kikai, machine	
kitte, (postage-) stamp	

Nouns

siyakusyo, City Hall
tyootyoo, Town Mayor
uta, song
zikan, time, hour

Adjectives

abunai, dangerous
hurui, old
mezurasii, rare

Verbs

haru, stick on, stretch over
kaeru, return
kamau, care about

kariru, borrow
neru, lie down, go to bed
oboeru, learn, remember
owaru, finish
utau, sing
utu, hit, strike

Adverbs

sugu (ni), immediately, soon
tabitabi, often
tokidoki, occasionally

Conjunctions

ga
keredo(mo)

Exercise 14

I. *Translate into English:* 1. Denwa de hanasite zikan o keizai simasu. 2. Huransu e wa tabitabi ikimasita ga Doitu e wa itta koto ga arimasen. 3. Ano kodomo no otoosan wa Igirisuzin de okaasan wa Huransuzin desu. 4. Sigoto ga owatte kara sugu dekakete mo ii desu ka. 5. Sina wa hurukute ookii kuni desu. 6. Ikura isoide mo ma ni awanai ka mo siremasen. 7. Eigo no bunpoo wa ikura benkyoo site mo oboeru koto ga dekimasen desita. 8. Sore kara nani o sitan' desu ka. Nanimo sinaide netan' desu. 9. Denpoo o utte mo utanakute mo watasi wa kamaimasen. 10. Kono niwa ni wa sakura no ki wa arimasu ga momo no ki wa arimasen. 11. Sityoo ga ikura uta o utatte mo daremo homemasen desita. 12. Issyuukan tatte kara doobutuen e itte mezurasii doobutu o mimasita. 13. Monbusyoo e dasu tegami wa watasi ga kaite mo ii desu. 14. Are wa yuubinkyoku de nakute siyakusyo desu. 15. Bukkyoo no hon o karimasita ga taihen muzukasikute hayaku yomu koto ga dekimasen.

II. *Translate into Japanese:* 1. He is a student, not a teacher. 2. Even if we went by car we might not be in time. 3. I have not put a stamp on a letter to go to the bank. 4. I have never been to the City Hall, but I know what the Mayor looks like. 5. Will it be all right to

broadcast a talk on Buddhism? 6. I have often bought new
books, but I have never bought second-hand ones. 7. After
the meeting was over I immediately came home. 8. However old this machine is, it is not dangerous. 9. After a
week (had passed) I went to the Ministry of Education.
10. Will it be all right if I don't go to bed early tonight?
11. I don't care whether we meet the (Town) Mayor or not.
12. Although I have been to China, I have never been to
Japan. 13. He sang some uncommon (unusual) and interesting songs. 14. I don't mind sending the telegram.
15. We went to the park and saw the cherry blossoms.

LESSON 15

You may have noticed that in some sentences the **-U**
(or " neutral ") form of verbs has been translated by the
future tense; in fact, the " present " and " future " tenses
have the same form in Japanese, but there is rarely any
confusion, because the context usually removes any
possible ambiguity—

> **Asita Koobe e ikimasu.** Tomorrow I shall go to Koobe.
> (Notice that the English idiom allows you to say
> here, " Tomorrow I am going to Koobe.")
> **Rainen Nihonzin no tomodati ga sannin Eikoku e
> kimasu.** Next year three Japanese friends of mine
> are coming (will come) to England.

But—

> **Mainen Koobe e ikimasu.** I go to Koobe every year.

This form indicates an action that is certain to take place;
there is another form which, in one of its most characteristic uses, requires a translation such as " I suppose
that . . .", and may be called the **DESYOO** form. This is
connected with, but distinct from, the **-OO** form.

The **DESYOO** form is obtained by adding **desyoo** to the
plain form of the verb, e.g., **kau desyoo; taberu desyoo;
ryokoo suru desyoo.** Notice that **desyoo** is the **-OO** form
of **desu,** and that **da desyoo** does not exist. If the adverb
tabun is used with this form (or with **ka mo siremasen**),

" perhaps " may be used with the English future. A past tense of the form is got by adding **desyoo** to the plain **-TA** form, and other tenses are possible—

> **Asita wa eigakan e iku desyoo.** Tomorrow he will probably go to the pictures. *Or* Tomorrow I expect he'll go the pictures.
>
> **Tabun Amerika e itte iru desyoo.** Perhaps he's in America. *Or* Perhaps he's gone to America.
>
> **Gakkoo e itte ita toki ni wa maiban benkyoo sita desyoo**? At the time when you were at school I suppose you studied every evening, didn't you?
>
> **Tonari no onna-no-ko wa itu iku desyoo ka.** I wonder when the girl next door is going.
>
> **Raigetu iku desyoo.** I expect she will go next month.
>
> **Kinoo atta hito wa Eikokuzin desyoo.** The man we met yesterday was probably an Englishman. (Notice that the Japanese prefer not to use a **-TA** form in the main clause of this sentence; being an Englishman is thought to be a permanent characteristic of the man in question. The use of a **-TA** form might imply that he was an Englishman at the time but has changed since.)

In the plain form of the **DESYOO** form, **daroo** replaces **desyoo**. Adjectives operate in the usual similar way to verbs; **-I** adjectives add **desyoo** (**daroo**) to the **-I** form, and **NA** adjectives replace **na** by **desyoo**—

> **Soto wa samui desyoo.** I expect it's cold outside.
>
> **Sono huku wa sukosi hen desyoo.** I expect that suit is a little odd.

As has been said before, however, all verbs have **-OO** forms independent of their **DESYOO** forms. The formation is as follows:

-Masyoo replaces **-masu**—

tabemasu	tabemasyoo
ikimasu	ikimasyoo
desu	desyoo

The plain **-OO** form of **-RU** forms is got by changing -ru to -yoo—

kowareru	kowareyoo
miru	miyoo

that of **-U** verbs by changing **-u** to **-oo**—

haku	hakoo
isogu	isogoo
herasu	herasoo
katu	katoo
sinu	sinoo
kau	kaoo
erabu	eraboo
kamu	kamoo

that of our usual " irregular " verbs thus—

kuru	koyoo
suru	siyoo
da	daroo

The uses of this form differ from those of the **DESYOO** form. As a main verb of a sentence it is used only with a subject of the first person (" I ", " we "); in an affirmative sentence it is to be translated by what is sometimes called a 1st person imperative in English, the form beginning with " Let us . . .".

Asatte Ueno kooen no doobutuen e ikimasyoo. Let's go to the Ueno zoo the day after tomorrow.

Yama no ue e nobotte umi no kesiki o nagamemasyoo. Let's climb to the top of the mountain and look out on the view of the sea.

(Notice how, in translation, the **-TE** form takes on the tense of the final verb.)

In an interrogative sentence, the translation becomes " Shall we (I) . . .", etc., with the idea of suggestion or proposition—

Asita hayaku okite hon o seiri simasyoo ka. Shall we get up early in the morning and arrange our books?

Anata ga deru koto ga dekinai hi ni wa watasi hitori de ikimasyoo ka. On days when you can't go out, shall I go by myself?

Ituka gaikoku e ryokoo simasyoo ka. Shall we make a journey abroad someday?

Do not forget that the **-OO** form is used as a final verb only when the subject is " I " or " we ", and then only when an imperative idea or a suggestion or a proposition is present. Otherwise the **DESYOO** form is used, an interrogative sentence being translated by the use of some such formula " I wonder if . . .", " Do you expect . . ."—

Watasi mo asita sinu desyoo ka. Shall I too die tomorrow? (I.e., " Do you expect that I too shall die tomorrow? ")

(**Watasi mo asita sinimasyoo ka** could also be translated in the same way, but would imply the will to die— " Shall I too kill myself tomorrow? ".)

Watasitati wa rainen wa Nihon ni itte iru desyoo. We shall probably be in Japan next year.

Tayama-san wa rainen wa Nihon ni itte iru desyoo ka. Will Mr. Tayama be in Japan next year, I wonder?

The plain **-OO** form is used as a final verb in appropriate circumstances in speech not on the polite level, and also in the middle of the sentence, in various constructions. One that we can deal with here consists of placing after the **-OO** form the particle **to** and the verb **suru**. The translation of this construction will often be " try to ", " be about to "—

Neko wa nezumi o korosoo to simasita ga nezumi wa nigemasita. The cat tried to kill the rat but it got away.

Nigeyoo to sita toki ni wa yuki ga hutte imasita. At the time I tried to escape, it was snowing.

Kawa no naka no sima ni tatte ita hito wa kawa o wataroo to site ita no desyoo ka. I wonder if the man who was standing on the island in the middle of the river was trying to get across.

The comparative of adjectives and adverbs in Japanese can be shown in more than one way, but never by changing

the form of the adjective or adverb. To translate a
sentence like " Apples are cheaper than oranges " two
basic constructions may be used. The first is **Orenzi yori
ringo no hoo ga yasui desu, yori** being a particle translatable
by " than ", and **hoo** being " direction ", " side " and
ringo no hoo being " apples (as opposed to anything
else) ". The second is **Ringo wa orenzi yori yasui desu.**
You will notice that **ringo no hoo** is followed by **ga** in the
first sentence, whereas **ringo** is followed by **wa** in the second.
The first may be thought of as the answer to " Which are
cheaper, apples or oranges? ". The second is a mere
description of apples—in talking about them you say they
are cheaper than oranges, just as you might mention their
colour, etc. Typically the sentence goes on to add further
information about them—

> **Ringo wa orenzi yori yasui desu ga amari oisiku
> arimasen.** Apples are cheaper than oranges, but
> they are not very tasty.
>
> **Aoyama-san yori Murata-san no hoo ga se ga takai
> desu. Murata-san wa Aoyama-san yori se ga
> takai desu.** Mr. Murata is taller than Mr. Aoyama.
> (**Se ga takai** is a kind of compound adjective.)
>
> **Kisya de iku no wa basu de iku yori benri desu ga
> takai desu.** It is more convenient to go by train
> than by bus but it is dearer.
>
> **Basu de iku yori kisya de iku hoo ga benri desu. Basu
> yori kisya no hoo ga benri desu.** The train is more
> convenient than the bus.
>
> **Kono hon wa sono hon yori omosiroi desu ka.** Is this
> book more interesting than that one?
>
> **Asita no hoo ga asatte yori ii desu.** Tomorrow will be
> better than the day after.
>
> **Watasi wa Aoyama-san yori hayaku okimasu.** I get
> up earlier than Mr. Aoyama.

One can also use the construction with the noun **hoo**
when that with which the comparison is made is not
expressed.

> **Yasui hoo o kaimasyoo.** Let's buy the cheaper one.
>
> **Hon-ya no hoo ga tikai desu.** The bookshop is nearer.

Yasui taipuraitaa no hoo o kaimasyoo. Let's buy the cheaper typewriter.

Kyooto e iku hoo ga kane ga kakarimasu. It costs more to go to Kyoto.

Kisya de iku hoo ga anzen desu. It is safer to go by train.

Note that when the noun is not expressed (as in **Yasui hoo o kaimasyoo**) **hoo** does imply a real comparison when used after the adjective. When, however, the noun is there, **hoo** normally follows it (**yasui tapuraitaa no hoo**), otherwise a different meaning arises; thus **yasui hoo no taipuraitaa** means " a cheapish typewriter ", " a fairly cheap typewriter ".

In connection with **hoo** preceded by a verb, there occurs another idiomatic use of the **-TA** form of the verb, in circumstances where English might use " would ", as in the following examples:

Kisya de itta hoo ga anzen desu. It would be safer to go by train.

Kisya de itta hoo ga anzen desita ga zikan ga nakatta no desu. It would have been safer to go by train, but I hadn't the time.

There is an adverb **motto** which can modify adjectives, adverbs, and verbs, and is translated by " more " or by the use of a comparative—

Eikoku de wa ame ga yoku hurimasu ga Nihon de wa motto hurimasu. It rains a lot in England but it rains more in Japan.

It is also used when a comparison is made between two things or persons, and then a further comparison is made, as in—

Watasi wa Aoyama-san yori hayaku okimasu ga Murata-san wa motto hayaku okimasu. I get up earlier than Mr. Aoyama, but Mr. Murata gets up earlier still.

To translate the construction " as . . . as . . . ", one can use the particle **hodo** (" to the extent of "), usually with a negative verb—

Orenzi wa ringo hodo yasuku arimasen. Oranges are not so cheap as apples.

Kamakura e iku no wa Hakone e iku hodo zikan ga kakarimasen. It doesn't take as long to go to Kamakura as it does to Hakone.

. Note that **hodo** follows immediately after a verb without an intervening **no.** When it follows an adjective and is used in this sense, **no** is necessary—

Atarasii zidoosya wa hurui no hodo gasorin o tukaimasen. A new car doesn't use as much petrol as an old one.

The construction " as . . . as . . ." with a positive can be expressed by the particle **gurai** (" to the degree of ")—

Anata no nooto wa watasi no gurai atui desu ka. Is your exercise-book as thick as mine?

Ie, anata no hodo atuku arimasen. No, it is not as thick as yours.

To translate " as . . . as possible ", the adverbial expression **dekiru dake** can be used—

Dekiru dake hayaku kimasu. I shall come as early as possible.

Dekiru dake osoku kaerimasyoo. Let's go home as late as possible.

To ask the question, " Which is the . . . er ? ", you should make use of **dotira**—

Dotira no pen ga nagai desyoo. I wonder which pen is longer.

Orenzi to ringo to (wa) dotira ga yasui desu ka. Which is cheaper, an apple or an orange?

Sometimes one has to use a more complicated construction—

Dotira ga Eikokuzin desu ka. Se ga takai hito desu ka, se ga hikui hito desu ka. (Which is the Englishman? Is it the tall person or the short person?) Is the Englishman the tall one or the short one?

To form a superlative, normally one places the adverb **itiban** before an adjective or adverb—

> **Itiban hayai kisya wa yozi zyuugohun ni demasu.**
> The fastest train leaves at 4.15.
> **Watasi ga itiban yoku iku onsen wa Atami desu.**
> The hot spring I go to most is Atami.

Vocabulary

Nouns

asatte (also adv.), the day after tomorrow
eigakan, cinema
gasorin, petrol
hon-ya, bookshop
hoo, direction, etc.
hune, boat, ship
kesiki, scenery
Koobe, Kobe
kooen, park
kotosi (also adv.), this year
maiban (also adv.), every evening
mainen (also adv.), every year
nezumi, rat, mouse
onna-no-ko, girl
onsen, hot spring
raigetu (also adv.), next month
rainen (also adv.), next year
se, back (of body), stature
seiri (**suru**), putting in order
soto, outside
taipuraitaa, typewriter
toki, time
tonari, next door
yama, mountain, hill

Adjectives

anzen na, safe
atui, thick
benri na, convenient
hikui, low
nagai, long
oisii, tasty, delicious
osoi, late, slow
tikai, near

Verbs

korosu, kill
nagameru, gaze at
nigeru, escape
noboru, go up
toru, take
wataru, cross over

Adverbs

amari, too much, (neg.) not very
itiban, most
motto, more, etc.
tabun, perhaps

Particles

dake
gurai (kurai)
hodo
yori

Prefix

mai-, every

Exercise 15

I. *Translate into English:* 1. Sono onsen e wa benri na kisya wa ikanai desyoo. 2. Kore wa tabun Tanaka-san no taipuraitaa desyoo. 3. Kono yama wa Hakone hodo takaku arimasen ga Hakone yori samui desu. 4. Asita no asa hayaku okite soto no kesiki o nagamemasyoo. 5. Motto tikai tokoro e nigeru koto ga dekinai desyoo ka. 6. Watasi no neko wa anata no gurai nezumi o korosu desyoo ka. 7. Ano onna-no-ko wa oyogoo to site imasu ga hune de watatta hoo ga anzen desyoo. 8. Nasi yori momo no hoo ga oisii desyoo ga momo wa amari tabeta koto ga arimasen. 9. Huru-hon no hoo ga yasui ka mo siremasen ga ano hon-ya de wa utte imasen desita. 10. Tamura-san wa Yamamoto-san hodo se ga takaku arimasen ga Yama-moto-san yori hayaku hasiru koto ga dekimasu. 11. Kotosi wa dekiru dake tiisakute karui kaban o kaimasyoo. 12. Amari atuku nai nooto o tukau hoo ga ii desu. 13. Dotira no zidoosya ga gasorin o keizai simasu ka. Aoi no desu ka, kuroi no desu ka. 14. Itiban osoku kita no wa se ga hikui hito datta desyoo ka. 15. Kooen de ki ni nobotte ita kodomotati wa tori no tamago o toroo to site ita no desyoo ka.

II. *Translate into Japanese:* 1. The one who will get up earliest tomorrow morning is probably Mr. Tanaka. 2. My younger brother is shorter than the girl next door, but his legs are longer. 3. On days when it rains and we can't go to the sea, shall we go to the cinema? 4. Every evening I tried to arrange the books on the bookshelf, but I hadn't the time. 5. That bookshop is nearer and more convenient, I suppose, but it may not sell that book. 6. Let us use as thick and heavy a lid as possible. 7. Every year my father goes to Kobe in March, but this year I expect he will go in April. 8. Next month shall we cross that river and climb the hill (which is) on the other side? 9. My elder brother will perhaps make a journey abroad next year. 10. The day after tomorrow let us go to the park and look at the view. 11. Let us buy a typewriter as good as Mr. Tamura's. 12. Even if we go by car it will be safe, but it will be safer still if we go by train. 13. It is not so late as yesterday, but we had better go home by bus, I suppose. 14. These peaches may not be very tasty, but they are cheap. 15. At the time the cat tried to kill it, the rat was running away.

LESSON 16

IN Lesson 14 we saw the use of **kara** following the **-TE** form. It is important to avoid confusing this construction with that consisting of **kara** following a verb in the **-U, -TA** or **DESYOO** form. In this instance the translation is "because", "as", "since" at the beginning of a clause, or "so" at the end of it (i.e., at the beginning of the following clause). A peculiarity is that the verb preceding **kara** is normally at the same level of politeness as the final verb, e.g., when the final verb is in the **-MASU** form, so is the verb preceding **kara**—

(a) **Kinoo sake o takusan nomimasita kara kyoo wa atama ga itai desu.** I drank a lot of *sake* yesterday, so my head aches today. *Or* My head is aching today because I drank a lot of *sake* yesterday.

(b) **Asita nagai ryokoo o surun' desu kara, konban wa hayaku neta hoo ga ii desu.** As you're going on a long journey tomorrow, it'd be better if you went to bed early tonight.

(c) **Gogo hakubutukan e iku ka mo siremasen kara hutuu yori hayaku hiru no syokuzi o simasyoo.** Perhaps we shall go to the museum this afternoon, so let's have lunch (our midday meal) earlier than usual.

(d) **Atarasii no o kaimasu kara kore wa minna tukatte mo ii desu.** As I'm going to buy some new ones, you may use all of these.

Another way of translating "as", "because", etc., is to use the **-TE** form of the **NO (N') DESU** construction, i.e., **no de,** sometimes abbreviated to **n' de**—

Nodo ga kawaite inakatta no de biiru o nomimasen desita. As I was not thirsty (my throat was not dry), I didn't drink any beer.

Ame ga yanda no de yama ga yoku miemasu. Since it's stopped raining, the mountains are clearly visible.

Sora ga hareta no de hosi ga yoku miemasu. One can see the stars clearly because the sky has cleared.

Unfortunately there is one restriction on the use of **no de**; it is not generally used when the main verb of the sentence is an imperative or implies some sort of obligation or permission. Thus, in the sentences with **kara** above, it could not be used in (*c*), which has a 1st person imperative, nor in (*b*) or (*d*), which have ideas of permission or obligation. However, in sentence (*a*) either **kara** or **no de** could be used. There are sentences in which, for the sake of euphony or economy of breath, **no de** is preferred to **kara**; such are—

> **Tekitoo na no ga nakatta no de nanimo kaimasen desita.** As there were no suitable ones I didn't buy anything.

which is preferred to—

> **Tekitoo na no ga arimasen desita kara nani mo kaimasen desita.**

to avoid the repetition of the long verb forms.

Similarly, to avoid the repetition of **desu,** many would prefer—

> **Kono hana wa ookii no de sukosi takai desu.**

to

> **Kono hana wa ookii desu kara sukosi takai desu.** These flowers are large so they are a little dear.

However, in neither case can **kara** be thought of as actually incorrect.

Thus you may consider it simplest to use **kara** for " because ", etc., in all circumstances. However, the use of **no de** is preferable where **kara** would involve the use or repetition of long -MASU forms. In any case, **no de** is not possible where the main verb is imperative or is in a form implying obligation or permission, nor, incidentally, is it

possible when the clause at the end of which it would come
already has its verb in the **NO DESU** form, i.e., one says
. . . **no desu kara** and not . . . **no na no de.**

The particle **ni** has up to the present in this book been
used mainly to indicate position or time—

> **Nyuu Yooku wa Amerika ni arimasu.** New York is in
> America.
> **Sanzi ni kimasita.** He came at three o'clock.

Sometimes it is used in places where you might expect **e.**
Thus, as well as **Amerika e itte imasu,** you will hear **Amerika
ni itte imasu,** which may indicate that the speaker is thinking more of the person's being in America than of his having
gone there. With expressions of paying attention, taking
interest, etc., it is used to show the direction of the attention
or interest—

> **Titi wa tabemono ni tyuui simasu.** My father is careful
> about his food. (. . . **ni tyuui suru,** " pay atten-
> tion to ", " be careful about ")
> **Yukiko-san wa Huransu no bungaku ni kyoomi o
> motte imasu.** Miss Yukiko is interested in French
> literature. (. . . **ni kyoomi o motte iru,** " have an
> interest in ", " be interested in ")
> **Ani wa uma ni noru koto ni kyoomi o motte imasu.**
> My elder brother is interested in horse-riding.
> (**uma ni noru,** " ride on a horse ")

Ni is used before expressions equivalent to " it is convenient
(inconvenient) ", etc., and can be translated as " for "—

> **Kono heya wa sigoto ni benri desu.** This room is con-
> venient for working in.
> **Kore wa sigoto ni benri na heya desu.** This is a room
> well suited for working in.
> **Benkyoo ni guai ga warui basyo desu.** It is a spot
> (place) in which conditions are bad for study.
> **Hon o yomu no ni koosen no guai ga warui desu.**
> The lighting (condition of the light-rays) is bad for
> reading (books).

Where the sentence requires **wa** after **no ni,** it is usual to
drop **no** and add **ni wa** direct to the verb—

Hon o yomu ni wa huben desu ga neru ni wa taihen benri desu. It's inconvenient for reading (books), but very good for sleeping.

Similarly, before certain verbs, such as **tukau,** " use "; **iru,** " be necessary ", and others of similar meaning, **ni** can be translated as " for " with a noun—

Hako o makura ni tukaimasita. He used the box for a pillow.
Kono hukuro wa kaimono ni irimasu. This bag is necessary for shopping. *Or* I need this bag for shopping.

No ni following a verb can also be used in this way, and can be translated by " for . . . ing ", " in . . . -ing ", or " to . . ."—

Teeburu o naosu no ni matu no ki o tukaimasita. He used deal (pine wood) for mending the table (to mend the table).
Enzin o ugokasu no ni gasorin o tukaimasu. One uses petrol to work the engine.
Hon o kau no ni takusan kane o tukaimasita. He spent (used) a lot of money in buying books.
Isu o tukuru (no) ni wa, nan no ki o tukaimasyoo ka. What kind of wood shall we use to make the chair?
Atarasii zidoosya o kau (no) ni wa kane ga takusan iru desyoo. I suppose it needs a lot of money to buy a new car.

Here are some more expressions with which this construction is used—

Ano ookii hoteru o tateru ni wa hizyoo ni kane ga kakarimasita. It took an awful lot of money to build that big hotel.
Menzyoo o toru ni wa taihen hone ga oremasita. It was very difficult getting the licence. (**Hone ga oreru,** " one's bones break ", is used figuratively for " it is hard work ".)
Ii ryokan o mitukeru ni wa sanzikan mo kakarimasita. It took me (as long as) three hours to find a good inn.

Another very common use is before verbs of motion, usually **iku** or **kuru,** where it shows the purpose of one's going or coming. It can be used after some nouns, such as **kaimono,** which means " shopping ", both in the sense of the act of shopping and of the things bought. Thus **kaimono ni iku** is " go shopping ". Usually, however, in this construction **ni** follows the " stem " of a verb. This " stem " is the part of the verb to which **-masu** is added, and it acts often as a kind of verbal noun or infinitive. The meaning of the construction " stem " + **ni** + verb of motion is usually most conveniently expressed by the infinitive " to . . ." after a verb of motion in English—

Atarasiku dekita hoteru o mi ni ikimasita. He went to see the newly completed hotel.

Daiku wa yane o naosi ni kite imasu. The carpenter is here to mend the roof.

Piano o hiki ni ikimasyoo ka. Shall we go and play the piano?

In some cases the first component of **suru** verbs can be thought of as equivalent to the " stem ". For instance, when the **suru** verb has no object, direct or otherwise, one can add **ni** + verb of motion directly to the first component—

Hatizi ni syokuzi ni ikimasyoo. Let's go and have a meal at eight o'clock.

Asita hiru-gohan o tabete kara sanpo ni dekakemasyoo ka. Shall we go for a walk tomorrow after we've had lunch?

When, however, there is an object, **ni** has to be added to " stem " of **suru**—

Buturigaku o benkyoo si ni Amerika e itte imasu. He has gone to America to study physics.

The idea of purpose, " in order to ", etc., can also be expressed by the use of **tame ni,** which occurs in constructions like that with **tumori desu** in Lesson 5. It may be used with a verb of motion in place of the construction mentioned above, especially when the clause giving the purpose is separated from the verb of motion—

>**Kai ni deru tame ni rainen Amerika e ikimasu.** He is going to America next year in order to attend a meeting.

It may also be used with verbs other than those of motion—

>**Eigo o narau tame ni Eikoku no hoosoo o kikimasu.** He listens to English broadcasts in order to learn English.

There is another, and quite distinct, use of **no ni** in which it has the same adversative sense as **ga** or **keredomo,** but with an emotional addition, most commonly of regret (including resentment or irritation), but sometimes merely of surprised awareness of incongruity. The translation into English will vary according to the circumstances; " in spite of " and " whereas " will sometimes come near it—

>**Maki-tabako ga takusan atta no ni naze suwanakattan' desu ka.** There were plenty of cigarettes; why didn't you smoke one?
>**Mae ni yakusoku sita no ni uti ni imasen desita.** In spite of the fact that we'd made an appointment previously, he wasn't at home.
>**Tenki ga ii no ni naze konain' desyoo ka.** The weather's all right; I wonder why he doesn't turn up.
>**Tyoonan wa hutuu wa syokuzi no ato de zassi o miru no ni konban wa sugu benkyoo o hazimemasita.** Whereas my eldest son usually looks at magazines after his meal, tonight he started on his work straight away.

Vocabulary

Nouns	
bungaku, literature	**guai,** condition
buturigaku, physics	**hakubutukan,** museum
daiku, carpenter	**hiru,** noon, daytime
gogo (also adv.), afternoon	**hiru-gohan,** midday meal
	hosi, star

D

Nouns

hukuro, bag, packet, sack
kaimono, shopping
koosen, (beam of) light
kyoomi, interest (not financial)
maki-tabako, cigarette
makura, pillow
matu, pine
menzyoo, licence, diploma
nodo, throat
piano, piano
ryokan, hotel (Japanese style), inn (ditto)
sake, rice wine
sanpo, stroll, walk
tabemono, food
tame, purpose, benefit
tyoonan, eldest son
tyuui (suru), attention, note
yakusoku (suru), promise, appointment
yane, roof

Adjectives

huben na, inconvenient
tekitoo na, suitable

Verbs

hiku, pull, play (stringed instrument)
iru, be necessary
kawaku, dry
mieru, be visible
mitukeru, find, discover
naosu, mend
nureru, get wet
oreru, break (bone, stick, etc.)
tateru, erect
ugokasu, move, set in motion
yamu, cease

Adverbs

hutuu (ni), usually, normally
mina, all
takusan, a lot

Exercise 16

I. *Translate into English:* 1. Kono kimono wa taihen nurete imasu ga tenki ga ii desu kara sugu kawaku desyoo. 2. Asa wa ame ga hutte imasita ga gogo yanda no de sanpo ni dekakemasita. 3. Kono hakubutukan wa koosen no guai ga warui no de yoku miemasen. 4. Ano daiku wa yane ni yoku tyuui site ie o tatemasu. 5. Kono maki-tabako wa taihen ii desu ga nodo ni warui desu kara amari suwanai hoo ga ii desyoo. 6. Buturigaku no benkyoo ni tekitoo na hon ga arimasu ka. 7. Kono niku wa hiru-gohan ni mina tukaimasyoo. 8. Ane wa piano o hiki ni ikimasu ga watasi wa uma ni nori ni ikimasu. 9. Asoko no ryokan de syokuzi o suru ni wa hizyoo ni kane ga kakarimasu. 10. Inoue-san wa bungaku ni kyoomi o motte imasu kara sono Huransuzin no hanasi o kiki ni iku desyoo. 11. Sono kire wa makura o naosu no ni irimasen kara kitte mo ii desu. 12. Tyoonan wa sensei no menzyoo o toru tame ni Tookyoo de benkyoo site imasu. 13. Ano matu no ki o ugokasu no ni wa taihen hone ga oremasita. 14. Sake o nomanai yakusoku o sita no ni maiban takusan nonde imasu. 15. Miti o naosu sigoto o hazimeta no de ie e hairu no ni huben desu.

II. *Translate into Japanese:* 1. As we may go shopping tomorrow morning, let us get up earlier than usual. 2. The sky was not clear, so we couldn't see the stars. 3. As this inn is a little inconvenient, I intend to find a more suitable one tomorrow. 4. My eldest son is interested in physics, so I expect he will buy that book. 5. The lighting is bad for playing the piano, so I will play it tomorrow afternoon. 6. We used a box for a table in order to have our lunch in the garden. 7. What do you use to work this machine? 8. I suppose it needs a lot of money to repair this roof. 9. It takes two years to get a teacher's diploma. 10. I came to drink some water because I was thirsty. 11. Let us go for a walk in the park after having a meal. 12. My father has gone to broadcast a talk on literature this evening. 13. In spite of the fact that he promised (to do so), he is not careful about his food. 14. He came to Japan in order to build a museum. 15. The packet is dry, I wonder why the cigarettes are wet.

LESSON 17

WE saw in Lesson 10 the effect of adding **-mo** to the interrogative words **dare, dore, doko, nani** and to a noun after **dono,** when used with a negative verb or adjective. The same thing can be done with any other interrogative word. For instance, the adjective **donna,** which can be translated by " what sort of ", " what kind of ", can be used in sentences like the following:

> **Donna sinbun o yomimasu ka.** What kind of newspaper do you read?
> **Roodootoo no sinbun o yomimasu.** I read the Labour Party newspaper.
> **Donna sinbun mo yomimasen.** I don't read any kind of newspaper (a newspaper of any kind).

Nan no is an interrogative expression similar in meaning to **donna,** but it is more often used when asking the name or title or function of something. For example, a sentence containing the words **donna ki** would enquire " what kind of wood " in the sense of hard or soft wood, red or white or black wood, etc., whereas **nan no ki** would expect the name of the wood in the answer—" oak ", " mahogany ", " pine ", etc. **Nan no e desu ka** is equivalent to " What is the subject of this picture? ", whereas **donna e** might refer to whether it was an oil-painting or a water-colour, etc. It should be possible to use **-mo** with a negative verb or adjective after **nan no,** but the occasion may not often arise.

With some other interrogative words the addition of **-mo** does not have quite the same effect. Thus to translate " How much *sake* is there? " you might say **Sake wa ikura arimasu ka.** To answer " There is no *sake* at all ", you must say **Sake wa sukosi mo arimasen** (There is not even a little *sake*; **sukosi,** " a small amount ", " a little "; **mo** with negative, " even "). **Sake wa ikuramo arimasen** is good Japanese but rather rare as a construction and would be translated as " There is not much *sake*". Similarly **ikutumo** with a negative verb or adjective would be translated as " not many ".

> **Kasi wa ikutu nokotte imasu ka.** How many cakes are left?
>
> **Kasi wa ikutumo nokotte imasen.** There aren't a lot of cakes left.
>
> **Kasi wa hitotu mo nokotte imasen.** There's not even one cake left.

Care must also be taken when translating " never ". At first glance, it might appear the **itumo** with a negative verb or adjective would serve, but this is rarely so. The most usual method when the construction in English is of the type " I have never . . ." is to use the **-TA** form of the verb before **koto ga arimasen**—

> I have never been to Kagosima. **Kagosima e itta koto ga arimasen.**

The whole thing can be put into the past—

> (At that time) I had never been to Kagosima. **Kago-sima e itta koto ga arimasen desita.**

Next, let us consider the ending **-demo,** which can be added to interrogative words in the same way as **-mo.** The basic meaning is like that expressed by the English construction ". . . ever it is " (**daredemo,** " whoever it is ", **itudemo,** " whenever it is ")—

> **Daredemo ii desu.** Whoever it is, it will do. Any-one will do. (Note this use of **ii desu.**)

English expressions such as " anyone ", " any time ", " at any place ", " either ", etc., can be used to translate these combinations of **-demo** with various interrogative words. If the word consisting of an interrogative followed by **-demo** is pronounced with stress on **-de,** it should be translated by an emphatic form of the indefinite pronoun, using expressions such as " every single one " (**daredemo, doredemo**), " at any time whatsoever " (**itudemo**), " as much as you like " (**ikurademo**)—

> **Daredemo soo itte imasu.** Everybody is saying so.
> **Ano hon-ya de wa donna hon demo utte imasu.** They sell books of every possible kind in that bookshop.
> **Biiru wa ikurademo atta no de, takusan nomimasita.** As there was any amount of beer, we drank a lot.

Normally these forms are used only with positive verbs or adjectives, with two exceptions, **itudemo** and **nandemo,** which can also be used with negative forms—

> **Maisyuu iinkai e ikoo to omotte imasu ga itudemo iku koto ga dekimasen.** Every week I think I will go to the committee meeting, but I *never* can.

The effect here is to add regret or irritation to one's state-ment. This could be expressed by adding strong stress to the pronunciation of the word " never ". In Japanese the **-de** of **-demo** tends similarly to be pronounced with strong stress when this meaning is present. **Nandemo** can have a parallel use—

Watasi no yuu koto wa nandemo kikimasen. He won't listen to *anything* I say.

Nandemo nai can have certain idiomatic uses; it can mean " There's nothing the matter " or " There is no difficulty about this ", " It is not worthy of anxiety "—

> **Kono mondai wa nandemo arimasen.** There's no difficulty about this problem. *Or* There's nothing in this problem.
> **Nandemo nai koto desu.** It's an unimportant matter.

We saw in Lesson 10 how **-ka** may be added to **dare, doko, dore, dotira, nani.** It is not added to expressions containing an interrogative adjective or its equivalent (**dono, donna, nan no**) nor usually to expressions using **nan** with a classifier, nor with **ikutu.** The word **ituka,** however, is widely used, with the translation of " at some time ", " at any time ", as we saw in Lesson 15—

> **Sina no sibai o ituka mi ni itta koto ga arimasu ka.** Have you at any time been to see a Chinese play?

We have also seen the use of **-mo** added to interrogatives with a negative verb or adjective. It is also possible to use them with positive verbs and adjectives, with a meaning like that of " all ", " every "; **daremo** would thus be equivalent to " everybody ", etc. Unfortunately the uses of these forms are very idiomatic, and it would only confuse you at this stage to discuss them in detail. The most satisfactory way of translating expressions involving " all ", " every " and the like, when they are not particularly emphasised (when you can use the **-DEMO** forms) is to use certain adverbs, of which the most useful is **mina**—

> **Mina narande imasu ka.** Are you all lined up?
> **Kodomo wa mina doobutuen e ikimasita.** All the children went to the Zoo.
> **Sono hon wa mina urimasita.** I have sold them (i.e., the books you mentioned) all.
> **Hoteru no heya o mina soozi simasita.** I have cleaned out all the hotel rooms.

Here are some other words which can be used—

> **Kono hon o zenbu yomimasita ka.** Have you read all this book?
>
> **Kono sinbun o sukkari yomimasita ka.** Have you read this newspaper right through?
>
> (**Zenbu** is something like " the whole of "; **sukkari** is more emphatic and should perhaps be used with caution.)
>
> **Tosyokan mo kyookai mo ryoohootomo yakemasita.** Both the library and the church burnt.
>
> (**Ryoohootomo** (" two sides together ") reinforces the . . . **MO** . . . **MO** construction; it can often be used to translate " both ".)

Itudemo can be used as mentioned in the section dealing with **-demo,** and also as an equivalent of " always "—

> **Itudemo kuzi ni kimasu.** He always comes at nine.

Itumo can have the same translation, but is less emphatic—

> **Itumo kuzi ni kimasu.** He always comes at nine.
>
> **Ano hito wa itumo sinsetu desita.** He was always kind.

If such a sentence with **itumo** is followed by **ga,** as in **Itumo kuzi ni kimasu ga kinoo wa zyuuzi ni kimasita,** one would have to translate **itumo** by " usually "—" He usually comes at nine but yesterday he came at ten ". In such a sentence **itumo wa** might be more usual. In addition, when **itumo** is followed by **no** or **to** it is also to be translated by " usual " or " usually "—

> **Itumo no zikan ni kimasen desita.** He did not come at the usual time.
>
> **Itumo no zikan ni kimasita.** He came at the usual time.
>
> **Itumo to onazi zikan ni kimasita.** He came at the same time as usual.
>
> **Kyoo no niku wa itumo no to tigaimasu.** Today's meat is different from the usual.

Vocabulary

Nouns

Doitugo, German (language)
kasi, cake
kyoo (also adv.), today
kyookai, church
maisyuu (also adv.), every week
mondai, question, problem
nitiyoo-bi, Sunday
roodootoo, Labour Party
ryoohootomo, both
seihu, government
siken, examination
sinpai (suru), anxiety
sizi (suru), support
soozi (suru), cleaning (room, etc.)
tatemono, building
yakusyo, official office

Pronouns

daredemo
nandemo (also adv.)

Adjectives

donna
modan na, modern
nandemonai
sinsetu na, kind

Verbs

nokoru, be left, remain
omou, think
yakeru, burn (intr.)

Adverbs

ikuramo
ikurademo
ikutumo
ikutudemo
itumo
itudemo
sukkari
zenbu

Exercise 17

I. *Translate into English:* 1. Donna tatemono o tatemasu ka. Ookii modan na no o tatemasu. 2. Nan no tatemono o tatete imasu ka. Seihu no yakusyo o tatete imasu. 3. Doitugo no hon wa donna no mo yonda koto ga arimasen. 4. Kono kyookai e wa daredemo hairu koto ga dekimasu. 5. Gasorin wa ikura nokotte imasu ka. Ikuramo nokotte imasen. 6. Sinsetu na hito ga ikurademo imasu kara sinpai sinakute mo ii desu. 7. Ano hito wa itumo (itudemo) roodootoo o sizi simasu. 8. Maisyuu nitiyoo-bi ni tomodati o uti e yobimasu ga Tanaka-san wa itumo (itudemo) kimasen. 9. Kaze ga itumo no to tigatte imasu kara ie ga takusan yakeru ka mo siremasen. 10. Itumo no hito ga soozi ni kuru to omoimasu ka. Soo

omoimasu. 11. Amai kasi wa nanimo (nandemo) tabemasen. 12. Kyoo no siken no mondai wa zenbu dekimasita.
13. Ano hito ga itte inai kuni wa ikutumo arimasen. 14.
Dare ga ii to omoimasu ka. Daredemo ii desu. 15. Zidoosya
mo densya mo ryoohootomo sukkari kowarete imasita.

II. *Translate into Japanese:* 1. What kind of cakes
do you eat? I don't eat any cakes. 3. What Ministry
(government office) is that? It is the Ministry of Education.
3. How much sugar is left? There is not much left. 4.
How many churches have you built? I have never built a
single church. 5. Anyone can clean this room. 6. As
there was any amount of cigarettes I smoked a lot. 7.
Every Sunday I think I will arrange my second-hand books,
but I never can. 8. I won't buy anything in that shop.
9. There's nothing in learning German, so you needn't
worry. 10. My friends all support the Labour Government.
11. Today's story is completely different from the usual
one. 12. Yesterday's examination questions were all easy.
13. Both my suit and my hat are quite wet. 14. Do you
think he will come at the same time as usual? I think so.
15. All the teachers in this school are kind.

LESSON 18

IF we leave to one side the brusque imperative used in
military circles and when speaking angrily to inferiors,
there are several more polite ways of giving orders or requests. One of the simplest is more or less equivalent
to the English use of " please ", and involves the use of
kudasai. Used as the main verb in a sentence, this word,
which is the imperative of the verb **kudasaru,** " give to
me ", can be translated as " Please give me ". Notice
that it can be used only in a request that something be
given to the speaker or to somebody closely connected
with the speaker—

Ringo o hitotu kudasai. Please give me (us) an apple.

When **kudasai** is used following the **-TE** form of another
verb the resulting construction can be translated as
" Please . . ."—

To o simete kudasai. Please shut the door (for me).

To make a negative request using **kudasai,** you should add it to a form of the verb made up of the plain negative with **-de** affixed (e.g., **uru, uranai, uranaide; miru, minai, minaide)**—

> **Mado no garasu o kowasanaide kudasai.** Please do not break the (glass of the) window.
> **To o akenaide kudasai.** Please don't open the door.

Strictly speaking, constructions with **kudasai** should be used only to request some action which is to the benefit of the speaker (to whom, as it were, is given, for instance, the closing of a door), but it is used generally to make polite requests. To give a polite order or instruction, one can use **nasai,** which is the imperative of the verb **nasaru,** used in certain circumstances for the verb " do ". **Nasai** follows the " stem " of the verb, the form that is left when you remove the **-masu** ending, to which is prefixed **o-;** this is one form of the expression that gets translated as " honourable " in popular literature—

> **Uti e kaette kara tegami o o-kaki nasai.** Write the letter after you've returned home.

In the case of **suru** verbs, **nasai** replaces **suru,** and the prefix **go-** (another form of the " honorific " **o-**) is added to the first part of the verb. Thus the polite imperative of **benkyoo suru** is **go-benkyoo nasai**—

> **Siken wa gogatu ni arimasu kara yoku go-benkyoo nasai.** The examination is in May, so work hard.

Certain verbs have special forms of the polite imperative. **O-agari nasai** is the polite imperative of verbs of eating and drinking; the translation of this will often be " Please eat (drink, take, have) . . ."—

> **Kono ringo o hitotu o-agari nasai.** Please have one of these apples.

Other special forms are: **miru, goran nasai; iku** and **kuru, irassyai** or **o-ide nasai,** both meaning " come " or " go "; **yuu, ossyai; suru, nasai**—

> **Kono syasin o goran nasai.** Look at this photo.

Asita zyuuzi ni irassyai. *Or* **Asita zyuuzi ni o-ide nasai.**
Come at ten tomorrow.

If you want to use a negative imperative it will probably be best to use the form with **kudasai** which was mentioned earlier in this lesson.

It should be noted that the constructions with **nasai** and **irassyai** express commands or orders, albeit polite, and are to be used either when speaking to persons over whom one has authority, such as servants or children, or in a friendly way to one's acquaintances. They should not, for instance, be used on formal occasions to a guest; in this case the form with **kudasai** is not out of place. However, some more or less fixed phrases, such as **o-yasumi nasai,** " sleep well ", can be used generally.

There are, of course, many semi-imperative expressions that can be used, some of which we have seen already—

To o simeta hoo ga ii desu. It would be better to shut the door. *Or* You had better shut the door.

To o akenai hoo ga ii desu. You had better not open the door.

When talking to children, too, one can use the **NO DESU** construction followed by **yo** to get a sentence with a meaning something like that of " The thing to do is to . . ."—

Benkyoo site kara niwa e dete asobun' desu yo. The thing to do is to go and play in the garden *after* studying. *Or* You should go out and play in the garden *after* you've done your work.

To introduce another expression of obligation we shall have to make something of a detour. There are several constructions which correspond to the English conditional clause beginning with " if ". The one you had better learn first because it seems to have the widest use consists of placing the verb in the conditional clause in the **-EBA** form. This obtained by cutting off the **-u** of the plain form and substituting **-eba** (**yobu, yobeba; kau, kaeba; isogu, isogeba; taberu, tabereba; miru, mireba; kuru, kureba; suru, sureba,** etc.). The **-EBA** form of **desu** is **de areba ;** that of **-I** adjectives is formed by substituting **-kereba**

for the final **-i** (oisii, oisikereba; ii, yokereba). The
negative **-EBA** form of verbs and adjectives is obtained
from the forms ending in **-nai** (uranai, uranakereba;
yoku nai, yoku nakereba)—

> **Rondon e ikeba Rondon-too o miru koto ga dekimasu.**
> If I go to London, I can see the Tower of London.
> **Tenki ga yoku nakereba soto e denaide kudasai.**
> Please don't go out if the weather is not fine.
> **Yuki ga hureba ongakkai e ikimasen.** If it snows, we
> won't go to the concert.
> **Hi ga dete inakereba itudemo ooba o kite imasita.**
> He always wore an overcoat if the sun was not
> out.

The use of the particle **sae** in a conditional clause with an
-EBA form gives a construction that can be translated by
" if only "—

> **Kane sae areba sibai e iku koto ga dekirun' desyoo
> ga** . . . If only we had the money we could go to
> the theatre (but we haven't).

Sae can follow the first component of a **suru** verb—

> **Benkyoo sae sureba seikoo surun' desyoo ga** . . . If
> only he studied, he would succeed (but he doesn't).

Should the clause contain only a verb, as in " If only he
would come, we could talk it over ", **sae** may be added to
the " stem " of the verb and be followed by **sureba**—

> **Ki sae sureba soodan dekirun' desu ga nee.**

The other expression of obligation that we have been
leading up to in this long diversion is made up of the
negative **-EBA** form of a verb or adjective, with **ikemasen**
in the main clause, and is to be translated as " must ",
" has to ", etc. If one considers the sentence **Gakkoo e
ikanakereba ikemasen,** one may say that it means " literally " " If I do not go to school it will not do ", in other
words, " I must go to school ". (**Ikemasen** is in fact the
negative potential form of **iku,** but is used here idiomatically.)

He had to get up at five o'clock every day. **Mainiti gozi ni okinakereba ikemasen desita.**

As my mother is not at home, I must clean the rooms myself. **Haha ga uti ni imasen kara watasi zibun de heya o soozi sinakereba ikemasen.**

Vocabulary

Nouns
garasu, glass (substance)
gin, silver
haizara, ash-tray
kekka, result
kippu, ticket
kudamono, fruit
ongakkai, concert
saiban (suru), trial
soodan (suru), consultation
uketori, receipt
zibun (also pron.), self
zimusyo, (unofficial) office
zyotyuu, maid servant

Adjectives
isogasii, busy

Verbs
agaru, rise
akeru, open
goran (-nasai)
irassyai (irassyaru)
kiru, put on, wear

kowasu, break, destroy
kudasai (kudasaru)
nasai (nasaru)
o-ide (nasai)
ossyai (ossyaru)
sawaru, touch
yameru, cease, resign, refrain
yasumu, rest

Adverb
yukkuri (ro) gently, slowly

Particle
sae

Interjections
ne (nee)
yo

Prefixes
o-
go-

Exercise 18

I. *Translate into English:* 1. Kore wa tomodati no desu kara uketori o kudasai. 2. Saiban no kekka o hanasite kudasai. 3. Heya no naka wa taihen atui desu kara to mo mado mo simenaide kudasai. 4. Ongakkai no kippu wa nimai o-kai nasai. 5. Kinoo hanasita koto o soodan simasu kara konban irassyai. 6. Asita no gogo watasi no zimusyo e o-ide nasai. 7. Garasu no haizara wa zyotyuu ga kowasimasita kara gin no o tukau hoo ga ii desu. 8. Soto wa samui desu kara ooba o kite derun' desu yo. 9. Zikan ga areba Rondoo-too mo mi ni iku tumori desu. 10. Siken sae nakereba sugu ryokoo dekirun' desu ga nee. 11. Seikoo suru tame ni wa yoku hatarakanakereba ikemasen. 12. Kudamono wa ikurademo arimasu kara takusan o-agari nasai. 13. Ani wa isogasikatta no de zibun de todana o akenakereba ikemasen desita. 14. Asoko o goran nasai; nanika hen na musi ga imasu yo. 15. Anata wa yukkuri yasumanakereba ikemasen kara kyoo no kai e iku no wa o-yame nasai.

II. *Translate into Japanese:* 1. Please give me five tickets for the concert. 2. Please shut the window because it is very cold. 3. Please refrain from smoking cigarettes in this room. 4. Come to my house on Sunday morning. 5. The thing to do is to have a good rest after (eating your) lunch. 6. If you haven't a receipt we can do nothing. 7. Please do not break the glass lid. 8. Come at five o'clock, as I am going to speak about the result of the trial. 9. The maid is busy, and so you had better clean your room yourself. 10. In order to go into his room you must open this door. 11. If only you would go to London you would be able to see him. 12. If there isn't an ash-tray an ordinary plate will do. 13. Look at that fine building! 14. Please don't come to the office if the weather is bad. 15. This fruit is delicious (very tasty); please take some.

LESSON 19

THE only use of the particle o that we have seen up to now is to indicate the direct object of a transitive verb, as in—

Kinoo tegami o mittu kakimasita. Yesterday I wrote three letters.
Eigo o benkyoo site imasu. I am studying English.

There is, however, another use, with verbs of motion, to indicate where or along what the movement takes place, the point of departure of the movement, etc.—

miti o aruku, walk along a road
mon o tooru, come, go, through a gate
yama o noboru, go up, climb, a mountain
Tookyoo o tatu, set out from Tokyo
ie o deru, go out of the house, leave one's home

Notice the use of the dictionary form of verbs in this kind of grammatical discussion; you will remember that it is form found in dictionaries.

Do not forget that the verbs **au,** " meet "; **deau,** " encounter (by chance) " do not take a direct object in Japanese, but that one says, for example, **tomodati ni au,** " meet a friend "—

> **Sinbasi de kyonen Kyooto de atta Doituzin ni deaimasita.** At Sinbasi I ran into (encountered) a German whom I met in Kyooto last year.

The verb **kiku** is to be translated as " hear " when used with **o,** but " ask " when used with **ni**—

> **Razio de syusyoo no hanasi o kikimasita.** I heard the Prime Minister's speech on the wireless.
> **Watasi wa sirimasen; hoka no hito ni kiite kudasai.** I don't know; please ask someone else.

Japanese verbs have a form which expresses a wish. It acts as an adjective and is obtained by substituting **-tai** for **-masu** in the **-MASU** form. Thus the **-TAI** form of **kiku** is **kikitai,** " want to hear (ask) "; that of **taberu** is **tabetai,** " want to eat "—

> **Watasi mo ikitai desu.** I want to go too.
> **Nanika tabetai desu ka.** Do you want something to eat?

What would in English be the object of the verb is usually followed by **ga** when the **-TAI** form is used. Thus one says **pan o taberu,** " eat bread ", but **pan ga tabetai,** " want to eat bread "—

> **Pan ga tabetakereba ano pan-ya de o-kai nasai.** If you want to eat some bread, buy some at that baker's.
> **Dareka itigo ga kaitakereba, mukoo no mise de yasuku utte imasu kara asoko de o-kai nasai.** If anyone of

you wants to buy some strawberries, buy them in that shop over there, because they sell them cheap.

Biiru ga nomitai desu ka. Do you want to drink some beer?

There is another adjective, **hosii,** that is most conveniently translated by the verb " want " in English—

Nani ga hosii desu ka. What do you want?

Kasi ga hosii desu. I want some cakes.

Anata mo kasi ga hosii desu ka. Do you want some (cakes) too?

Ie, watasi wa kudamono ga hosii desu. No, I want some fruit.

There now follows a list of representative pairs of verbs that resemble pairs in English like " fall ", " fell "; " rise ", " raise "; " lie ", " lay " in that one of them is intransitive and the other transitive, i.e., takes a direct object with **o.** There are far more of such pairs in Japanese, and it is often difficult to find convenient equivalents for them in English. In some cases, however, the same verb in English can act as either transitive or intransitive, and in others a passive may be used to translate the intransitive form. Typical translations for each of the verbs are given. Unfortunately there is no way of recognizing merely from the sound of a verb whether or not it is transitive, but the list gives examples of most of the possible groups of forms.

(a) *Intransitive in* **-aru,** *transitive in* **-eru**

atumaru, gather, collect	**atumeru,** gather, collect
Tomodati ga atumaru. One's friends meet (gather).	**Tomodati o atumeru.** Gather one's friends together.

(b) *Intransitive in* **-u,** *transitive in* **-eru**

todoku, arrive, be delivered, reach	**todokeru,** deliver, report (to authorities)
Denpoo ga todoku. A telegram arrives.	**Denpoo o todokeru.** Deliver a telegram.
	Keisatu ni nanika o todokeru. Report something to the police.

(c) *Intransitive in -eru, transitive in -u*

nukeru, come out (tooth, cork, etc.), be extracted

Ha ga nukeru. A tooth falls out.

Ha ga nukete iru. A tooth is missing.

Nezikugi ga nukeru. A screw comes out.

nuku, extract, pull out

Ha o nuku. Extract a tooth.

(d) *Intransitive in -u, transitive in -asu*

ugoku, move, begin to move

Kikai ga ugoite iru. The machinery is running.

ugokasu, move, set in motion

Enzin o ugokasu. Start a (car-) engine.

Omoi nimotu o ugokasu. Move heavy luggage.

(e) *Intransitive in -reru, transitive in -su*

kakureru, hide (oneself).

To no usiro ni kakurete iru. Be hidden behind the door.

Hebi ga kusa no naka ni kakureru. A snake hides in the grass.

kakusu, hide, conceal.

Kane o hako no naka ni kakusu. Hide money in a box.

Sugata o kakusu. Hide oneself (hide one's shape).

(f) *Intransitive in -ru, transitive in -su*

tooru, go through, go along

Miti o tooru. Go along a road.

Densya ga ie no mae o tooru. The trams pass in front of the house. (Remember that this **o** does not indicate a transitive verb, see above.)

toosu, pass through, send along

Ito o toosu. Pass a thread (through a needle).

(g) *Intransitive in -eru, transitive in -asu*

nureru, get wet

Kimono ga nurete iru. One's clothes are wet.

nurasu, make wet, soak

Kimono o nurasu. Get one's clothes wet.

(h) *Intransitive in -iru, transitive in -osu*

okiru, rise, get up

Asa sitizi ni okiru. Get up at seven in the morning.

okosu, rouse, wake up

Sitizi ni otooto o okosu. Call (rouse) one's younger brother at seven o'clock.

(i) *Miscellaneous*

Intransitive

kikoeru, be heard, be audible

Neko no nakigoe ga kikoeru. The cry of a cat is heard.

mieru, be seen, be visible

Tookyoo kara Huzi-san ga mieru. Mt. Huzi is visible from Tokyo.

wakareru, part, say goodbye

Ginkoo no mae de wakareru. Part outside the bank.

kieru, go out, be extinguished

Dentoo ga kieru. The electric light goes out.

neru, sleep, go to bed

Zyuuzi ni neru. Go to bed at ten o'clock.

Transitive

kiku, listen to, hear

Seiyoo no ongaku o kiku. Listen to Western music.

miru, see

Mado kara zidoosya no syoototu o miru. See a motor-car collision from a window.

wakeru, divide, separate

Zaisan o mittu ni wakeru. Divide property into three.

kesu, extinguish, put out

Hi o kesu. Extinguish the fire (light).

Enpitu de kaita zi o kesu. Rub out writing written with a pencil.

nekasu, put to sleep, put to bed.

Ko o nekasite kara eiga o mi ni iku. Go and see a film after putting the child to bed.

noru, mount, ride

noseru, put on (a horse, etc.), put in (a boat, carriage, etc.).

Hune ni noru. Embark on a ship. *Or* Go aboard.

Nimotu o kuruma ni noseru. Put luggage on a cart.

Uma ni noru. Ride on a horse.

Vocabulary

Nouns

Doituzin, a German
eiga, film
ha, tooth
hi, fire, light
hoka, elsewhere (**hoka no,** another)
itigo, strawberry
ito, thread
keisatu, police
kugi, nail
kuruma, cart, carriage
kusa, grass, plant (other than trees and crops)
mon, gate(way)
mukoo, opposite side
nakigoe, cry
nezikugi, screw
pan-ya, baker('s)
razio, radio
seiyoo, the Occident
sugata, shape, form, appearance
syoototu (suru), collision
syusyoo, Prime Minister
yuubin-gitte, postage stamp

Verbs

atumaru, gather
atumeru, collect
deau, encounter
kakureru, hide
kesu, extinguish
kieru, go out, be extinguished
kikoeru, be heard
nekasu, put to bed
noseru, put on
nukeru, come out, be extracted
nuku, pull out, extract
nurasu, wet, soak
okosu, wake up, rouse
todokeru, deliver, report
todoku, be delivered, reach
tooru, go through, go along
toosu, send through, send along
ugoku, move
wakareru, separate, say good-bye
wakeru, divide

Adjective

hosii, desirous

Suffix

-tai

Exercise 19

I. *Translate into English:* 1. Syusyoo no kuruma wa gakkoo no mae o toorimasu ka. Watasi wa sirimasen. 2. Hen na hito ga kusa no naka ni kakurete imasita kara keisatu ni todokemasita. 3. Itigo ga sukosi hosii desu kara itiban ii no o todokete kudasai. 4. Seiyoo no yuubin-gitte o atumeyoo to site imasu ga amari atumarimasen. 5. Miti de Ooyama-san ni deatta no de sukosi hanasi o site kara wakaremasita. 6. Mizu de hi o kesoo to site huku o sukkari nurasimasita. 7. Siroi ito ga hosii' desu; kuroi no wa takusan arimasu. 8. Nakigoe wa kikoemasu ga sugata wa miemasen. 9. Razio o kikoo to sita toki ni dentoo ga kiemasita. 10. Eiga o mi ni ikitakatta no de kodomo o itumo yori hayaku nekasimasita. 11. Neko no syasin ga toritai no desu ga ugoite iru no de toru koto ga dekimasen. 12. Nezikugi wa nukete imasita ga hoka no kugi wa ani ga nukimasita. 13. Kinoo todoita matu no ki wa amari ookikute mon o toosu koto ga dekimasen desita. 14. Watasitati ga wakete tabeta pan wa mukoo no pan-ya de katta no desu. 15. Asita no asa rokuzi ni okosite kudasai; hatizi ni deru hune ni nimotu ga nosetain' desu.

II. *Translate into Japanese:* 1. When I was coming through the school gate I ran into Mr. Ooyama. 2. He is collecting a lot of second-hand books, but I don't suppose he intends to read them all. 3. I wanted to hear the Prime Minister's talk on the wireless, but I heard somebody else's. 4. If you want some postage-stamps, go to the shop opposite and buy them. 5. Shall we put on the cart the luggage which arrived yesterday? 6. The room is very cold because the fire has gone out. 7. My friends have gathered, but my younger brother has hidden himself and is not to be seen. 8. When did that German leave Germany? I don't know. 9. If your father agreed, I suppose it would be better to report it to the police. 10. Snakes may be hiding in the grass, so let's walk along that road over there. 11. I saw the tram collision from the window of a moving bus. 12. If you want to see an occidental film, go to the cinema in front of the station. 13. Please don't put the electric light out, because I want to pull out

this nail.   14. After putting the child to bed, I went to the
baker's and the butcher's.   15. I want to leave earlier than
usual tomorrow morning, so please wake me at six o'clock.

LESSON 20

CERTAIN expressions of space were mentioned in Lesson 4,
where it was indicated that their function was that of a
noun.   In addition to **ue, naka, sita,** we have **mae,** " front ",
usiro, " behind "—

> **Ie no mae ni hatazao ga tatte imasu.**   A flagpole stands
> in front of the house.
> **Undoozyoo wa gakkoo no usiro ni arimasu.**   The play-
> ground is behind the school.

Mae can be used also as an expression of time, " before ".

> **Ruuzuberuto no mae wa dare ga daitooryoo desita ka.**
> Who was President before Roosevelt?
> **Kono tatemono wa, mae wa, ryokan desita.**   This
> building was formerly an inn.

Expressions of time of day often precede **mae** immediately,
without an intervening **no,** e.g., **sanzi mae ni,** " before three
o'clock "; **zyuuzi sukosi mae ni,** " a little before ten
o'clock ".   Notice that **zippun mae** means " ten minutes
to ", thus **sanzi zippun mae** is " ten to three ".   The word
for " after " in these expressions is **sugi,** and the method of
its use is similar to that of **mae.**

The same construction is used with expressions of duration of time, e.g., " for the past three years ", **sannen mae
kara ;** " three hours before ", " three hours ago ", **sanzikan
mae ni.**   Note that expressions of duration of time, except
-syuukan, before **mae** do not have **-kan** suffixed to them—

> **Gonen mae kara Nihongo o naratte imasu.**   He has been
> learning Japanese for the last five years.
> **Sansyuukan mae kara asoko ni tomatte imasita.**   He
> had been staying there for the last three weeks.

Note the translation of the **-TE IRU** and **-TE ITA** forms
when used with this construction.

As **mae** functions as a noun, it may be preceded by an adjective or, more commonly, by an adjectival clause—

> **Issyo ni ikimasu ga sono mae ni tyotto denwa o kakete mo ii desu ka.** I shall go with you, but before that will it be all right if I just phone somebody?
>
> **Deru mae ni tya o nomimasyoo.** Let's have some tea before we go out.
>
> **Amerika e iku mae ni wa Sina ni sunde imasita.** Before he went to America he was living in China.

Notice that the verb in the adjectival clause preceding **mae** is not put in the **-TA** form.

An expression of duration of time, or an adverb, may be inserted immediately before **mae**—

> **Kisya ni noru sanpun mae . . .** Three minutes before boarding the train . . .
>
> **Yokohama e iku sugu mae . . .** Immediately before he went to Yokohama . . .

" After " can be rendered by **ato**—

> **Kono ato ni wa nani ga arimasu ka.** What is there after this?
>
> **Ato de kuru hito . . .** People who are coming later . . .
>
> **Hito no ato o tukeru.** Follow a person, trail somebody.

Ato can be used preceded by an adjectival clause—

> **Daigaku o deta ato de . . .** After he had left his university . . .

but do not forget that often the use of the **-TE** form followed by **kara** will do as well.

Note that **ato** can also mean " remains ", " traces ", etc.—

> **tera no ato,** the ruins of a temple
> **asiato,** footprint

" While Father was alive " can be translated as **Otoosan ga ikite iru uti ni,** using **uti,** which can also be used both for time and place, and may be translated by " among ", " while ", " during ", etc.—

Yasumi no uti ni kuru desyoo. He will probably come during (the course of) the holiday.

In addition, certain sentences in which English uses " before " may be translated by a special idiom in Japanese, involving the use of a negative verb and **uti.**

Sensei ga minai uti ni nigemasita. They ran away before the teacher saw them (while the teacher did not see them).

Sentences of this type show some purpose or precaution or preparation. In the sentence above the children ran away so that the teacher should not see them. A similar thought lies behind—

O-kyaku-san ga konai uti ni kono heya o katazuke-masyoo. Let us clear this room up before the guest comes.

Here the purpose is to avoid letting the guest see what an untidy state the room is in.

Position between objects is expressed by the use of **aida**—

Ki no aida ni ido ga arimasu. There is a well between the trees.

Kawasaki wa Yokohama to Tookyoo (to) no aida ni arimasu. Kawasaki is between Yokohama and Tokyo.

There now follow a number of useful expressions to put after verbs and adjectives in Japanese.

(1) **soo desu,** " it is said that . . .", " I hear that . . .", " it seems (from what I have heard) that . . .", etc.—

Gaikoku e ikanai soo desu. I hear that he is not going abroad.

Eikokuzin da soo desu. He is said to be English.

Tanaka-san ga katta zidoosya wa taihen hurui soo desu. I hear that the car that Mr. Tanaka has bought is very old.

Kyonen Suisu e sukii o si ni itta soo desu. It is said that they went skiing in Switzerland last year.

(2) **yoo desu**: **yoo** is equivalent to "appearance", and **yoo desu** can be translated as "it seems that . . .", "it looks as if . . .", etc.

> **Gaikoku e ikanai yoo desu.** It looks as if he is not going abroad.
>
> **Ueda-san ga sunde iru ie wa atarasii yoo desu.** It looks as if the house Mr. Ueda is living in is new.

Note that whereas one says **Eikokuzin da soo desu**, " I hear he is an Englishman ", the correct construction with **yoo** is with **no** replacing **da**: **Eikokuzin no yoo desu**, " He looks like an Englishman ". Similarly, " I hear it is so " is to be translated as **Soo da soo desu** and " It looks as if it is so ", by **Sono yoo desu**.

(3) **tumori desu**, intend (see also Lesson 5)—

> **Kinoo syasin o toru tumori desita ga ame ga hutte dekimasen desita.** I intended to take some photographs yesterday, but it rained and I couldn't.
>
> **Indo e wa dare to ryokoo suru tumori desu ka.** With whom do you intend to travel to India?

(4) **-soo desu**, " it looks as if . . ." It is better to write this with a hyphen to distinguish it from **soo desu** ((2) above); it is attached to the stem of the verb or adjective—

> **Ame ga hurisoo desu.** It looks as if it will rain.
>
> **Kodomo wa nakidasisoo desita.** The child looked as if it would burst into tears.
>
> **Ano buturigaku no sensei wa nakanaka wakasoo desu.** That physics teacher looks remarkably young.

The difference between **-soo desu** and **yoo desu** is that the former nearly always refers to a real appearance that may be seen with the eyes, whereas **yoo desu** covers appearance to any of the senses, unless hearing is precisely intended, when one uses **soo desu**. When used with a verb **-soo desu** normally refers to future likelihood judged from appearance—

> **Ame ga yande haresoo desu.** It looks as if the rain will stop and it will clear up.
>
> **Ookaze ga hukisoo desita.** It looked as though a gale would blow.

With an adjective **-soo desu** refers to present appearance.
Note that **yosasoo** is the irregular formation from **ii**
(" good ") and **-soo**, and **nasasoo** from **nai** and **-soo**.

(5) **rasii** is also to be translated as " it looks as if . . .",
" it seems as if . . .", " it appears that . . .", etc., but
has a meaning that embraces those of **yoo desu, soo desu**
and **-soo desu**.   It can follow a verb—

> **Yuki ga hutte iru rasii desu.** It seems that it is snowing.

or an adjective—

> **Yoru ano miti o tooru no wa abunai rasii desu.** It
> seems that it is dangerous to go along that road at
> night.

or even a noun—

> **Hoteru no mae ni tatte iru hito wa Sinazin rasii desu.**
> The man standing in front of the hotel looks as if he
> is a Chinese.

You will have realized that **rasii** is an adjective; it can
be used in front of a noun, **isya rasii hito**, " someone who
looks like a doctor "; **hontoo rasiku nai hanasi**, " a story
that has not the appearance of truth ".

Adjectives may also be formed from **yoo** and **-soo** by the
addition of **na**.   The meaning of **yoo na** may differ slightly
from what one might expect from **yoo desu**—

> **Eikokuzin no yoo desu.** He looks like an Englishman.
> **Eikokuzin no yoo na hito.** *Either* A person who looks
> like an Englishman.   *Or* Such people as the English.

In fact, **kono yoo na, sono yoo na,** etc., may be thought of
as having the same meaning as **konna, sonna,** etc., i.e.,
" this . . . and others like it ", etc.—

> **Amerika e iku yoo na hito** . . . Persons such as go
> to America . . .

-soo na has the meaning one would expect from that of
-soo desu—

> **Ame ga hurisoo na hi . . .** A day on which it looks
> as if rain will fall . . .

Omosirosoo ni hito no hanasi o kiku. Listen with interest to a person's story.

With human beings it is often used before **kao o suru,** "look", i.e., show emotion, etc., on the face—

Kanasisoo na kao o suru. Look sad.

Tumori may be joined to a following noun by **no**—

Zidoosya de kuru tumori no hito . . . Persons who intend to come by car . . .

Soo desu has no adjectival form.

Vocabulary

Nouns

aida, interval, space between

ato, what is left behind, time after

byooki, illness

daigaku, university

daitooryoo, president (U.S.A., etc.)

doroboo, robber

getuyoo-bi, Monday

hatazao, flag-pole

hontoo, truth

ido, well

ima (also adv.), present time

Indo, India

kyaku, guest

kyakusitu, drawing-room

mura, village

oka, hill

ookaze, gale

otoko, male

otoko-no-ko, boy

soo

Suisu, Switzerland

sukii, ski, skiing

syokudoo, dining-room

taisi, ambassador

tera, temple (Buddhist)

tya, tea

undoozyoo, playground, playing-field

yasumi, holiday, vacation

yoo

yoru, night

Adjectives

hiroi, wide, large

kanasii, sad

rasii

wakai, young

yoo na

Verbs

katazukeru, tidy up, finish off

nakidasu, burst into tears

tomaru, stay, stop

tukeru, fix, etc.

Adverbs

issyo ni, together

tyotto, a little, just

Suffix

-soo

Exercise 20

I. *Translate into English:* 1. Tera no mae ni tatte iru no wa hatazao no yoo desu. 2. Kono mura no mae wa umi de usiro wa oka desu. 3. Imai-san no mae wa Torii-san ga taisi desita ga ato wa dare datta desyoo ka. 4. Nisyuukan mae no getuyoo-bi kara yakusyo o yasunde iru rasii desu. 5. Kyakusitu o soozi suru mae ni syokudoo o katazukete kudasai. 6. Yasumi ga hazimaranai uti ni Suisu e sukii o si ni itta yoo desu. 7. Daigaku to kawa to no aida ni hiroi undoozyoo ga dekiru soo desu. 8. Amerika no daitooryoo ga byooki da soo desu ga hontoo desu ka. 9 Ido no usiro ni tatte ita no wa Sinazin no yoo desita ga yoru datta no de yoku miemasen desita. 10. Ato de kita o-kyaku wa wakai Amerikazin de omosirosoo ni titi no hanasi o kiite imasita. 11. Ame ga yamisoo desu kara syokuzi no ato de issyo ni dekakemasyoo. 12. Kyonen no yoo na ookaze ga huku ka mo siremasen kara hune de ikanai hoo ga ii desyoo. 13. Ano hito wa Indo no tya wa nomanai rasii desu kara Sina no tya o kaimasyoo. 14. Doroboo rasii otoko o mita no de ato o tuketa soo desu. 15. Uti ni tomatte iru otoko-no-ko wa kodomo rasiku nai koto mo simasu ga sakuban neru tyotto mae ni wa kanasisoo na kao o site nakidasimasita.

II. *Translate into Japanese:* 1. Three days before the vacation started a gale blew, and the University gateway was completely smashed. 2. After the meal he was looking with interest at photographs of Swiss scenery. 3. They say that this playground was formerly a field. 4. It seems that it is this ship that the Indian ambassador will go aboard. 5. It was at night that I tried to follow the robber so I didn't see his face. 6. Among the guests there were also some Chinese, it seems. 7. The boy burst into tears on seeing someone who looked like a foreigner. 8. In the front of this temple is a garden and the back a field. 9. That young man did not wear the overcoat even on days when it looked as if it would snow. 10. I hear that they are going to erect a tall flag-pole in front of the gate. 11. After hearing the President's speech I went with a friend to drink some tea. 12. It looks as if they talked a little about this affair in the drawing-room before going to the dining-room. 13. They say there is no illness in that village, but that's a story that doesn't seem true. 14. On Monday afternoon it looked as if the rain would stop and it would clear up, so we set off for the church on the hill. 15. In this hotel a lot of people are staying who look as though they do skiing.

LESSON 21

LET us examine first three adverbs which often cause confusion to Western students of Japanese. They are **mada, mata, moo.**

Mada is to be translated as " still ", " yet ", and refers to an action that has gone on in the past up to the present or some specified time—

> **Mada ikite imasu ka.** Is it still alive?
> **Sono toki ni wa mada ikite imasita ka.** At that time was it still alive?
> **Asita mada ikite iru desyoo.** I expect it will still be alive tomorrow.

The verb may be negative, and then " yet " will be the more usual translation—

> **Sore wa watasi ga mada kekkon site inai toki desita.** That was when I was not yet married (still not married).

Notice that in English the verb form with " has " is used where the Japanese has the **-U** form—

> **Mada dekakemasen ka.** Hasn't he started yet?

Note also the elliptical use of **mada** with **desu.**

> **Syatyoo-san wa kaerimasita ka. Mada desu.** Has the (company) president gone home? Not yet.

Mata, " again "—

> **Kyoo wa mata kiri desyoo.** I suppose there will be fog again today.

Sonna tokoro wa itido ikeba mata ikitaku wa nai desyoo. If you go to a place like that once you probably won't want to go again.

Moo: (*a*), "already", "by then", "by now", "now"—

Sono toki wa moo taisi o yamete itan' desu. At that time he had already given up the ambassadorship.

Rokuzi desu kara syatyoo wa moo kaetta desyoo. It's six o'clock, so I expect the president has gone home by now.

Moo ikimasyoo ka. Shall we go now?

Moo ii desu ka. Will it be all right now? *Or* Do you want this any more? *Or* Have you finished with this?

Note that **Mada ii desu ka** is " Is it still all right? ", " Is there still time? "

(*b*) " more " with an expression of number or quantity: **moo hitotu,** " one more "; **moo hutari,** " two more (people) "; **moo sukosi,** " a little more "; **moo itido,** " once more ".

Reported Speech

In Japanese, as in English, the exact words of the speaker may be reproduced when reporting speech; they are followed by **to** and a verb of saying or its equivalent—

" **Asita kimasu** " **to iimasita.** He said, " I shall come tomorrow."

" **Ame ga huranakereba tooka ni issyo ni umi e ikimasen ka** " **to kikimasita.** " If it doesn't rain, won't you come (go) to the sea(side) with me on the tenth? " he asked.

" **Ano hito wa dare desu ka** " **to kikimasita.** " Who is that? " he asked.

Isya wa " **mizu o takusan o-nomi nasai** " **to iimasita.** The doctor said, " Drink a lot of water."

O-kyaku wa " **yuubin ga areba sirasete kudasai** " **to iimasita.** My guest said, " Please tell me if there is any mail."

" **Kanai wa asita taiin simasu** " **to iimasita.** " My wife is coming out of hospital tomorrow," he said.

This procedure, however, is the exception rather than the rule, and is used only when the exact words spoken are for some reason important. Normally certain changes are made, although the basic construction is maintained. It is usual for the verb in the reported words to be in the plain form, and no change of tense is made—

> **Asita kuru to iimasita.** He said he would come to-morrow.
>
> **Ame ga huranakereba tooka ni issyo ni umi e ikanai ka to kikimasita.** He asked me if I wouldn't go with him to the seaside on the tenth if it didn't rain.
>
> **Are wa itoko da to iimasu.** He says that that's his cousin.

In reported questions **da** tends to be omitted. You have already encountered this in expressions involving **ka mo siremasen**—

> **Ano hito wa dare ka to kikimasita.** He asked who that was.

When reporting orders given to the speaker, or in general cases, one transposes the polite imperative (**o- . . . nasai**), into the plain imperative, which is formed in **-U** verbs by substituting **-e** for final **-u** (**iku, ike; kau, kae; matu, mate,** etc.) and in **-RU** verbs by substituting **-ro** for **-ru** (**taberu, tabero; miru, miro,** etc.)—

> **Isya wa mizu o takusan nome to iimasita.** The doctor told me to drink a lot of water.
>
> **Isya wa mizu o takusan nome to iimasu.** Doctors tell one to drink a lot of water.

The **kudasai** which concludes a polite request is transposed into **kure,** which is used for making requests when one is using plain language. You will probably never have occasion to use **kure** except in reported speech—

> **O-kyaku wa yuubin ga areba sirasete kure to iimasita.** My guest asked me to tell him if there was any mail.

When a reported question is followed by the verb **sitte iru**, " know ", **to** is omitted—

> **Asita anata ga doko e iku ka watasi wa sirimasen.**
> I don't know where you are going tomorrow.
> **Inu wa doko ni iru ka sitte imasu ka.**
> Do you know where the dog is?

But it may be inserted before other verbs—

> **Inu wa doko ni iru ka to kiite kudasai.** Please ask where the dog is.

" I wonder . . ." followed by a positive verb in the reported question is best rendered by the use of the **DESYOO** form of the verb—

> **Inu wa doko ni iru desyoo ka.** I wonder where the dog is.

In other cases, " wonder " can be translated by **omou,** e.g. when " wonder " is followed by a negative verb in the reported question, the following construction with **n' d'ya nai ka . . .** is usual—

> **Yama e nigetan' d'ya nai ka to omoimasu.** I wonder whether he hasn't escaped into the mountains.

A similar construction is used with **sinpai site imasu,** " I am worrying ", etc., from **sinpai suru,** " be anxious "—

> **Yokohama e gozi mae ni tukanakattan' d'ya nai ka to sinpai site imasu.** I am worried that he mightn't have got to Yokohama before five o'clock. (I am anxious, thinking, " Is it not that he did not arrive . . .").
> **Kawa no naka e otitan' d'ya nai ka to sinpai site imasu.** I'm afraid he may have fallen into the river. *Or* I'm worried that he may have fallen into the river.

Another useful construction with **omou** is following a **-TAI** form; thus **ikitai to omoimasu** may be thought of as a less definite form of **ikitai desu,** to be translated as " I should like to go "—

Asita doobutuen e ikitai to omoimasen ka.   Wouldn't you like to go to the zoo tomorrow?

Huzi-san no e ga kakitai to omoimasu.   I should like to draw a picture of Mt. Huzi.

Alternative questions, of the kind expressed by " whether . . . or . . ." in English are simply rendered as follows:

I asked whether the dog was in the garden or upstairs. **Inu wa niwa ni iru no ka nikai ni iru no ka to kikimasita.**

I wondered if the dog was upstairs or in the garden. **Inu wa nikai ni irun' daroo ka niwa ni irun' daroo ka to omoimasita.**

If the second alternative is " or not ", it can be expressed by **doo ka**—

Tuita ka doo ka sitte imasu ka.   Do you know whether he has arrived or not?

Tuita desyoo ka doo desyoo ka.   I wonder whether he has arrived or not.

Tuita ka doo ka denwa o kakete kikimasyoo ka. Shall I ring up and ask whether he has arrived or not?

Earlier in this exercise we saw the use of the plain imperative in reported speech.   In ordinary circumstances this is limited to general cases or where the recipient of the order is the speaker.   The normal way to report an order made to another person is to use the adverbial expression **yoo ni . . .** ; in such a sentence as " I told the child to wash his hands ", " to wash " is translated by **arau yoo ni**—

Kodomo ni te o arau yoo ni iimasita.

This **yoo ni** is the adverbial form of **yoo na,** and it can also be used as equivalent to " in such a way as "—

Hankati o huru yoo ni ude o ugokasite imasita.   He was moving his arm as if he were waving a handkerchief.

In certain cases there is the possibility of confusion arising between these two constructions, thus—

Omosiroi hanasi o suru yoo ni iimasita.

This might mean " He said it as if he was telling a funny story " or " He told him to tell a funny story ". The ambiguity can be avoided by adding **to** after **yoo ni** in the case of the reported order—

Omosiroi hanasi o suru yoo ni to iimasita.

Vocabulary

Nouns

bara, rose
hankati, handkerchief
henzi (suru), reply
itoko, cousin
kaisya, company, firm
kanai, (one's own) wife
kayoo-bi, Tuesday
kekkon (suru), marriage
kesa (also adv.), this morning
kiri, fog, mist
ozi, uncle
saru, monkey
sensyuu (also adv.), last week
syatyoo, president, chairman (company)
syoki, secretary
taiin (suru), leaving hospital
ude, arm (limb)
yuubin, mail
zinzya, Shinto shrine

Adjectives

anna, that sort of, such a . . . as that

konna, this sort of, such a . . . as this
sabisii, lonely
sonna, that sort of, such a . . . as that
tumaranai, frivolous, insignificant

Verbs

huru, wave, shake
ikiru, be alive
kimeru, decide
saku, bloom (flower)
siraseru, inform
tomeru, stop, put up (guest)
ueru, plant

Adverbs

anna ni, to that extent
daibu, quite a lot
itido, one time, once
mada
mata
moo

E

Exercise 21

I. *Translate into English:* 1. " Sono zinzya e wa mada itta koto ga arimasen ga itido ikitai to omoimasu " to iimasita. 2. Moo zyuuzi na no ni mada kite imasen kara nanika attan' d'ya nai ka to sinpai site imasu. 3. Daibu hurui ga moo itinen wa tukau koto ga dekiru daroo to henzi simasita. 4 Syatyoo wa ano otoko wa kaisya o yamerun' d'ya nai ka to omou kara tyuui site kure to iimasita. 5. Syoki wa kayoo-bi ni suru ka doo ka mada kimete inai yoo desu. 6. Ookawa-san wa itu kekkon suru ka sitte imasu ka. Tooka da to omoimasu. 7. Konna sabisii tokoro de kurasite iru to wa omoimasen desita. 8. Inoue-san wa moo kite iru ka doo ka denwa o kakete kiite kudasai. 9. Sensyuu no nitiyoo-bi ni watasitati ga itta toki ni wa mada ikite ita doobutuen no saru wa kesa sinda soo desu. 10. Ozi wa o-kyaku ni " ano bara wa kyonen ueta no desu ga moo anna ni saite imasu " to hanasimasita. 11. Kanai wa asatte taiin simasu kara moo konakute mo ii to itoko ni tegami de sirasemasita. 12. Asita mo mata kiri d'ya nai ka to omoimasita ga kaze ga sukosi huite imasu kara hareru ka mo siremasen. 13. Akai hankati o hutte kisya o tomeyoo to simasita ga ma ni aimasen desita. 14. Sensei wa sonna tumaranai hon o yomanai yoo ni (to) iimasita. 15. Ano otoko wa tera no niwa o tootte nigetan' desyoo ka.

II. *Translate into Japanese:* 1. It was when I was still at the university that I went to that shrine. 2. Do you know where last Tuesday's newspaper is? 3. I planted this rose some time ago, but I'm afraid that it's not going to bloom this year. 4. I don't want to live in such a lonely village as this again. 5. The chairman asked the secretary whether it was foggy or not. 6. He said, " My wife was still alive when the doctor came." 7. It's nine o'clock, is it still all right? Yes, it is (still all right). 8. I was already married when I resigned from that firm. 9. The guest asked me to ring up again. 10. My younger brother replied that he did not know whether or not there had been any mail this morning. 11. It's ten o'clock, so I suppose he has already set out for the temple. 12. My uncle told my cousin not to tell frivolous stories. 13. Won't you like to go to such a place? 14. He put his arm out of the train window and moved it as if he was waving a handkerchief. 15. My friend said he had never seen so splendid a monkey.

LESSON 22

Verbs of Giving and Receiving

Two series of verbs are used in Japanese to translate "give", depending upon whether the speaker, or someone that the speaker considers in the same group as himself, is the giver or receiver of the gift. Which of the various words in each series is used depends upon the respect, actual or formal, due to or from the persons involved. We shall deal with "respect language" in Lesson 30, and for the moment we shall consider mainly those verbs that conform with the use of the **-MASU** form and are used when any third party is considered as more or less on a level with the speaker or the person he is speaking to.

The verb "give" to someone else is **ageru** (originally "raise")—

> I gave a book to my elder brother. **Ani ni hon o agemasita.**
> My mother gave the (city) mayor an oil-painting. **Haha wa sityoo-san ni abura-e o agemasita.**
> My mother gave my father six handkerchiefs. **Haha wa titi ni hankati o rokumai agemasita.**

(When one third person gives something to another third person the tendency is for the speaker to put himself with the giver; thus **ageru** is used.)

> I gave my mother a new hat. **Haha ni atarasii boosi o agemasita.**
> May I give you some water? **Mizu o agemasyoo ka.**

The verb "give" to the speaker or to a person that the speaker considers in his group is **kureru**—

> My elder brother gave me a book. **Ani wa hon o kuremasita.**

The (city) mayor gave my mother an oil-painting. **Sityoo-san wa haha ni abura-e o kuremasita.**

My mother gave me a new hat. **Haha wa atarasii boosi o kuremasita.**

Note that " Please give me . . ." is **kudasai. Kureru** has an imperative **kure,** but this is found only in sentences using the plain forms of verbs, and does not concern us at the moment. You should note, therefore, that while **kuremasu** is suitable for use in normal **-MASU** language, **kure** is not, for the reason given. The verb **kudasaru,** of which the **-MASU** form is **kudasaimasu,** will often replace **kureru** when the speaker owes some respect to the giver, even though respect language is not otherwise being used—

> **Sensei wa kono hon o kudasaimasita.** My teacher gave me this book.

The verb " receive ", " be given " is **morau,** which can be used of any person, first, second or third—

> **Kyoo obaasan kara nani o moraimasita ka.** What were you given by Grandmother today?
>
> **Tanzyoobi ni rippa na okurimono o moraimasita.** I had some splendid gifts on my birthday.
>
> **Ano oziisan wa mainiti siyakusyo kara nihyakuen moraimasu.** That old man receives ¥200 from the City Hall every day.

Each of the verbs of giving and receiving mentioned above, and their corresponding verbs in the " honorific system " (see Lesson 30), may be used following the **-TE** form of a verb.

-te ageru—perform an action for the benefit of somebody else—

> **Haha ni atarasii boosi o katte agemasita.** I bought my mother a new hat.
>
> **Kutu o migaite agemasyoo ka.** Shall I polish your shoes for you?

-te kureru—perform an action for the benefit of the speaker, or somebody that the speaker considers as in his group—

Eigo no zibiki o kasite kuremasita. He lent me an English dictionary.

Hi o tukete kuremasen ka. Won't you please set fire to it?

-te morau—get someone to do something for one—

Tonari no hito ni pan o katte moraimasita. I got the people next door to buy me some bread.

Kyuuzi ni koruku o nuite moraimasyoo ka. Shall we get the waiter to pull the cork out?

Note that with the **-te morau** construction the word indicating the person whom one gets to perform the action is followed by the particle **ni**. When **morau** is used without the **-TE** form the word indicating the giver is usually followed by **kara,** though in this case, too, **ni** is not impossible.

A useful construction can be formed with **-te moraitai,** " I want you (him) to . . .", and **-te moraitai to omou,** " I should like him (you) to . . ."—

Tanaka-san ni mo itte moraitai desu. I want Mr. Tanaka to go too.

Okaasan ni kono tane o maite moraitai to omoimasu. I should like your mother to sow these seeds.

Kondo no doyoo-bi ni ongakkai ga arimasu kara neesan ni mo uta o utatte moraitai to omoimasu. As there is a concert next Saturday, I should like your elder sister to sing (as well as the other performers).

Further Uses of the -TE Form

The uses of the **-TE** form that we have seen up to now have been:

(1) Use at the end of a clause to join it to the next, the " co-ordinating " use—

Tenrankai e itte e o mimasyoo. Let's go to the exhibition and see some pictures.

(2) The **-TE IRU** construction—

Tegami o kaite imasu. He is writing a letter.

Kono hako no naka ni nani ga haitte imasu ka. What is there in this box?

(3) The **-TE KARA** construction—

Hon o seiri site kara syokuzi ni ikimasyoo. Let's go and eat after we have arranged the books.

(4) The **-TE** form with verbs of giving and receiving.

The rest of this lesson is given up to the consideration. of further more or less idiomatic constructions where the **-TE** form immediately precedes another verb.

(*a*) The **-TE** form before verbs of motion—
(i) The construction may have the same meaning as that of the normal co-ordinating **-TE** form as in (1) above—

Tamago o too katte soto e demasita. He bought ten eggs and went outside.
Nimotu o tukutte dekakemasita. He packed his bags and set off.

When the second verb is **kuru** the meaning is basically the same as above; thus one may telephone to someone asking him to buy, say, some oranges, and bring them to where the speaker is. **Orenzi o katte kite kudasai.** The answer may be something like **Hai, katte ikimasu.** You will not have forgotten that **kuru** is strictly reserved for motion to the place where the speaker is.

A very characteristic use of **-te kuru** occurs where English would rather use " go and . . .". That is to say, if the three actions of (1) going, (2) doing something, and (3) coming (back) are involved, as when one goes and posts a letter and comes (back), English mentions the first two (" I shall go and post a letter "), Japanese the last two (**Tegami o dasite kimasu**)—

Please go and wash this knife. **Kono naihu o aratte kite kudasai.**

Another example of this construction, **Itte kimasu,** is the usual formula spoken when leaving one's house, said to whoever remains behind, and is something like " Au revoir ". On returning, one says **Tadaima kaerimasita** or merely **Tadaima.**

However, if circumstances demand it, one can, of course, express the idea of going, especially when the destination is mentioned—

I went next door and borrowed a pound. **Tonari e itte itipondo karite kimasita.**

(ii) The verb of which the **-TE** form is used may show the method of the motion. The situation in Japanese is similar to that in French, where some such expression as *traverser en courant* has to be used to translate " to run across ". Some examples in Japanese are **oyoide kuru,** " come swimming "; **hasitte wataru,** " cross running ", " run across "; **dete iku** " go out "; **tonde iku,** " fly away "—

Hikooki ga nizyuudai tonde kimasita. Twenty planes flew over (came flying).

Asoko ni aru hune e oyoide ikimasyoo. Let's swim to that boat over there.

Inu wa sippo o hutte dete kimasita. The dog came out wagging its tail.

Special mention may be made here of combinations formed with **motte** and a verb of motion. **Motte imasu** can be translated, you will remember, by " has ", " possesses ". **Motte kuru** is " fetch ", " bring "—

Inaka kara mezurasii hana o motte kimasita. He brought some rare flowers from the country.

Motte iku is " take away "—

Sutete mo ii yoo na mono o takusan motte ikimasita. He took away a lot of things that I had no more use for (that were of the sort that it would be all right to throw away).

Motte kaeru is " take back ", " go home with (something) "—

Matigatte tomodati no kaban o motte kaerimasita. I made a mistake and went off (home) with my friend's bag.

This is a good place to mention the uses of **kaeru**—

> **Suugaku no sensei wa nanzi ni kaerimasu ka.** At what time does the mathematics master go back (home)?

That is to say, **kaeru**, not followed by a verb of motion, is to be translated as " go back ", " return ", " leave ", especially one's place of work or the place one is visiting. Notice that it is better not to use it for " come home ", which is **kaette kuru.** The point may be illustrated by the following two sentences—

> **Takata-san ga kaette konai uti ni gohan o tabemasyoo.** Let us eat before Mr. Takata comes home.
> **Takata-san ga kaeranai uti ni gohan o tabemasyoo.** Let us eat before Mr. Takata goes home.

Kaette iku can be used for " going back " instead of **kaeru** to avoid ambiguity. For instance **Nimotu o tori ni eki e kaerimasita** might mean " He has gone (or come) back to the station to fetch his luggage ", but **Nimotu o tori ni eki e kaette ikimasita** can only mean " He has gone back . . .".

(iii) *Idioms.* There are two idiomatic uses of **kuru** after a **-TE** form that should be mentioned. The first is normally used in the **-TA** form, with the meaning of ". . . is beginning to . . .". It is characteristically used when referring to the weather.

> **Yuki ga hutte kimasita.** It is beginning to snow.

The second is restricted to the combination **itte kuru** (from **yuu**, " say ") and the use is seen in the following sentence—

> **Terada-san kara tegami de asita konai to itte kimasita.** A letter has come from Mr. Terada saying that he will not be coming tomorrow. *Or* Mr. Terada has sent me a letter saying that he will not come tomorrow.

(*b*) Further uses of the **-TE** form before verbs other than those of motion.

(i) **-te miru.** This use shows the co-ordinating use of the **-TE** form, with a meaning of " do something and see ". Hence it comes to something like " see what happens when . . .", " try . . . -ing "—

> **Kai o mimi ni atete mimasita ga nani mo kikoemasen desita.** He tried putting the shell to his ear but he heard nothing.
> **Yuubinkyoku wa doko ni aru desyoo ka.—Soo desu nee; kiite mimasyoo.** I wonder where the Post Office is.—Yes, let's ask. (Let's try asking.)

You should notice the difference between this construction and **-OO TO SURU.** In the latter case one tries to perform the action; in the former one performs the action to see what happens—

> **Kai o mimi ni atete mimasita.** He tried putting the shell to his ear.
> **Kai o mimi ni ateyoo to simasita.** He tried to put the shell to his ear.

(ii) **-te oku. Oku** is " put ", " place ". After a **-TE** form it gives the idea of doing something and leaving it in the state of having been done, for some purpose or other. There is no stock translation, but the following examples will give you some guidance:

> **Dentoo o tukete okimasu.** I shall leave the light on.
> **Kane wa hikidasi ni irete okimasyoo.** Let us put the money in the drawer.
> **Are wa teeburu no ue ni oite okimasita.** I left it on the table (deliberately, not from forgetfulness).
> **Kangaete oite kudasai.** Please think it over.

The last sentence should be considered as an idiom and learned as such.

(iii) **-te simau. Simau** is " finish ", and added to the **-TE** form of a verb it gives the idea of completion. It is commonly used with verbs which in themselves have some feeling of finality (" die ", " escape ", etc.) or in conjunction with certain adverbs such as **sukkari,** " completely "; **tootoo,** " finally ".

Ii kikai ga areba nigete simaimasu. If there is a good opportunity I shall run away.

Gozi mae ni sukkari yonde simau desyoo ka. Do you think he will finish reading it before five o'clock?

Kyonen tootoo Indo e itte simaimasita. Last year he finally went off to India.

Vocabulary

Nouns

abura-e, oil-painting
bin, bottle
doyoo-bi, Saturday
hikooki, aeroplane
kagi, key, lock
kai, shell(-fish)
kasa, umbrella, lamp-shade
kikai, opportunity
koe, voice
kondo (also adv.), this time, next time
koori, ice
koruku, cork, stopper
kyuuzi, waiter, office boy
mainiti (also adv.), every day
mimi, ear
nyuuin (suru), entering hospital
obaasan, grandmother, old woman
okurimono, gift
oto, sound, noise
oziisan, grandfather, old man
sippo, tail
suugaku, mathematics
tane, seed

tanzyoo-bi, birthday
tenrankai, exhibition
todana, cupboard

Adjective

yakamasii, noisy

Verbs

ageru
ateru, put, guess
kangaeru, consider
kudasaru
kureru
maku, sow, scatter
matigaeru, mistake
migaku, polish
mitukaru, be discovered
morau
oku
simau
suteru, abandon, throw away
tobu, fly, jump
torikaeru, exchange

Adverbs

tadaima
tootoo

Exercise 22

I. *Translate into English:* 1. Kono abura-e wa ryoohoo-tomo tomodati kara moratta no desu ga anata ni dotiraka hitotu agemasu. 2. Obaasan wa bin no koruku o nuku koto ga dekinai yoo desita kara watasi ga nuite agemasita. 3. Todana no kagi wa hikidasi no naka ni irete oita to omoimasita ga ikura sagasite mo mitukarimasen desita. 4. Kyonen kara byooki de nyuuin site ita itoko wa kinoo tootoo sinde simaimasita. 5. Sensyuu no doyoo-bi ni Amerika kara kaette kita Tanaka-san ga kono tokei o kuremasita. 6. Kyuuzi wa koori o motte kite kuremasita ga hosiku arimasen desita kara mata motte kaette morai-masita. 7. Teeburu no ue ni oite oita ooki na hukuro wa dareka sutemasita ka. 8. Akai-san wa matigatte watasi no kasa o motte itta yoo desu kara asita torikaete kuru tumori desu. 9. Kondo no tenrankai e wa kikai ga areba anata ni mo itte moraitai to omoimasu. 10. Ame ga hutte kimasita kara tane wa ituka hoka no hi ni makimasyoo. 11. Suugaku no sensei wa amari muzukasiku nai siken no mondai o kangaete oku to itte kaette ikimasita. 12. Mezurasii kai o hirotta no de akete mimasita ga naka ni wa nanimo arimasen desita. 13. Hikooki ga takusan tonde kite, oto ga amari yakamasikatta no de mimi ni te o atemasita. 14. "Tadaima", to itte haitte kita ani no koe o kiite inu wa sippo o hutte dete ikimasita. 15. Asatte wa tonari no oziisan no tanzyoo-bi desu kara nanika okurimono o agetai to omoimasu.

II. *Translate into Japanese:* 1. Before I went to the exhibition I had my shoes cleaned. 2. Won't you please come home immediately, as I am going into hospital next Saturday? 3. Grandmother took some cakes out of the cupboard and gave me one. 4. The dog heard my voice and came in wagging its tail. 5. As I brought back a lot of rare shells, I should like to get you to come to see them. 6. He put his hands to his ears because the child's crying was very noisy, but finally he went out of the room. 7. Let us go and change it before my father comes home. 8. Yesterday was the birthday of the old man next door, and so I gave him a present. 9. I intend to sow tomorrow the seeds I've been given by a friend. 10. The fountain-pen that the mathematics master uses every day could not be found, so we, too, looked for it for him. 11. I've thrown the ice away by mistake, so please go to the shop opposite and buy me a little. 12. I heard the noise of the aeroplane flying over, and so I went out into the garden and had a look, but nothing could be seen. 13. I don't mind going if there is an opportunity, but please think over whether or not somebody else can go. 14. Please lend me an umbrella, as it's starting to rain. 15. A letter has come saying that he would like to consult you too because it is a difficult matter.

LESSON 23

In this lesson you will see some more particles and have examples of some of their uses. They are **bakari, dake, sika** (all of which have in common that at times they can be translated as " only "), **hodo,** and **made.** In addition, there is one adverb, **tada,** which is introduced at this point because it, too, can be translated as " only ". We shall also consider the translation of " about " when it modifies numerical expressions, and discuss ordinal numbers.

bakari. (*a*) After a numerical expression, it may be translated by " about " (see later in this lesson)—

> **Undoozyoo ni wa kodomo ga zyuunin bakari imasita.** In the playground there were about ten children.

(*b*) (i) Between a **-TA** form and **da,** it can be translated by " only just ".

> **Sono hon wa katta bakari desu kara ii ka doo ka mada wakarimasen.** I've only just bought that book, so I don't know yet whether it is good or not.

(ii) When an adverb of point of time precedes the **-TA** form, the translation of **bakari** will be " only "—

> **Sono huku wa kesa kawakasita bakari na no ni mata sukkari nurete simaimasita.** I only dried that suit this morning and it's quite wet again!

(c) Following a noun, it can be translated by expressions such as " nothing but ", " all that one does is . . .", etc.

Syoosetu bakari yonde imasu.   He reads nothing but novels.   *Or* All he reads is novels.

(d) When the verb is in the **-TE IRU** form **bakari** may be placed between the **-TE** form and **iru**—

Ano ko wa asonde bakari imasu.   All that child does is play.

Syoosetu o yonde bakari imasu.   All he does is read novels.

Any other particle used with **bakari** normally follows it; **ga** and **o** are generally omitted. Note, however, that when **to** is used with **bakari** a different translation is involved according to whether it precedes or follows—

Hontoo no hana bakari to omoimasita.   I thought they were nothing but real flowers.

Hontoo no hana to bakari omoimasita.   I thought all the time that they were real flowers.

dake can in most sentences be translated as " only "—

Eikokuzin ga zyuunin dake kimasita.   Only ten Englishmen came.

Ano hito wa syoosetu nado wa yomimasen ; yomu no wa keizai no hon dake desu.   He doesn't read things like novels; he reads only books on economics (what he reads is only books on economics).

Gaikokugo wa eigo dake hanasimasu.   English is the only foreign language I speak.   (As for foreign languages, I speak only English.)

Ano hito wa hon wa kaimasen, kariru dake desu.   He doesn't buy books, he only borrows them.

Doyoo-bi dake aite imasu.   It is open only on Saturdays (*or* I am free only on Saturdays).

Notice the difference between the last sentence and—

Doyoo-bi ni katta bakari desu.   I only bought it on Saturday.

Generally speaking, the same rule about further particles applies to **dake** as to **bakari**.

There are other idiomatic uses of **dake,** but the only one you need at the moment is **dekiru dake,** which you have seen before—

> **Dekiru dake hayaku okimasyoo.**   Let us get up as early as possible.

sika is always used with a negative verb or adjective, the translation " only " always being applicable. The construction is comparable with the English " nothing but ". If another particle is required, it precedes **sika,** but **ga** and **o** do not have to be expressed.

> **Zyuunin sika kimasen desita.**   Only ten people came.
> **Oosaka e sika ikimasen desita.**   I went only to Osaka.
> **Eigo sika hanasimasen.**   He only speaks English.

tada is not a particle, but normally an adverb.   It often serves to reinforce **dake**—

> **Kyoo wa tada sansatu dake urimasita.**   Today he sold only three (books).

but it can be used with **sika**—

> **Hon wa tada sansatu sika urimasen desita.**   He sold only three books.

or one can even say—

> **Hon wa tada sansatu dake sika urimasen desita.**

It can also support **bakari**—

> **Ano ko wa tada asonde bakari imasu.**

Sometimes it occurs alone as " only ", especially with numerical expressions of unity—

> **Tada issatu urimasita.**   He only sold one (book).

but it can also have other meanings.   **Tada no** can mean " mere ", " ordinary ", as in **tada no hito** " an ordinary man (with no titles, etc.) "—

> **Tada no kaze desu.**   It's just a cold.

With this meaning **tada** is often used with a negative—

> **Kore wa tada no e-hon de wa arimasen.**   This is not just a picture book.

Tada no can also be used adjectivally as " free ", the corresponding adverb being **tada de**—

> **Tada no kippu o moraimasita.**   I was given a free ticket.
> **Tada de hairimasita.**   I got in free.

From what you have seen above, you will realise that there are many ways of translating " only " into Japanese. The advice we would give you is to use **sika** with a negative whenever you can, for it is not so open to ambiguity as other words, and you will be able to use it without fear of misunderstanding.   There are, however, certain circumstances which make **sika** unsuitable.   One is when the verb in the sentence is **desu**.   In this case **dake** will have to be used.

> **Huransugo o yomu no wa ani dake desu.**   It is only my elder brother who reads French.

but it can be expressed with **sika** by using the verb **iru** and saying something like—

> There is only my elder brother who reads French.
> **Huransugo o yomu no wa ani sika imasen.**

This means, too, that **sika** will not follow a verb.   Here you will have to use **dake** or **bakari** according to the sense.

Another construction which you may hear and which may be translated with the help of " only " is of the following type:

> **Doyoo-bi de nakereba iku koto ga dekimasen.**   If it isn't Saturday I can't go.   *Or* I can go only on Saturdays.

Here again, **sika** could replace **de nakereba**.
The second sentence in—

> Do you think I'll like Japanese food?
> You'll only find out by eating it.

would be in Japanese—

> **Tabete minakereba wakarimasen.**   If you don't try eating some, you won't know.

made is a particle, to be translated by such expressions as " as far as ", " to ", " until ", etc.

(a) With expressions of place; " as far as ", " to ".

Doko made ikimasita ka. How far did you go?
Eki made ikimasita. I went as far as (to) the station.

(b) With expressions of time, " till ", " until "—

ima made, up to now, hitherto
Itu made imasu ka. Until when will you be here?
Or How long will you be here?
**Zyuuzi made matimasita ga otooto-san wa kimasen
desita.** I waited until ten o'clock, but your younger
brother didn't come.

(**otooto,** " my younger brother "; **otooto-san,** " your
(his, etc.) younger brother ". In circumstances where in
English the Christian name would be used, the personal
name would likewise be used in Japanese. The use of
imooto(-san), " younger sister ", is similar.)

(c) After verbs the translation is usually as in (b)—

sinu made, until I die, until death
Otoosan ga dekakeru made matte kudasai. Please
wait until Father sets out.

If other particles are used with **made** they generally
follow. **made ni** follows either an expression of time or a
verb, and is to be translated as " by "—

Itizi made ni tuita hoo ga ii desu. We had better get
there by one o'clock.
**Okaasan ga kaette kuru made ni heya o o-katazuke
nasai.** Clear the room up by the time Mother comes
back.

made ga is not often met with, but it does occur and is
equivalent to " even " with the subject of the sentence—

Kimura-san made ga kite imasita. Even Mr. Kimura
was present.

made mo is more common than **made ga,** and has a similar
meaning, although its use is not restricted to the subject
of the sentence—

Kodomo made mo korosite simaimasita. They killed even the children.

Kono zidoosya wa zyuunin made mo noru koto ga dekimasu. As many as ten people can ride in this car.

hodo is a word of wide use.

A. (*a*) Its basic use is as a noun with the meaning of " degree ", " limit ", etc. With this meaning it is used in such expressions as—

Mono ni wa hodo ga arimasu. There is a limit to everything.

(*b*) **Hodo** can come after a verb with more or less its basic meaning—

Byooki de wa nai ka to omou hodo kao-iro ga warukatta desu. He looked so bad that I wondered if he was ill. (His face-colour was bad to the degree that I thought, " Isn't he ill? ")

Tenzyoo kara yuka made todoku hodo no ito ga arimasu ka. Is there enough string to stretch from the ceiling to the floor?

B. **Hodo** can often be used as a particle.

(*a*) In comparative expressions, to translate " as . . . as ", as has been explained in Lesson 15.

(*b*) With numerical expressions it shows approximation—

Gozyuunin hodo haitte imasu. About fifty people are inside.

(*c*) To translate " The . . . the . . .", a construction is used in which the **-EBA** form of a verb or adjective is followed by the plain form of the verb or adjective with **hodo** to make the first half of the sentence.

Natu wa atukereba atui hodo suki desu. The hotter summer is the more I like it.

Hon o kaeba kau hodo uresiin' desu. The more books I buy the happier I am.

Hayakereba hayai hodo ii desu. The quicker the better.

When the second part of the sentence is **ii desu,** it is not absolutely necessary to use the **-EBA** form—

Hayai hodo ii desu.

Numerical Approximations, etc.

In this lesson you have seen that **bakari** and **hodo** can be used with numerical expressions to give the idea of approximation. To these two can be added **gurai.** There is, of course, a slight difference of meaning between them. **Bakari** does not make much of the approximation at all; it can be used very often where in English " about " or some similar word is not used, particularly where in English we use a round number. It does tend, however, to suggest that the number it accompanies is at the upper limit of the approximation. **Gurai** is nearest to " about ", **hodo** tends to suggest the lower limit of the approximation. Probably **gurai** will be the one that you will use most of all. If you wish to express exactness, you can use **tyoodo** in front of the numerical expression.

With expressions of point of time, typically with times o'clock, **-goro (-koro)** is used to express approximation. Here again, " about " is not always necessary in the translation.

> **Nanzi goro tukimasita ka.** At what time did you get there?
> **Sanzi goro desita.** (About) three o'clock.

Goro is a form of **koro,** a noun which can be translated as " time ", " period ", though **toki** is now more common. The combinations **imagoro** " about this time ", " nowadays "; **konogoro,** " recently ", " of late "; **sonokoro,** " at that time "; **itugoro** " when ", " at what period ", are frequently heard. Note that with expressions of duration of time, **gurai, hodo, bakari** are used for approximations, as with other numerical expressions.

Ordinal Numbers

There are various ways of forming ordinal numbers (" first ", etc.) in Japanese. Here again we shall give you examples of what you may expect to hear Japanese speakers use, but give you advice about what it is most useful to learn to speak yourself.

-me. (1) This suffix can be added to numerals of the **hitotu** series; the resulting ordinal number can be used only with things that are counted with those numerals.

> **Koko kara hutatume no kado o migi e o-magari nasai.** Turn left at the second corner from here.

(2) It is also added to expressions of time, as, for example, in **itinenme,** " the first year "; **nikagetume,** " the second month "; **sansyuume,** " the third week "; **tookame,** " the tenth day "; **zyuugonitime,** " the fifteenth day "; **sanzikanme,** " the third hour ". You do not have to be told, of course, that these forms are not used for dates, in which the ordinary (" cardinal ") numerals are used. The expressions with **-me** are used in sentences such as—

> **Beikoku e tuite kara ninenme ni Amerikazin to kekkon simasita.** In the second year after reaching America he married an American.
> **Doku o nonde kara nizikanme ni sinde simaimasita.** He died in the second hour after taking poison.

(3) In theory, **-me** can follow any combination of numeral and unit, and you may hear expressions made up in this way, but normally **-banme** directly following a numeral of the **iti** series is used with any noun other than those mentioned in (2) above. Instead of the sentence given in (1), it is more usual to say—

> **Koko kara nibanme no kado o migi e o-magari nasai.**

Other examples are—

> **Yuubinkyoku kara nibanme no ie ni sunde imasu.** They live in the second house from the Post Office.
> **Itibanme ni deta hito wa Nihonzin de, nibanme no wa Eikokuzin desu.** The man who came out first was a Japanese, and the second an Englishman.

dai-. Another set of ordinal numbers can be obtained by prefixing **dai-** to a numeral of the **iti** series. In practice, these tend not to be used in spoken Japanese, with one or two exceptions. The most important of the latter are formed with **peizi,** " page (of book etc.) "; **gyoo,** " line (of writing, etc.) ".

Tanaka-san no e wa zassi no dainipeizi ni dete imasu.
Mr. Tanaka's picture appears on page 2 of the magazine.

syuu, " week ", too, is preceded by **dai-** when you are talking of a certain week in a calendar month; thus " the second week in January " is **itigatu no dainisyuu.** Whereas " the second week after reaching Japan " is **Nihon e itte kara nisyuume.**

Thus, if you have to use an ordinal number, the normal thing is to use **-banme** except for expressions of time, and the one or two exceptions with **dai-.** It should be noted, however, that ordinal numbers are not in fact greatly used in Japanese. For instance, instead of **daiitipeizi,** etc., the cardinal forms **itipeizi,** etc., are common.

Tanaka-san no e wa zassi no nipeizi ni dete imasu.

We have already said that they are not used in dates, and with other expressions of time some other way of saying it is often found. Instead of **sansyuume,** for instance, one might hear **nisyuukan tatte kara,** " after two weeks had passed ".

-ban. Following numerals of the **iti** series, **-ban** forms expressions corresponding to " No. 1 ", etc. These are used for numbers of buses, trams, etc. (**itiban no basu,** " No. 1 bus "), and for telephone numbers, car registration numbers, etc. We saw earlier that **itiban** can be used to translate " most ". It can also form words like **itiban-ressya,** " the first train (of the day) "; **itiban-bosi,** " the first star to appear "; later members of the series (**niban-ressya,** etc.) are possible.

-goo has a similar meaning to **-ban,** but is not greatly used in spoken Japanese. It is, however, common with room numbers (**hyakugoo no heya,** " Room 100 "). It is also suffixed to names of foreign ships, e.g., **Kuiin-**

meerii-goo, " S.S. *Queen Mary* "; Japanese merchant ships have **-maru** at the end of their names, e.g., **Atorasu-maru,** " S.S. *Atlas* ".

It will be convenient here to mention Japanese addresses. Houses are not given an individual number in a street; instead, they are identified by the plot of ground on which they are built (**-banti**), in a district (**-tyoome**). Larger units are **-tyoo,** or **-mati,** which may be a small town in a country area or, in a large city, may vary in size, the smallest ones not being divided into **tyoome; -ku,** which is normally a subdivision of a large city, about the size of a London metropolitan borough; **-si,** " city "; **-ken,** " department " (comparable to a county in England); Osaka and Kyoto are classified as **-hu,** which are similar to **ken,** and Tokyo is unique in being a **-to,** or metropolitan area. In country districts there are also **mura,** " villages ", and **gun,** " sub-prefectures ", the last not being a unit of local government, but purely a postal area. Thus, to give a sample address in Tokyo, one might live at—

> **Tookyoo-to, Sinagawa-ku, Gotanda** (this is a **mati**), **5 tyoome, 60 banti** (the last two are usually shortened to **go no rokuzyuu**).

Vocabulary

Nouns

aki, autumn	**kaoiro,** complexion
deguti, exit	**ken**
doku, poison	**ku**
e-hon, picture book	**mati (tyoo)**
gakusya, scholar	**migi,** right
gun	**natu,** summer
haru, spring	**Oosaka,** Osaka
hidari, left	**otooto,** younger brother
hu	**si**
huyu, winter	**sirase,** news, information
imooto, younger sister	**syatu,** vest
iriguti, entrance	**to**
Itariizin, an Italian	**warukuti,** insulting remark
kado, corner	**yuka,** floor

Adjectives
uresii, pleased
warui, bad

Verbs
kawakasu, dry
magaru, turn, twist
okoru, be angry, lose one's temper
ukeru, receive, get
wakaru, be clear, be understandable
yurusu, forgive, permit

Adverbs
imagoro
itugoro
kanari, considerably

konogoro
matigai naku, without fail
tada
tyoodo, just, exactly

Particles
bakari
made
sika

Prefix
dai-

Suffixes
-goro (koro)
-gurai (kurai)
-maru

Exercise 23

I. *Translate into English:* 1. Sono mati e wa natu sika itta koto ga arimasen kara huyu taihen samui ka doo ka wa sirimasen. 2. Yozi made ni matigai naku migi no iriguti e kite iru to iimasita kara kuru made matte imasyoo. 3. Sono sirase o uketa imooto wa tada naku bakari desita. 4. Ototosi no aki ni wa Sina made sika ikimasen desita ga kondo wa Indo made ikitai to omoimasu. 5. Kyonen no tyoodo imagoro Oosaka no eigakan no deguti de atta dake desu. 6. Nurete iru yuka no ue ni syatu o otosite nurasimasita kara sanzi made ni kawakasite kuremasen ka. 7. Ano Itariizin wa konogoro Nihon e kita bakari desu ga Nihongo o kanari yoku hanasimasu. 8. Tosyokan wa asoko no kado o hidari e magatte itte nibanme ni aru tatemono desu. 9. Haru no yasumi ni wa dono gurai arukimasita ka. Sanzyuuri gurai arukimasita. 10. Kimura-san wa warukuti bakari itte hito ga okoreba okoru hodo uresii rasii desu. 11. Moo sinai to yakusoku sae sureba kyoo dake wa yurusite agemasu. 12. Sono hito ga tada no gakusya ka doo ka wa atte minakereba wakarimasen. 13. Nyuuin site iru otooto ni e-hon o gosatu hodo okurimasita. 14. Sanbanme no onna-no-ko wa itugoro kekkon simasu ka. Rainen no sigatu goro desu. 15. Nanika doku o nonda yoo de kaoiro ga taihen warui desu.

II. *Translate into Japanese:* 1. All my younger brother did was to cry, and didn't ask me to forgive him. 2. It is only the third bottle from the left which has poison in it. 3. About how many people live in this town? About six thousand, I suppose. 4. He was saying that he would come back by three o'clock without fail, but it seems that he is not back yet. 5. It is only in summer that one can dry clothes out of doors. In winter they don't get dry. 6. How long will your younger sister be in Paris? I think she will be there till autumn. 7. Only Japanese scholars are gathering at the conference this time, but I hear that next spring many foreign scholars will come too. 8. On this side there is only an entrance, and there doesn't appear to be an exit. 9. Recently he has been getting nothing but bad news, and he doesn't look well. 10. That Italian spoke only French at the time when I met him. 11. I have only just dropped the money, so it should be still somewhere on the floor. 12. I am pleased to have been given a free ticket, but as the exhibition is open only during the daytime I may not be able to go. 13. Yesterday I sent about five picture books to the child next door who is in hospital, and so I expect he is looking at them about now. 14. The more I look at the man who turned right at that corner, the more I think he doesn't look like a Japanese. 15. Mr. Tamura who used to say only bad things about people went off to Osaka in the second week after I lost my temper with him.

LESSON 24

THIS lesson will be used for tying up loose ends and disposing of some remaining problems.

(*a*) **Dareka Eikokuzin ga imasu ka.**
 Dokoka ame ga huranai tokoro wa arimasen ka.
 Ituka atatakai hi ni umi e ikimasyoo ka.
 Nanika omosiroi eiga o mi ni ikitai to iimasita.

The above examples show that it is possible to prefix a noun phrase by an appropriate pronoun in **-KA** to add a certain note of indefiniteness to the sentence. Translations such as " some . . . or other ", " any " will be appropriate.

Is there any Englishman here?
Isn't there some place where it doesn't rain?
Shall we go to the seaside some day when it's warm?
He said he wanted to go and see some interesting film.

As you see, the meaning is not greatly different from what it would be without the pronoun.

(b) We have already seen that **doo** is in the same group as **aa, koo, soo,** and means " in what way ", " how ".

Doo ikimasita ka.   How did you go?

Doo is often used with the verb **yuu** to form an adjectival phrase more or less equivalent to **donna**—

Doo yuu hito desu ka.   Or **Donna hito desu ka.**   What sort of person is he?

Compare this with **nan to yuu,** which normally asks the name of something or somebody—

Nan to yuu hana desu ka.   What is the name of the flower?

The use of **doo** in reported speech was mentioned in Lesson 21; another expression in which it occurs is **Doo sitan' desu ka,** to be translated as " What is wrong? ", " What have you done to yourself? ", etc. If the answer is " I'm not hurt ", " Nothing is wrong ", the Japanese will be **Doo sitan' de mo arimasen.**

The derivatives of **doo** have rather unexpected uses. **Dooka** is most commonly used in the expression **Dooka sitan' desu ka,** which is normally to be translated as " Is something wrong? ", " Have you hurt yourself? "

Doomo is most commonly used in expressions of begging pardon, etc.—

Doomo sumimasen.   Please forgive me.
Doomo siturei simasita.   I beg your pardon.   Or I am sorry to have bothered you.
Doomo arigatoo gozaimasu.   Thank you very much.

The above expressions may be used without **doomo,** in which case they are somewhat less polite and more informal.

Doodemo is used regularly to mean "in any way", especially with **ii desu.** For example, in reply to **Doo ikimasyoo ka,** "How shall we go?", one might say **Doodemo ii desu,** "Any way will do". **Doodemo ii desu** can also be translated as "It doesn't matter", and also occurs in such sentences as—

> **Soozi wa doodemo ii desu kara ryoori o site kudasai.** Please don't worry about the cleaning but get on with the cooking.

Doosite. "Why?", "How does it come about that?" (see Lesson 13).

Doositemo, "whatever happens", etc., especially with expressions of wishing, intention, etc.—

> **Doositemo ikitai desu kara kippu o katte kudasai.** Whatever happens, I want to go, so please buy me a ticket.
> **Asita wa doositemo iinkai e ikimasen ka.** Are you quite decided that you will not go to the committee meeting tomorrow?

Doozo is used with imperatives and requests to make them more agreeable—

> **Doozo, o-hairi nasai.** Come in, please.

(c) **de mo.** This combination of particles will, of course, occur in many sentences in which each element has its normal meaning—

> **Tya wa Sina de mo Nihon de mo dekimasu.** Tea is grown both in China and Japan.

Then there is the construction derived from **desu** (**de arimasu**) of which the following is an example:

> **Kono gakkoo no Eigo no sensei wa Amerikazin de mo Eikokuzin de mo arimasen.** The teacher of English in this school is neither an American nor an Englishman.

Do not forget, either, the use of **de mo** with an interrogative pronoun—

> **Ano hito wa zibun de tukutta mono o nandemo tada de otooto ni kuremasu.** Everything he makes (himself) he gives to my (younger) brother free of charge.
>
> **Nanika yoo ga areba itudemo go-enryo naku kite kudasai.** If ever you want me for anything, please do not hesitate to come at any time.

(**go-enryo naku,** " without keeping yourself at a distance ", is used as seen above, to invite someone not to stand on ceremony, not to be affected by considerations of politeness.)

A similar kind of **de mo** to that used with interrogative pronouns can follow a noun, followed by **ii desu** or some equivalent expression—

> **Huru-hon de mo ii desu ka.** Will a second-hand copy do? (Even if it is a second-hand book will it do?)

de here is rather to be thought of as the **-TE** form of **desu,** and a negative construction is possible—

> **Huru-hon de nakute mo ii desu.** It doesn't have to be second-hand. (Even if it is not a second-hand book it will do.)

de mo can be used with other expressions than **ii desu** and the like, and is then often to be translated as " even ", when it is not greatly different from **mo,** though a little more emphatic.

> **Hutuu Nihon no koto wa nanimo siranai Eikokuzin de mo syoogun to yuu kotoba wa kiite imasu.** Even Englishmen who do not know anything about Japan have usually heard the word *syoogun.*

A further use of **de mo,** in which it may be considered as a particle in its own right, requires the translation ". . . or something ", " for instance ".

> **Kyoo wa taihen ii tenki desu kara sanpo ni de mo ikimasyoo.** It's fine today so let's go out for a walk or something.

Omosiroi syoosetu de mo yonde zikan o sugosimasyoo.
Let's pass the time reading an interesting novel or
something.

If, instead of this sentence, we said—

Omosiroi syoosetu nado (o) yonde . . .

the translation would be—

. . . reading an interesting novel and similar things.

Another similar sentence might have—

Omosiroi syoosetu ka nanika yonde . . .
. . . reading an interesting novel or something.

The difference between this and the construction with **de
mo** is that this one means " reading an interesting novel
or some other book or paper ", whereas the one with **de
mo** implies " reading an interesting novel or carrying on
some such pursuit ".

Vocabulary

Nouns

enryo (suru)
hasami, scissors
imi, meaning
kagami, mirror
keikaku, plan
kotoba, word, language
noozyoo, farm
setumei (suru), explanation
sinamono, goods
siturei (suru), lack of politeness
son, loss (as against profit)
syoogun, title of (military)
ruler of Japan before
1868, general
tooyoo, the Orient
yoo, business, what one has
to do
yunyuu (suru), importation

Adjectives

kitanai, dirty
kurusii, full of suffering,
hardship
kuwasii, detailed
mittomonai, disgraceful
raku na, easy, comfortable
sumanai, regrettable

Verbs

gozaimasu (see Lesson 30)
okureru, be late, be backward
sugosu, spend (time), pass
(time)
tasukeru, help, rescue

Adverbs   *Interjection*
doodemo   **arigatoo**
dooka
doomo
doositemo
doozo

Exercise 24

I. *Translate into English:* 1. Kono hasami wa doo sitan' desu ka, nani mo kiru koto ga dekimasen yo. 2. Tooyoo kara wa doo yuu sinamono o yunyuu simasu ka. 3. Doomo sumimasen, matigaeta no wa watasi desu, kore kara wa yoku tyuui simasu. 4. Kisya ga deru made ni wa mada zikan ga takusan arimasu kara eki no mae no mise de mo mite kimasyoo ka. 5. Sensei wa dareka Torii-san o tasukete agetai hito wa inai ka to kikimasita. 6. Kane sae kakaranakereba doo yuu keikaku de mo kamaimasen. 7. Ima no kurusii sigoto o yamete nanika raku na koto ga sitai to itte imasu. 8. Ano hito ga natu no yasumi o sugosita no wa Suisu de mo Itarii de mo arimasen. 8. Boosi wa doodemo ii desu yo; kagami de kao o mite goran nasai, kitanakute mittomonai desu kara sugu aratte o-ide nasai. 10. Noozyoo wa doo sitan' desu ka. Son ga ookii no de utte simaimasita. 11. Eikoku e wa doo ikimasu ka. Amerika o tootte ikimasu. 12. Doozo syoogun to yuu kotoba no imi o kuwasiku setumei site kudasai. 13. Nandemo go-enryo naku hanasite kudasai, dekiru dake no koto o site miru tumori desu kara. 14. Kyoo de nakute mo iin' desu; mokuyoo-bi ni de mo kite kudasai. 15. Doomo siturei simasita; doositemo sinakereba ikenai yoo ga atta no de okurete simattan' desu.

II. *Translate into Japanese:* 1. Is something wrong? No, nothing. 2. What sort of scissors are best, I wonder, to cut this? 3. Please forgive me; I'm late because I went shopping. 4. We still seem a little early, so shall we go for a stroll or something? 5. Any English dictionary will do. 6. He was asking whether there wasn't someone who wanted to go with him to the concert. 7. No doubt he is considering some new plan or other. 8. Yesterday I spent a busy day cleaning, but today I am doing only

easy jobs. 9. The meaning of this word is neither " mirror "
nor " clock ". 10. What happened to the imported goods?
I had to sell them cheaply, so my losses were great. 11.
How are you going to the East? I want to go as quickly
as possible, but I haven't yet decided how. 12. Please
ask him whether or not he is going to the farm tomorrow.
13. Please do not hesitate to ask me anything; I will
explain it in detail for you. 14. What I have to do doesn't
matter; I shall go with you (for your benefit). 15. I'm
quite decided that I should like to help him, so please tell
me if there is any suitable work for him.

LESSON 25

IN English the passive verb is widely used with all kinds
of subject—

> The cat was killed by the dog.
> The tree was cut down by the woodman with a saw.
> This house was built in seven weeks.
> My uncle was given a new car.

In English all verbs (except imperatives and infinite
verbs) must have the subject expressed, and the passive is
commonly used to avoid mentioning the doer of the action
(the subject of the active verb). There is not the need for
this device in Japanese, where the subject of the verb does
not, of course, have to be expressed. Japanese, too, is
well provided with pairs of corresponding transitive and
intransitive verbs, the second of which will often serve where
English might have a passive.

> **Itu denpoo o todokemasita ka.** When did he deliver
> the telegram?
> **Denpoo wa itu todokimasita ka.** When did the tele-
> gram arrive? *Or* When was the telegram delivered?

Another Japanese procedure is to use a transitive verb,
but to place the object early in the sentence, following it
with **wa** instead of **o**. The result is to put the object into
a position of prominence which it would not usually occupy;
a translation using the passive in English will often be
suitable.

Kono hon wa itu kakimasita ka.   When was this book written?

Kono hana wa haha ga hasami de kirimasita.   This flower was cut by my mother with her scissors.

Nevertheless, Japanese does possess a verb form which is commonly called the passive.   Its mode of formation is as follows—

-RU verbs: change **-ru** of dictionary form to **-rareru.**

taberu	taberareru
miru	mirareru

-U verbs: change **-u** of dictionary form to **-areru,** except that in verbs where a vowel immediately precedes the **-u** of the dictionary form one adds **-wareru.**

korosu	korosareru
okosu	okosareru
warau	warawareru.

suru, kuru, yuu:

suru	sareru (serareru)
kuru	korareru
yuu	iwareru

A fundamental condition of the use of these forms is that, at least theoretically, they can have only animate subjects, that is, their subjects must be living.   With transitive verbs, where the subject is the direct recipient of the action, the construction should cause no difficulty.

Kinoo zyunsa ga sannin korosaremasita.   Yesterday three policemen were killed.

The noun representing the person by whom the action was done is followed by **ni,** and the thing by which it was done by **de.**

Tyoonan wa siken ni seikoo simasita kara kootyoo ni homeraremasita.   My eldest son was praised by his headmaster for being successful in the examination.

Zinan wa tomodati to kenka o sita no de hutaritomo sensei ni gakkoo ni tomeraremasita.   My next son

had a fight with a friend, and they were both kept
in (school) by their teacher.

Syookoo wa teki ni utarete uma kara otimasita. The
officer was shot by the enemy and fell from his horse.

Neko wa inu ni kamaremasita. The cat was bitten
by the dog.

The above may be called the " direct passive ", and
much more difficult than it is what may be called the
" indirect passive ".   With this, the human subject of the
passive verb is the person who suffers inconvenience from
the action.   The translation may not be a passive in
English, but will often include the idiomatic construction
with " have " as in " I had my purse stolen ", **Kaneire o
nusumaremasita** (" I suffered the inconvenience of having
my purse stolen ").   You will see from this that the object
of the active verb is still followed by **o**.   Notice, too, that
an English idiom allows you to translate this particular
sentence by " I was robbed of my purse ".   Generally,
however, such a device is not available—

Hune ni noru mae ni nimotu o siraberaremasita.
Before going aboard, I had my luggage examined.

Zyunsa ni katana o toraremasita. He had his sword
taken away by a policeman.

The active forms of these three sentences would, of course,
be—

Kaneire o nusumimasita.   (Someone) stole my purse.

Hune ni noru mae ni nimotu o sirabemasita.   (They)
examined my luggage before I went aboard.

Zyunsa wa katana o torimasita.   The policeman took
the sword.

The difference between the two sets of sentences is that
those with the active verbs merely relate an event objectively, and those with the passive place the event in
relation to the person who suffered from it.

This accounts for the possibility of intransitive verbs
having a passive in Japanese.   The event is placed in
relation to the person who suffers from the action, and the

noun representing the subject of the active verb is followed
by **ni**—

> **Kyaku ni korarete kai e iku koto ga dekimasen desita.**
> I had some guests come and couldn't go to the party.
> **Titi ni sinarete gaikoku e no ryokoo ga dekimasen
> desita.**   I lost my father (I had my father die) and
> was unable to travel abroad.

Another verb form that may be termed passive is that
consisting of the **-TE** form of a transitive verb with the
verb **aru** as an auxiliary. The subject of this is normally
inanimate, and the form refers to a state resulting from some
person's action—

> **Heya wa kirei ni katazukete arimasu.**   The room has
> been neatly tidied up.
> **Kanzyoo wa moo haratte arimasu.**   The bill has already
> been paid.
> **Himo wa kitte arimasita.**   The string had been cut.

Note that this construction can refer only to a state resulting from an action, and not to an action (it could not,
for example, be used to translate " This door is opened at
eight o'clock every morning ").   Nevertheless, the state
must be the result of an action, and it implies that somebody
carried out the action.   The sentence **Himo wa kirete
imasita** would imply that the string was broken, but not
that anyone had done it—

> **E wa kabe ni kakatte imasu.**   The picture is hanging
> on the wall.
> **E wa kabe ni kakete arimasu.**   The picture has been
> hung on the wall.

To return for a moment to the passive in **-(r)areru,**
although, theoretically, it is used only with a personal
subject, there is a growing tendency to use it with impersonal subjects, perhaps under the influence of English.

> **Kore wa itiban hutuu ni tukawarete iru hikooki desu.**
> This is the aeroplane which is the most used.

You will be well advised to avoid this use, however, until
you have considerable experience of talking in Japanese,

when you will know with what verbs it is possible. It seems, for example, that there are no restrictions on the use of **tukawareru**.

Potential Verbs

In addition to the construction with **koto ga dekiru**, there exist special forms of the verb to render the idea of " can ", etc. With **-RU** verbs the form is the same as the passive (**miru, mirareru ; taberu, taberareru**). With **-U** verbs one inserts **-er-** before the final **-u** (**kau, kaeru ; yomu, yomeru**) ; these potential verbs are all **-RU** verbs (**yomeru, yomemasu**). The potential of **kuru** is **koreru** ; it is most convenient to consider **dekiru** as the potential of **suru**.

Usually what would in English be the object is followed by **ga** before a potential verb, and what would be the subject by **wa** or **ni (wa)**, the latter especially before a negative—

> **Imo ga taberaremasu ka.** Can you eat potatoes?
> **Watasi wa taberaremasen.** I can't eat them.
> **Watasi ni wa kono zi ga yomemasen.** I can't read this character.
> **Watasi ni yomenai zi ga arimasu.** There is a character that I can't read.

Whether this form or the one with **koto ga dekiru** is used depends to a large extent on the whim of the speaker ; the present tendency seems to be that the potential forms are more widely used, and that **koto ga dekiru** is a little more formal. Its use may also avoid some of the ambiguity that can arise from the identity of the passive and potential forms of **-RU** verbs, and that of some intransitive verbs (e.g., **kireru**) with the potential of the transitive form (also **kireru**).

Note the various ways of forming the potential of **suru** verbs—

> **Yoru wa ongaku o rensyuu suru koto ga dekimasen.**
> **Yoru wa ongaku ga rensyuu dekimasen.**
> **Yoru wa ongaku no rensyuu ga dekimasen.**

One cannot practise music at night.

F

Vocabulary

Nouns

boo, stick, bar
hazime, beginning
hutaritomo, both, (with neg.) neither
imo, potato, sweet potato, etc.
katana, sword
kaneire, purse
kanzyoo (suru), account, bill
kawa, skin, peel, leather, bark
kenka (suru), quarrel, fight
kootyoo, headmaster (-mistress)
ningyoo, doll
omote, front (of house, etc.)
onna, woman
oya, parent
rensyuu (suru), practice
ryokoo-menzyoo, passport
syookoo, (military) officer
teki, enemy
tizu, map
zinan, the second son
zyooriku (suru), going ashore, landing
zyunsa, policeman

Adjectives

kirei na, pretty, clean, neat
zyoozu na, skilful, good at

Verbs

kau, keep (animals)
naraberu, put in line
nusumu, steal
sawagu, make disturbance
sikaru, scold, tell off
simaru, shut (intr.)
siraberu, investigate, search
tukamaeru, capture
tukamaru, be captured
tureru, take someone with you
yorokobu, rejoice

Adverb

sibaraku, for some time, for a while

Exercise 25

I. *Translate into English:* 1. Doroboo wa zyunsa ga tukamaeyoo to simasita ga tukamarimasen desita. 2. Omote no niwa de asonde ita onna-no-ko ga inu ni asi o kamarete nakidasimasita. 3. Sono syookoo wa kaneire o nusumarete kanzyoo ga haraemasen desita. 4. Imo wa mina kirei ni kawa ga totte arimasu. 5. Sono mati ga doko ni aru ka sirabetakereba kabe ni kakete aru tizu o goran nasai. 6. Kodomotati wa amari sawaida no de oya

ni sikararemasita. 7. Kono ningyoo wa imooto ga tukutta
no desu ga yoku dekite iru no de tonari no ko ga hosii to
itte imasu. 8. Hazime wa zi ga zyoozu ni kakemasen
desita ga yoku rensyuu sita no de konogoro wa nakanaka
rippa ni kakimasu. 9. Simeta to omotta to ga yoku
simatte imasen desita. 10. Kootyoo ni homerareta tyoonan
wa taihen yorokonde imasu ga, gakkoo ni tomerareta zinan
wa kanasisoo na kao o site imasu. 11. Sono obaasan
wa wakai onna no hito ni tasukerarete basu ni norimasita.
12. Sibaraku ryokoo-menzyoo o siraberareta no de sugu
zyooriku suru koto ga dekimasen desita. 13. Teki ga
sutete itta katana ga takusan narabete arimasu. 14. Kenka
o sita otoko wa hutaritomo keisatu e turerarete ikimasita.
15. Tonari no hito ga katte ita neko wa boo de utarete
sinde simaimasita.

II. *Translate into Japanese:* 1. When will the luggage
arrive? I think it will arrive tomorrow or the day after.
2. My second son was praised by his teacher because his
writing (characters) was good. 3. I had some guests
come and couldn't do my music practice. 4. We can't
go in because the gate is shut. 5. The young man who
tried to catch the cat belonging to that woman fell from the
tree. 6. The parents of the boy whose leg was bitten by
the dog brought back a policeman with them. 7. He was
looking at a sword in a room which had been neatly tidied
up. 8. Yesterday three enemy officers were captured.
9. My younger brother had a fight in front of the school,
and was told off by the headmaster. 10. That old man was
hit by a big fellow with a stick, and had his purse stolen.
11. The map that has been hung up on the wall is very
old, so look at the one on the table. 12. My younger
sister, who was playing in the front garden, had her doll
broken. 13. I was very worried because I was unable to
pay the bill for some time. 14. You can't eat that potato
skin, you know. 15. Neither of them had a passport, so
they could not land.

LESSON 26

SURU is a generalised verb very often equivalent to the English " do ". This lesson will be concerned with many other uses of **suru,** and with **naru,** " become ", which often acts as an intransitive counterpart of **suru.**

Suru can, as we have seen in earlier lessons, be used independently in such sentences as—

Nani o site imasu ka. What are you doing?
Soozi o site imasu. I am doing the cleaning.

Note that in this use **suru** may be replaced by **yaru**—

Nani o yatte iru ka. What are you doing?

In this case the context tends to be rather more informal than with **suru;** it is advisable not to use **yaru** with this meaning in a sentence using **-MASU** forms.

The **SURU** verbs show **suru** in its role as an auxiliary whose function is to give verbal status to a word, such as **ryokoo,** which is normally a noun. In fact, as we have just seen in **soozi o site imasu,** words which form **SURU** verbs can also be used as the object of **suru,** excepting those with which **suru** enters into close combination, often becoming **-siru.** A list of these verbs follows, with their negative and passive forms:

ai-suru	ai-sanai	ai-sareru
bas-suru	bas-sinai	bas-serareru
kan-ziru	kan-zinai	kan-zirareru
sas-siru	sas-sinai	sas-serareru
sin-ziru	sin-zinai	sin-zirareru
tuu-ziru	tuu-zinai	tuu-zirareru

When the **SURU** verb of the normal type is transitive, as is **soozi suru,** the form **soozi o suru** will tend to be used when the object is not expressed; **soozi o suru** is then something like " do the cleaning ". Apart from **heya o soozi suru** you may hear **heya no soozi o suru;** the difference between these two expressions may vary according to the context, but the second will be used when **heya no soozi** is thought of as a task to be done, as an item in a timetable, etc.

It was said in Lesson 16 that in some circumstances the first component of a **SURU** verb can be thought of as equivalent to the " stem ". The examples given there were with **ni** and a verb of motion, but there are others. One of these occurred in Lesson 18, when we had the two expressions **benkyoo sae sureba** and **ki sae sureba ;** another common usage involves the particle **wa,** which is placed between the first component of a **SURU** verb, or the stem of a verb, and **suru.** The effect then is to emphasize the verb, as when one stresses the verb in English. Usually, when the verb is positive the sentence in which it occurs will be followed by **ga,** " but ", or some similar expression.

> **Soodan wa simasu ga sansei no yakusoku wa simasen.**
> I will *discuss* it, but I won't promise to agree.
> **Benkyoo wa site imasu ga amari susumimasen.** I am *studying*, but I'm not making much progress.
> **Sakuban Matuo-san wa kimasita ka. E, ki wa sima-sita ga, sugu kaerimasita.** Did Mr. Matuo come last night? Yes, he *came*, but he went home straight away.

This construction occurs with a negative verb often in reply to a question, but only in circumstances where a fairly forceful rejection of the idea behind the question is expressed.

> **Sumimoto-san wa Amerika e iku to itte imasita ga hontoo desyoo ka. Iya, iki wa simasen yo, kane ga nain' desu kara ne.** Mr. Sumimoto says he's going to America; I wonder if it's true. No, he won't go; he's got no money, has he?

You will also recall that the polite imperative (e.g., **o-kaki nasai**) involves the stem of a verb with a **suru** equivalent.

Another use of **suru** as an auxiliary is with **-tari,** which is formed by adding **-ri** to the **-ta (-da)** of the **-TA** form of verbs (**tabetari, kaitari, sitari,** etc.). A typical use is shown in the sentence **Uti no mae de ittari kitari site imasu,** " He is going to and fro in front of the house ". There should normally be at least two verbs in the **-TARI** form before **suru,** and the general meaning is a frequentative one, " keeps on . . .", etc.—

Piano o hiitari, uta o utattari nado site seikatu site imasu. He gets his living by playing the piano, singing songs and so on.

It is possible for a single **-TARI** form to be followed by **nado**—

Piano o hiitari nado site . . .

You have already seen **suru** following the **-OO** form with **to**. The **-TE** form of **suru** (**site**) may also follow **to**, after a noun, and be translated by " as "—

Yakusya to site wa dame desu ga ongakka to site wa nakanaka rippa desu. He's no good as an actor but as a musician he's really fine.

Ano kai e wa kozin to site ikimasu. I am going to that meeting as a private person (as an individual).

There now follow certain idioms involving **suru.**

(i) *nioi ga suru,* " *there is a smell* "—

Kono heya wa hen na nioi ga site imasu ne. There is a funny smell in this room, isn't there?

Titi no niwa wa itudemo bara no nioi ga simasu. There is always a scent of roses in my father's garden.

(ii) *oto ga suru,* " *there is a noise* "—

Yoru no itizi-goro garasu-mado o kowasu oto ga simasita. At one o'clock at night there was a noise of a (glass) window breaking.

Koko wa taihen sizuka de sukosi mo oto ga simasen. It is very quiet here and there's not the slightest noise.

(iii) *ki ga suru,* " *have a feeling* "—

Amari narete inai no de hen na ki ga simasu. I'm not very accustomed to it so I feel odd.

A verb, however, is normally linked to **ki ga suru** by **yoo na**—

Mae ni mo kita yoo na ki ga simasu. I feel that I have been here before.

(iv) **kega o suru,** "*be hurt*", "*hurt oneself*"—

> **Te ni hidoi kega o simasita.** He had a very bad injury to his hand.

It will be convenient now to introduce the verb **naru**, "become", etc., which is usually preceded by the particle **ni**—

> **Kemusi wa tyootyoo ni narimasu.** The caterpillar becomes a butterfly.
> **Nihon e kaette Eigo no sensei ni narimasita.** He returned to Japan and became a teacher of English.

It can be used of the weather—

> **Ame ni naru to omoimasu.** I think it will turn to rain.

With sums of money, it can be translated by "fetch", "amount to", etc.—

> **Ureba sen-en ni mo naru ka mo siremasen.** If you sell it, it may fetch as much as ¥1,000.
> **Zenbu de ikura ni narimasu ka. Goman-en ni narimasu.** How much does it amount to altogether? ¥50,000.

It can be used with expressions of duration of time—

> **Haha ni sinarete gonen ni narimasu.** It is five years since my mother died.

The meaning of **tame ni naru** can be seen from the following examples—

> **Eikoku e itta koto wa hontoo ni tame ni narimasita.** My going to England did me a lot of good.
> **Nihongo o naraeba anata no tame ni naru to omoimasu.** If you learn Japanese, I think it will be of service to you.

The expression . . . **koto ni natte imasu** is to be translated as "It has been decided that . . .", "It has been arranged that . . ."

Asatte syokubutuen e iku koto ni natte imasu. It's been decided to go to the botanical gardens the day after tomorrow.

Notice the difference in meaning between **doo** and **nan ni** before **naru**—

(*a*) **Otoosan ga sineba watasitati wa doo naru desyoo ka.** What will become of us if Father dies?

(*b*) **Yakunin o yamete nan ni naru desyoo ka.** I wonder what he'll become when he gives up the civil service.

In (*a*) the general fate of the person is wondered about, in (*b*) what profession, etc., will he take up.

An **-I** adjective goes into the **-KU** form before **naru**, and the **na** of **NA** adjectives becomes **ni**.

Sora ga akaku natte imasu. The sky has turned red.

Obaasan wa mekura ni narimasita. Grandmother has become blind.

Sigoto ga iya ni natte imasu. I no longer take any pleasure in my work. (My work has become distasteful to me.)

It is possible to add **naru** to the **-KU** form of the plain negative of verbs to make an expression that may sometimes be translated by ". . . has left off . . ." or by the use of "no longer".

Eiga o mi ni ikanaku narimasita. I have left off going to the cinema.

Asita ikenaku narimasita. I can no longer go tomorrow.

Otooto ga sake o nomanaku naru kanoosei ga aru desyoo ka. I wonder if there is the possibility of my younger brother giving up *sake*.

To suffix **naru** to a positive verb, one has to place **yoo ni** between them.

Sake o nomu yoo ni natta no wa kyonen no koto desu. It was last year that he started to drink *sake*.

Many of the above uses of **naru** have corresponding uses of **suru**. **sensei ni naru**, " become a teacher "; **sensei ni suru**, " make . . . a teacher "; . . . **koto ni natte imasu**, " it has been decided that . . ."; . . . **koto ni suru**, " decide to . . .", " arrange to . . ." (**Asatte syokubutuen e iku koto ni simasita**, " We arranged to go to the botanical gardens the day after tomorrow "); **doo naru ka**, " what will become of . . ."; **doo suru ka**, " what shall we do with . . ." (**Kore o doo simasyoo ka**, " What shall we do with this? "); **nan ni naru ka**, " what will (he) become? "; **nan ni suru ka**, " make into what " (**Sono ki wa nan ni simasu ka**, " What will you make that wood into ", " What will you make with that wood? "); **akaku naru**, " become red ", " redden (intransitive) "; **akaku suru**, " make red ", " redden (transitive) "; **kirei ni naru**, " become pretty "; **kirei ni suru**, " make pretty ".

Vocabulary

Nouns

garasu-mado, glass window
kanoosei, possibility
kega, injury
kemusi, caterpillar
ki, feeling, spirit
kozin, individual
mekura, blindness, blind man
nikai, upstairs, first floor
ningen, human being
nioi, smell, scent
ongakka, musician
sakuban (also adv.), last evening
sansei (suru), agreement
seikatu (suru), life, living
syokubutuen, botanical garden
unten (suru), driving (car, etc.)
yakunin, government official
yakusya, actor, actress

Adjectives

dame na, no good
hidoi, terrible, awful
sizuka na, quiet

Verbs

ai-suru, love
bas-suru, punish
kaesu, give back
kan-ziru, feel
kumoru, cloud over
nareru, become used to
naru
sas-siru, guess
sin-ziru, believe in
susumu, go forward
tuu-ziru, get through (telephone, etc.), be well acquainted with (a subject)
yaru

Adverb

nakanaka, considerably

Exercise 26

I. *Translate into English:* 1. Kono tokei wa susundari okuretari simasu kara dame desu. 2. Sakuban taberu tumori de katta sakana wa iya na nioi ga site taberarenaku narimasita. 3. Ano ongakka ni wa mae ni atta yoo na ki ga simasu. 4. Isya wa byooki ga hidoku naru ka mo sirenai kara sizuka ni nete iru yoo ni to iimasita. 5. Mekura to site no seikatu ni wa mada narete imasen. 6. Zidoosya no unten wa simasu ga mada amari zyoozu ni natte inai yoo desu. 7. Ame ga huru desyoo ka. Iya, sukosi kumotte kimasita ga huri wa sinai desyoo. 8. Nikai de nanika hen na oto ga simasu yo; dareka aruite iru yoo na oto desu. 9. Ano hito ga sansei suru kanoosei ga aru to sin-zimasu ka. 10. Otooto wa rainen daigaku o dete yakunin ni naru koto ni natte imasu. 11. Karita kane o kaesi wa simasita ga nagaku tatte kara no koto desita. 12. Yakusya to site wa nakanaka omosiroi ningen desu ga, kozin to site wa hontoo ni tumaranai desu. 13. Garasu mado ga kowarete kao to te ni hidoi kega o simasita. 14. Kodomotati wa syokubutuen e itte kimasita ga taihen tame ni natta to itte imasu. 15. Sono otoko o bas-suru koto ni sita no wa watasi de wa arimasen.

II. *Translate into Japanese:* 1. He has now become a government official, and it seems the life is easy for him. 2. Mr. Matuo did go to the botanical garden, but it seems that he did not stay very long. 3. He is saying that he will return the money he borrowed, but I wonder if that is true. No, he won't return it; he hasn't got any money, has he? 4. He is an interesting man, you know; he has been an actor and a musician. 5. This rose has a very good scent, hasn't it? 6. I have a feeling that I saw it last night upstairs. 7. At the time that I hurt myself I didn't feel anything, but now it is extremely painful. 8. I think you will come to be able to drive by yourself when you get used to it. 9. If it's too noisy let's arrange to go somewhere quiet. 10. As an individual he is all right, but he is no good as a Prime Minister. 11. I'm going with a friend who has become blind, so I may be a little late. 12. I no longer take any pleasure in working in the garden because there are a lot of caterpillars. 13. It turned to rain, but we had to go forward. 14. There is no possibility of his consenting. 15. There were some glass windows, but it started to cloud over, and I was no longer able to read my book in the room.

LESSON 27

IN Lesson 18 you saw that one way of expressing a conditional sentence, with " if ", is to use the **-EBA** form; it was also said in that lesson that **-EBA** had the widest use and was recommended to you. Other forms you will hear, however, are as follows:

(i) **TO.** This is formed by adding **to** to the plain form. Note that it never follows the **-TA** form in this construction.

(ii) **TARA.** This is formed by adding **-ra** to the **-TA** form.

(iii) **-TE WA.** This is formed by adding **wa** to the **-TE** form.

(iv) **NARA.** This is formed by adding **nara** to plain neutral form of verbs and **-I** adjectives, and to stem of **NA** adjectives.

We can immediately dispose of (iii), for it is most commonly used in expressions involving " must " in the English translation—

Soo site wa ikemasen. (If you act thus it will not do.)
    You mustn't do that.
Sono hon wa nantoka site kawanakute wa ikemasen.
    By some means or another, you must buy that book.

In sentences of the above types, **ikemasen** may be replaced by **narimasen** without a change of meaning. In so far as your own Japanese is concerned, our advice is that in the early stages you confine your use of the **-TE WA** form to the **-TE** form of the positive verb or adjective, followed by **wa ikemasen,** to make a fairly blunt negative imperative. You will, however, hear other people use it as in the second sentence we have just quoted, and in other conditional clauses.

(iv) is most usefully employed in forming a conditional for **da** and **NA** adjectives, to avoid the awkward forms **de areba** and **rippa de areba**.

Zi ga zyoozu nara tukaimasyoo. If he writes well, let's employ him.

(i) and (ii) and the **-EBA** form are all widely used not only in conditional clauses, but also in temporal ones, that is in clauses starting not only with " if " but also with " when ". You will be safe if you confine yourself to **-EBA** for all " if " clauses, and for most " when " clauses, but we shall give you a few instances of how the meaning can sometimes be changed by the use of (i) or (ii). Notice, however, that a great deal of personal idiosyncrasy is involved, certain persons preferring certain forms—

(1) **Ame ga huru to kooen e ikimasen.**

(2) **Ame ga hureba kooen e ikimasen.**

(3) **Ame ga huttara kooen e ikimasen.**

(1) would normally be a general statement and might be thought of as meaning: " When (If) it rains, one doesn't go to the park ". (2) would refer to a particular occasion: " If it rains I shall not go to the park." (3) seems a more remote possibility: " If it rained I should not go to the park." Many people, however, would make little difference between (2) and (3).

When the verb in the main clause is in the **-TA** form, the tendency will naturally be, with all three forms, to use " when " in the translation, though " if " will still sometimes be possible.

Ame ga huru to (hureba, huttara) kooen e ikimasen desita. When (If) it rained, we didn't go to the park.

(Note again that, with this meaning, **to** never follows the **-TA** form.)

The examples we have given have all been translatable by the use of " if " as well as by " when " in some cases. However, these three forms may be used occasionally, in cases where the subordinate clause places no condition on the main clause, and where " if " would be impossible as a translation.

To o akeru to tomodati ga sannin haitte kimasita.
When I opened the door, three of my friends came in.   *Or* I opened the door, and three friends came in.

Note, however, that here is some connection of cause and effect between the two clauses; it was because he opened the door that his friends came in. Sometimes this connection is not so clearly present, as in—

Mado kara mitara yuka no ue ni sitai ga arimasita.
When I looked in through the window, there was a corpse lying on the floor.

The corpse was there whether one looked or not, but it was only by looking that he saw it.

Heya e hairu to kirei na onna-no-hito ga imasita.
When he went into the room, a pretty woman was there.

Here again, it was only by going in that he knew the woman was there.

Sometimes there is no connection at all but the temporal one, as in the sentence—

When I reached the age of six, I was living in Akita.
Muttu ni natta toki ni wa Akita ni sunde imasita.

Toki is used in sentences of this sort, and is often preceded by the **-TA** form. It is normally used only when pure contemporaneity is to be expressed—

Koobe e itta toki wa muttu desita.   I was six when I went to Koobe.

but—

Itutu ni naru to gakkoo e ikimasita.   When I reached the age of five, I went to school.

Here the going to school results from one reaching the age of five.

" While ", with a verb, in sentences in which the subject of the main clause is the same as that in the subordinate clause, and the two actions go on together, may be translated by **-nagara,** which follows the stem of the verb—

> **Razio o kiki-nagara zidoosya o unten suru hito ga ooi desu.** There are many people who listen to the wireless while driving (their car).
>
> **Asa no syokuzi o si-nagara sinbun o yonde imasita.** He was reading a newspaper while having his breakfast.

In sentences of other types, e.g., when the subjects of the two clauses are different, or when one action is of short duration, **toki** and **aida** can be used—

> **Ryoosin ga nete iru aida ni watasi wa mado kara nigemasita.** While my parents were in bed I fled through the window.
>
> **Kooen e sanpo site ita toki tonari no hito no kaneire o mitukemasita.** While I was taking a walk to the park I found a purse belonging to the man next door.

We shall finish this rather miscellaneous lesson with a consideration of **hazu, tame,** and **mama.** These are all nouns, and can follow verbs or adjectives.

The meaning of **hazu** can be expressed by " is due to ", " is expected to ", " ought to ", though it must be realised that in this case " ought to " is only an inferential expression and does not apply to moral or ethical obligation—

> **Rokuzi desu kara moo eki e tuite iru hazu desu.** It is six o'clock, so he ought to have reached the station by now.
>
> **Kono hune wa kinoo minato o deru hazu desita ga sentyoo ga sinda no de mada dete imasen.** The ship was due to leave harbour yesterday, but it hasn't done so yet because the captain has died.
>
> **Watasi mo iku hazu desita ga byooki ni natte yamemasita.** I was to go, but I fell ill and gave it up.
>
> **Mada konai hazu desu.** He shouldn't be here yet.

The expression **hazu ga (wa) arimasen** is used as in the following sentences:

Sonna hazu ga nai to omoimasu. I don't think that that can be so.

Mada Tookyoo e tuite iru hazu wa arimasen. He shouldn't have reached Tokyo yet. (In reply, perhaps, to someone saying that he'd seen the person in question in Tokyo.)

You have met **tame** in Lessons 16 and 26; the basic meaning of the word seems to be " benefit ", as in **tame ni naru,** " be of benefit ". This meaning can also be found in expressions like **kuni no tame (ni),** " for the sake of one's country "—

Kodomo no tame no hon o kaite seikatu site imasu. He gets his living by writing books for children.

Another common use of **tame** is in the meaning of " because ", " on account of "—

Kaze no tame ni hune wa deraremasen desita. The ship was unable to leave on account of the wind.

Kaze no tame ni itiniti-zyuu uti ni imasita. I was at home all day because of a cold.

Nan no tame ni yakunin o yametan' desu ka. For what reason did he resign from the government service?

Following a verb, **tame** sometimes is to be translated as " in order to " (see Lesson 16) and sometimes " because of ", " by reason of ". The tendency is for the first of these to apply when the verb is in the **-U** form—

Asi wa aruku tame ni arimasu. One's legs are there in order that one may walk. *Or* One has legs for walking.

Kane o keizai suru tame ni zimusyo e aruite ikimasu. He walks to the office in order to save money.

When the verb is in the **-TA** form, usually the second translation (" because of ", etc.) is appropriate—

Oomizu ga atta tame ni, hasi ga toorenaku narimasita. Because there were floods, it became impossible to go across the bridge.

However, when **tame** is used with this meaning, it can be replaced by a construction with **no de,** and a similar construction can be used when **tame** has this meaning when not following a verb—

> **Kaze no tame ni (Kaze ga atta no de) hune ga derare-masen desita.**

Mama can be thought of as meaning " unchanged state "; it is often followed by the particle **de.** You will hear it preceded by **kono,** etc., (**kono mama de,** " just as I am ", " without doing anything more ") or the **-TA** form of a verb. The translation of this word will vary considerably with the context—

> **Konban kono mama de itte mo ii desu ka.** Will it be all right for me to go as I am this evening?
> **Boosi o kabutta mama de heya e haitte wa ikemasen.** You must not go into a room with your hat on.
> **Dentoo o tuketa mama de nete imasita.** He was asleep with the light on.

Vocabulary

Nouns

bannin, watchman
byooin, hospital
hazu
kagakusya, scientist
kaiin, member (of club, etc.)
kazu, number
komeya, rice merchant('s)
koohii, coffee
kyooiku (suru), education
mama
minato, harbour, port
mori, wood, forest
netu, heat, temperature (of body)
oomizu, flood
ryoosin, parents
sentyoo, ship's captain
sitai, corpse
syoogakkoo, primary school

tyuumon (suru), order (from shop)

Verbs

gakkari suru, be disappointed
hakaru, measure
heru, decrease (intr.)
huyasu, increase (tr.)
miseru, show
odoru, dance

Adverbs

itinitizyuu, the whole day
nantoka site, by some means or another

Suffix

-nagara

Exercise 27

I. *Translate into English:* 1. Uti no kodomo wa ookiku nattara kagakusya ni narun' da to itte imasu. 2. Soto e deru to samui desu kara kyoo wa itinitizyuu uti ni tomatte iru hoo ga ii desu yo. 3. Hitobito ga odotte iru aida ni watasitati wa niwa e demasita. 4. Oomizu no tame ni kawa no soba ni sunde iru hito wa oka no hoo e nigenakute wa narimasen desita. 5. Bannin no sitai wa mori no naka ni sutete arimasita ga nan no tame ni korosareta no ka sukosi mo wakarimasen. 6. Kaiin no kazu ga hette simaimasita kara nantoka site mata huyasanakute wa ikenai to omoimasu. 7. Yasumi ni nattara sugu umi e iku tumori desita ga mainiti ame ga huru no de gakkari site imasu. 8. Kaze d'ya nai ka to omotte netu o hakatte mitara sanzyuuhatido arimasita. 9. Titi ga Amerika e itta toki wa watasi wa too desita. 10. Koohii o nomi-nagara soodan simasita. 11. Ryoosin wa asita kono minato ni tuku hazu no hune ni notte imasu. 12. Kono syoogakkoo wa mekura no kodomo o kyooiku suru tame ni arimasu. 13. Sono mama de byooin e itte wa ikemasen. 14. Sentyoo wa kuzi made ni kaette kuru hazu desita ga zyuuzi ni natte mo sugata o misemasen desita. 15. Kome o tyuumon suru tame ni komeya e denwa o kakeyoo to simasita ga itu made tatte mo tuu-zimasen desita.

II. *Translate into Japanese:* 1. My parents were disappointed because my younger brother, who was expected to come home yesterday, did not arrive. 2. That girl is singing while she is dancing. 3. He left at three o'clock, so he should have reached the hospital by now. 4. Will it be all right if you take my temperature just as I am? 5. When eleven o'clock came they all went off to have coffee. 6. For what reason do you educate children in such a place as that? 7. By some means or another I must see that scientist. 8. When the ship entered the harbour the captain fell ill. 9. Because there were floods the number of children coming to the primary school had grown less. 10. Yesterday I spent the whole day reading a book in a quiet wood. 11. When I went inside the building the watchman showed me the corpse. 12. If you become a

member you will be able to buy these goods very cheaply.
13. Please hand me over the money while he is not here.
14. They say that rice merchant is expected to increase the
number of carts which deliver rice. 15. The man who
ordered the suit went out of the shop, leaving the door
open.

LESSON 28

THE last verb form that we shall explain to you is the
causative, the formation of which is as follows:

   -RU verbs change **-ru** to **-saseru**—

taberu	**tabesaseru**

   -U verbs change **-u** to **-aseru,** those with a vowel immediately preceding **-u** add **-w-**—

nomu	**nomaseru**
warau	**warawaseru**

Others—

suru	**saseru**
kuru	**kosaseru**

The causative form carries the meanings of " make to do
something " and " let do something ". When the verb is
transitive the noun standing for the person who is made or
allowed to do the action is followed by **ni,** and the direct
object by **o**—

   Kodomo ni e o kakasemasita. He made the children
      draw pictures.

When the verb is intransitive the noun standing for the
person who is made to do the action may be followed by **o,**
but when permission is implied **ni** is more usual—

   Iguti-san wa zyosyu o hayaku kaerasemasita. Mr.
      Iguti sent his assistant home early. *Or* Mr. Iguti
      let his assistant go home early.
   **Musuko ni ban no kuzi made tomodati no tokoro e
   ikasemasita.**   I allowed my son to visit a friend until
      nine o'clock in the evening.

As you would expect, the person who is caused or allowed to do the action is very often in a subordinate position, under the authority of the person who causes or allows the action—

> **Zyotyuu ni to o simesasemasyoo ka.**　Shall we have the maid shut the door?
>
> **Imooto ni tegami o mittu kakasemasita.**　I made my younger sister write three letters.
>
> **Isya wa byoonin ni budoo o tabesasemasita.**　The doctor allowed the sick man to eat some grapes. *Or* The doctor made the sick man eat some grapes.
>
> **Neko ni miruku o sukosi nomasete kudasai.**　Please give the cat a little milk to drink.

Do not forget the construction with **-te morau,** which occurred in Lesson 22, and which allows you to express an idea similar to that of the causative when the doer of the action is not necessarily subordinate, and when the feeling is present that the action is for the benefit of the person who causes it—

> **Tomodati ni tegami o mittu kaite moraimasita.**　I got my friend to write three letters for me.

Notice, too, that, as a practical point of politeness, whereas one would say **Zyotyuu ni to o simesasemasyoo ka** when the maid was not present, if she was there one would say **Zyotyuu ni to o simete moraimasyoo ka.**

Nevertheless, there are some contexts in which the causative is used even though the doer of the action is not in a subordinate position. The verbs involved are such as " cry ", " get angry ", " get tired ", where the **-te morau** form would not be possible because the action is not for the benefit of the causer of it—

> **Itumo okaasan o nakaseru yoo na koto o site imasu.**　He is always doing things that make his mother cry.
>
> **Mainiti watasi o okoraseru yoo na koto o simasu.**　Every day he does things that make me angry.

Although every verb can have a causative formed on this model, in some instances alternative forms are used. In

Lesson 19 we listed some intransitive verbs which have transitive forms in **-ASU, -OSU,** and **-SU.** The latter have some of the feeling of causatives and may replace the normal causative forms at least on some occasions. For example, **nigasu** (transitive of **nigeru,** " escape ") is " allow to escape ", " let go ". **Dasu** (transitive of **deru,** " go ", " come out ") is " send out ", " put out ", " let out ". **Toosu,** " pass through ", " let through ", is used rather than **tooraseru.** Other instances of transitive verbs doing the work of causatives are **ireru,** " put, let, in ", and **yaru,** " send ", " cause to go ".

> **Mon no mae ni takusan no hito ga matte imasita ga watasi ga byooki da to omotte toosite kuremasita.** In front of the gate there were a lot of people waiting, but they thought I was ill and let me through.
>
> **Soto wa samui desu kara irete kuremasen ka.** Please won't you let me in, it's cold outside.
>
> **Pan o kai ni kodomo o yarimasita.** I sent my child to buy some bread.
>
> **Ikura nigasite kure to iwarete mo nigasimasen desita.** However much he asked me to let him go, I wouldn't.

You may hear some Japanese say **nomasite, nomasita,** etc., instead of **nomasete, nomaseta.** This change from **-se** to **-si** occurs only before **t,** and its use depends very much upon personal choice. You will not be wrong to use the forms with **-se-** and, in fact, will be well advised to keep to them until you are sure of your ground. Certain verbs in **-asu** (e.g., **ugokasu**) look as though they may be causatives, but, whatever the historical aspect of the matter may be, such verbs are not causatives now, because they can have inanimate things for objects, whereas true causatives can clearly have only animate beings as the doers of the action.

The passive of causative verbs is sometimes used. That of **-RU** verbs is regular—

| taberu | tabesaseru | tabesaserareru |

but that of most **-U** verbs is formed by dropping **-eru** from the causative and adding **-areru—**

| nomu | nomaseru | nomasareru |

Others—

kuru	kosaseru	kosaserareru
suru	saseru	saserareru
naosu	naosareru	naosaserareru

This last shows that, possibly under the influence of **saserareru,** verbs in **-su** often have a passive causative in **-saserareru.**

This form may be used with a subject in the first person to translate ". . . got me to . . .", etc.; i.e., it is complementary to **-te morau—**

> **Ano hito ni imo o katte moraimasita.**   I got him to buy some potatoes.
>
> **Ano hito ni imo o kawasaremasita.**   He got me to buy some potatoes.
>
> **Zitensya o naosaseraremasita.**   He had me mend his bicycle.

The form can, however, be used with subjects in the second or third person, provided they are personal subjects—

> **Hanako wa tonari e itte takusan kasi o tabesaserare-masita.**   Hanako went next door and was made to eat a lot of cakes.
>
> **Amari sake o nomasarenai yoo ni ki o tukete kudasai.** Please take care that you are not made to drink too much *sake.*

There follow some further examples of uses of the causative which, although of rare occurrence, come quite naturally to a Japanese, so that you should be able to understand them—

> **Zyotyuu ni rokuzi ni okosasete kudasai.**   Please have your maid wake me at six.
>
> **Uti no zyotyuu ga kaimono ni ikimasu ga, nanika hosii mono ga arimasu ka.**   My maid is going out to buy some things; do you want anything?
>
> **Hai, orenzi o kawasete moraeru desyoo ka.**   Yes, do you think I could get you to have her buy some oranges?
>
> **Tanaka-san no soobetukai e ikimasu ka.**   Are you going to Mr. Tanaka's farewell party?

Iya, ikimasen; asita itiban-ressya ni noranakereba narimasen kara, konban wa amari nomasaretaku nain' desu. No, I've got to catch the early train tomorrow, and I don't want to have to drink too much this evening.

Vocabulary

Nouns

byoonin, person who is ill
daihyoo (suru), representative, representation
hoogen, local dialect
kanzume, tinned goods
kyuuryoo, salary
miti-annai, guide
musuko, son
musume, daughter
namae, name
onaka, abdomen, inside, stomach
ressya, train
riyuu, reason
soobetukai, farewell party
tama, ball, jewel
tigai, difference
zyosyu, assistant
zyuusyo, address, residence

Adjectives

kawaisoo na, pitiable
muri na, unreasonable
sukunai, few
zyoobu na (ni), strong, healthy

Verbs

ireru, put in, etc.
nageru, throw
nigasu, allow to escape
sasou, induce, invite
tamaru, accumulate (intr.)
tameru, accumulate (tr.)
tanomu, request, rely on

Exercise 28

I. *Translate into English:* 1. Kono niwa de wa kodomotati ni tama o nagesasenai yoo ni site kudasai. 2. Kinoo tukamaeta tori o kago na naka e ireyoo to omoimasita ga kawaisoo na no de nigasimasita. 3. Issyo ni itte moraitaku nai hito made mo sasowasareta to itte imasita. 4. Ano byoonin wa dare ni mo onaka o sawarasenai yoo ni to isya ni tanomimasita. 5. Musume ni sono seinen to issyo ni eiga o mi ni ikasemasita. 6. Watasi wa ikemasen kara tyoonan ni daihyoo saseru tumori desu. 7. Zyuusyo to namae o kakaseyoo to simasita ga zi ga kakenai hito

ga ita no de hoka no hito ni kaite morawasemasita. 8.
Itiban-ressya ni okurenai yoo ni okosasete moraeru desyoo
ka. 9. Sensei wa zyosyu ni hoogen no tigai o sirabesasemasita. 10. Kane o tamesaseyoo to simasu ga ima no
sukunai kyuuryoo de wa dekinai to itte imasu. 11. Otooto
wa itu mo hito o warawaseru yoo na koto o simasu. 12.
Kanzume no niku o zyotyuu ni akesasete motte kosasete
kudasai. 13. Watasi ga itiban yoku sitte iru no ga riyuu
de miti-annai o saseraremasita. 14. Uti no mae ni wa hito
ga takusan tatte imasita ga watasi no kao o miru to nani
mo iwanaide toosite kuremasita. 15. Musuko wa amari
zyoobu de nai no de muri na benkyoo wa sasetaku nain'
desu.

II. *Translate into Japanese:* 1. I didn't want to go
at all, but in the end I was made to (go). 2. In the afternoon I let the child amuse himself throwing the ball.
3. My son does something every day which makes the
patient angry. 4. I sent my daughter to buy some tinned
fruit. 5. I was sorry for it, so I let it go. 6. I want to
make him save a little money, but with things as they are
now I don't think he can. 7. My stomach was very
painful, so I had my maid call the doctor. 8. I asked him
to get them to wait till the train arrived. 9. Shall I have
my wife ask their name and address? 10. The headmaster told the teacher not to allow the children to use the
local dialect. 11. Let the dog into the house because it's
very cold today. 12. I am made to work unreasonably for
a small salary. 13. Please have people to represent this
school invited too. 14. I tried to get him to act as guide,
but he didn't consent. 15. The difference was too great,
so I had my assistant investigate the reason.

LESSON 29

This lesson has as its object to widen your vocabulary by
giving some examples of verb formation and also some
notes on uses of some verbs whose translation often causes
difficulty.

When a compound verb (or adjective) is formed, the
second component is joined to the stem of the first. A
convenient example of a second component is **sugiru,**

which adds the idea of excessiveness, too much, to a verb or adjective.

> **ookisugiru,** be too large
> **samusugiru,** be too cold
> **rippasugiru,** be too splendid
> **tabesugiru,** eat too much
> **nomisugiru,** drink too much
> **sinpai sisugiru,** be too anxious
> **ikisugiru,** go too far

sugiru may be added to any verb or adjective whose meaning is appropriate.

Other second components of wide distribution are the adjective forms **-yasui, -ii,** and **-nikui,** and the verb **hazimeru.**

-yasui adds a meaning of " easy to . . ." to a verb; when used independently it is usually to be translated as " cheap ", " easy " being **yasasii.** Thus **kakiyasui tegami** is " a letter which is easy to write " **wakariyasui,** " easy to understand ", " easily understood "—

> **Sumisu-san no bunsyoo wa kantan de wakariyasui desu.** Mr. Smith's sentences (writing) are simple and easy to understand.
> **Kono yama wa noboriyasui desu.** This mountain is easy to climb.

The use of particles in a sentence with one of these compound adjectives can be seen from the following example:

> **Sonna hon wa otona ni wa yomiyasui ka mo siremasen ga kodomo ni wa zenzen yomenai desyoo.** A book like that may be easy to read for an adult, but I should think that a child would be quite unable to.

In some instances **-yasui** is to be translated as " apt to ", " prone to ", " easily . . ."; this use occurs mainly with intransitive verbs—

> **Onna no kokoro wa kawariyasui to iimasu.** They say that woman is fickle. (A woman's heart changes easily.)

-ii. This is the adjective " good " when used independently, but may be added to some verbs, particularly when the noun qualified by the resulting adjective refers to the instrument by means of which the action of the verb is performed—

> **Kono pen wa kaki-ii desu.** This pen is easy to write with.
>
> **Kinoo katta binsen wa hontoo ni kaki-ii desu ne.** The notepaper you bought yesterday is really easy to write on, isn't it?

-nikui. " difficult to . . .", etc.

> **Eigo no bunpoo wa wakarinikui desu ne.** English grammar is difficult to understand, isn't it?
>
> **Kono tegami wa kakinikui desu.** It's hard to write this letter.
>
> **Kono pen wa kakinikui desu.** This pen is difficult to write with.

Notice that **minikui** normally means " ugly ", " unpleasant to look at ".

Hazimeru is " begin " (transitive)—

> **Sigoto o hazimemasyoo ka.** Shall we start on the work?

It has the same meaning when used as a second component after another verb—

> **Benkyoo sihazimeta no wa kuzi sugi desita.** It was after nine when I started to study.
>
> **Kutusita o amihazimemasita ga totyuu de te ni kega o sita no de yamete simaimasita.** I started to knit some socks, but while I was doing so I hurt my hand and gave it up.

Notice that when " begin ", " start " has the meaning of doing something for the first time, one uses **hazimete**, " for the first time ".

> **Imooto ga kutusita o hazimete anda no wa kyonen no koto desu.** My younger sister started knitting socks a year ago.

Imooto ga kutusita o amihazimeta no wa kyonen no koto desu. It was last year that my younger sister started knitting the socks.

The method of making compound verbs, as with **sugiru** and **hazimeru,** is widespread in Japanese, but there are many pitfalls in the path of beginners who seek to make them up for themselves. We shall, however, now give you a selection of these verbs, and you will be able to get an idea of the translations of the various components. It would be unwise, however, to try innovations. You will recognize most of the verbs, and will in many cases see how the compound verb acquires its meaning; some, however, are idiomatic.

dekiagaru, be completed (**dekiru,** be produced, etc., **agaru,** rise)

deau, meet by chance, encounter (**deru,** go out; **au,** meet)

dekakeru, start out (**deru, kakeru**—*see later*)

hikiukeru, undertake (responsibility, etc.) (**hiku,** pull; **ukeru,** receive)

hikkakaru, be caught up (on wire, etc.) (**hiku, kakaru**—*see later*)

hipparu, drag away, pull (**hiku, haru,** stretch)

iidasu, utter, come out with (remark, etc.) (**yuu,** say; **dasu,** go out)

iitukeru, command, tell (someone to do something) (**yuu, tukeru,** fix)

Iitukerareta yoo ni suru. Do as one is told.

kakiireru, fill in (form) (**kaku,** write; **ireru,** put in)

kakinaosu, rewrite (**kaku, naosu,** repair)

kakitoru, take down (from dictation) (**kaku, toru,** take)

kakitori, dictation

kamikiru, bite off (**kamu,** bite; **kiru,** cut)

kumitateru, assemble, fit together (**kumu,** assemble; **tateru,** erect)

kumitate-honbako, sectional bookcase

kumitate-isu, collapsible chair

miageru, look up (at) (**miru, ageru**)

miokuru, see off (departing guests, etc.) (**miru, okuru,** send)

miorosu, gaze on from above (**miru, orosu,** lower)

mitukeru, find (**miru, tukeru,** fix). (This verb has an intransitive form **mitukaru,** " be found ".)

nagedasu, throw out, throw away (**nageru,** throw; **dasu**). (This verb is used literally and as a vivid equivalent of **suteru,** " abandon ".)

nakidasu, burst into tears (**naku,** weep; **dasu**)

nigedasu, run away (**nigeru,** escape; **dasu**)

nomikomu, swallow (**nomu,** drink; **komu,** plunge in)

nuitukeru, sew on (**nuu,** sew; **tukeru**)

omoidasu, call to mind, remember (**omou,** think; **dasu**)

omoikiru, give up thoughts of, resign oneself to losing (**omou, kiru**)

   ryokoo o omoikiru, give up the idea of travelling

otituku, become settled, become calm (**otiru,** fall; **tuku,** be attached)

otitukeru, settle, calm (**otiru, tukeru**)

   ki o otitukeru, calm one's feelings

   kodomo o otitukaseru, calm down the children

suikomu, inhale (**suu,** suck; **komu**)

suitoru, soak up, absorb (**suu, toru**)

   suitori-gami, blotting-paper

tobiagaru, jump up, fly up (**tobu,** jump, fly; **agaru**)

tobidasu, jump out, fly out (**tobu, dasu**)

tobikomu, jump in (**tobu, komu**)

   kawa no naka ni tobikomu, jump into the river

   mado kara tobikomu, jump in through the window

torikaeru, exchange, replace (**toru, kaeru,** change)

   Kono rekisi no hon o syoosetu to torikaete kudasai. Please exchange this history book for a novel.

   kutu no soko o torikaeru, resole shoes

torikaesu, recover (something from somebody) (**toru, kaesu,** return)

   nusunda mono o torikaesu, recover stolen property

torikesu, cancel (**toru, kesu,** extinguish)

   yakusoku o torikesu, cancel an appointment

tukiau, become friendly with (**tuku, au**)

tumekomu, cram in, force in (**tumeru,** pack; **komu**)

   yoohuku o kaban ni tumekomu, cram a case with suits

   tumekomi-benkyoo, cramming

utitukeru, nail on, drive in a nail (**utu,** strike; **tukeru**)

> **kowareta mado ni ita o utitukeru,** nail a board on a broken window

> **kabe ni kugi o utitukeru,** drive a nail in a wall

waraidasu, burst out laughing (**warau,** laugh; **dasu**)

-garu is a second component that is added only to certain adjectives; a list of those in your vocabulary is given later in this exercise, and in addition **-garu** may be added to the **-TAI** form of verbs. These adjectives might perhaps be termed subjective, since they are peculiar in referring to an emotion or sensation only as experienced, while to refer to the same emotion or sensation as objectively regarded, the **-GARU** form must be used.

Thus they may all be used to describe what the speaker is feeling, **samui desu,** " I am cold "; **kowai desu,** " I am afraid ". They may also be applied to the cause of the emotion or sensation, **iya na hito,** " an unpleasant person " (" a person who causes a feeling of repugnance "); **samui hi,** " a cold day " (" a day that makes one feel cold "); **itai kutu,** shoes which hurt one. One adjective will often have two different translations—

abunai	it is dangerous	I feel apprehensive
atui	it is hot	I am hot
hosii	it is desirable	I want it
itai	it hurts, it is painful	I feel a pain
iya	it is unpleasant	(I have a feeling of repugnance) I don't like it.
kayui	it itches	I feel an itch
kitanai	it is dirty	(I am repelled by the dirtiness)
kowai	it is frightening	I am frightened
kurusii	it is painful	I am suffering
mezurasii	it is unusual	I feel curious
okasii	it is funny, it is suspicious	(I am made to laugh), I feel suspicious
omosiroi	it is interesting, it is amusing	I am interested
osii	it is precious	I regret it, I don't want to part with it

sabisii	it is lonely, remote	I am lonely
samui	it is cold	I am cold
-tai		I want to

Note that these adjectives may be applied to words meaning " feeling ", " experience ", etc., in particular with the expression . . . **me ni au**, " meet with a . . . experience ". A common use is with the adjective **hidoi**—**hidoi me ni au**, " meet with an awful experience "—but it can be used with adjectives in our present list, e.g., **kurusii me ni au, itai me ni au**—

> **Imooto wa itai me ni aimasita.**   My younger sister had quite a lot of pain.

Now, to say directly that another person experiences the emotion or sensation designated by one of these adjectives, recourse must be had to the corresponding **-GARU** verb, formed by adding **-garu** to the adjective stem (**iyagaru, samugaru**). Of these verbs, **iyagaru, kitanagaru, kowagaru, mezurasigaru, okasigaru,** and **osigaru** may be used transitively—

> **Ano hito wa neko o iyagarimasu.**   Cats disgust him. *Or* He hates cats.
> **Ano ko wa inu o kowagarimasu.**   That child is afraid of dogs.

The rest are intransitive. Note that one does not use the verb when reporting what someone said of his own feelings—

> **Ano hito wa neko ga iya da to itte imasu.**   He says that he hates cats.

or when asking a second person about his feelings—

> **Samui desu ka.**   Are you cold?

or in a conditional or concessive clause when the subject is in the second person—

> **Hasiritaku nakattara doosite hasittan' desu ka.**   How was that you ran if you didn't want to?
> **Kowakute mo nigenain' desu ka.**   Won't you run away even if you're frightened?

One does use **-GARU,** however, when asking about the feelings of a third person, because the person of whom you ask the question can have no direct experience of the feeling, and also in conditional or concessive clauses with the subject in the third person—

> **Abunagatte ikanakattan' desyoo ka.** Do you suppose they thought it too risky and didn't go?
>
> **Dozin wa hikooki o mezurasigaranakattan' desu ka.** Wasn't the curiosity of the natives excited by the aeroplane?
>
> **Sonna ni osigatte mo anata ni kuretan' desu ka.** He gave it to you even though he was so much attached to it?

In point of fact **-GARU** occurs rather uncommonly in spoken Japanese partly because there are other verbs and adjectives which do not come within the category (e.g., **osoreru,** " fear "), and partly because with the second and third person one can use reported speech or reported thought. Nevertheless, you should make yourself familiar with its uses.

Finally, in this lesson which has dealt with various matters connected with verbs, we will give you some information about particular verbs in English and Japanese, especially about some cases in which one language uses one verb where the other has several.

The verb " wear " can be used with any article of attire from shoes to hats, but in Japanese different verbs must be used, according to the articles worn. **kiru** is used for garments hanging from the shoulders (**kimono, ooba, yoohuku,** etc.) and for suits (**huku**); **haku** for articles covering legs or feet (**zubon, kutu, sukaato,** etc.); **kaburu** for headgear. Miscellaneous examples are **megane o kakeru,** " wear glasses "; **tebukuro o hameru,** " wear gloves "; **nekutai o tukeru,** " wear a tie ". Note, incidentally, that the **-U** form of the verbs mentioned can also be translated as " put on "; " is wearing " is expressed, of course, by the use of the **-TE IRU** form.

Here are some examples of Japanese verbs which have many translations in English, according to the context:

kakeru (kakaru), hang up—

    kabe ni e o kakeru, hang a picture on the wall

    kabe ni e ga kakatte iru, a picture hangs on the wall

    hito ni denwa o kakeru, telephone somebody

    denwa ga kakatte kuru, somebody rings up

    megane o kakeru, wear glasses

    kosi o kakeru (kosikakeru), sit down (in chair)

    (suwaru, sit in Japanese style)

    hasi o kakeru, build a bridge

    hasi ga kakatte iru, a bridge has been built, there is a bridge

    mizu (sio) o kakeru, sprinkle water (salt)

    razio o kakeru, switch on wireless

    kane o kakeru, wager money

tukeru, attach—

    to ni kagi o tukeru, fix (fit) a lock on a door

    ie ni hi o tukeru, set fire to a house

    dentoo o tukeru, switch on the electric light

    gasu o tukeru, light the gas

    hito no ato o tukeru, follow somebody

tuku, be attached to—

    pen ni pensaki ga tuite iru, a pen nib is attached to the pen

    penki ga tuita zubon, trousers with paint on them

    minato ni tuku, reach harbour

    sensei ni tuite benkyoo suru, study under a teacher

    sensei ni zyosi ga tuite iru, an assistant is attached to the teacher

    ne ga tuku, take root

    ie ni hi ga tuku, the house catches fire

    kimono ni musi ga tuku, clothes have the moth in them

Vocabulary

Nouns

binsen, notepaper

botan, button

bunsyoo, sentence, writing

dozin, native

gasu, gas

hadaka, nakedness

hanabi, fireworks

Nouns

hanbun, half
hei, wall
karada, body, health
kazi, fire (conflagration)
keito, wool
kemuri, smoke
kin, gold
kokoro, heart, mind
kosi, waist
kutusita, socks, stockings
manzoku (suru), satisfaction
me, eye
ne, root
oogoe, loud voice, shout
otona, adult
penki, paint
pensaki, pen-nib
suitorigami, blotting-paper
tabako, tobacco, cigarette
tabakoire, tobacco-pouch, cigarette-case
tatami, mat, *tatami*
tebukuro, glove
totyuu, midway
ura, rear, back
zubon, trousers

Adjectives

abekobe na, back to front

kantan na, simple
mazime na, serious
osorosii, frightful
suki na, fond of

Verbs

amu, knit
damaru, become silent
hameru, fit round, insert
kawaru, change, be different
osoreru, fear
sakeru, avoid
uturu, change position, move (house)
wasureru, forget

Adverbs

hazimete, for the first time
sonna ni, to that extent
totemo, very
zenzen, completely

Interjection

maa

Suffixes

-garu
-ii
-nikui
-tagaru
-yasui

Exercise 29

Translate into English, then put back into Japanese:
1. Moo aki desu; ha no iro ga kawarihazimemasita. 2. Sukosi iinikui koto na no de damatte iyoo ka to omoimasu. 3. Kono tebukuro wa tiisasugite hameru koto ga dekimasen. 4. Kinoo anata ga katte kita penki wa totemo tukai-ii desu ne. 5. Kono hanabi wa hi ga taihen tukiyasui desu

kara anzen na tokoro e oite okimasyoo. 6. Kyonen tatehazimeta no desu ga mada dekiagatte imasen. 7. Koko no dozin o kyooiku suru sigoto o hikiuketa no wa watasi ga hazimete desu. 8. Sono hito no boosi wa ki ni hikkakari-masita. 9. Akai kao no otoko wa osorosii me o site mini-kui otoko no mimi o hipparimasita. 10. Ano ko wa hoka no hito ga kayugatte iru no o miru to zibun mo " kayui " to iidasimasu. 11. Kantan na koto sika iitukenain' desu ga hanbun wa wasurete simaun' desu. 12. Kinoo kaita bunsyoo wa manzoku de nai no de kakinaosite imasu. 13. Kono hon ni wa Hayakawa-san ga akai enpitu de kakiireta tokoro ga takusan arimasu. 14. Osii koto desu ga zyuusyo wa kakitotte arimasen. 15. Inu wa imooto ga ande iru kutusita no keito o kamikirimasita. 16. Hazime wa hanasi o mazime ni kiite imasita ga totyuu de waraidasite simaimasita. 17. Kono hon-dana wa otona de nakute mo kumitateru koto ga dekimasu. 18. Ano hito wa hizyoo ni se ga takai no de watasi wa miage-nagara hanasanakute wa narimasen. 19. Ani wa tomodati o miokuri ni eki e ikimasita. 20. Yama e nobotte sita no kesiki o miorosu no ga suki desu. 21. Zinan wa gakkoo kara kaette kuru to hon o teeburu no ue e nagedasite soto e dete ikimasita. 22. Hone o nomikomanai yoo ni tyuui nasai (go-tyuui nasai). 23. Kodomotati wa inu o kowagatte nigedasimasita. 24. Botan ga toremasita kara nuitukete kudasai. 25. Kao wa oboete imasu ga namae wa doositemo omoidasemasen. 26. Amerika e iku koto wa ima de mo omoikirenain' desu. 27. Ano hito ni attara otituite yukkuri hanasun' desu yo. 28. Maa sonna ni sawaganaide sukosi kokoro o otitukete kudasai. 29. Tabako no kemuri o suikomu no wa karada ni warui desu. 30. Kono suitorigami wa amari yoku suitorimasen ne. 31. Ura no to o akeru to ki ni tomatte ita tori ga mina tobiagarimasita. 32. " Kazi da, kazi da," to oogoe de ii-nagara hadaka no hito ga tobidasite kimasita. 33. Kodomo ga kawa ni otita no o mita seinen wa zubon o haita mama mizu no naka e tobikomimasita. 34. Byooki de soto e deraremasen kara asita no yakusoku wa torikesite kudasai. 35. Kin no tabakoire o torikaesi ni ittara abekobe ni hidoi me ni awasarete simaimasita. 36. Kondo tonari e ututte kita hito wa taihen tukiainikui hito desu. 37. Gohan o tumekomu yoo ni tabete isoide

G

dete ikimasita. 38. Kodomo o sakeyoo to site hei ni
utituketan' da soo desu. 39. Hito ni iyagarareru no o
osorete kaisya o yamemasita. 40. Tatami no ue ni suwari-
tagatte imasita ga asi ga itaku narun' d'ya nai ka to omotte
isu ni kosikakete moraimasita.

LESSON 30

THIS last lesson is concerned with the respect language of
Japanese. We have throughout the book confined ourselves to the " polite " forms represented by -MASU
forms of verbs, and if you keep to them you will not commit
any mistakes. However, you will no doubt have many
people speak to you using respect language, and you should
know how it works. Women are much more prone to use
it than men, but men use it too. The explanation which
follows is strictly speaking applicable to men only, but
women's language is basically similar, though differing
in detail.

The varying uses depend upon the amount of respect
the speaker shows to others, and this depends to a great
extent on relations within the family, relations between
persons of different ages and sex, between pupils and
teachers, subordinates and persons in charge, and upon
the degree of intimacy between people. These relations
and differences are expressed by the use of different vocabulary which includes, to some extent, nouns (you will remember the different nouns for various members of the
family) and pronouns, but which mainly consists of verbs.
To some extent it may be said that respect language,
among those who use it, replaces personal pronouns because verb forms will vary with the person that is the
subject, etc., of the verb. It also affords valuable clues
about the relations between persons when one listens to
their conversation, to the dialogue in films, etc.

The essential thing to grasp about respect language in
non-imperative sentences—imperatives being treated late
in this lesson—is that it is divisible into two main sections,
according to whether one is paying respect to the person
who is spoken to, or to the person one is speaking about.
These two sections are independent, but often intertwine

because the person spoken to and the one spoken about are often one and the same. In the sentence " Has Mr. Smith gone to Spain? " Mr. Smith is the one spoken about, and the person spoken to is the one from whom the information is sought. In " Are you going to Spain? " the person spoken to and the person spoken about are the same. The respect language which has to do with the person spoken about we shall call the " honorific system " and that which has to do with the person spoken to is the " system of levels ".

It will be easier to start with the latter, for you are already familiar with some of it, namely, the two levels of speech we have called plain and polite. The plain level is used to a person to whom you do not have to be polite, that is, to a school friend, to a fellow student, to a member of your family of your own age or younger, to a subordinate, perhaps to a colleague at work if he is a fairly close friend, to one's wife. One cannot lay down complete rules for this kind of thing—it will vary with all the social and psychological factors involved. Obviously, if you are a cheerful extrovert you may soon get on friendly terms with all sorts of people and use the plain level widely; if you are more reticent and retiring you may use the polite level to nearly everyone. Women use the plain level far less than men.

The plain level is characterized by the use of the plain forms of verbs and adjectives at the end of the sentence (you will, of course, remember that plain forms are used in the interior of a sentence in speech at the polite level using **-MASU** forms). This does not bring with it many grammatical problems, but you may note that when a sentence at the polite level ends in (**n'**) **desu ka,** at the plain level it will normally end with (**no**) **ka**—

> *Polite:* **Ano hito wa Eikokuzin desu ka.**
> *Plain:* **Ano hito wa Eikokuzin ka.**
> *Polite:* **Itu asoko e iku n' desu ka.**
> *Plain:* **Itu asoko e iku no ka.**

Speech at the plain level uses different forms for the first and second person pronouns from those used at the polite level. In so far as men's speech is concerned, at least, one must separate the uses of plain level speech into three types. The first of these, which may be called " brusque ", is used, for example, when giving military or similar orders, when angry, etc. On these occasions the second person pronoun, when used, will generally be **omae(tati)**, and the first person **ore(tati)** or **watasi(tati)**. The second type is often used within the family, by a father to children, husband to wife, older to younger child, etc. Here the pronouns get a little complicated, in so far as they are used at all; the name of the person spoken to is more generally used in Japanese than in English, and, of course, the subject, etc., of a verb need not be expressed. However, if a father does use a second person pronoun when addressing his child, he tends to use **omae,** and will use of himself **ore** (if he is elderly or old-fashioned) or **watasi**. An older brother will probably, and this is a modern development, use **kimi** to his brothers and even to his sisters. He will use **boku** for the first person. A modern husband will use **kimi** to his wife and **boku** for himself. His wife will call him **anata** and herself **watasi**, but will probably not use plain level speech. The third type of use of this level one may call friendly and occurs between male friends and acquaintances; here **kimi** and **boku** constitute the normal usage. Of recent years, among, for example, university students, this use has spread to young women, and the use of **kimi, boku** among members of a family is probably an extension of this friendly use.

The next level of speech is the polite, characterized by the use of **-MASU** forms at the end of the sentence and plain forms in other positions. It is the level that has been taught throughout this book and which it is advised that foreign students, men and women, should use.

We must now consider the means of expressing one's respect for the person spoken about, who may or may not be the person spoken to. From the very nature of the factors involved it is not possible to give anything like a complete statement of the circumstances in which a Japanese man will use the honorific system, for it will depend upon all sorts of factors, and it is quite permissible not to use it at all.   However, if you listen to Japanese conversation you will hear the system used on formal occasions, when the parties do not know each other very well, when speaking to or of one's own or somebody else's parents or grandparents, or one's superiors or one's teachers.

The system is characterized by the use of different verbs or verb forms according to the relation the particular verb has to the persons speaking or being spoken about.   There are three categories of verbs within the system—verbs which refer to the actions of the persons to whom respect is being paid and of others whom the speaker associates with him, that is, honorific verbs proper; verbs which refer to the actions of the speaker and others whom the speaker associates with himself, in so far as these actions relate to the person to whom respect is being shown, that is, depreciatory (or negative honorific) verbs; and, finally, verbs which refer to the actions of the speakers or some person whom the speaker associates with himself, in so far as they relate to some other person to whom he is not showing respect, or which refer to the actions of some person other than the speaker or the person to whom the speaker is showing respect, that is, indifferent verbs.

Honorific verbs are either special forms of the corresponding indifferent verbs, or are special verbs not derived from the indifferent equivalent.   The special forms consist of the stem of the indifferent verb prefixed by **o-** and followed by **ni naru** or **nasaru, ni naru** being perhaps a little more usual, or, in the case of **SURU** verbs, **go-** is prefixed and **suru** changed to **nasaru**.   The special verbs are set out in the table at the end of this lesson.

While it is true to say that all honorific verbs have indifferent equivalents, and vice versa, there are only a certain number of depreciatory verbs; **SURU** verbs normally have a depreciatory equivalent with **itasu** replacing **suru,** and the others are special forms.   Where no depreciatory verb exists, one uses the appropriate indifferent verb.   The table at the end should make things clear, but perhaps some examples now will be of assistance.

Indifferent	*Honorific*	*Depreciatory*
yomu	o-yomi ni naru	(yomu)
benkyoo suru	go-benkyoo nasaru	benkyoo itasu
miru	goran ni naru	haiken suru
kureru	kudasaru	(kureru)
yuu	ossyaru	(yuu)

All these verbs can be used at either of the levels of speech which we have mentioned. In the case of the honorific and the depreciatory, if the person to whom one is showing respect is also the person being spoken to, final verbs will be at the polite level, though those within the sentence will, of course, be in the plain form. Notice that the honorific verbs ending in **-aru** have **-MASU** forms in **-aimasu** (e.g., **nasaru, nasaimasu**).

> **Sensei, nan to ossyaimasita ka.** What did you say, sir?
> **Eiga o goran ni natta koto ga arimasu ka.** Have you ever seen a film?

When the person to whom one is showing respect is not the person spoken to, the level of speech used in final verbs depends entirely upon one's relations with the person being spoken to. For example, if a boy asks a servant about his father's whereabouts, he may say

> **Otoosan wa doko ni irassyaru ka.** Where is Father?

The verbs **ageru** and **yaru** require some comment. **Ageru** is " give to equal or superior " (in the sense of " give to a superior " **sasiageru** is often used) and **yaru**, " give to inferior ", provided in both cases that the recipient is not the speaker, in which instance **kureru** (**kudasaru**) is appropriate. The following examples will show how these verbs are used, but do not forget their construction with the **-TE** form :

> **Inu ni hone o yarimasita.** I gave the dog a bone.
> **Sensei ni gindokei o sasiagemasita.** I gave my teacher a silver watch.
> **Sensei wa inu ni hone o o-yari ni narimasita.** The teacher gave the dog a bone.
> **Sensei wa kootyoo ni okurimono o o-age ni narimasita.** The teacher gave his headmaster a present.

There is a further level of speech, used only when one is using honorifics to the person one is speaking to and wishes to show him even more respect. This may be called the deferential level, and manifests itself by the replacement of the verbs **desu, arimasu, imasu, ikimasu, kimasu** and **iimasu** by, respectively, **de gozaimasu, gozaimasu, orimasu, mairimasu, mairimasu** and **moosimasu.** The plain forms, used in the middle of a sentence, of **de gozaimasu** and **gozaimasu** are as for **desu** and **arimasu,** those of the others are **oru, mairu** and **moosu,** as you would expect. It is extremely unlikely that you will ever have to use the deferential level, but you should be able to recognize it and its significance. Since it can be used only when honorific verbs are also used, you must realize that actions performed by the person to whom you are showing respect, or someone you consider to be connected with him, are always expressed by the use of honorific verbs, and the deferential style is applicable to all other actions, whether performed by you (or someone connected closely with you), or by somebody else, or by impersonal subjects, whether or not the action has any relation to the person to whom one is paying respect. Notice here the difference between the depreciatory verbs and the deferential style.

Suppose A is telling B that C has told him that he (C) is going to the seaside tomorrow. In the Japanese we have taught you in this book, that is, using speech at the polite level, the sentence will be—

(*a*) **C-san wa asita umi e iku to iimasita.**

Now if the relation between A and B is friendly to the extent that they use the plain level to each other, then the sentence will be—

(*b*) **C-san wa asita umi e iku to itta.**

The use of **-san** here indicates that A and C do not use the plain level when talking to each other; **-san** indicates the polite level. It is replaced by **-kun** at the plain level in circumstances where **kimi** is used for " you ", but only among males. Thus—

(*c*) **C-kun wa asita umi e iku to itta.**

indicates that A, B and C are all on terms of friendship, and—

(d) **C-kun wa asita umi e iku to iimasita.**

indicates that A and C are on those terms, whereas A is not intimate enough with B to use the plain level with him.

Now if A wishes to show respect to B to such an extent that he would use the system of honorific and depreciatory verbs, the sentence would be as (a) or (d), according to the relation between A and C, since there are no words describing B's actions. If, however, A's attitude to B is such that he uses the deferential level when speaking to him, and if A considers C as connected with himself, he will say—

(e) **C wa asita umi e iku (mairu) to moosimasita.**

with the omission of **-san** or its equivalent after C, his name being used by itself. If, however, A links B and C in his mind, the sentence will be—

(f) **C-san wa asita umi e irassyaru to ossyaimasita.**

The effect on the imperatives of verbs used in respect language requires especial treatment. You will have noticed that the polite imperatives we gave you in Lesson 18 are reminiscent of honorific verbs, and care must be taken to avoid confusion.

The imperatives we are dealing with here are all of the second person, so that we are only concerned with the person spoken to. For true imperatives we have the normal three levels of speech, and the plain level is divided into the three sub-sections we mentioned with regard to personal pronouns in the plain level—" brusque ", " family, etc." and " friendly ". The brusque imperative is formed in **-U** verbs by substituting **-e** for the final **-u** in the plain form, and in **-RU** verbs by substituting **-o** for the final **-u** of the plain form. The brusque imperatives of **kuru** and **suru** are **koi** and **siro**. The " family, etc." imperative is the same as the polite with the initial **o-** or **go-** omitted, and the friendly imperative adds **-tamae** to the stem. The polite true imperative is also used to persons to whom one would use honorific verbs, and the deferential imperative adds **-masi** to the polite forms. Note, however, the rarity with which these forms are used, by the very nature of things.

The plain forms of the imperative with the implication of " for my benefit " consist of the **-TE** form of the verb followed by **kure, o-kure** and **kure-tamae,** in the brusque, family and friendly sub-sections respectively. The polite level has two forms; the first, consisting of the **-TE** form followed by **kudasai,** is used when the polite level is being used without honorifics; the second, consisting of the **-TE** form of the honorific followed by **kudasai,** is used at the polite level with honorifics. Notice the special forms of the **-TE** form of the honorific verbs as set out in the table in the Appendix, and that the form with **ni naru** is not used except in **oide ni natte kudasai,** which is an alternative of **irassite kudasai.** The deferential level of this imperative is obtained by adding **-masi** to the **kudasai** of the honorific form.

There follow a few miscellaneous notes on respect language. (i) Some formal greetings used at the polite level were originally depreciatory or deferential—

> **Hazimete o-me ni kakarimasu**—used when introduced to someone. (I meet you for the first time.)
> **O-hayoo gozaimasu.** Good morning. (It is early.)
> **Arigatoo gozaimasu.** Thank you. (**arigatoo** by itself is at the plain level.)
> **O-medetoo gozaimasu.** Congratulations. (**o-medetoo** is plain level.)
> **Itadakimasu**—see (iii) below.

(ii) Some expressions derived from honorific or depreciatory uses have come into use in sentences where no honorifics are otherwise being used, for example—

> **. . . o o-moti desu ka** (slightly formal polite), Have you . . .
> **Tyotto haiken** (plain friendly). Let me have a look.
> **Sore o mite goran** (plain family). Have a look at this.

Siturei itasimasita (polite). Please excuse me (for some action performed).

Doo itasimasite (polite).   Not at all.

(iii) **itadaku** is a depreciatory verb equivalent to **morau, taberu, nomu. Itadakimasu** is a fixed expression at the polite level uttered before eating or drinking. Another construction is with the **-TE** form of the causative of some verbs. Thus **haiken sasete itadakimasu** is a depreciatory expression used when one is allowed to look at something. **Haiken sasete itadakitoo gozaimasu** is a deferential level expression asking permission to look at something.

RESPECT LANGUAGE
(to be studied in conjunction with Lesson 30)

(1) HONORIFIC SYSTEM (Degrees of Respect to Person or Thing Spoken of)

Indifferent	Honorific Proper	Depreciatory (Neg. Hon.)
	Verbs	
da	de irassyaru	
aru	o-ari ni naru *	
iru ⎫ iku ⎬ kuru ⎭	oide ni naru,* irassyaru	
yuu	ossyaru	
suru	nasaru	itasu
morau	o-morai ni naru *	⎫
taberu	mesiagaru, o-agari ni naru *	⎬ itadaku, tyoodai suru
nomu	mesiagaru, o-nomi ni naru,* o-agari ni naru *	⎭
sinu ⎫ nakunaru ⎭	o-nakunari ni naru *	NONE
yaru (ageru)	o-yari ni naru * (o-age ni naru *)	ageru, sasiageru ("give" only)
kureru	kudasaru	NONE
siru	go-zon-zi ni naru *	zon-ziru
omou	o-omoi ni naru *	zon-ziru
miru	goran ni naru *	haiken suru †
au	o-ai ni naru *	o-me ni kakaru ("meet person" only)
miseru	o-mise ni naru *	o-me ni kakeru, goran ni kakeru
kariru	o-kari ni naru *	haisyaku suru †
negau	o-negai ni naru *	o-negai suru,‡ ukagau
tanomu	o-tanomi ni naru *	o-tanomi suru,‡ ukagau
kiku (*ask*)	o-kiki ni naru *	o-kiki suru,‡ ukagau
tazuneru	o-tazune ni naru *	o-tazune suru,‡ ukagau
benkyoo suru	go-benkyoo nasaru	benkyoo itasu
ALL OTHERS	*stem* + ni naru *	NONE

* OR nasaru IN PLACE OF ni naru.
† OR itasu IN PLACE OF suru.
‡ OR itasu OR moosu IN PLACE OF suru.

(2) System of Levels (*Degrees of Respect to Person Addressed*)

Plain	Polite	Deferential
	Verbs	
da (no, na)	desu (no, na)	de gozaimasu (no, na)
aru	arimasu (aru)	gozaimasu (aru)
iru	imasu (iru)	orimasu (oru)
iku	ikimasu (iku)	mairimasu (mairu)
kuru	kimasu (kuru)	mairimasu (mairu)
yuu	iimasu (yuu)	moosimasu (moosu)
ALL OTHERS	*stem* + -masu	
	Adjectives	
anzen da (na)	anzen desu (na)	anzen de gozaimasu (na)
takai	takai desu (takai)	takoo gozaimasu (takai)
ookii	ookii desu (ookii)	okyuu gozaimasu (ookii)
hikui	hikui desu (hikui)	hikuu gozaimasu (hikui)
hiroi	hiroi desu (hiroi)	hiroo gozaimasu (hiroi)

(*Forms in brackets are those normally used before nouns.*)

(3) IMPERATIVE

	Plain		Polite	Deferential
Brusque	Family	Friendly		

Affirmative

iro	i-nasai	i-tamae	irassyai *or* o-íde nasai	irassyaimasi *or* o-íde nasaimasi *and so forth throughout ; deferential is polite plus* -masi
ike	iki-nasai	iki-tamae	do.	
koi	ki-nasai	ki-tamae	do.	
ie	ii-nasai	ii-tamae	ossyai	
siro	(si-)nasai	si-tamae	nasai	
morae	morai-nasai	morai-tamae	o-morai nasai	
tabero	tabe-nasai	tabe-tamae	mesiagare *or* o-agari nasai	
nome	nomi-nasai	nomi-tamae	do. *or* o-nomi nasai	
yare	yari-nasai	yari-tamae	o-yari nasai	
agero	age-nasai	age-tamae	o-age nasai	
kure	o-kure	kure-tamae	kudasai	
miro	mi-nasai	mi-tamae	goran nasai	
ae	ai-nasai	ai-tamae	o-ai nasai	
misero	mise-nasai	mise-tamae	o-mise nasai	
kariro	kari-nasai	kari-tamae	o-kari nasai	
negae	negai-nasai	negai-tamae	o-negai nasai	
tanome	tanomi-nasai	tanomi-tamae	o-tanomi nasai	
kike	kiki-nasai	kiki-tamae	o-kiki nasai	
tazunero	tazune-nasai	tazune-tamae	o-tazune nasai	
benkyoo siro	benkyoo (si-)nasai	benkyoo si-tamae	go-benkyoo nasai	

Negative

iru na	i-nasaru na	i-tamoo na	irassyaru na *or* o-íde nasaru na	irassyaimasu na *or* o-íde nasaimasu na

etc. BUT *generally replaced by* -te wa ikenai, *etc.*

Kaiwa Iti

(Linguaphone Course, Side 5)

1. Ano teeburu no ue ni nani ga arimasu ka.
   Syasin ga arimasu.
2. Nan no syasin desu ka.
   Miki-san no gakkoo no syasin desu.
3. Miki-san no gakkoo wa doko ni arimasu ka.
   Tookyoo ni arimasu.
4. Anata no gakkoo wa doko ni arimasu ka.
   Watasi no gakkoo mo Tookyoo ni arimasu.
5. Tosyokan ga arimasu ka.
   Arimasu.
6. Anata wa tosyokan de nani o yomimasu ka.
   Nihongo no syoosetu o yomimasu.
7. Eigo no syoosetu mo yomimasu ka.
   Eigo no syoosetu wa arimasen.
8. Sono hako no naka ni nani ga arimasu ka.
   Hude ga arimasu.
9. Sono hude de nani o kaku tumori desu ka.
   Tegami o kaku tumori desu.
10. Sore wa dare no zibiki desu ka.
    Kore wa watasi no zibiki desu.
11. Zibiki no usiro ni wa nani ga imasu ka.
    Neko ga imasu.
12. Sono neko wa sakana o tabemasu ka.
    Sakana mo niku mo tabemasu.
13. Mado no sita no sutekki wa anata no sutekki desu ka.
    Are wa Tanaka-san no sutekki desu.
14. Tanaka-san wa doko ni imasu ka.
    Eki no mae no mise ni imasu.
15. Anata wa Tanaka-san ni au tumori desu ka.
    Eki de Tanaka-san o matu tumori desu.

Kaiwa Ni

(Linguaphone Course, Side 6, Sections 1–16)

1. Sono hako ni wa nani ga haitte imasu ka.
   Hon toka zassi toka sinbun nado ga haitte imasu.
2. Dareka e okuru tumori desu ka.
   Yamasita-san e okuru tumori desu.

Conversation I

1. What is there on that table?
   There is a photograph.
2. What is it a photograph of?
   It's a photograph of Mr. Miki's school.
3. Where is his school?
   It is in Tokyo.
4. Where is *your* school?
   My school is in Tokyo too.
5. Has it a library?
   Yes.
6. What do you read in the library?
   I read Japanese novels.
7. Do you also read English novels?
   It has no English novels.
8. What is in that box?
   A writing-brush.
9. What do you propose to write with that brush?
   A letter.
10. Whose dictionary is that?
    It's mine.
11. What is there behind the dictionary?
    There is a cat.
12. Does that cat eat fish?
    It eats both fish and meat.
13. Is the stick underneath the window yours?
    It is Mr. Tanaka's.
14. Where is Mr. Tanaka?
    He is in the shop in front of the station.
15. Do you intend to meet him?
    I intend to wait for him at the station.

Conversation II

1. What is there in that box?
   Books, magazines, newspapers, and so on.
2. Are you intending to send them to someone?
   I intend to send them to Mr. Yamasita.

3. Yamasita-san wa doko ni sunde imasu ka.
   Kyooto ni sunde imasu.
4. Nani o site imasu ka.
   Huransugo o osiete imasu.
5. Hon wa doko de kaimasita ka.
   Tookyoo no ooki na mise de kaimasita.
6. Zassi to sinbun mo onazi mise de kaimasita ka.
   Zassi to sinbun wa Huransu de kaimasita.
7. Anata wa Huransugo o hanasu koto ga dekimasu ka.
   Dekimasu.
8. Huransugo wa muzukasii desu ka.
   Muzukasiku wa arimasen; yasasii desu.
9. Huransu de ekaki no Miki-san ni aimasita ka.
   Aimasita.
10. Hen na boosi o kabutte imasita ka.
    Boosi wa kabutte imasen desita.
11. Huransu kara dokoka e ryokoo simasita ka.
    Eikoku e ryokoo simasita.
12. Eikoku ni wa tomodati ga imasita ka.
    Honda-san to Kimura-san ga imasita.
13. Honda-san wa nani o site imasita ka.
    Eikoku no nyuusu o Nihon e hoosoo site imasita.
14. Kimura-san wa.
    Ano hito wa eigo o benkyoo site imasita.
15. Honda-san wa zidoosya o tukatte imasita ka.
    Rippa na zidoosya o tukatte imasita.
16. Zidoosya no iro wa nan desita ka.
    Kuroi zidoosya desita.
17. Eikoku wa samukatta desu ka.
    Samukatta desu.
18. Yuki ga hurimasita ka.
    Yuki wa hurimasen desita.
19. Huransu mo samukatta desu ka.
    Huransu wa atatakakatta desu.
20. Amerika e mo ikimasita ka.
    Amerika e wa ikimasen desita.

3. Where does he live?
   In Kyoto.
4. What does he do?
   He teaches French.
5. Where did you buy the books?
   In a big Tokyo shop.
6. Did you buy the magazines and newspapers in the same
   shop?
   I bought them in France.
7. Can you speak French?
   Yes, I can.
8. Is French difficult?
   No, it's not; it's easy.
9. Did you meet Mr. Miki, the artist, in France?
   Yes, I did.
10. Was he wearing a funny hat?
    He wasn't wearing one.
11. Did you travel anywhere from France?
    I travelled to England.
12. Were there any friends of yours in England?
    Mr. Honda and Mr. Kimura were there.
13. What was Mr. Honda doing?
    He was broadcasting English news to Japan.
14. And Mr. Kimura?
    He was studying English.
15. Was Mr. Honda using a car?
    He was using a magnificent one.
16. What was the colour of his car?
    It was a black car.
17. Was it cold in England?
    Yes, it was.
18. Did it snow?
    No, it didn't.
19. Was it cold in France too?
    It was warm in France.
20. Did you go to America too?
    No, not to America.

Kaiwa San

(Linguaphone Course, Side 7, Sections 1–12)

1. Yuubinkyoku wa doko ni arimasu ka.
   Kono toori no mukoogawa ni arimasu.
2. Ano ooki na tokei no aru tokoro desu ka.
   Ie, are wa yuubinkyoku de nakute siyakusyo desu.
   Yuubinkyoku wa sono tonari desu.
3. Asoko de denpoo o utu koto ga dekiru desyoo ka.
   Saa, dekiru ka mo siremasen.　Watasi wa kitte o katta
   koto wa arimasu ga, denpoo o utta koto wa arimasen.
   Denpoo wa dare ni utun' desu ka.
4. Atami no onsen ni iru ani ni utun' desu.
   Anata no niisan ni wa ituka atta koto ga arimasu.
   Anata yori se ga takai desyoo.
5. Soo desu.　Watasi yori sukosi takai desu ga, otooto
   hodo takaku wa arimasen.
   Otootosan wa niisan yori mo takain' desu ka.
6. Soo desu.　Watasi ga itiban hikuin' desu.
   Watasi mo yuubinkyoku e ikimasyoo ka.
7. Ie, anata wa konakute mo ii desu.
   Watasi wa itte mo ikanakute mo kamaimasen ga,
   nagaku matte iru no wa iya desu.
8. Dekiru dake hayaku simasu.
   Watasi wa ano mise no mae de matte imasu.
9. Hayakatta desyoo.
   E, hayakatta desu.　Kono mise wa amari benri de wa
   arimasen.　Bukkyoo no hon o issatu kaoo to simasita ga, dono hon-dana ni mo nain' desu.
10. Naze bukkyoo no hon o kaoo to sitan' desu ka.
    Asatte razio de bukkyoo no koto no hoosoo ga arun'
    desu.
11. Hon o yomu yori hoosoo o kiita hoo ga ii desyoo.
    Hon o yonde kara hoosoo o kiita hoo ga motto ii
    desu.
12. Sore mo soo desu ga, hon o kau no wa kane ga kakaru
    desyoo.
    Biiru o nomu hodo wa kakarimasen.
13. Watasi wa biiru o nomu koto mo hon o kau koto mo
    dekimasen.
    Naze desu ka.

Conversation III

1. Where is the Post Office?
   On the other side of this street.
2. Is it the place with a big clock?
   No, that's not the Post Office; it's the City Hall.
   The Post Office is next door.
3. Do you think I can send a telegram there?
   Well, you may be able to.   I have bought stamps there,
   but never sent a telegram.   Who are you sending it
   to?
4. To my elder brother who is at the Atami hot spring.
   I met your brother once.   He is taller than you, I
   think.
5. That's right.   He is a little taller than I am, but he is
   not as tall as my younger brother.
   Is he taller than your elder brother?
6. Yes, he is.   I am the shortest.
   Shall I come to the Post Office too?
7. No, you needn't come.
   I don't mind whether I come or not, but I hate waiting
   about for a long time.
8. I shall be as quick as possible.
   I shall be waiting in front of that shop.
9. That was quick, wasn't it?
   Yes, it was.   This shop is not much good to me.   I
   wanted to buy a book on Buddhism, but there wasn't
   one on any of the shelves.
10. Why did you want to buy a book on Buddhism?
    The day after tomorrow there is to be a broadcast on
    the wireless about it.
11. Rather than reading a book I should think it would be
    better to listen to the broadcast.
    It will be better still to read a book and then listen to
    the broadcast.
12. That may be so, but it costs money to buy books.
    Not so much as beer does.
13. I can't afford either beer or books.
    Why?

14. Eigakan e tabitabi ikun' desu.
    Issyuukan ni nando ikimasu ka.
15. Sando ikimasu.
    Watasi wa itinen ni itido ka nido ikimasu.
16. Basu ga kimasita.   Are ni norimasyoo ka.
    Are wa eki e ikimasen.
17. Nanban no ga ikun' desu ka.
    Sitiban no desu.
18. Densya de eki e iku koto wa dekimasen ka.
    Dekimasu ga basu yori zikan ga nagaku kakarimasu.
19. Kisya wa zyuuzi nizippun ni tukun' desu ga, ma ni au
    desyoo ka.
    Ma ni au desyoo.   Watasitati ga sukosi osokute mo
    Aoyama-san wa matte iru desyoo.
20. Sitiban no basu ga kimasita.
    Isoide norimasyoo.

Kaiwa Si

(Linguaphone Course, Side 8, Sections 1–15)

1. Yamasita-san wa Tookyoo de nani o site irun' desu ka.
   Sensei no menzyoo o toru tame ni benkyoo site iru soo
   desu.
2. Nani o benkyoo site irun' desu ka.
   Buturigaku da soo desu.
3. Buturigaku wa muzukasii desyoo ne.
   Muzukasii to omoimasu; yoku sirimasen ga.
4. Gakkoo e itte ita toki ni wa naratta koto mo arimasu
   ga, omosiroi to wa omoimasen desita.
   Watasi mo onazi desu.
5. Anata wa donna mono ni kyoomi o motte imasu ka.
   Saa, bungaku desyoo ne.
6. Gaikoku no bungaku desu ka.
   Gaikoku no bungaku no koto wa nanimo sirimasen.
7. Otootosan wa.
   Otooto wa Doitugo ni hizyoo ni kyoomi o motte imasu.
     Itumo Doitugo no hon o yonde iru yoo desu.
8. Otootosan wa rainen daigaku e ikun' desyoo.
   Daigaku e iku koto wa muzukasii desyoo.

14. Because I go to the pictures a lot.
    How many times a week do you go?
15. Three times.
    I go once or twice a year.
16. Here is a bus.   Shall we get on it?
    It doesn't go to the station.
17. What number does?
    Number seven.
18. Can't we go to the station by tram?
    We can, but it takes longer than the bus.
19. The train arrives at ten twenty;   do you think we shall
    be in time?
    Yes, I think so.   Even if we are a bit late, Mr. Aoyama
    will wait.
20. Here is a Number Seven bus.
    Let's get on it quickly.

Conversation IV

1. What is Mr. Yamasita doing in Tokyo?
   I hear he is studying for his teacher's diploma.
2. I wonder what he is studying.
   Physics, I hear.
3. Physics must be difficult.
   Yes, I think it is.   I don't know much about it,
   though.
4. I *did* learn some at school, but I didn't think it was
   interesting.
   The same with me.
5. What kind of thing are you interested in?
   Well, literature, I suppose.
6. Foreign literature?
   I don't know anything about that.
7. What about your younger brother?
   He is very interested in German.   He always seems to
   be reading German books.
8. He is going to a university next year, I suppose.
   It will be difficult for him to go to a university.

9. Naze desu ka.
   Ima itte iru gakkoo o deta ato de sugu hatarakanakereba ikenai to omoimasu.
10. Ima de wa daredemo daigaku e ikimasu yo.
    Uti ni kane sae areba motiron iku koto ga dekirun'
    desu ga nee.
11. Anata wa daigaku e ittan' desyoo.
    Watasi ga itta no wa titi ga sinanai uti desita kara
    ikurademo benkyoo suru koto ga dekitan' desu.
12. Otootosan wa daigaku e ikitain' desyoo ne.
    Soo desu. Daigaku e hizyoo ni ikitai no de hiruma
    hataraite yoru benkyoo suru tumori rasii desu.
13. Sore wa sukosi muzukasii desu ne.
    Daigaku e ikanakute mo tekitoo na sigoto o mitukeru
    koto ga dekiru to omoun' desu.
14. Asoko o goran nasai. Nakagawa-san ga yaoya no mae
    o aruite imasu yo. Nimotu ga otisoo desu.
    Soo desu ne. Itumo no to tigau huku o kite imasu ne.
15. Yobimasyoo ka.
    Yobanaide kudasai. Ano hito wa hitotu no koto o
    hanasu no ni mo hizyoo ni nagai zikan ga kakarun'
    desu.
16. Watasi wa hiru no syokuzi o si ni ikun' desu ga anata
    mo kimasen ka.
    Anata sae yokereba ikimasyoo.
17. Watasi wa sukosi mo kamaimasen.
    Soo desu ka.
18. Watasi wa itumo wa hiru no syokuzi wa itizi mae ni wa
    sinain' desu ga, kyoo wa gogo iku tokoro ga arimasu
    kara sukosi hayaku sitain' desu.
    Watasi mo gogo nizi ni hito ni au yakusoku ga arimasu.
19. Ima zyuunizi nizippun desu kara zikan wa takusan aru
    desyoo.
    Soo desu nee.
20. Anata wa donna mono ga tabetai desu ka.
    Watasi wa tabetaku nai mono wa nanimo arimasen yo.

9. Why?
   He'll have to start work straight away after leaving the school he is at now, I think.
10. Everybody goes to a university now.
    If only we had the money, of course he could go.
11. You went to a university, didn't you?
    It was before my father died that I went, so I could study as much as I liked.
12. I expect he wants to go, doesn't he?
    Yes, he does. It seems that he is so eager to go that he intends to work by day and study at night.
13. That will be a bit difficult, won't it?
    Even if he doesn't go to a university, I think he will be able to find some suitable job.
14. Look over there. Mr. Nakagawa is walking past the greengrocer's. It looks as if he is going to drop his luggage.
    It does, doesn't it? He is wearing a different suit from his usual one, isn't he?
15. Shall we call him?
    Please don't. He takes such a long time to tell you even the least thing.
16. I'm going to have my lunch; won't you come with me?
    If it is all right with you, I'll come.
17. I don't mind in the least.
    All right, then.
18. I don't usually have my lunch before one o'clock, but as I have somewhere to go this afternoon, I want to have it a little earlier.
    I have an appointment to meet someone at two.
19. It's now twenty-past twelve, so you will have plenty of time.
    That's right.
20. What would you like to eat?
    There is nothing that I don't like.

Kaiwa Go

(Linguaphone Course, Side 9, Sections 1–1st sentence of 16)

1. Inoue-san wa imasu ka.
   Moo kuru zikan desu ga mada kite imasen. Nanika yoo desu ka.

2. Sukosi kikitai koto ga arun' desu.
   Koko de sukosi o-mati nasai. Moo sugu kuru desyoo.

3. Moo hitori aitai tomodati ga imasu kara sono hito no tokoro e itte kimasu.
   Soo desu ka. Inoue-san ni wa anata ga aitai to itte okimasu.

4. Mata kimasita yo. Inoue-san wa moo kite iru desyoo.
   Anata ga koko o dete kara zippun bakari ato de kimasita ga, sugu mata syatyoo to issyo ni dete ikimasita.

5. Soo desu ka. Watasi no koto o hanasite kuremasita ka.
   E, hanasimasita ga tada matte ite moraitai to itta dake desita.

6. Doko e itta ka anata sitte imasu ka.
   Saa, sirimasen. Amari nagai koto wa nai desyoo. Sukosi watasi to hanasi de mo site irassyai.

7. Watasi wa ii desu ga anata wa isogasiin' desyoo.
   Iie, sore hodo de mo arimasen. Hiru mae wa amari sigoto ga arimasen.

8. Hontoo desu ka.
   Hontoo desu. Anata ga atte kita tomodati wa doko de hataraite irun' desu ka.

9. Siyakusyo desu. Nanika tumaranai sigoto sika site inai hito nan' desu.
   Nan to yuu hito desu ka.

10. Kitamura to yuun' desu.
    Kitamura-san wa watasi mo sukosi sitte imasu yo.

11. Soo desu ka. Kyoo ano hito wa sityoo ga yameru rasii to itte imasita yo.
    Doosite desu ka.

12. Ima yamenakereba ato rokkagetu gurai sika ikite irarenai ka mo sirenain' da soo desu.
    Sonna ni waruin' desu ka. Doo sitan' desu ka.

Conversation V

1. Is Mr. Inoue in?
   It is time for him to come, but he hasn't yet.   Do you
   want him for something?

2. There is just something that I would like to ask him.
   Wait here a little.   I expect he'll come presently.

3. There is another friend that I want to see, so I'll go
   to his place and come back.
   Very well, then.   I'll tell Mr. Inoue that you want to
   see him.

4. Here I am again.   I expect Mr. Inoue has arrived now.
   He arrived about ten minutes after you left, but he
   went out again straight away with the chairman.

5. Did he?   Did you tell him about me?
   Yes, I did.   All he said was that he'd like you to wait.

6. Do you know where he went?
   No, I don't.   I don't suppose he will be very long.
   Stay here and talk to me a little.

7. It's all right by me, but I expect you are busy.
   No, not awfully.   I haven't much work to do before
   midday.

8. Are you sure?
   Quite sure.   Where does the friend you've just been
   to see work?

9. In the City Hall.   He just does some trifling job there.
   What is his name?

10. Kitamura.
    I know Mr. Kitamura a little too.

11. Do you?   Today he was saying that it seems the Mayor
    is resigning.
    Why?

12. He said that if the Mayor didn't resign now, he might
    have only six months to live.
    Is it as serious as all that?   What's wrong with
    him?

13. Sityoo wa mae kara mimi ga warukattan' desu ga, tikagoro wa hotondo nanimo kikoenain' da soo desu. Sore de nanimo sigoto o sinaide yukkuri yasumana-kereba ikenain' desu ne.

14. Soo nan' desu. Atarasii sityoo wa dare desyoo ka.

15. Dare ka wakarimasen ne. Ima no sityoo no otooto wa syookoo de zyuunen bakari mae ni korosaretan' d'ya nain' desu ka.

16. Soo desu yo. Nanika warui hito kara kane o moratta koto ga wakatte keisatu ni siraberareyoo to sitan' desyoo.

17. Soo desu. Siraberare ni iku tyotto mae ni korosaretan' desita ne. Kane o kureta hito ga korositan' d'ya nai daroo ka to iwarete imasita ne.

18. Sinbun wa hizyoo ni sawagimasita nee. Anna koto de sinbun ni kakaretaku nai desu ne.

19. Inoue-san wa doo sitan' desyoo ne. Konna ni nagai to wa omoimasen desita yo.

20. Watasi wa moo matemasen. Mata kimasu kara soo itte oite kudasai. Doomo sumimasen desita ne.

Kaiwa Roku

(Linguaphone Course, Side 10, Sections 1–1st sentence of 16)

1. Kagakusya no Aoyama-san no hanasi o kiki ni iki-masen ka. Itu desu ka.

2. Raigetu no yokka desu. Nanyoo-bi ni narimasu ka.

3. Kinyoo-bi ni narimasu. Sitizi ni hazimarimasu. Iketara ikimasyoo.

4. Nanika hoka no yakusoku de mo arun' desu ka. Nanika aru yoo na ki ga surun' desu.

5. Ookawa-san mo kuru hazu ni natte imasu. Hanasi wa doko de surun' desu ka.

13. He has had something wrong with his ears for some time
     now, and lately he can hardly hear a thing, it seems.
     In that case, he must take things easy and not do any
     work, mustn't he?
14. You are quite right.
     I wonder who will be the new Mayor.
15. I don't know who will be.
     His younger brother was an officer and was killed about
     ten years ago, wasn't he?
16. Yes, he was.
     It was discovered that he had accepted money from
     some bad character, and he was about to be questioned
     by the police.
17. That is so. He was killed just before going to be
     questioned, wasn't he?
     The story went round that he might have been killed
     by the man who gave him the money.
18. The newspapers made a terrible fuss about it.
     One doesn't want one's name in the papers for such a
     thing as that, eh?
19. I wonder what has happened to Mr. Inoue.
     I didn't think he'd be as long as this.
20. I can wait no longer. Please tell him that I'll call
     again.
     I'm very sorry.

Conversation VI

1. Won't you come and hear the talk by Mr. Aoyama,
    the scientist?
    When is it?
2. On the fourth of next month.
    What day of the week is it?
3. Friday.   It starts at seven.
    If I can, I will.
4. Have you another engagement, or something?
    I have a feeling that I have something on.
5. Mr. Ookawa is expected to come too.
    Where is the talk?

6. Daigaku de suru koto ni natte imasu.
    Wasureru to ikemasen kara mae no hi ni denwa o
    kakete kudasai.
7. Denwa no bangoo wa nanban desita ka ne.
    Nakano no nisen sanbyaku gozyuusanban desu.
8. Hoka ni mo kitai hito ga attara turete kite kudasai.
    Ikitagaru hito ga itara soo simasu.
9. Takai-san wa doo desu ka.
    Doo desu ka nee. Ikitai to ittara issyo ni ikimasu.
10. Konogoro Takai-san no karada no guai wa doo desu ka.
    Ima de wa ii yoo desu.
11. Ano hito wa karada o kowasiyasui hito no yoo desu ga
    doo desu ka.
    Hatarakisugirun' desu. Ano hito to site wa ima no
    sigoto wa raku-sugite gakkari site imasu ga, karada
    no tame to omotte site imasu.
12. Sore wa soo to, Simoda-san wa tootoo ano onna-no-
    hito to kekkon suru koto ni narimasita.
    Soo desu ka.
13. Ryoosin ni nagai aida damatte imasita ga kondo
    yakunin ni natta no de kimeta rasiin' desu.
    Ano onna-no-hito ni atte kara moo zyuunen gurai ni
    narun' desyoo.
14. Soo desu. Simoda-san wa syoogakkoo no sensei o
    site imasita.
    Yakunin ni naru tumori de totemo benkyoo site imasita
    ne.
15. E, ano koro wa seikatu ga kurusikatta yoo desu.
    Ano hito no ozisan wa kanai no titi no hurui tomodati
    desu yo.
16. Soo desu ka. Sore wa sirimasen desita.
    Kanai no titi wa Simoda-san no ozisan ni tokidoki
    sake o nomasaresugita koto ga arun' desu.
17. Hutaritomo wakai toki no hanasi nan' desyoo.
    Soo desu. Sake o nomi-nagara kenka o sitari oogoe
    de uta o utattari site sawaida to yuu koto desu.
18. Mitakatta desu ne.
    Kanzyoo o harawanai mama de dete itte simatta koto
    mo aru soo desu.
19. Watasi ni wa tyotto kangaeraremasen.
    Wakai toki ni wa dare de mo yoku suru koto desu yo.

6. It is planned to hold it at the university.
   In case I forget please give me a ring the day before.
7. Now, what was your telephone number?
   Nakano 2353.
8. If any others want to come, please bring them along.
   If there is anyone, I will.
9. What about Mr. Takai?
   I wonder. If he says he wants to come, I'll bring him with me.
10. How is his health these days?
    He seems to be better now.
11. He gives the impression of falling ill very quickly; is that right?
    He works too hard. He is very disappointed because his present work is too easy for him, but he is doing it for the sake of his health.
12. By the way, Mr. Simoda is getting married to that girl, after all.
    Is he?
13. He didn't tell his parents about her for a long time, but now that he has become a government official he seems to have made his mind up.
    It must be about ten years since he met her.
14. Yes. He was working as a primary school teacher.
    He was studying very hard with the object of becoming a government official, wasn't he?
15. Yes. His life then seems to have been very hard.
    Did you know that his uncle is an old friend of my wife's father?
16. Is that so? I didn't know that.
    It sometimes happened that my wife's father was made to drink too much by Mr. Simoda's uncle.
17. That was when they were both young, I should think.
    Yes. The story is that while they were drinking they used to make a disturbance by quarrelling and singing songs in a loud voice.
18. I wish I could have seen them!
    It seems that sometimes they left the place without paying the bill.
19. I just can't imagine it.
    It is the kind of thing we all do when we are young.

20. Moo sanzi ni narimasita. Yokka ni wa watasi o gakkari sasenaide kudasai.
Dekiru dake iku yoo ni simasu.

Kaiwa Siti

(*Linguaphone Course, Side 11, Sections 1–1st sentence of 16*)

1. Anata wa asa nanzi ni okimasu ka.
Taitei rokuzi ni okosaremasu.
2. Naze desu ka. Me ga samenain' desu ka.
Ie, omote ga yakamasiku natte kuru no de nete irarenain' desu.
3. Watasi wa kao o arattari ha o migaitari hige o sottari suru no ni sanzippun mo kakarimasu ga anata wa doo desu ka.
Watasi wa zyuugohun sika kakarimasen yo.
4. Asa no syokuzi wa nanzi ni simasu ka.
Sitizi ni simasu. Pan o tabete koohii o nomu dake desu kara sugu owatte simaimasu.
5. Watasi wa Nihon no syokuzi o simasu.
Sore de wa zikan ga sukosi kakaru desyoo.
6. Ee. Sono ue uti o deru mae ni asa kita tegami to sinbun o yomimasu. Dakara eki made hasitte ikanakereba naranai koto ga tabitabi arimasu.
Watasi wa sinbun wa densya no naka de yomimasu.
7. Zimusyo ni wa nanzi ni tukimasu ka.
Hatizi-han desu. Sigoto o hazimeru no wa kuzi desu.
8. Hiru no yasumi wa dono kurai arimasu ka.
Zyuunizi kara itizi made no itizikan desu.
9. Syokuzi ni wa soto e derun' desu ka.
E, tomodati to issyo ni dekakemasu.
10. Watasi wa bentoo o tyuumon site motte kosasemasu.
Denwa de tyuumon surun' desu ka.
11. Soo desu. Hoka no hito ga mina soto e deru no de watasi wa nokotte inakereba naranain' desu.
D'ya ban ni wa hoka no hito yori hayaku uti e kaererun' desyoo.
12. Sonna ni hayaku mo arimasen. Hutuu wa rokuzi-han ni kaerimasu.
Watasi wa uti e kaeru no wa hatizi sugi ni narimasu.

20. It's now three o'clock. Please don't disappoint me on the fourth.
I'll try my best to come.

Conversation VII

1. At what time do you get up in the morning?
I am usually woken up at six.

2. Why? Don't you wake up by yourself?
No. It's because it gets so noisy in front of my house that I can't stay asleep.

3. It takes me a good half-hour to wash my face, clean my teeth, and shave; what about you?
It only takes me fifteen minutes.

4. What time do you have your breakfast?
At seven. As I have only bread and coffee I soon get it over.

5. I have a Japanese breakfast.
It must take a little longer, then.

6. Yes. In addition, I read my morning mail and the newspapers before I leave. So, I often have to run to the station.
I read my newspaper in the train.

7. At what time do you reach the office?
Half-past eight. We start work at nine.

8. How long is your lunch break?
One hour, from twelve to one.

9. Do you go out to lunch?
Yes, I go with a friend.

10. I order a packed lunch and have it brought to me.
Do you order it by telephone?

11. Yes. Everybody else goes out, so I have to stay in.
In that case, I suppose, you can get home earlier than the others.

12. It's not so early as all that. Usually I get home at half-past six.
When I get home it's gone eight o'clock.

13. Yoku sonna ni hatarakimasu ne.
    Binboonin ni wa hima ga arimasen.
14. Doyoo-bi wa han-niti nan' desyoo.
    Watasi no tokoro de wa doyoo-bi mo hoka no hi to
    tigai ga arimasen.
15. Ban ni wa donna koto o simasu ka.
    Ban ni wa sukkari tukarete iru no de syokuzi ga owaru
    to nani o suru ki mo arimasen.
16. Watasi wa maiban razio o kikimasu.
    Maiban desu ka.
17. Syuukan desu ne.   Kikitaku nakereba kikanaide mo
    iin' desyoo ga.
    Watasi wa soo yuu mono o tanosimu zikan mo genki
    mo arimasen.
18. Neru toki ni wa itumo hon o ni-sansatu yomu tumori
    de motte ikimasu.
    Toko ni haitte kara yomimasu ka.
19. Ee, taitei itizikan gurai yomimasu.
    Sore de wa nemuru zikan ga tarinai desyoo.
20. Tariru to omoimasu ne.   Donna ni hon ni nettyuu
    site mo zyuunizi made ni wa nemurimasu.
    Yoku sonna koto ga dekimasu ne.   Watasi wa zyuuzi-
    han yori osoku okite iru koto wa hotondo arimasen.

Kaiwa Hati

(Linguaphone Course, Side 12)

1. Isoganai to okuremasu yo.
   Ee, kono tegami o kaitara sugu dekakemasu.
2. Kinoo moratta hon no o-rei desu ka.
   Ie, Nagoya ni iru oba ni dasun' desu.
3. Kaette kite kara kaitara ii d'ya arimasen ka.
   Sanzi made ni dasanai to ma ni awanain' desu.
4. Sonna ni isoganakereba naranain' desu ka.
   E, konsyuu no doyoo-bi made ni okutte moraitai
   mono ga arun' desu.
5. Okane desu ka.
   Ie, itoko no huku desu.
6. Karirun' desu ka.
   E, tomodati no kekkonsiki ni deru tame ni irun' desu.

13. You do work hard, don't you?
    The poor have no leisure.
14. I suppose Saturday is a half-day.
    In my firm Saturday is no different from the rest of
      the week.
15. What do you do in the evening?
    I am completely exhausted in the evening, and so after
      my meal is finished I don't feel like doing anything.
16. I listen to the wireless every evening.
    Every evening?
17. It's a habit.   I suppose I wouldn't have to listen to it
      if I didn't want to.
    I have neither the time nor the energy to enjoy things
      like that.
18. When I go to bed I always take two or three books to
      read.
    Do you read in bed?
19. Yes, I usually read for about an hour.
    In that case you don't get enough sleep.
20. I think I do.   No matter how absorbed I am in a book,
      I get to sleep by twelve.
    How do you manage to do it!   I scarcely ever stop up
      later than half-past ten.

Conversation VIII

 1. You'll be late if you don't hurry, you know.
    Yes, I will go as soon as I've written this letter.
 2. Is it a letter of thanks for the book you got yesterday?
    No, it's to my aunt in Nagoya.
 3. Wouldn't it be better to write it after you get back?
    If I don't post it before three, it will miss the post.
 4. Does it have to be in such a hurry?
    Yes, there is something I want her to send me by next
      Saturday.
 5. Some money?
    No, my cousin's suit.
 6. Are you borrowing it?
    Yes, I need it to go to a friend's wedding.
    H

7. Kekkonsiki wa itu nan' desu ka.
Getuyoo-bi na no de doyoo-bi made ni tukanai to
komarun' desu.

8. Karita huku ga aimasu ka.
Au to omoimasu.

9. Mosi doyoo-bi made ni konakattara doo simasu ka.
Sono toki wa watasi no tomodati o hitori-zutu kiite
mawarimasu.

10. Siki ni tukau huku o kattara ii d'ya arimasen ka.
Huku toka kimono nado o kau no wa kane o suteru
yoo na ki ga surun' desu.

11. Sonna koto o itta'tte * itumo hito kara karite bakari
wa iraremasen yo.
Sore mo soo desu ga ne. Maa hontoo no koto o ieba
watasi ni wa kane ga nain' desu ne.

12. Moo nizi-han desu yo.
Oya, soo desu ka. Hanasi bakari site ite tegami ga
kakemasen.

13. Anata ga binsen o motte kono heya e haitte kite kara
itizikan gurai ni narimasu yo.
Hito ni mono o tanomu tegami wa kakinikui mono
desu.

14. Huutoo mo kitte mo arimasu ka.
Sore wa anata kara moraoo to omotte itan' desu ga ne.

15. Anata wa nandemo hito no mono o tukaoo to simasu
ne.
Soo yuu koto ni narimasu ka ne. Watasi no seikatu no
sosiki ga warui kara nan' desyoo.

16. Dotiraka to ieba soo desu ne.
Watasi no yoo ni isogasii ningen wa sosikiteki na
seikatu ga dekinain' desu.

17. Isogasii nan'te zibun de isogasiku saseru kara ikenain'
desu yo.
Anata no baai wa mata hantai desu ne. Nandemo
sosikiteki de matigai ga nain' desyoo.

18. Sore hodo de mo arimasen.
Saa, dekimasita. Sumimasen ga huutoo to kitte o
o-negai simasu.

---

* itta'tte = itte mo.

7. When is the wedding?

It's on Monday, so if it doesn't arrive by Saturday I shall be in a fix.

8. Will a borrowed suit fit you?

I think it will.

9. What will you do if it doesn't come by Saturday?

Then I shall have to go round to all my friends one by one.

10. Hadn't you better buy a suit to use on formal occasions?

I feel that it's just like throwing money away to buy suits and kimonos and things.

11. It's all very well for you to talk like that, but you can't just keep on borrowing other people's things.

I suppose you are right. Well, to tell you the truth, I haven't any money.

12. It's already half-past two.

Oh dear, is it? I've been talking so much; I can't get on with my letter.

13. It's a good hour since you came into this room with your note-paper.

It's difficult to write a letter asking someone for something, isn't it?

14. Have you got an envelope and a stamp?

I was hoping to get them from you.

15. You are always trying to use other people's things, aren't you?

I suppose that's what it comes to. My life is badly organized or something.

16. It is rather.

The fact is that people as busy as I am cannot live an organized life.

17. Busy? It's because you give yourself so much work; that's the trouble with you.

It's just the opposite in your case, isn't it? Everything is well organized and nothing goes wrong.

18. Not so well organized as all that, you know.

Well, I've finished. I am very sorry, but could I have an envelope and a stamp?

19. Kondo kara wa anata mo katte okanakereba ikemasen
   yo.
   Matigai naku soo simasu kara kyoo dake wa kasite
   kudasai.
20. Sanzi gohun mae desu yo.
   Soo desu ka.   D'ya moo dekakenakereba ikemasen.

Kaiwa Ku

(Linguaphone Course, Sides 13 and 14)

1. Konniti wa.   Doo desu, ie wa mitukarimasita ka.
   E, yatto mitukarimasita.

2. Sore wa kekkoo desu.   Nagai aida sagasite itan' desyoo.
   Soo desu.   Ani to hutari de hooboo sagasimasita yo.

3. Doko nan' desu ka.
   Kunitati no tikaku desu.

4. Atarasii ie desu ka.
   Kanari atarasii desu.   Hanbun wa nihon-siki de
   hanbun wa seiyoo-siki nan' desu.   Nihon-siki no
   hoo wa sukosi hurui yoo de ikkai sika arimasen.
   Seiyoo-siki no hoo wa nikai ga arimasu.

5. Heya wa ikutu arun' desu ka.
   Soo desu nee, yattu arun' da to omoimasu.   Genkan
   ga sanzyoo de sono usiro ni yozyoo-han no heya ga
   arimasu.   Genkan no yoko ni zyuuzyoo no kyakusitu, sono usiro ni hatizyoo to rokuzyoo no heya ga
   arimasu.   Ato wa seiyoo-siki de sita ni wa nagasa
   ga gomeetoru haba ga yonmeetoru no heya to
   huroba to benzyo to daidokoro ga arimasu.   Nikai
   ni wa heya ga hutatu arimasu.

6. Huroba to daidokoro ga seiyoo-siki na no wa hen desu
   ne.
   Soo desu.   Seiyoozin ga sunde ita rasiin' desu.

7. Naruhodo ne.   Sono ie wa kasiya desu ka.
   Ima wa soo desu.   Ani wa itinen gurai sunde mite
   guai ga ii yoo nara katte mo ii to itte imasu.

19. In future you must buy some and keep them by you.
I'll do so without fail, so please lend me them just this
once.

20. It's five to three, you know.
Is it? Well, I must go now.

Conversation IX

1. Hello. How are you getting on—have you found a
house yet?
Yes, we have, at last.

2. That's fine. You've been searching for a long time,
haven't you?
Yes. My elder brother and I looked all over the place.

3. Where is it?
Near Kunitati.

4. Is it a new house?
It's fairly new. Half of it is in Japanese style and half
in Western. The Japanese-style part looks a bit
old and has only one floor. The Western part is on
two floors.

5. How many rooms are there?
Let me see now; I think there are eight. The hall
measures three tatami, and behind it there is a room
of four and a half. At the side of the hall there is a
ten-tatami drawing-room, and behind that there
are two rooms, one eight tatami and the other six.
The remainder of the house is in Western style.
Downstairs there is a room five metres long by four
wide and a bathroom, lavatory, and kitchen. On
the second floor there are two rooms.

6. It's odd for the bathroom and the kitchen to be in
Western style, isn't it?
Yes, it is. It looks as if some Westerners lived there.

7. Oh, I see. Is it a rented house?
It is now. My brother says that we'll live there for
about a year, and if things are all right he would
buy it.

8. Anata wa niisan no ie ni tomatte iru koto ni narun'
desu ne.
Maa soo desu. Watasi no ima no kyuuryoo de wa itu
zibun no ie o motu koto ga dekiru ka wakarimasen
kara.

9. Anata no heya wa dore desu ka.
Ani wa nikai no heya o hutatutomo tukatte ii to itte
kuretan' desu. Sore de watasi wa hitotu o sinsitu
ni, moo hitotu o benkyoo suru heya ni tukatte
imasu.

10. Anata wa siawase desu yo. Niisan to niisan no okusan
no heya wa doko nan' desu ka.
Nihon-siki no hatizyoo no heya desu. Ani wa Nihon-
siki de mo seiyoo-siki de mo kamawanai to itte imasu
ga, ane wa seiyoo-siki no sindai de wa nerarenai to
itte imasu.

11. Anata no sinsitu ni wa donna mono ga arimasu ka.
Sindai, tansu, tiisai teeburu, isu ga hutatu; sono hoka
kabe ni wa tomodati kara moratta abura-e to ryoosin
no syasin to kagami ga kakete arimasu.

12. Benkyoo suru hoo no wa ookiin' desu ka.
Sukosi ookii ka mo siremasen ga, ooki na teeburu ga
hitotu, tiisa na no ga hutatu, isu ga hutatu, hon-
bako ga mittu mo arimasu kara amari ookiku miemasen.

13. Todana wa nain' desu ka.
E, yuka kara tenzyoo made todoku hosonagai no ga
hitotu arimasu. Heya no higasigawa ni hitotu,
kitagawa ni hutatu mado ga atte, minamigawa ni wa
to ga arimasu. To no hidarigawa no kabe ni wa
todana ga atte, heya no migigawa no kabe ni hon-
bako ga narande imasu. Dentoo wa tenzyoo no
mannaka to ookii teeburu no ue to ni arimasu.

14. Sono heya wa kita o muite irun' desu ka.
Soo desu. Watasi wa sigoto o suru toki ni wa hi ga
ataru no ga kirai nan' desu.

15. Syokudoo wa doko desu ka.
Daidokoro ni itiban tikai rokuzyoo no heya desu.
Sikasi watasi wa asa no syokuzi no hoka wa zibun
no heya de simasu.

8. What it comes to, then, is that you are staying in your
   brother's house.
   I suppose it does, for I don't know when I shall be
   able to have my own house on my present salary.

9. What are your rooms?
   My brother told me that I might use both the two
   rooms on the second floor.   So I am using one for a
   bedroom and the other to study in.

10. You are lucky.   Where is the room belonging to your
    brother and his wife?
    It's the eight-tatami Japanese-style room.   My brother
    says that he doesn't mind whether it's Japanese or
    Western style, but my sister-in-law says that she
    can't sleep on a Western-type bed.

11. What have you got in your bedroom?
    A bed, a chest of drawers, a small table, and two chairs.
    Besides these, on the wall there are hanging an oil-
    painting I got from a friend, a photograph of my
    parents, and a mirror.

12. Is the study larger?
    It may be a bit, but it doesn't look very big, because
    there are a large table, two small ones, two chairs,
    and three bookcases.

13. Are there no cupboards?
    Yes, there is a high, narrow one, reaching from the
    floor to ceiling.   On the east side of the room there
    is one window and on the north two; on the south
    side of the room there is a door.   On the wall to the
    left of the door there is a cupboard, and on the right-
    hand wall of the room there is a row of bookcases.
    There are two electric lights, one in the middle of the
    ceiling and the other on the large table.

14. Does the room face north?
    Yes.   I don't like the sun shining on me when I work.

15. Where is the dining-room?
    It's the six-tatami room, the one nearest to the kitchen.
    But I have all my meals except breakfast in my
    own room.

16. Niwa wa hiroin' desu ka.
    Hyakugozyuu-heihoomeetoru bakari arimasu. Ima
    no tokoro amari kirei de wa arimasen.
17. Ura ni mo niwa ga arimasu ka.
    E, tiisai no ga arimasu. Ima wa sentakumono o
    kawakasu no ni tukatte imasu ga, yasai o tukuru
    hatake ni suru tumori desu. Daikon toka imo toka
    mame nado o tukuroo to omotte imasu.
18. Nanika doobutu o katte imasu ka.
    Ie, nanimo katte imasen. Watasitati wa soto e deru
    koto ga ooi desu kara doobutu no sewa o suru koto
    wa muzukasii desu.
19. Hatake no sewa wa dare ga surun' desu ka.
    Ane daroo to omoimasu. Ani mo watasi mo amari
    zikan ga arimasen kara. Motiron tokidoki wa
    watasitati mo tetudau tumori desu ga ne.
20. Denki mo gasu mo denwa mo arun' desu ka.
    Gasu wa arimasen. Zenbu denki desu. Denwa wa
    hosii no desu ga mada hiite arimasen.

Kaiwa Zyuu

(*Linguaphone Course, Sides 15 and 16*)

1. Hidoi ooame na no ni yoku kimasita ne.
   Kesa ryokan o deta toki wa konna ni huru to wa
   omoimasen desita yo. Konna ooame ga tuzuku
   to mata oomizu no koto ga sinpai ni naru desyoo.
2. Soo desu. Ningen wa donna ni sinpo site mo sizen ni
   wa nakanaka katemasen. Tonikaku ototosi no yoo
   na koto ni naranakereba ii to omotte imasu.
   Ano oomizu wa ototosi desita ka; watasi wa kyonen
   da to omotte imasita.
3. Ototosi desu.
   Anata no tokoro wa oomizu no songai wa nakattan'
   desyoo.
4. Siawase ni mo arimasen desita. Sikasi aki no ookaze
   no tame ni wa hidoi me ni aimasita.
   Kome ni mo yasai ni mo ooki na songai ga atta soo
   desu ne.

16. Is the garden large?
    It is about 150 square metres. At the present it's not
    very much to look at.

17. Is there a garden at the back too?
    Yes, there is a small one. It's used now for drying
    washing, but we hope to make it into a plot for
    vegetables. We are thinking of growing things like
    giant radishes, potatoes, and beans.

18. Have you got any animals?
    No, none. We go out very often, and so it would be
    difficult to look after them.

19. Who will look after the vegetable plot?
    My sister-in-law, I expect. Neither my brother nor I
    have much time for it. Of course, we intend to help
    from time to time.

20. Have you got electricity, gas, and the telephone?
    There is no gas. It's all electric. We want a tele-
    phone, but it is not installed yet.

Conversation X

1. How nice of you to come in this terrible downpour!
    When I left my hotel this morning I didn't think it
    would rain like this. If this heavy rain goes on
    there will be anxiety about floods again.

2. Yes, there will. However much we progress, we are
    quite unable to overcome nature. However, I hope
    it won't be as it was the year before last.
    Were those floods the year before last? I thought they
    were last year.

3. No, the year before last.
    There wasn't any flood damage at your place, was
    there?

4. Fortunately there wasn't. But we suffered badly from
    the autumn gales.
    I hear that you had heavy damage to your rice and
    vegetables.

5. Sore bakari d'ya nain' desu. Hayasi no ki ga hanbun-izyoo taosarete simattan' desu.

   Kono hen wa kikoo wa warui hoo d'ya arimasen ga, aki no owari to huyu no hazime ni wa totemo hidoi kaze ga huku soo desu ne.

6. Soo desu. Ano tonari no mura no ookazi mo huyu no hazime desita.

   Asoko wa kawa kara hanarete iru no de oomizu no sinpai wa arimasen ga, kazi no toki ni wa mizu ga nakute komatta desyoo ne.

7. Soo desu. Kawa wa kono mura made wa higasi kara nisi ni mukatte nagarete imasu ga, ano hayasi no usiro ni aru oka no tame ni migi ni mawatte kita e iku no de tonari no mura e wa ikanain' desu.

   Ogawa mo ike mo nain' desu ka.

8. Arimasen. Dakara tuti ga kawaite ite kome o tukuru no ni wa tekitoo de wa arimasen.

   Sore de mo mura no hitobito wa mina noozyoo de hataraite irun' desyoo.

9. Ie, hanbun dake desu.

   Hoka no hito wa nani o site irun' desu ka.

10. Tiisa na koogyoo desu ne. Noogyoo ni tukau doogu o tukuru koozyoo ga arun' desu.

    Kono hen wa huyu ni wa kiri toka yuki ga ooin' desu ka.

11. Huyu ni wa kuuki ga kawaite iru no de kiri mo yuki mo sukunai desu.

    Samuku wa arimasen ka.

12. Kaze no tuyoi toki wa kanari samui desu ga, taitei wa atatakai desu.

    Ondo wa dono kurai made sagarimasu ka.

13. Kandankei o miru koto wa amari nai no de yoku sirimasen ga, gozyuudo-ika ni naru koto wa hotondo nai to omoimasu.

    Sore wa kekkoo desu ne.

14. Anata no tokoro wa umi ni tikain' desyoo.

    Saa, itiri bakari hanarete imasu ne.

15. Minami wa umi ni muite ite ato wa yama ni kakomarete iru no de kesiki ga ii desyoo.

    Ee; sono kawari doko e iku ni mo yama o noboru no ni kurusimimasu yo.

5. That's not all.   More than half the trees in my woods
   were blown down.

   The weather in these parts is not so bad, but I hear
   that the most terrible winds blow at the end of autumn
   and the beginning of winter.

6. Yes, they do.   The big fire in the neighbouring village
   was at the beginning of winter.

   There is no anxiety about floods, as they are away
   from the river there, but at the time of the fire I
   expect they suffered from the lack of water, didn't
   they?

7. Yes.   The river flows from east to west as far as this
   village, but as it turns to the right and goes north-
   wards because of the hill behind those woods, it
   doesn't go in the direction of the next village.

   Have they neither streams nor ponds?

8. No, they haven't.   So the earth is dry and unsuitable
   for growing rice.

   Even so, everyone there works on the farms, don't they?

9. No, only half of them.

   What do the rest of them do?

10. They are engaged in small industry.   There are work-
    shops which make tools used in agriculture.

    Is there a lot of fog and snow here in winter?

11. In winter the air is dry, so there isn't very much of
    either fog or snow.

    Isn't it cold?

12. It's fairly cold when there is strong wind, but generally
    it's warm.

    How long does the temperature drop?

13. I don't often see a thermometer, so I don't know
    exactly, but I think it scarcely ever goes below fifty
    degrees.

    That's fine, isn't it?

14. You are near the sea, I think.

    I should say we are about two and a half miles away.

15. What with facing the sea at the south, and for the rest
    being shut in by mountains, the scenery must be
    good.

    Yes.   But, on the other hand, wherever we go we
    are afflicted by having to climb mountains.

16. Natu wa suzusikute huyu wa atatakain' desyoo.
    Soo desu nee; koko to kurabereba soo ieru ka mo
    siremasen.

17. Tooge kara wa taihen tooku made nagameru koto ga
    dekiru soo desu ne.
    Ee, toku ni haru to aki wa ii desu ne.   Haru ni wa me
    no todoku kagiri usui midori no naka ni samazama
    na hana ga sakimasu.   Aki ni wa ki no ha ga aka
    ka kiiro ni natte sizen no utukusisa ni ningen-sekai
    no koto o sukkari wasureru koto ga dekimasu.

18. Ano tooge wa naze Tukibasi-tooge to yuun' desu ka.
    Are wa tikyuu kara tuki e iku hasi ga kakatte iru
    tokoro to yuu hanasi ga aru kara nan' desu.

19. Sore kara nanika zisin no koto no hurui hanasi ga arun'
    desyoo.
    Soo desu.   Mukasi oo-zisin ga atte tatimati ano yama
    ga dekita to yuu hanasi desu.

20. Oo-zisin, oo-kazi, ooame, oomizu, ookaze; Nihon wa
    hen na mono de yuumei desu ne.
    Sikasi Nihon wa soo yuu mono ga ooi kuni desu kara
    sizen wa utukusikute hitobito wa yoku hatarakun'
    da to omoimasu ne.

Kaiwa Zyuuiti

Oono: Kyoo wa minasan to omosirokatta koto, kanasikatta koto, osorosikatta koto, uresikatta koto no hanasi
o sitai to omotte atumatte moratta no desu.   Hazime
ni Koyama-san, nanika omosirokatta hanasi wa arimasen
ka.

Koyama: Soo desu ne.   Tai-sita mono wa arimasen ga ne.
Itiban omosiroi to omotta koto de ima de mo hakkiri to
oboete iru no wa, ima kangaereba bakabakasii hanasi
nan' desu.
   Watasi ga mada too gurai no toki no koto desita.   Aru
hi haha ni turerarete otooto to issyo ni zidoosya no
kyoosoo o kenbutu si ni itta no desu.   Kono toki made
wa Nihon ni wa zidoosya no kyoosoo wa mattaku nakatta
to omoimasu.   Dakara watasi no kokoro wa kono

16. I expect it is cool in summer and warm in winter.
    Well, I suppose one could say that in comparison with
    here.
17. I hear that you can see a very long way from the
    pass.
    Yes. It is particularly good in spring and autumn.
    In spring all kinds of flowers bloom against the fresh
    verdure which extends as far as the eye can see. In
    autumn the leaves turn red or yellow and we can
    entirely forget the world of men in the beauty of
    nature.
18. Why do they call that pass the Tukibasi pass?
    It's because there is a story that it is the place where a
    bridge crosses from the earth to the moon.
19. And isn't there some old story about an earthquake?
    Yes. The tale is that long ago there was a great
    earthquake and suddenly these mountains were
    formed.
20. Great earthquakes, great fires, great rains, floods,
    gales; Japan is famous for queer things, isn't it?
    But, I think it is because Japan is a country where
    such things are frequent that nature here is beautiful
    and her people work hard.

Conversation XI

Oono: Today, I have brought you together because I want
all of us to tell stories about something that was interesting, something that was sad, something frightening, and
something happy. First, Mr. Koyama, haven't you a
story about something you found interesting?

Koyama: Well, now. I haven't got very much of a story.
The most interesting thing that I can still clearly
remember is really rather stupid when I come to think
of it.

   It happened when I was about ten. One day I was
taken by my mother with my younger brother to see
some car racing. Up to this time there had been no car
racing in Japan at all, I think. Therefore, I was completely fascinated by this spectacle which had come from

Amerika kara kita misemono ni sukkari hikasarete simattan' desu. Gozen zyuuzi kara gogo yozi made hiru no syokuzi mo sinaide kenbutu site imasita.

Haha wa amari omosiroi to wa omowanakatta no desyoo ga, kodomotati no tame ni huhei mo iwanaide imasita. Aka, ao, kuro, siro, ki nado no iroiro na iro ga nutte aru tiisa na zidoosya ga hizyoo na hayasa de hasitte iku no o mite imasita. Kyoosoo ga owaru to unten site ita hitobito wa nandemo nakatta yoo na yoosu de hanasitari zyoodan o ittari site iru no de yoku anna koto ga dekiru to omoimasita.

Oono: Kondo wa Nitta-san, anata wa nanika kanasikatta koto o hanasite kudasai.

Nitta: Sore wa watasi ga otooto ni sinareta toki desu. Watasi wa zyuugo no toki titi o nakusimasita ga sono toki wa amari kanasii to omoimasen desita. Sore kara sannen tatta haru ni, otooto wa netu ga sukosi aru no de gakkoo o yasunde nete imasita. Hazime wa haha mo watasi mo tai-sita koto wa nai to omotte imasita ga, netu wa itu made tatte mo sagarimasen desita.

Byooki ni naru mae otooto wa hutotte wa imasen desita ga yasete iru hoo dè mo arimasen desita. Sore ga, byooki ni natte kara dandan yasete itte, asi mo ude mo take no boo no yoo ni hosoku natte simaimasita. Me wa ookikute hen ni hikatte imasita. Hoo no niku wa otite hana ga hakkiri to ukabiagatte imasita. Kuti-biru wa kao to onazi yoo ni tutiiro ni natte kuti ga doko ni aru no ka wakaranai kurai desita. Hontoo ni miru dake de mo namida ga deru hodo desita.

Koo site itinen bakari nete imasita ga gogatu no owari ni tikai ame ga huru ban ni, sinu koto o isiki sinaide nemutta mama iki o hikitorimasita. Watasi wa tiisai toki kara amari naku koto ga nakatta no desu ga, kono toki bakari wa nan to mo ienaku kanasikute oogoe o agete nakimasita.

Oono: Watasitati mo nakasaremasu ne. Otootosan wa hai ga warukattan' desu ka.

Nitta: Soo desu. Sono ue sinzoo mo amari zyoobu de nakatta yoo desu.

Oono: Kondo wa Hurukawa-san, anata wa nanika osorosi-katta hanasi wa arimasen ka.

America.   From ten in the morning to four in the afternoon, we watched the racing without even having our
lunch.

I suppose my mother didn't find it very interesting,
but for the sake of us children she didn't complain.
We watched tiny cars, painted in all kinds of colours, red,
blue, black, yellow, etc., as they rushed round at an
extraordinary speed.   When a race was over, the drivers
chatted and joked as if nothing remarkable had happened, and I was amazed at their ability to do so.

Oono: Now, Mr. Nitta, please tell us a story of something
sad.

Nitta: It was when my younger brother died.   I lost my
father when I was fifteen, and at that time I didn't feel
particularly sad.   Three years afterwards in spring, my
younger brother stayed home from school and was in bed
with a slight temperature.   At first both my mother and
myself thought it was nothing serious, but his temperature
refused to drop.

Before he fell ill my brother was not fat, but neither
was he thin.   But then he got thinner and thinner, and
his arms and legs became as thin as bamboo sticks.   His
eyes were large and had a strange glitter in them.   His
cheeks became hollow, and his nose stood out clearly
from his face.   His lips became the same earthy colour
as his face, so that one could hardly tell where his mouth
was.   Truly, just to look at him was enough to cause one
to weep.

He lay like this for about a year, and on one spring
evening, near the end of May, he passed away in his sleep,
not realizing that he was dying.   Ever since I was an
infant I had scarcely ever shed a tear, but on this one
occasion an indescribable sadness came over me and I
wept aloud.

Oono: Your story makes us cry too.   Was it his lungs
that were affected?

Nitta: Yes, they were.   Moreover, his heart, too, wasn't
very strong, it seems.

Oono: Now, Mr. Hurukawa, haven't you a tale of something that frightened you?

Hurukawa: Saa, osorosikatta hanasi desu ne. Watasi wa taitei no koto ni heiki de irareru no de hontoo ni osorosii to omotta koto ga nain' desu ga ne. Maa, yama e nobotte miti ga wakaranaku natta toki no keiken desyoo.

Mada gakusei datta toki sitasii tomodati to hutari de natu no yasumi ni yama e iku koto ni simasita. Tookyoo kara hatizikan bakari kisya de nisikita no hoo e itte tiisa na mura no eki de orimasita. Soko kara kitanai basu ni notte yama no sita ni aru onsen ni tukimasita. Onsen to wa iimasu ga sono ban ni haitta ryokan no huro wa totemo tumetakattan' desu. Watasi wa huro wa atui no ga suki na no de kore ni wa komarimasita. Itu made haitte ite mo atuku narimasen desita. Huro kara deyoo to suru to samusa ni hurueru arisama desita. Tonikaku itizikan mo haitte imasita ne.

Tugi no hi ni wa asa yozi ni okimasita. Tenki wa zyootoo de watasitati wa ooyorokobi de noborihazime-masita. Miti wa dandan kyuu ni natte ikimasita ga watasitati wa kaette genki ni naru bakari desita.

Ooki na ki no kage de bentoo o tabete mata susumi-masita. Tokoro ga asa no uti yokatta tenki wa gogo nizi goro kyuu ni waruku natte kimasita. Kiri ga dete kita no desu. Hazime no uti wa amari sinpai sinaide imasita ga, tootoo nimeetoru gurai sika saki ga mienai yoo ni natte simaimasita. Soko de tomatte kiri ga hareru no o mateba yokatta no desu ga, wakai watasitati wa sono mama arukituzukemasita.

Sibaraku makkura na yoru ni te de mono o saguru yoo ni site aruite ikimasita ga, tootoo hutaritomo sukkari tukarete nanimo iwanaide kosi o orosite simaimasita. Sosite soko ni taoreta mama inoti ga nakunarun' d'ya nai ka to omou to kyuu ni taihen osorosiku natte simaimasita.

Nanzikan tatta ka sirimasen ga, kiri ga sukosi harete kimasita. Mamonaku tuki no hikari ga bonyari to miete kitan' desu. Watasitati wa yorokonde arukoo to simasita ga miti wa zenzen arimasen. Ki to kusa no naka o sukosi orite iku to miti ga arimasita. Mata nobotte ikimasita ga mokutekiti ni tuita no wa yoru no zyuunizi tikaku desita.

Hurukawa: Ah, it's a frightening tale, is it? I am able to
keep my head in the face of nearly anything, and so I
haven't anything that I thought really frightening. If
anything, it would be an experience I had when I was
climbing a mountain and lost my way.

When I was still student a close friend and I planned
to go into the mountains during our summer holiday.
We travelled north-west from Tokyo for about eight
hours by train and got off at the station at a small
village. Then we got on a dirty bus and arrived at a
hot spring at the bottom of the mountain. They called
it a hot spring, but the bath we got in at the inn that
evening was very cold. I like my bath to be hot, so I
couldn't get on with this one at all. No matter how long
I stayed in it, I couldn't get warm. When I tried to
get out, I shivered with cold. And so I stayed in it for a
whole hour.

On the next day we woke at four in the morning. The
weather was first class and we joyfully started to climb.
Our path grew steeper and steeper, but nevertheless our
spirits grew higher and higher.

We ate our lunch in the shade of a large tree, and re-
sumed our climb. However, the weather, which had
been fine in the morning, suddenly deteriorated at two
o'clock in the afternoon. Fog appeared. At first we
were not particularly anxious, but finally we could see
only two yards ahead of us. It would have been better
to stay where we were until the fog lifted, but we were
young and kept on walking.

After a while we were groping our way along as if it
was in the depth of night, but eventually we sat down
without saying a word, completely exhausted. Then we
suddenly felt frightened, wondering if we were going to
die there where we had fallen.

I don't know how long we stayed there, but the fog
lifted a little. Soon we could see the faint light of the
moon. We joyfully tried to walk on, but there was
absolutely no path. We descended a short way through
shrubs and grass, and found a path. We climbed up
again, but it was nearly midnight when we reached our
destination.

Oono: Owari ni watasi ga uresikatta koto no hanasi o
simasu.   Watasi wa kodomo no toki kara bunsyoo o kaku
no ga suki desita.   Amari zyoozu de wa arimasen desita
ga nantonaku suki dattan' desu.   Gakkoo ni itte iru
aida wa siken no koto bakari sinpai sinakute wa naranai
no de amari kaku hima wa arimasen desita.

Tookyoo no daigaku e haitta tosi no koto desu.
Watasi no umareta mati ni atta tiisa na sinbun ga wakai
hito no kaita mono o yoku nosete imasita.   Sore de
watasi wa natu no yasumi ni kuni e kaetta toki, "Tookyoo
no gakusei no seikatu" to yuu ronbun no yoo na syoosetu
no yoo na mono o kaite okurimasita.

Yasumi ga owatte watasi wa mata Tookyoo e dete
ikimasita.   Tookyoo de wa ozi to oba no ie ni tomatte
imasita ga hutaritomo tosiyori datta no de watasi wa
asa hayaku okite soozi no tetudai nado o site imasita.
Aru asa kita yuubin no naka ni kuni no sinbun ga arimasita.   Sugu akete miru to itiban owari no peizi ni
watasi ga okutta bunsyoo ga notte itan' desu.   Watasi
wa zibun ga kaita mono ga hazimete insatu ni natte iru
no o mite totemo uresiku natte, uta o utai-nagara nan-do
mo yomikaesimasita.   Sono toki watasi wa sekaiiti no
syoosetuka ni de mo natta yoo na ki ga simasita ne.

Kyoo wa kore dake ni simasu.   Mata raisyuu ka
saraisyuu atumatte iroiro na hanasi o sitari kiitari sitai
to omoimasu.

Kaiwa Zyuuni

(Linguaphone Course, Sides 17–20, Selected Passages)

Asami Zyun-iti (Z)	Nizyuugo	Ginkooin
Ikawa Matiko (M)	Nizyuusan	Tyuugakkoo no sensei
Asami Syuuzoo (S)	Gozyuugo	Zyun-iti no titi
Maeda Akio (A)	Sizyuusi	Kaisyain
Maeda Noriko (N)	Sanzyuusi	Akio no tuma, Matiko
		no ane
Hirata Takao (H)	Sizyuugo	Ginkoo no zyuuyaku
Ookawa Yataroo (O)	Sisyuusiti	Hirata no tomodati

(i)

Matiko: Nagai koto o-matase itasimasite?
Zyun-iti: Iie, boku mo ima kita bakari no tokoro desu.

Oono: Finally, I'll tell you about a time when I was happy. Since my childhood I have been fond of writing. I wasn't very good at it, but I just liked doing it. When I was at school I had to concentrate on worrying about examinations, and I didn't have much time for writing.

What I'm going to tell you happened in the year I entered a Tokyo university. A small newspaper in my native town often published things written by young people. So, when I went home in the summer holiday, I wrote something half essay and half story entitled "Life of a Tokyo Student", and sent it in.

When the summer holiday was over, I went off to Tokyo again. There I was staying with my uncle and aunt, and as they were both elderly, I used to get up early in the morning and help with the cleaning and so on. In the mail one morning there was a newspaper from my home. I opened it at once and saw that the article I had sent in was on the last page. I was extremely happy at seeing something that I had written appearing in print for the first time, and I read it again and again, singing a song as I did so. At that time I felt as though I had become the best novelist in the world.

That's all for today. I hope we shall meet next week or the week after and tell and listen to various stories once more.

Conversation XII

Asami Zyun-iti (*Z*)	25	Bank clerk.
Ikawa Matiko (*M*)	23	Middle school-teacher.
Asami Syuuzoo (*S*)	55	Zyun-iti's father.
Maeda Akio (*A*)	44	Company employee.
Maeda Noriko (*N*)	34	Akio's wife, Matiko's sister.
Hirata Takao (*H*)	45	Bank director.
Ookawa Yataroo (*O*)	47	Hirata's friend.

(*i*)

Matiko: Have I kept you waiting long?
Zyun-iti: No, I've only just come.

M.: Osoku narun' d'ya nai ka to omotte tobu yoo ni site mairimasita no yo.

Z.: Nanika attan' desu ka.

M.: Ee, seito no hitori ga hen na mondai de batu o ukemasita no. Ano gakkoo no tikaku ni wa iroiro warui mono ga aru no de seitotati wa tada no kodomo d'ya nain' desu no. Dakara watasi totemo komaru koto ga arimasu wa.

Z.: Soo desyoo ne. Doosite hoka e kawaranain' desu ka.

M.: Datte mada itinen mo inai no ni kawaru no wa ikemasen wa. Watasi mada hontoo no sensei d'ya [1] nain' desu mono.

Z.: Maa anata no gakkoo no hanasi wa ato de yukkuri kiku koto to site doko e ikimasyoo ka.

M.: Dokodemo anata no o-suki na tokoro e.

Z.: Boku no suki na tokoro nan'te toku ni arimasen ga; mazu nanika tabemasyoo.

M.: Watasi amari onaka ga suite inain' desu keredo.

Z.: Nanika ki ni kakaru koto de mo arun' desu ka.

M.: Ee.

Z.: Nan desu ka. Bokutati no koto?

M.: Ee.

Z.: Okaasan ga nanika ossyattan' desu ka.

M.: Iie, haha wa iin' desu no. Ani to ane nan' desu. Ane wa ne, haha ga tosi ga tosi desu kara watasi no koto wa zibuntati no sekinin to kangaete iru desyoo. Dakara watasi no koto o nandemo siranakut'ya [2] ki ga sumanai rasiin' desu no. Sosite watasi no hanasu koto wa minna ani ni yuu desyoo. Dakara watasi no syoorai o kimeru no wa ani nan' desu wa.

Z.: Sore wa amari sansei dekinai koto desu ne.

M.: Go-sinpai nasaranakute mo ii koto nan' desu wa. Ani ga itido anata ni o-ai sitai 'tte [3] itte'masu [4] no.

Z.: Naruhodo ne. Sore wa atarimae no koto desyoo ne. Sikasi ima boku wa hoka no hito ni haitte koraretaku nain' desu. Anata sae wakatte ite itadakereba ii to omotte'run' [5] desu.

---

[1] d'ya = de wa. [2] siranakut'ya = siranakute wa.
[3] 'tte = to *or* to yuu to; *here* = to.

M.: I thought I might be late, so I flew here as fast as I could.

Z.: Did something keep you?

M.: Yes. One of my pupils was punished for something rather unusual. There are all kinds of unsuitable things going on near the school, so that the pupils are rather more than children. The result is that some things crop up which I find quite awkward to deal with.

Z.: I suppose they do. Why don't you transfer somewhere else?

M.: But, I can't go transferring when I haven't been there a year yet. You see, I'm not a real teacher yet.

Z.: You can tell me all about your school later at your leisure; let's leave it for now and think where we shall go.

M.: Wherever you fancy . . .

Z.: Wherever I fancy?—there isn't anywhere in particular. Let's have something to eat first.

M.: I'm not very hungry myself.

Z.: Have you got something on your mind?

M.: Yes.

Z.: What is it? Something to do with us?

M.: Yes.

Z.: Has your mother said something?

M.: No, my mother is all right. The trouble is Noriko and Akio. As you know, Noriko thinks that, my mother being old as she is, I am their responsibility. So she is not satisfied if she doesn't know all about me. Then she tells Akio everything that I tell her. So what it comes to is that he is the one who decides my future.

Z.: I don't think I can accept that, you know.

M.: You don't have to worry about it. Akio says he'd like to meet you, sometime.

Z.: Oh, I see. I suppose that's to be expected. But for the present I don't want to bring other people into it. All I ask is that *you* should understand how I feel.

---

[4] itte'masu = itte imasu.
[5] omotte'run' = omotte iru no.

M.: Watasi mo motiron onazi kangae desu wa.   Dakedo
ani wa sukosi huruin' desu wa ne.   Soo wa omoun' desu
kedo ani o okorasetaku wa nain' desu no.
Z.: Yorosii.   Aimasyoo.   Anata kimete kudasai.   Boku
wa itu de mo ii desu.
M.: Kore kara itte kudasaimasu ka.
Z.: Ima kore kara?   Bokutati mada ban-gohan o tabete
inain' desu yo.
M.: Anata sae yokereba watasi tyotto ane no tokoro e
denwa site iku to ieba ban-gohan no koto wa ane ga
sinpai site kuremasu wa.
Z.: Soo?   D'ya ikimasyoo.   Anata wa denwa o kakete
irassyai.   Boku wa takusii o sagasite kimasu.

. . . . .

(ii)

Matiko: Oneesan, kono kata Asami-san.
Noriko: Hazimete o-me ni kakarimasu. . Imooto ga
itumo o-sewa ni natte orimasu soo de.
Zyun-iti: Iie, watasi no hoo koso.   Konban wa doomo
totuzen mairimasite . . .
N.: Saa, doozo o-agari ni natte.   Otto mo sugu kaette
mairu to omoimasu kara sibaraku o-mati ni natte . . .
Matiko-san, Asami-san o kyakusitu no hoo e go-annai
site kudasai ne.
M.: O-neesan, nanika o-tetudai simasyoo ka.
N.: Iie, ii no yo.   Anata wa Asami-san no o-aite site
agete ne.   Watasi wa siturei sasete itadaite tyotto
daidokoro e itte kuru wa.
Z.: Doomo, iroiro sumimasen.

. . . . .

(iii)

Zyun-iti: O-neesan no tokoro nakanaka rippa desu ne.
Matiko: Iie, sonna koto arimasen wa.   Moo daibu huruin'
desu wa.
Z.: Itugoro kara o-sumi desu ka.
M.: Anetati ga Amerika kara kaette kita tugi no tosi;
moo zyuugonen kurai ni naru desyoo.
Z.: Neesan mo Amerika ni o-ide dattan' desu ka.
M.: Ee, itinen bakari itte imasita wa.

M.: Naturally I think the same as you.   But my brother-
in-law is a bit old-fashioned.   That's what I feel, but I
don't want to make him angry.

Z.: All right, then.   I will meet him.   Will you please
arrange it?   Any time will suit me.

M.: Could you come straight away?

Z.: What, now?   We haven't had dinner yet.

M.: If you don't mind, I'll just phone Noriko, and if I
tell her we are coming she will see about dinner for us.

Z.: Will she?   All right, then, let's go.   You go and telephone ; I'll go and look for a taxi.

.   .   .   .   .

(*ii*)

Matiko: Noriko, this gentleman is Mr. Asami.

Noriko: I'm very pleased to meet you.   How nice of you
to give up such a lot of time to her.

Zyun-iti: No, not at all.   I'm the one to be grateful.   I'm
afraid we've descended upon you rather suddenly this
evening.

N.: Please come in.   I think my husband will be here
soon, so would you mind waiting a little?   Matiko,
please take Mr. Asami to the drawing-room.

M.: Can I help you, Noriko?

N.: No, it's all right.   You look after Mr. Asami.   If
you'll excuse me I'll just get on with what I'm doing in
the kitchen.

Z.: I'm sorry to give you so much trouble.

.   .   .   .   .

(*iii*)

Zyun-iti: Your sister's house is very nice, isn't it?

Matiko: Oh, I don't know . . .   It's quite old, you know.

Z.: How long have they been living here?

M.: Ever since the year after they came back from
America.   I suppose it's about fifteen years now.

Z.: Did your sister go to America too?

M.: Yes, she was there for about a year.

Z.: D'ya Amerika de kekkon nasattan' desu ne.

M.: Soo nan' desu no. Watasi mo itido itte mitain' desu kedo . . .

Z.: Ikeru ka mo siremasen yo. Boku no ginkoo wa Igirisu ni mo Amerika ni mo mise ga arun' desu yo.

M.: Watasi ga anata no okusan ni nareba ikeru 'tte [6] yuun' desyoo. Dame desu wa yo. Mada hayasugimasu. A, ani ga kaette kita rasii wa.

. . . . .

(iv)

Matiko: O-niisan, konban wa. Mata kite'masu no yo. Anoo, kono kata, Asami-san.

Akio: Yaa, yoku irassyaimasita.

Zyun-iti: Doomo totuzen o-zyama ni agarimasite.

A.: Sa doozo, o-kake kudasai.

Z.: D'ya siturei simasu.

M.: O-niisan, watasi tyotto o-neesan no tokoro e itte kuru wa.

A.: Soo ka ne. D'ya Asami-san wa boku ga hikiuketa. Asami-san, anata no koto wa Matiko kara kiite imasite ne. Are no haha wa daibu tosi o totte ite, karada mo zyoobu de nai hoo nan' de watasi ga maa are no titi no yoo na katati ni natte irun' desu. Go-syooti desyoo ga, tuma to Matiko to wa tosi ga too-izyoo mo tigai, watasi wa mata too bakari ue nan' desu kara.

Z.: Iya, doomo go-sinpai o-kake site sumimasen.

A.: Daigaku wa itu demasita ka.

Z.: Ototosi desu.

A.: Hooritu desu ka.

Z.: Soo desu. Sikasi ima site iru sigoto wa hooritu to wa mattaku kankei ga arimasen.

A.: Iya, dokodemo sonna mon' desu yo. Sosite ima wa donna koto o. . . .

Z.: Ima wa Amerika no keizai-zyootai o sirabete imasu.

A.: Soo desu ka. Watasi mo wakai toki wa Amerika ni ite keizai no koto o sukosi sirabeta koto ga arimasu yo. Sikasi ima wa nanimo wakaranaku narimasita.

---

[6] 'tte = to.

Z.: Did they get married in America, then?

M.: Yes, they did.   I wish I could go there once.

Z.: You may be able to.   My bank has branches in both England and America.

M.: You mean that I could go if I were your wife.   That won't do.   It's too soon yet.   Ah, it seems as if Akio is back.

.   .   .   .   .

(iv)

Matiko: Good evening, Akio.   I'm here again.   Er, this is Mr. Asami.

Akio: How do you do.

Zyun-iti: Please excuse me for calling on you without warning.

A.: Please sit down.

Z.: Thank you.

M.: Akio, I'll just go and see if I can help Noriko.

A.: Oh, yes?   Well, I'll look after Mr. Asami.   Mr. Asami, I've heard about you from Matiko.   Her mother is getting on and she is not very strong either, so, you might say, I've taken on the job of being Matiko's father.   As you may know, there is more than ten years' difference between my wife and Matiko, and I'm about ten years older still, so you can see what I mean.

Z.: It's nice of you to concern yourself about her.

A.: When did you leave the university?

Z.: The year before last.

A.: Did you graduate in law?

Z.: Yes, I did.   But, the work I'm doing at the moment has no connection at all with the law.

A.: It's the same everywhere.   And what are you doing now?

Z.: I'm going into economic conditions in America.

A.: Are you?   When I was younger, I was in America and did a bit of work on the American economy too. But I've quite lost touch with it now.

Z.: Sonna koto wa nai desyoo. Anata no kaisya wa
Amerika to hukai kankei ga arun' d'ya nain' desu ka.

A.: Arimasu yo. Sikasi watasi wa moo dame nan' desu
ne. Amerika no koto nado to wa zenzen kankei ga nai
koto o site irun' desu.

Z.: Siturei desu ga ima wa donna o-sigoto o. . . .

A.: Wakai hito no soodan-aite desu yo. Atarasii hito o
ireru toki no siken no yoo na mono mo simasu. Titi mo
kaisya ni kankei site imasita kara nanimo dekinai
watasi o yamesaseru koto wa dekinain' desu.

Noriko: Doomo o-matase itasimasita. O-syokuzi no
sitaku ga dekimasita kara doozo.

A.: D'ya, syokudoo e itte tabe-nagara hanasi o simasyoo.

. . . . .

(v)

Akio: Matiko wa doo ka ne. Moo sensei no sigoto ni
sukkari nareta ka ne.

Matiko: Hazime wa kurusikatta kedo moo nareta wa.
Sono kawari yoosu ga wakatte kuru to iroiro kangaesa-
serareru koto ga dete kuru no yo.

A.: Tatoeba?

M.: Tatoeba siken no koto. Ima no yoo ni siken siken de
kurusimerarete ite wa kodomotati wa hontoo ni kyooiku
o ukeru koto wa dekinai to omou wa.

Zyun-iti: Kyooiku wa mondai no tada hitotu dake desu.
Genzai no Nihon no iroiro na mondai no gen-in wa hito
ga oosugiru koto ni aru to omoimasu ne. Nantoka site
zinkoo o herasanakereba ikenain' desu.

A.: Kodomo ni zei o kakerun' da ne. Sore mo nibanme no
wa itibanme no nibai, sanbanme wa sanbai to yuu yoo
ni dandan takusan kakerun' da ne.

Noriko: Sonna koto sitara o-tonari nado taihen da wa.
Sitininme ga kuru tokoro na no yo.

Z.: Sitinin mo arun' desu ka.

N.: Soo nan' desu no.

Z.: Tyotto siturei simasu ga ano tokei wa atte imasu ka.

A.: Saa gohun gurai susunde imasu ka ne.

Z.: I find that difficult to believe. Your firm has a close connection with America, hasn't it?

A.: Yes, it has. But I'm no good at all in that line. What I'm doing at the moment has no connection at all with America.

Z.: Excuse my asking, but what is your work now?

A.: I'm acting as adviser to the young members of the staff. I also occupy myself with things like the examination we hold when we take on new people. My father was connected with the firm, and they can't get rid of me, although I'm no good.

Noriko: I'm afraid I've kept you waiting. The dinner is ready, so please come along.

A.: Well, now, let's go into the dining-room and talk while we have dinner.

.   .   .   .   .

(v)

Akio: How are you getting on, Matiko? Are you quite used to teaching now?

Matiko: It was hard at first, but I've got used to it now. On the other hand, now that I can see what's going on, all kinds of things crop up which make me think.

A.: For example?

M.: For example, examinations. Children are so harassed by examination after examination under the present system that they can't acquire a real education, I think.

Zyun-iti: Education is only one of the problems. In my opinion, the cause of various problems besetting Japan at the moment is that there are too many people. Somehow or other we must decrease our population.

A.: The best thing would be to tax children. Not only that, they ought to increase the rate progressively— twice as much on the second as on the first, three times on the third.

Noriko: If that happened it would be terrible for people like those next door. They are expecting their seventh.

Z.: Seven children?

N.: That's right.

Z.: Excuse me, but is that clock right?

A.: Let me see, it was about five minutes fast, wasn't it?

Z.: Sore de wa moo o-itoma sinakereba narimasen. Konban wa titi ga Kyooto kara kaette kimasu kara. Matiko-san, anata wa doo simasu ka.

M.: Watasi wa konban wa koko ni tomarimasu.

Z.: D'ya asita no ban mata . . .

M.: A, asita wa siturei sasete itadakitain' desu no. Gakkoo de kai ga arimasu kara.

Z.: D'ya asatte no ban . . .

M.: E, itu mo no tokoro de?

Z.: Soo simasyoo. De wa, doomo iroiro gotisoo-sama desita. Kore de siturei sasete itadakimasu.

. . . . .

(vi)

Kyuuzi: Asami-san, Hirata-san ga o-yobi desu.

Zyun-iti: A, soo.

Z.: Nanika go-yoo desu ka.

Hirata: Aa, tyotto hanasitai koto ga atte ne. Sigoto wa doo da ne. Susunde iru ka ne.

Z.: Dekiru dake no koto wa yatte orimasu.

H.: Zitu wa Nyuuyooku ni itte iru Kawada-kun ga rainen no syoogatu ni kaette kuru koto ni natte irun' da ga sono ato ni kimi ni itte moraoo ka to omotte irun' da. Zissai no sigoto o suru yori mo benkyoo no tame nan' da. Sore de kimi no tugoo o kikitain' da ga ne.

Z.: Doomo arigatoo gozaimasu. Watasi no yoo na mono de yorosikereba ikasete itadakitai to omoimasu.

H.: Sore wa kekkoo. Tokorode kimi wa mada hitori datta ne.

Z.: Ima no tokoro wa soo desu.

H.: Ima no tokoro 'tte [7] nanika kekkon no hanasi de mo arun' ka ne.

Z.: Mada kekkon to yuu tokoro made wa itte orimasen ga.

H.: Tumari sono hookoo ni susunde iru to yuun' da ne.

Z.: Maa sonna tokoro desu.

H.: De wa ninen gurai wa materu ne.

Z.: Ninen desu ka. Soo desu ne. Dekiru to omoimasu.

---

[7] 'tte = to yuu to.

Z.: That being so, I'm afraid I must take my leave. You see, my father is coming back from Kyoto this evening. What will you do, Matiko?

M.: I'll stay here tonight.

Z.: Well, I'll see you again tomorrow evening.

M.: I'm afraid I can't manage tomorrow—there is a meeting at the school.

Z.: The day after tomorrow, then.

M.: Yes, at our usual place?

Z.: Agreed. Well, thank you very much for your hospitality. Now I really must go.

.   .   .   .   .

(vi)

Office boy: Mr. Asami, Mr. Hirota wants you.

Zyun-iti: Does he?

Z.: You wanted me, sir?

Hirata: Yes, there is something I wanted to tell you. How's your work getting on? Making progress?

Z.: I'm doing the best I can.

H.: The fact is that Kawada in New York is due to come home in January next year, and we are thinking of getting you to succeed him. It would be more for study than actual work. So I'd like to know how you're fixed.

Z.: Thank you very much. If you think I would do, I should like to be sent there.

H.: Excellent! By the way, you are still single, aren't you?

Z.: I am at the moment.

H.: At the moment, you say. Does that mean that you are going to get married?

Z.: Well, it hasn't gone as far as that yet.

H.: But, you are moving towards it, eh?

Z.: Yes, I suppose you are right.

H.: In that case, you can wait two years, eh?

Z.: Two years? Ye-es, I think I can.

H.: Zitu wa ima mo itta toori kimi no wa benkyoo ni ikun' de kazoku no teate wa denain' da. Sono koto mo syooti site oite moraitai.

Z.: Yoku wakarimasita ga hakkiri sita gohenzi wa ni-sanniti tatte kara moosiagetain' desu ga.

H.: Aa, motiron. Toku ni isogun' d'ya nain' da ga raisyuu no suiyoo-bi no zyuuyaku no kai made ni henzi o site moraoo ka ne.

Z.: Kasikomarimasita.

.   .   .   .   .

(vii)

Zyun-iti: Otoosan wa o-kaeri ni natte iru?

Zyotyuu: Hai, o-kaeri ni natte irassyaimasu.

Z.: O-heya ni irassyarun' da ne.

Zyotyuu: Hai, sayoo de gozaimasu.

Z.: Anoo, tyotto o-hanasi sitai koto ga arun' desu ga.

Syuuzoo: Nan no yoo ka ne.

Z.: Kinoo Hirata-san kara Nyuuyooku e itte moraitai to no o-hanasi ga attan' desu ga, hakkiri kimeru mae ni o-negai sitai koto ga arun' desu ga.

S.: Nani ka ne.

Z.: Zitu wa sankagetu bakari mae kara aru onna no hito to tukiatte irun' desu ga, ginkoo no hoo de wa hitori de ninen itte koi to itte imasu kara gaikoku e iku mae ni watasitati no kankei o hakkiri sasetai to omotte irun' desu.

S.: Konyaku sitai to yuun' da ne.

Z.: Maa soo nan' desu.

S.: Saa, sore wa yoku kangaeru hituyoo ga aru ne. Watasi wa sono hito no koto o moo sukosi siranakute wa. . . .

Z.: Sore de otoosan ni kono hito ni atte itadakitai to omoun' desu ga.

S.: Sore wa doo ka ne. Watasi ga atte simau to omae no ziyuu ga nakunarun' d'ya nai ka ne. Konyaku wa kaette kite kara ni site wa doo ka ne.

Z.: Watasi no ima no kimoti to site wa sore wa dekisoo mo nain' desu ga.

S.: Yorosii. Au dake wa au koto ni siyoo.

H.: Actually, as I've just said, you would be going to study, so we couldn't pay a family allowance. I should like you to agree to that.

Z.: I understand. I should like to give you a definite answer in two or three days.

H.: Of course. There is no particular hurry, but I'd like you to give me your reply before the directors meeting Wednesday next week.

Z.: Very good, sir.

.   .   .   .   .

(*vii*)

Zyun-iti: Is Father in?

Maid: Yes, sir. He has just returned.

Z.: He is in his room, is he?

Maid: Yes, sir.

Z.: Father, there's something I should like to talk to you about.

Syuuzoo: What is it?

Z.: Yesterday Mr. Hirata told me that he wanted me to go to New York. There is something I should like you to do for me before I accept.

S.: What?

Z.: The fact is, I've been going about with a young woman for the last three months or so. The bank is having me go away by myself for two years, and I thought that before I went abroad I should like to put my relationship with her on a firm footing.

S.: You mean, get engaged?

Z.: Yes, that's what I mean.

S.: Now, that calls for consideration. I must know more about this person.

Z.: Yes; so I should like you to meet her, Father.

S.: I'm not sure about that. If once I see her, you'll lose your freedom of action, won't you? What about getting engaged when you come back?

Z.: As I feel now, that doesn't seem possible.

S.: Very well, then. I will see her, but that's all.

Z.: Doomo arigatoo gozaimasu. Go-tugoo wa itu ga ii desu ka.

S.: Soo da ne. Raisyuu no getuyoo-bi no ban watasi no zimusyo e issyo ni kite moraoo ka.

Z.: Nanzi goro ga ii desu ka.

S.: Sitizi to yuu koto ni siyoo.

Z.: Kasikomarimasita.

.   .   .   .   .

(viii)

Zyun-iti: Ookawa-san wa o-ide ni narimasu ka.

Zyotyuu: Hai, irassyaimasu.

Z.: O-me ni kakareru ka doo ka tyotto ukagatte itadaki-tain' desu ga.

Zyotyuu: Donatasama de irassyaimasu ka.

Z.: Asami Zyun-iti to yuu mono desu.

Zyotyuu: Tyotto o-mati kudasaimasi.

Zyotyuu: Doozo o-agari ni natte itadakitoo gozaimasu.

Z.: Watasi Asami Zyun-iti to moosu mono de gozaimasu. Hirata-san kara o-hanasi ga atta koto to zonzimasu ga.

Ookawa: Arimasita. Maa, o-kake kudasai. Tikaku Amerika e iku soo desu ga.

Z.: Sayoo de gozaimasu.

O.: Kekkoo desu ne. Dono kurai itte irun' desu ka.

Z.: Ninen bakari to zonzimasu.

O.: Hirata-kun kara kimi ga Amerika e iku to yuu koto o kiita no de watasi kara kimi ni aitai to o-negai sitan' desu yo. Zitu wa watasi no zinan ga atira e itte ite ne. Sore de kimi ga mukoo ni tuitara itido atte moraoo to omotte irun' desu. Nanimo toku ni kore to yuu yoo ga arun' de wa nain' desu ga ne. Tada watasitati wa kenkoo de iru kara ansin site iro to itte moraereba iin' desu yo.

Z.: Sore wa matigainaku itasimasu.

O.: O-hitori de ikun' desu ka.

Z.: Hazime wa hitori de mairimasu ga ato de ginkoo no hoo no yurusi ga areba konyaku site iru hito ni kite moratte, mukoo de kekkon siyoo to omotte imasu.

Z.: Thank you very much.   When will it be convenient?

S.: Let me see.   Do you think you could bring her to my office next Monday?

Z.: What time do you prefer?

S.: Let's make it seven.

Z.: Very well, Father.

.   .   .   .   .

(*viii*)

Zyun-iti: Is Mr. Ookawa in?

Maid: Yes, sir, he is.

Z.: Could you ask him if he could spare me a moment?

Maid: Can I have your name, sir?

Z.: It is Asami Zyun-iti.

Maid: Please wait a moment, sir.

Maid: Please come in, sir.

Z.: My name is Asami Zyun-iti.   You may have heard of me from Mr. Hirata.

Ookawa: Yes, I have.   Well, please sit down.   I hear you are going to America soon.

Z.: That is so.

O.: That's excellent, isn't it?   How long for?

Z.: About two years, I think.

O.: I heard from Hirata that you are going to America, so I asked him whether I could see you.   The point is my second son is over there, so I wondered whether I could get you to look him up when you arrive.   There is nothing in particular that I want to say to him; just that we are well and he is not to worry about us.

Z.: Certainly I shall do that.

O.: Are you going alone?

Z.: I shall be alone at first, but if I get permission from the bank I should like to send for my fiancée, and get married over there.

I

APPENDIX II

NUMERALS AND UNITS

(a) *Numbers*

1	iti, hito	16	zyuuroku
2	ni, huta	17	zyuusiti
3	san, mi	18	zyuuhati
4	si, yo	19	zyuuku
5	go, itu	20	nizyuu
6	roku, mu	30	sanzyuu
7	siti, nana	40	sizyuu (yonzyuu)
8	hati, ya	50	gozyuu
9	ku, kokono	60	rokuzyuu
10	zyuu, to	70	sitizyuu (nanazyuu)
11	zyuuiti	80	hatizyuu
12	zyuuni	90	kuzyuu (kyuuzyuu)
13	zyuusan	100	hyaku
14	zyuusi	365	sanbyaku rokuzyuugo
15	zyuugo		

5,824	gosen happyaku nizyuusi
13,006	itiman sanzen roku
500,890	gozyuuman happyaku kuzyuu
1,000,000	hyakuman
80,000,000	hassenman

(b) Numbers and Units Combined

The sign * indicates that the number and unit combine with no change of spelling, e.g., nanbai.

The sign — indicates that the combination does not exist.

When the spelling of only one of the two elements changes it is printed in the table by itself and must be combined with the other element. When both change, the complete combination is given. Words in brackets replace the whole combination.

	nan	iti	ni	san	si	go	roku	siti	hati	ku	zyuu	hyaku	
bai	*	*	*	*	yon / *	*	*	* / nana	*	* / kyuu	*	*	"times as much," e.g., sanbai, three times as much
ban	*	*	*	*	yon / yo	*	*	nana	*	kyuu	*	*	"No." forms ordinals
banti	*	*	*	*	yon	*	*	* / nana	*	* / kyuu	*	*	Plot number (in address)
bun	*	*	*	*	* / yon	*	*	* / nana	*	* / kyuu	*	*	"part," "fraction"
byoo	*	*	*	*	* / yon	*	*	nana	*	kyuu	*	*	"second"
dai	*	*	*	*	yon / yo	*	*	* / nana	*	* / kyuu	*	*	used for counting vehicles, planes
do	*	*	*	*	yo / yon	*	*	* / nana	*	* / kyuu	*	*	"times," nido, twice; degree, o
en	*	*	*	*	yon	*	*	* / nana	*	kyuu	*	*	"yen"
goo	*	*	*	*	* / yon	*	*	* / nana	*	kyuu	*	*	"No."

Counter	nan-	1	2	3	4	5	6	7	8	9	10	100	Meaning
guramu	*	*	*	*	* yon	*	*	* nana	*	* kyuu	*	*	"grams"
gyoo	*	*	*	*	* yon	*	*	* nana	*	* kyuu	*	*	"line (of print, etc.)"
hai	bai	ippai	*	bai	*	*	roppai	* nana	happai	kyuu	zippai	hyappai	"cupfuls", "glasses"
hiki	biki	ippiki	*	biki	* yon	*	roppiki	* nana	happiki	* kyuu	zippiki	hyappiki	used for counting animals
hon	bon	ippon	*	bon	* yon	*	roppon	* nana	happon	* kyuu	zippon	hyappon	used for counting cylindrical objects
hun(kan)	pun	ippun	*	pun	* yonpun	*	roppun	* nana	happun	kyuu	zippun	hyappun	"minutes"
hyaku	byaku	(hyaku)	*	byaku	* yon	*	roppyaku	* nana	happyaku	* kyuu	—	—	"100"
kagetu	*	ik	*	*	* yon	*	rok	* nana	hak	* kyuu	zik	hyak	"months"
kai	gai	ik	*	gai	* yon	*	rok	* nana	hak	* kyuu	zik	hyak	"floors", "storeys"
kan	gan	ik	*	gan	yon	*	rok	nana	hak	kyuu	zik	hyak	unit of weight. "kan" = 8·27 lb.
kiro	*	ik	*	*	yon	*	rok	* nana	hak	kyuu	zik	hyak	"kilogrammes", "kilo-metres"
mai	*	*	*	*	yo / yon	*	*	* nana	*	* kyuu	*	*	used for counting flat things, "sheets (of paper)", etc.
man	*	*	*	*	yon	*	*	nana	*	kyuu	*	*	10,000
meetoru	*	*	*	*	yon	*	*	* nana	*	* kyuu	*	*	"metres"

	nan	iti	ni	san	si	go	roku	siti	hati	-ku	zyuu	hyaku	
monme	*	*	*	*	yon	*	*	*	*	*	*	*	unit of weight, "monme" = $\frac{1}{1000}$ kan; 2·117 dr.
nen(kan)	*	*	*	*	yo / yon	*	*	nana	*	kyuu	*	*	"years"
niti(kan)	*	*	hutuka	mikka	yokka	ituka	muika	nanoka	yooka	kokonoka	tooka	*	"days" (see note below)
nin	*	hitori	hutari	*	yo	*	*	*	*	kyuu	*	*	used for counting human beings
oku	*	*	*	*	*	*	*	nana	*	kyuu	*	*	100,000,000
paasento	*	*	*	*	yon	*	rop	nana	hap	kyuu	zip	hyap	"per cent"
peizi	*	*	*	*	yon	*	rop	nana	hap	kyuu	zip	hyap	"page"
ri	*	*	*	*	yo / yon	*	*	nana	*	kyuu	*	*	unit of length, "ri" = 2·445 miles
rittoru	*	*	*	*	yon	*	*	nana	*	kyuu	*	*	"litres"
satu	*	is	*	*	yon	*	*	nana	has	kyuu	zis	*	used for counting books
sen	*	is	*	*	yon	*	*	nana	has	kyuu	zis	—	"sen", $\frac{1}{100}$ of yen
sen	zen	is (sen)	*	zen	yon	*	*	nana	has	kyuu	—	—	1,000
soku	zoku	is	*	zoku	yon	*	*	nana	has	kyuu	zis	*	used for counting pairs of footwear, "pair"

											Notes
soo	*	zis	kyuu	has	*nana	*	*	*yon	*zoo	*	is	used for counting ships
sun	*	zis	kyuu	has	*nana	*	*	yon	zun	*	is	unit of length, "sun" = 1·193 in.
syaku	*	zis	kyuu	has	nana	*	*	yon	zyaku	*	is	unit of length, "syaku" = 10 sun = 0·995 ft.
syoo	—	—	kyuu	has	*nana	*	*	yon	*zyoo	*	is	unit of volume, "syoo" = 3·17 pints
syurui	*	zis	*kyuu	has	nana	*	*	yon	*	*	is	"sorts", "kinds"
syuu(kan)	*	zis	*kyuu	has	nana	*	*	yon	*	*	is	"weeks"
ten	*	zit	kyuu	hat	*nana	*	*	yon	*	*	it	"marks", "points"
to	—	zit	*kyuu	hat	nana	*	*	*yon	*	*	it	unit of volume, "to" = 10 syoo = 15·88 quarts
tyoo(me)	*	zit	kyuu	hat	nana	*	*	*yon	*	*	it	"tyoo" = 360 syaku = 119·16 yards; "tyoome", "ward"
zi(kan)	*	*	*	*	*	*	*	yo	*	*	*	"hours"
zyoo	*	*	*kyuu	*	*	*	*	yo	*	*	*	unit of size of room, "zyoo", "mat", "tatami", approx. 6 ft. × 3 ft.
zyuu	—	—	*kyuu	*	*	*	*	*yon	*	*	—	10

	iku	hito	huta	mi	yo	itu	mu	nana	ya	kokono	to	hyaku	
ban	*	*	*	*	*	*	*	*	—	*	—	*	"evenings"
hako	*	*	*	*	si	go	oku	siti	hati	ku	zippako	hyappako	"boxes", "boxfuls"
hukuro	*	*	*	*	*	*	*	*	*	*	*	*	"bags", "sacks"
kumi	*	*	*	*	si	go	rok	siti	hak	ku	zik	hyak	"sets", "suits", etc.
tu	*	*	*	mit	yot	*	mut	*	yat	*	(too)	(hyaku)	used for counting objects which have no other special units

When two forms are given, the one above is the more usual, e.g., yonbai and sibai are both found, but yonbai is more usual.

Combinations of numbers and niti(kan) above 10 are normal (zyuuitiniti, "11 days", etc.) except that yokka is used in all numbers ending in 4 (zyuuyokka, "14 days", etc.).

For the purposes of this table the interrogatives nan and iku are included in the numbers, and hyaku, man, oku, sen (1,000), and zyuu among the units.

(c) *Hours and Minutes*

1.25	itizi nizyuugohun
2.37	nizi sanzyuusitihun
4.24 a.m.	gozen yozi nizyuuyonpun
5.33 p.m.	gogo gozi sanzyuusanpun
half past six	rokuzi han
quarter to eight	hatizi zyuugohun mae
quarter past eight	hatizi zyuugohun (sugi)
ten to nine	kuzi zippun mae

(d) *Days of the Month*

1st	tuitati		17th	zyuusitiniti
2nd	hutuka		18th	zyuuhatiniti
3rd	mikka		19th	zyuukuniti
4th	yokka		20th	hatuka
5th	ituka		21st	nizyuuitiniti
6th	muika		22nd	nizyuuniniti
7th	nanoka		23rd	nizyuusanniti
8th	yooka		24th	nizyuuyokka
9th	kokonoka		25th	nizyuugoniti
10th	tooka		26th	nizyuurokuniti
11th	zyuuitiniti		27th	nizyuusitiniti
12th	zyuuniniti		28th	nizyuuhatiniti
13th	zyuusanniti		29th	nizyuukuniti
14th	zyuuyokka		30th	sanzyuuniti
15th	zyuugoniti		31st	sanzyuuitiniti
16th	zyuurokuniti			

(e) *Days of the Week*

Sunday	nitiyoo-bi	*Thursday*	mokuyoo-bi
Monday	getuyoo-bi	*Friday*	kinyoo-bi
Tuesday	kayoo-bi	*Saturday*	doyoo-bi
Wednesday	suiyoo-bi		

(f) Months

January	itigatu		July	sitigatu
February	nigatu		August	hatigatu
March	sangatu		September	kugatu
April	sigatu		October	zyuugatu
May	gogatu		November	zyuuitigatu
June	rokugatu		December	zyuunigatu

(g) Years

Meizi	gannen	1868	Taisyoo	gannen	1912
,,	gonen	1872	,,	gonen	1916
,,	zyuunen	1877	,,	zyuunen	1921
,,	zyuugonen	1882	(,,	zyuugonen	1926)
,,	nizyuunen	1887	Syoowa	gannen	1926
,,	nizyuugonen	1892	,,	gonen	1930
,,	sanzyuunen	1897	,,	zyuunen	1935
,,	sanzyuugonen	1902	,,	zyuugonen	1940
,,	yonzyuunen	1907	,,	nizyuunen	1945
(,,	yonzyuugonen	1912)	,,	nizyuugonen	1950
			,,	sanzyuunen	1955

Appendix III

ROMANIZATION

(a) *Our system* (= " *kunrei-siki* ")

(Forms shown in italics are different in the Hepburn system)

a	ka	sa	ta	na	ha	ma	ya	ra	wa	ga	za	da	ba	pa
i	ki	*si*	*ti*	ni	hi	mi		ri		gi	*zi*	*zi*	bi	pi
u	ku	su	*tu*	nu	*hu*	mu	yu	ru		gu	zu	zu	bu	pu
e	ke	se	te	ne	he	me		re		ge	ze	de	be	pe
o	ko	so	to	no	ho	mo	yo	ro		go	zo	do	bo	po

a	kya	*sya*	*tya*	nya	hya	mya	rya	gya	*zya*	bya	pya
u	kyu	*syu*	*tyu*	nyu	hyu	myu	ryu	gyu	*zyu*	byu	pyu
o	kyo	*syo*	*tyo*	nyo	hyo	myo	ryo	gyo	*zyo*	byo	pyo

The independent consonant is *n*.

(b) *Hepburn System*

(Only differences from the above have been shown)

a					
i	shi	chi		ji	ji
u		tsu	fu		
e					
o				wo (*accusative case particle*)	

a	sha	cha	ja
u	shu	chu	ju
o	sho	cho	jo

The independent consonant is *n* except before *b*, *m*, *p*, when it is *m*.

Note that in our romanization long vowels are written with the vowel duplicated; you will see that length is often shown (in other books than this) by overlining the vowel, except in the case of *i*, which is always duplicated.

KEY TO EXERCISES

Exercise 1 (p. 9)

I. 1. There is a book there (by you). 2. There is a pin over there. 3. It is here. 4. There is a pen here. 5. There is some paper. 6. There is an exercise-book here. 7. There is a pencil over there. 8. It is over there. 9. There is some ink there (by you). 10. It is there (by you).

II. 1. Koko ni nooto ga arimasu. 2. Koko ni arimasu. 3. Asoko ni hon ga arimasu. 4. Koko ni enpitu ga arimasu. 5. Soko ni arimasu. 6. Asoko ni inki ga arimasu. 7. Pen ga arimasu. 8. Soko ni pin ga arimasu. 9. Asoko ni arimasu. 10. Soko ni kami ga arimasu.

Exercise 2 (p. 12)

I. 1. What is there here? 2. There is a fork there (by you). 3. The tea-cup (rice-bowl) is there (by you). 5. There is a window here too. 5. The apples, too, are here. 6. Both the plate and the knife are there (by you). 7. What is there over there? 8. There are both bread and butter. 9. Is there a chair too there? 10 The door is here.

II. 1. Koko ni bata ga arimasu. 2. Mado wa koko ni arimasu. 3. Asoko ni wa nani ga arimasu ka. 4. Asoko ni wa teeburu ga arimasu. 5. Ringo mo orenzi mo koko ni arimasu. 6. Soko ni nani ga arimasu ka. 7. Koko ni wa isu ga arimasu. 8. Asoko ni tyawan ga arimasu. 9. Soko ni to ga arimasu. 10. Koko ni sara ga arimasu ka.

Exercise 3 (p. 15)

I. 1. Where is the child? He is in the house. 2. Who is in that room? There is a child. 3. There are both birds and insects in this garden. 4. Where are you? 5. I am in London. 6. Is there a fish there (by you)? 7. London is in England. 8. Is there a friend (of yours) in London? In London is there Mr. Miki. 9. They are in Tokyo. 10. In Japan, too, there are both cats and dogs.

II. 1. (Anata wa) niwa ni imasu ka. 2. Ano hito wa Rondon ni imasu ka. 3. Kodomotati wa koko ni imasu. 4. Koko ni sakana ga imasu. 5. Neko wa asoko ni imasu. 6. Soko ni mo neko ga imasu. 7. Kono heya ni kodomo ga imasu. 8. Ano heya ni nani ga imasu ka. 9. Ano hitotati wa uti ni imasu. 10. Niwa ni mo hito ga imasu. 11. Eikoku ni mo Nippon ni mo neko ga imasu. 12. Rondon ni mo tori ga imasu ka. 13. Rondon ni wa tori mo musi mo imasu. 14. Miki-san wa doko ni imasu ka. Eikoku ni imasu. 15. Tookyoo ni wa dare ga imasu ka. Tomodati ga imasu.

Exercise 4 (p. 18)

I. 1. There is a dictionary on top of the bookshelf too. 2. Is that your hat too? 3. This is a photograph of the school library. 4. There is a knife under the box. 5. Are both the teacher and the student in the room? 6. Whose suit is that? It is my suit. 7. There is a cat in front of the window. 8. Whereabouts in the drawer is the pencil? 9. What is he a student of? He is a student of Japanese. 10. Behind the chair there is his stick. 11. What is that (by you)? It is an English novel. 12. What is there on his head? A hat.

II. 1. Zibiki wa hako no mae ni arimasu. 2. Kore wa Nihongo no syoosetu desu ka. 3. Are wa nan no syasin desu ka. 4. Are wa gakkoo no syasin desu. 5. Hon no sita ni pen ga arimasu. 6. Anata no atama no ue ni boosi ga arimasu. 7. Kore wa Ueda-san no sutekki desu ka. 8. Are wa Nihongo no gakkoo desu ka. 9. Zibiki wa heya no doko ni arimasu ka. 10. Sore wa dare no hondana desu ka. 11. Mado no mae ni teeburu ga arimasu. 12. Watasi no huku wa hikidasi no naka ni arimasu ka. 13. Kono zibiki wa gakkoo no tosyokan ni mo arimasu. 14. Hako no usiro ni tori ga imasu. 15. Sensei mo gakusei mo to no mae ni imasu.

Exercise 5 (p. 22)

I. 1. Does this cat eat fish? 2. He lends magazines too. 3. Will you sell that kimono too? 4. What do you intend to smell? 5. I shall wash both the chopsticks and the rice-bowls with cold water. 6. Do you, too, intend to wait for a bus? 7. I intend to look at some insects with these glasses. 8. I both write characters and draw pictures with this brush. 9. I intend to read both the newspaper and the magazine. 10. I intend to stay (be) in the shop. 11. Do you intend to call a doctor? 12. I intend to eat the apple on the table. 13. I will meet Mr. Tanaka at the station. 14. I intend to die in England. 15. Where do you intend to sell meat?

II. 1. Ano heya de hon o yomu tumori desu. 2. Sutekki mo kasimasu ka. 3. Kono megane de e o miru tumori desu. 4. Dare ga kagimasu ka. 5. Sono (ano) gakuseitati wa zi o kakimasu. 6. Sono (ano) hito wa ano mise de sinbun o urimasu. 7. Niku mo sakana mo hasi de tabemasu. 8. Nippon no syasin o miru tumori desu. 9. Denwa de tomodati o yobu tumori desu ka. 10. Doko de sara o araimasu ka. 11. Anata mo eki de matimasu ka. 12. Neko wa mizu no naka de sinimasu. 13. Tosyokan de sensei ni aimasu. 14. Niwa de tegami o kaku tumori desu. 15. Kono kimono mo arau tumori desu ka.

Exercise 6 (p. 27)

I. 1. He is living in Tokyo. 2. Where do you live? I live in Kyoto. 3. Does this door open too? 4. Some friends are swimming in that river. 5. A teacher is standing in front of the hotel. 6. Students come from England to this school. 7. Your hat has

fallen under the table.   8.   Some books are in a row on the bookshelf.
9.   Mr. Yamasita is in (has gone to) the library.   10.   They are broadcasting news to America.   11.   Does it snow, too?   12.   The insect
in the water is dead.   13.   Is he, too, an American?   No, he's not
(He is different);   he's an Englishman.   14.   Where is the dog?
It is out in the garden.   15.   He is travelling from America to
Europe.

II.   1.   Nani o site imasu ka.   Eigo o benkyoo site imasu.   2.
Ano Eikokuzin wa Eikoku kara Nippon e ryokoo site imasu.   3.
Anata no zibiki ga otite imasu.   4.   Tosyokan no mae ni gakusei ga
narande imasu.   5.   Hito mo inu mo sinde imasu.   6.   Ano Amerikazin
wa tomodati no hoteru e itte imasu.   7.   Kono boosi wa tigaimasu
(tigatte imasu).   8.   Sensei mo syooti site imasu.   9.   Nippon no
nyuusu o hoosoo simasu.   10.   Kono hito wa Rondon kara kite
imasu.   11.   Kono kawa ni sakana ga sunde imasu ka.   12.   Sora
wa harete imasu ka.   13.   Anata mo oyogimasu ka.   14.   Tori wa
heya no naka e haitte imasu.   15.   Ano Eikokuzin wa Kyooto ni
sunde imasu.

Exercise 7 (p. 31)

I.   1.   This black cow is big.   2.   The hat which the small child is
wearing is blue.   3.   The horse that is over there is white.   4.   Is the
French book that you are reading interesting?   5.   He can talk
difficult Japanese.   6.   That Frenchman's cooking is fine.   7.   Can
you study in a cold room?   8.   The flowers on the table are the same
colour.   9.   The man using the red pencil is our teacher.   10.   The
shoes that my friend is wearing are black.   11.   That artist is wearing
a peculiar hat.   12.   On the bookshelf there is a peculiar insect.   13.
It is unpleasant to travel on rainy days.   14.   Can you drink the
milk that is in the big cup?   15.   On that tree there is a small bird.
II.   1.   Asoko ni siroi uma ga imasu.   2.   Ano hito no boosi wa
akai desu.   3.   Tiisai uti ni sunde imasu.   4.   Niwa de e o kaite iru
hito wa rippa na ekaki desu.   5.   Ano hito no megane wa ookii desu.
6.   Omosiroi hoosoo ga dekimasu ka.   7.   Teeburu no ue ni hen na
musi ga imasu.   8.   Kono syasin ni (mo) onazi hito ga imasu.   9.   Siroi
niku mo taberu koto ga dekimasu ka.   10.   Mise no mae ni iya na
inu ga imasu.   11.   Yuki no hi wa samui desu.   12.   Omosiroi syoosetu
o kaku koto wa muzukasii desu.   13.   Kuroi neko wa miruku o
nonde imasu.   14.   Ano ooki na usi wa rippa desu.   15.   Tiisai ki
no sita ni aru hana wa aoi desu.

Exercise 8 (p. 36)

I.   1.   They don't sell cars in the country.   2.   There aren't any
easy books in this bookcase.   3.   Are there any Japanese who don't
eat rice?   4.   A library in which there are no French novels is not a
good one.   5.   People without legs, too, are working.   6.   There are
insects in places which aren't warm, too.   7.   In this garden there
are no white butterflies.   8.   On days when the weather isn't good
there are some people who don't come.   9.   Isn't that clock peculiar?

10. This gravy is not salty. 11. Is there any sugar that isn't sweet? 12. It is unpleasant to drink bitter medicine. 13. Are there any animals that do not breathe air? 14. The juice of this orange is not sour. 15. The luggage on the bicycle is not heavy; it is light.

II. 1. Karai siru mo iya de wa arimasen. 2. Kono tosyokan ni wa omosiroi hon ga arimasen. 3. Gakkoo e ikanai kodomo ga imasu ka (arimasu ka). 4. Zidoosya ga nai tokoro wa arimasen. 5. Suppaku nai mikan (orenzi) ga arimasu ka. 6. Koko ni wa ari mo tyootyoo mo imasen. 7. Kono doobutu wa atatakai tokoro ni sunde imasu. 8. Ano kodomo wa amai orenzi no siru o nonde imasu. 9. Inaka de wa ii kuuki o suu koto ga dekimasu. 10. Koko ni wa omoi nimotu wa arimasen. 11. Karui zitensya o tukau koto wa yasasii desu. 12. Ano hon-bako no ue ni wa tokei ga arimasen. 13. Tenki ga yoku nai hi ni wa umi e ikimasen. 14. Nigaku nai kusuri o nomimasu. 15. Kome o uru mise de hataraite imasu.

Exercise 9 (p. 41)

I. 1. The furniture that he has bought is not splendid. 2. That is the snake that bit my foot. 3. He decreased the weight of the heavy trunk. 4. A tall chimney was broken. 5. They did not resemble each other. 6. The fountain-pen that I chose was cheap. 7. There were some people who didn't hurry. 8. That young man didn't win. 9. A basket without a lid arrived. 10. The face of the child who cried was hot. 11. He joined the chains with some strong string. 12. I met a teacher who taught French at that school. 13. The chairman's speech was interesting. 14. My overcoat was not dear. 15. His gramophone was peculiar.

II. 1. Kono nimotu no mekata o herasimasita. 2. Doogu o (wa) erabimasita ka. 3. Ano hito wa anata ni nite imasita. 4. Kuroi inu wa siroi neko o kamimasita. 5. Kaban wa omoku wa arimasen desita. 6. Dare ga katimasita ka. 7. Kowareta tikuonki wa doko ni arimasu ka. 8. Kusari wa tuyoku arimasen desita. 9. Tori wa kago no naka de naite imasita. 10. Kaityoo no hanasi o hoosoo simasita. 11. Are wa Eigo o osieta sensei desu. 12. Watasi mo isogimasen desita. 13. Yasui mannenhitu wa kaimasen desita. 14. Huta wa atukatta desu. 15. Sono seinen wa tukimasen desita.

Exercise 10 (p. 46)

I. 1. Did you go off somewhere? I didn't go off anywhere. 2. Do you intend to send something to your friend abroad? I intend to send things like books, newspapers, and magazines. 3. Where is it warm? It's not warm anywhere. 4. Can I buy some eggs at the greengrocer's or the butcher's? 5. Which foreign language did you learn? I didn't learn any. 6. We are going in this car. 7. Mr. Honda and Mr. Kimura are walking. 8. Did you cut any of them? I cut some branches which had no leaves. 9. Which one did you pick up in the road? 10. Which is the parcel of books? That one. 11. Is someone living on this island? Nobody. 12. I do not intend to buy any of the pictures. 13. Will you drink some beer too? I shan't drink anything. 14. Do you intend to send that trunk too? 15. Do you intend to use one of them? I may not use either of them.

II. 1. Huransugo o dokoka de naraimasita ka. 2. Teeburu no ue ni wa pen toka inki toka nooto nado ga arimasu. 3. Yaoya ka nikuya ga kuru ka mo siremasen. 4. Dono hana o kirimasita ka. Akai hana o kirimasita. 5. Ano mise ni aru kutu no doreka o kau tumori desu ka. 6. Kotira no kozutumi mo okurimasu ka. 7. Niwa de nanika hiroimasita ka. Tori no tamago o hiroimasita. 8. Dareka biiru o nomimasita ka. Daremo nomimasen desita. 9. Asoko ni iru hito no dotira ga Honda-san desu ka. 10. Nanika kakimasu ka. Nanimo kakimasen. 11. Te wa dotiramo itaku arimasen. 12. Ano heya ni aru kaban no dore ga kowarete imasu ka. 13. Gaikoku wa doko e mo ikanai tumori desu. 14. Dokoka de ano Amerikazin to Eikokuzin ni aimasita. 15. Watasi no tomodati wa asoko ni aru hoteru no dotiraka ni imasu.

Exercise 11 (p. 54)

I. 1. I arrived in Japan on the 1st of March, 1945. 2. What did he talk about? Well now, I don't know. 3. The train leaves at 9.14. 4. Do you grow grapes too? No, I don't. 5. Mr. Yamasita was born in 1910. 6. That dog is walking on three legs. 7. The first year of Taisyoo was 1912. 8. This bridge cost ¥185,743,500. 9. What is the weight of this baggage? One *kan* 600 *monme*. 10. Were those five books dear? Yes, they were.

II. 1. Basu wa yozi nizyuusanpun ni tukimasu. 2. Ano hito wa Amerikazin desu ka. Saa, sirimasen. 3. Watasi wa Taisyoo zyuunen sitigatu mikka ni umaremasita. 4. Meizi gannen wa sen happyaku rokuzyuuhatinen desu. 5. Ano tosyokan wa gohyaku-man-en kakarimasita. 6. Eki de sannin no tomodati ni aimasita. 7. Kome mo tukurimasu ka. E, tukurimasu. 8. Ano Eikokuzin wa Syoowa sannen ni Nippon e kimasita. 9. Anata wa hatigatu ni umaremasita ka. Ie, kugatu ni umaremasita. 10. Kono mado no haba wa ikura arimasu ka. Gosyaku rokusun arimasu.

III. 1. How many times does three go into nine? Three times. 2. What is your telephone number? 3058. 3. At what number does Mr. Nakayama live? He lives at number sixteen. 4. What fraction of nine is three? One-third. 5. How many cars are lined up in front of the school? There are seven. 6. How many times did you go to America? I went twice. 7. How much (How many yen) did you send? I sent ¥94. 8. In what number room are you? Number six. 9. How many grams does this letter weigh? Thirty. 10. How many lines did you read? I read twelve lines. 11. How many glasses of beer did you drink? Six. 12. How many dogs are there in the garden? There are two. 13. How many fountain-pens do you intend to choose? Three. 14. At how many minutes past four do we arrive? We arrive at twenty-seven minutes past. 15. For how many minutes did you swim? I swam for fifteen minutes. 16. How many months were you in France? Four. 17. How many storeys has this hotel? Ten. 18. How many *kan* does that animal weigh? It weighs seventy *kan*. 19. How many kilometres does that car go in an hour? It goes one hundred. 20. How many kilograms does this meat weigh? Five. 21. How many sheets of letter-paper did you use? I used six. 22. How many metres long is this string? Ten metres. 23. How many *monme* of meat does that dog eat? A hundred. 24. In what year did you go to England? In 1936. 25. How many years were you in America? I was there for three years. 26. On what day did you leave? On the tenth. 27. How many days did you work? I worked ten days. 28. How many teachers are there in this school? There are thirty. 29. What percentage of Japanese speak English? Ten per cent. 30. How many pages are there in this book? Two hundred and thirty-six. 31. How many *ri* is your house from Tokyo? Twenty. 32. How many litres of milk are there? One. 33. How many English novels have you read? I have read nine. 34. How many pairs of black shoes will you buy? Two pairs. 35. How many steamers are there that go to that island? Three. 36. How many *sun* of red cloth will you cut? Five. 37. How many *syaku* high is that chimney? Nine. 38. In your house how many *syoo* of rice are eaten in one day? One. 39. How many kinds of gramophone are there? There are fifteen kinds. 40. How many weeks did the journey take? It took three weeks. 41. How many marks did you get? Seventy-five. 42. How many *to* of rice arrived? Four. 43. How long is this road? Twenty *tyoo*. 44. In what *tyoome* is the library? In five *tyoome*. 45. At what time do you broadcast? At five o'clock. 46. How long will you broadcast? Five hours. 47. How big is this room? Eight mats (*tatami*). 48. How many boxes of oranges will you send? Ten. 49. How many bags of sugar did you buy? Two. 50. How many pairs of chopsticks did you sell? I sold forty-five pairs. 51. How many windows are there in this room? Two.

Exercise 12 (p. 63)

I. 1. Of course my father hasn't a car. 2. The things that that teacher says are very difficult. 3. The kimono which your elder sister sewed is very well made. 4. I'll never see him! 5. The man who picked up the fountain-pen which I dropped in the street was not wearing a hat. 6. My mother has hardly ever run. 7. When will you pay the money? Tomorrow. 8. The person to whom my elder sister is handing over the parcel is the mother of a friend of mine. 9. The shoes which I bought just recently are a little small. 10. The picture which my elder brother is hanging on the wall we bought yesterday in the shop on the other side of the street. 11. How long has your father been abroad? 12. At some time I shall tell you about a man who succeeded. 13. Is the man washing the brush your elder brother? 14. He is certainly not skilful. 15. Last year we often saw in the garden butterflies whose colour was black.

II. 1. Niisan wa atarasii kutu o haite imasita ka. 2. Ituka gaikoku e iku ka mo siremasen. 3. Sore wa otoosan ni okuru kozutumi desu ka. 4. Toori no mukoogawa no taihen ooki na mise desu ka. 5. Okaasan ga kasita Huransugo no hon o yomimasita ka. 6. Ano uma wa taihen hayaku hasitte imasu. 7. Neesan wa itu kara osiete imasu ka. Kyonen kara osiete imasu. 8. Ano hito no uti e wa kessite ikimasen. 9. Ani wa miti de hirotta kane o otosita hito ni watasimasita. 10. Kinoo nonda kusuri wa nigakatta desu. 11. Titi wa hotondo boosi o kabutta koto ga arimasen. 12. Taguti-san wa Tookyoo de hizyoo ni seikoo simasita. 13. Ane wa haha no syasin o kabe ni kakete imasu. 14. Ano hito ga yuu koto wa sukosi okasii desu. 15. Iro ga akai tori o mita koto ga arimasu ka.

Exercise 13 (p. 68)

I. 1. Was it this picture that he praised? 2. The one who is playing in the garden is the child of (one of) my relatives. 3. The thing which my elder sister is taking out of the drawer is my mother's kimono. 4. It was the day before yesterday that a strong wind blew. 5. When is it that the new play starts? 6. The one the tip of which is shining is yours. 7. Why are they digging a big hole in the field? 8. Why did he hide his face? 9. The thing to do in Italy is to listen to good music. 10. The thing is, my elder brother doesn't look for work. 11. Why don't we get on this tram? 12. What happened was that Mr. Arita, who lost his fortune, committed suicide yesterday. 13. What are they laughing at? 14. Why don't you get up early in the morning? 15. Why don't you shut the window?

II. 1. Parii de kiita no wa kono ongaku desu. 2. Kono sinrigaku no hon wa anata no desu ka. 3. Niwa de ana o hotte iru no wa sinrui no kodomo desu. 4. Hikidasi kara dasita no wa atarasii waisyatu desu ka. 5. Boosi o nakusita no wa tuyoi kaze ga huite iru hi desita. 6. Naze to o simerun' desu ka. 7. Koko de densya ni norun' desu ka. 8. Beikoku de sigoto o sagasun' desu. 9. Itu sibai e ittan' desu ka. Ototoi desu. 10. Doosite zaisan o kakusanain' desu ka. 11. Asa wa gozi ni okirun' desu. 12. Naze hatake de asobun' desu ka. 13. Dono e mo homenain' desu ka. 14. Asita hazimaru eiga wa Itarii no (no) desu ka. 15. Saki ga hikatte iru no o waratte irun' desu.

Exercise 14 (p. 74)

I. 1. I save time by speaking on the telephone. 2. I have often been to France, but I have never been to Germany. 3. The child's father is English and his mother is French. 4. Will it be all right to leave as soon as I finish my work? 5. China is an old and large country. 6. However much you hurry, you may not be in time. 7. However much I studied English grammar, I couldn't learn it. 8. What did you do after that? I went to bed without doing anything. 9. I don't mind whether you send a telegram or not. 10. In this garden there is a cherry-tree but not a peach. 11. However much the (city-)mayor sang songs, nobody praised him. 12. After a week had elapsed we went to the Zoo and saw some rare animals.

13. I don't mind writing the letter to the Ministry of Education. 14. That is not the post-office; it is the City Hall. 15. I borrowed a book on Buddhism, but it is very difficult and I cannot read it quickly.

II. 1. Ano hito wa sensei de wa nakute gakusei desu. 2. Zidoosya de itte mo ma ni awanai ka mo siremasen. 3. Ginkoo e dasu tegami ni kitte o harimasen desita. 4. Siyakusyo e itta koto wa arimasen ga sityoo no kao wa sitte imasu. 5. Bukkyoo no hanasi o hoosoo site mo ii desu ka. 6. Atarasii hon wa tabitabi kaimasita ga huru-hon wa katta koto ga arimasen. 7. Kai ga owatte kara sugu kaerimasita. 8. Ikura hurukute mo kono kikai wa abunaku arimasen. 9. Issyuukan tatte kara monbusyoo e ikimasita. 10. Konban hayaku nenakute mo ii desu ka. 11. Tyootyoo ni atte mo awanakute mo watasi wa kamaimasen. 12. Sina e itta koto wa arimasu keredomo (ga) Nihon e itta koto wa arimasen. 13. Ano hito wa mezurasikute omosiroi uta o utaimasita. 14. Denpoo wa watasi ga utte mo ii desu. 15. Kooen e itte sakura no hana o mimasita.

Exercise 15 (p. 83)

I. 1. No convenient trains go to that hot spring, I suppose. 2. This is probably Mr. Tanaka's typewriter. 3. This mountain is not so high as Hakone, but it is colder. 4. Let us get up early tomorrow morning and view the scenery outside 5. I wonder if we can't escape to some nearer place. 6. I wonder whether my cat kills as many mice as yours. 7. That girl is trying to swim, but it would be safer if she crossed by boat. 8. I suppose peaches are more delicious than pears, but I've not eaten very many peaches. 9. Second-hand books may be cheaper, but they didn't sell them at that bookshop. 10. Mr. Tamura is not so tall as Mr. Yamamoto, but he can run faster. 11. This year let us buy a trunk that is as small and light as possible. 12. You had better use a notebook that is not too thick. 13. Which car saves petrol, the blue one or the black one? 14. I wonder if the one who came last was a short man. 15. I wonder if the children who were up in the tree in the park were trying to take birds' eggs.

II. 1. Asita no asa itiban hayaku okiru no wa Tanaka-san desyoo. 2. Ototoo wa tonari no onna-no-ko yori se ga hikui desu ga asi wa nagai desu. 3. Ame ga hutte umi e iku koto ga dekinai hi ni wa eigakan e ikimasyoo ka. 4. Maiban hon-dana no hon o seiri siyoo to simasita ga zikan ga arimasen desita. 5. Ano hon-ya no hoo ga tikakute benri desyoo ga sono hon wa utte inai ka mo siremasen. 6. Dekiru dake atukute omoi huta o tukaimasyoo. 7. Titi wa mainen sangatu ni Koobe e ikimasu ga kotosi wa sigatu ni iku desyoo. 8. Raigetu ano kawa o watatte mukoogawa ni aru yama ni noborimasyoo ka. 9. Ani wa tabun rainen gaikoku e ryokoo suru desyoo. 10. Asatte kooen e itte kesiki o nagamemasyoo. 11. Tamura-san no gurai ii taipuraitaa o kaimasyoo. 12. Zidoosya de itte mo anzen desu ga kisya de iku hoo ga motto anzen desu. 13.

Kinoo hodo osoku arimasen keredomo (ga) basu de kaeru hoo ga ii desyoo. 14. Kono momo wa amari oisiku nai ka mo siremasen ga yasui desu. 15. Neko ga korosoo to sita toki ni wa nezumi wa nigete imasita.

Exercise 16 (p. 90)

I. 1. This kimono is very wet, but as the weather is fine I expect it will soon get dry. 2. In the morning it was raining, but as it left off in the afternoon we went off for a walk. 3. As the lighting is bad in this museum, one cannot see very well. 4. That carpenter builds houses taking great care over the roof. 5. These cigarettes are very nice, but as they are bad for the throat, it would be better not to smoke too many of them. 6. Is there any book suitable for the study of physics? 7. Let's use up all this meat for lunch. 8. My elder sister is going in order to play the piano, but I am going horse-riding. 9. Having meals at that hotel over there costs a lot of money. 10. Mr. Inoue is interested in literature, so I expect he'll go and listen to that Frenchman's talk. 11. That cloth will not be needed to mend the pillow, so it is all right to cut it. 12. My eldest son is working in Tokyo to get his teacher's diploma. 13. It was a terrible job moving that pine-tree. 14. In spite of the fact that he promised not to drink *sake*, he drinks a lot every evening. 15. As they've started on the job of mending the road, it's inconvenient for getting into the house.

II. 1. Asita no asa kaimono ni iku ka mo siremasen kara hutuu yori hayaku okimasyoo. 2. Sora ga harete inakatta no de hosi wa miemasen desita. 3. Kono ryokan wa sukosi huben na no de asita motto tekitoo na no o mitukeru tumori desu. 4. Tyoonan wa buturigaku ni kyoomi o motte imasu kara sono hon o kau desyoo. 5. Piano o hiku no ni koosen no guai ga warui desu kara asita no gogo hikimasu. 6. Niwa de hiru-gohan o taberu no ni hako o teeburu ni tukaimasita. 7. Kono kikai o ugokasu no ni wa nani o tukaimasu ka. 8. Kono yane o naosu ni wa kane ga takusan iru desyoo. 9. Sensei no menzyoo o toru ni wa ninen kakarimasu. 10. Nodo ga kawaite imasita kara (ita no de) mizu o nomi ni kimasita. 11. Syokuzi o site kara kooen e sanpo ni ikimasyoo. 12. Titi wa konban bungaku no hanasi o hoosoo si ni itte imasu. 13. Mae ni yakusoku sita no ni tabemono ni tyuui simasen. 14. Hakubutukan o tateru tame ni Nihon e kimasita. 15. Hukuro wa kawaite iru no ni naze maki-tabako wa nurete irun' desyoo ka.

Exercise 17 (p. 96)

I. 1. What sort of building will you erect? I shall erect a large modern one. 2. What sort of building are they erecting? They are building a government office. 3. I have not read any sort of German book. 4. Anybody can go into this church. 5. How much petrol is left? Not very much. 6. There are lots of kind people, so you do not have to worry. 7. He always supports the Labour Party. 8. I invite friends to my house every Sunday, but Mr.

Tanaka never comes. 9. This is no ordinary wind, so a lot of houses may be burned down. 10. Do you think the usual person will come to do the cleaning? Yes, I do. 11. I don't eat sweet cakes at all. 12. I was able to do all the questions in today's examination. 13. There aren't many countries that he hasn't visited. 14. Who do you think will be best? Anyone will do. 15. Both the car and the train were completely smashed.

II. 1. Donna kasi o tabemasu ka. Donna kasi mo tabemasen. 2. Are wa nan no yakusyo desu ka. Monbusyoo desu. 3. Satoo wa ikura nokotte imasu ka. Ikura mo nokotte imasen. 4. Kyookai wa ikutu tatemasita ka. Kyookai wa hitotu mo tateta koto ga arimasen. 5. Daredemo kono heya o soozi suru koto ga dekimasu. 6. Makitabako wa ikurademo atta no de takusan suimasita. 7. Maisyuu nitiyoo-bi ni huru-hon o seiri siyoo to omotte imasu ga itudemo suru koto ga dekimasen. 8. Ano mise no mono wa nandemo kaimasen. 9. Doitugo o narau no wa nandemo arimasen kara sinpai sinakute mo ii desu. 10. Watasi no tomodati wa mina roodootoo no seihu o sizi simasu. 11. Kyoo no hanasi wa itumo no to sukkari tigaimasu. 12. Kinoo no siken no mondai wa mina yasasikatta desu. 13. Huku mo boosi mo ryoohootomo sukkari nurete imasu. 14. Ano hito wa itumo to onazi zikan ni kuru to omoimasu ka. Soo omoimasu. 15. Kono gakkoo no sensei wa mina sinsetu desu.

Exercise 18 (p. 101)

I. 1. This belongs to a friend, so please give me a receipt. 2. Please tell me about the result of the trial. 3. Please do not shut either the door or the window, as it is very hot in the room. 4. Buy two tickets for the concert. 5. Come this evening, since we are going to discuss the matter which I told you about yesterday. 6. Come to my office tomorrow afternoon. 7. The maid has broken the glass ashtray, so we had better use the silver one. 8. It's cold outside, so you should wear your coat when you go out. 9. If there is time I intend to go and see the Tower of London too. 10. If only there were not an examination we could set off on our trip straight away. 11. In order to succeed one must work hard. 12. We have plenty of fruit, so please eat a lot. 13. As my elder brother was busy, I had to open the cupboard by myself. 14. Look over there; there's a peculiar insect or something! 15. Give up going to the meeting today, for you must rest quietly.

II. 1. Ongakkai no kippu o gomai kudasai. 2. Taihen samui desu kara mado o simete kudasai. 3. Kono heya de maki-tabako o suu no wa yamete kudasai. 4. Nitiyoo-bi no asa watasi no uti e irassyai (o-ide nasai). 5. Hiru-gohan o tabete kara yukkuri yasumun' desu yo. 6. Uketori ga nakereba nanimo dekimasen. 7. Garasu no huta o kowasanaide kudasai. 8. Saiban no kekka o hanasimasu kara gozi ni o-ide nasai (irassyai). 9. Zyotyuu wa isogasii desu kara zibun de heya o soozi sita hoo ga ii desu. 10. Ano hito no heya e hairu ni wa kono to o akenakereba ikemasen. 11. Rondon e iki sae sureba ano hito ni au koto ga dekirun' desu ga nee. 12. Haizara ga nakereba hutuu no sara de ii desu. 13. Ano rippa na tatemono o goran nasai.　14. Tenki ga warukereba zimusyo e konaide kudasai.　15. Kono kudamono wa taihen oisii desu; sukosi o-agari nasai.

Exercise 19 (p. 108)

I.　1. Will the Prime Minister's carriage pass in front of the school? I don't know.　2. As a suspicious-looking man was hiding in the grass, I reported (the matter) to the police.　3. I want a few strawberries, so please deliver some of your best ones.　4. I am trying to collect Western postage stamps, but the collection doesn't grow very quickly.　5. I ran into Mr. Ooyama in the street, so we talked a little and then separated.　6. I got my suit quite wet trying to put the fire out with some water.　7. What I want is some white thread; I've got plenty of black.　8. I can hear it crying, but I can't see it.　9. When I tried to listen to the wireless the light went out.　10. As we wanted to go to the cinema we sent the children to bed earlier than usual.　11. I want to take a photograph of the cat, but it is moving and I can't.　12. The screws were out, but my elder brother removed the (other) nails.　13. The pine-tree that was delivered yesterday was too big, and we couldn't get it through the gate.　14. The bread that we shared out and ate I bought at the baker's opposite.　15. Please wake me at six o'clock; I want to get some luggage on the ship that leaves at eight.

II.　1. Gakkoo no mon o tootte ita toki ni Ooyama-san ni deai-masita.　2. Ano hito wa huru-hon o takusan atumete imasu ga zenbu yomu tumori de wa nai desyoo.　3. Razio de syusyoo no hanasi ga kikitakatta no desu ga hoka no hito no hanasi ga kikoe-masita.　4. Yuubin-gitte ga hosikereba mukoo no mise e itte o-kai nasai.　5. Kinoo todoita nimotu o kono kuruma ni nosemasyoo ka.　6. Hi ga kiete iru no de heya wa taihen samui desu.　7. Tomodati wa atumarimasita ga, otooto wa sugata o kakusite miemasen.　8. Ano Doituzin wa itu Doitu o tatimasita ka. Watasi wa sirimasen.　9. Otoosan ga syooti sureba keisatu ni todoketa hoo ga ii desyoo.　10. Kusa no naka ni hebi ga kakurete iru ka mo siremasen kara atira no miti o arukimasyoo.　11. Ugoite iru basu no mado kara densya no syoototu o mimasita.　12. Seiyoo no eiga ga mitakereba eki no mae no eigakan e o-ide nasai.　13. Kono kugi ga nukitai desu kara dentoo wa kesanaide kudasai.　14. Kodomo o nekasite kara pan-ya to nikuya e ikimasita.　15. Asita no asa wa itumo yori hayaku dekaketai desu kara rokuzi ni okosite kudasai.

Exercise 20 (p. 115)

I.　1. The thing standing in front of the temple looks like a flag-pole.　2. In front of the village is the sea and at the back some hills.　3. Before Mr. Imai, Mr. Torii was ambassador, but who was after him, I wonder.　4. He seems to have been away from the office since Monday of the week before last.　5. Before you clean the drawing-room, please tidy the dining-room.　6. He seems to have gone to Switzerland to do some skiing before the holiday starts.

7. Between the University and the river they say a large playing-field is being made. 8. They say the American President is ill; is that true? 9. The man standing behind the wall looked like a Chinese, but as it was night I couldn't see very well. 10. The guest who came afterwards was a young American, and he was listening interestedly to my father's story. 11. It looks as if it will leave off raining, so let's set out together after our meal. 12. A gale like the one last year may blow, so it would probably be better not to go by boat. 13. It seems that he doesn't drink Indian tea, so let's buy some China. 14. He says that, seeing a fellow who looked like a thief, he followed after him. 15. The boy who is staying with us does some things that are not childish, but just before he went to bed yesterday evening he looked sad and burst into tears.

II. 1. Yasumi ga hazimaru mikka mae ni ookaze ga huite daigaku no mon ga sukkari kowaremasita. 2. Syokuzi no ato de Suisu no kesiki no syasin o omosirosoo ni mite imasita. 3. Kono undoozyoo wa mae wa hatake datta soo desu. 4. Indo no taisi ga noru no wa kono hune rasii desu. 5. Doroboo no ato o tukeyoo to sita no wa yoru desita kara kao wa mimasen desita. 6. O-kyaku no uti ni wa Sinazin mo ita rasii desu. 7. Otoko-no-ko wa gai-kokuzin no yoo na hito o mite nakidasimasita. 8. Kono tera no mae wa niwa de usiro wa hatake desu. 9. Sono wakai otoko wa yuki ga hurisoo na hi ni mo ooba o kimasen desita. 10. Mon no mae ni takai hatazao o tateru soo desu. 11. Daitooryoo no hanasi o kiita ato de tomodati to issyo ni tya o nomi ni ikimasita. 12. Syokudoo e iku mae ni kyakusitu de sono koto o tyotto hanasita yoo desu. 13. Ano mura ni wa byooki ga nai soo desu ga hontoo rasiku nai hanasi desu. 14. Getuyoo-bi no gogo ame ga yande haresoo datta no de oka no ue ni aru kyookai e dekakemasita. 15. Kono ryokan ni wa sukii o suru rasii hito ga takusan tomatte imasu.

Exercise 21 (p. 122)

I. 1. He said, " I have never yet been to that shrine, but I should like to once." 2. It's already ten o'clock and he hasn't come yet ; I'm worried lest something may have happened to him. 3. He replied that it was fairly old, but that he thought it would be possible to use it for another year. 4. The Chairman said that he was wondering whether that chap mightn't be resigning from the company, so we ought to keep an eye on him. 5. The secretary doesn't seem to have decided yet whether he will do it on Tuesday or not. 6. Do you know when Miss Ookawa is getting married? On the tenth, I think. 7. I didn't think you were living in such a lonely place as this. 8. Please ring up and ask whether Mr. Inoue has come yet or not. 9. The monkey in the Zoo that was still alive when we went there last Sunday is said to have died this morning. 10. My uncle said to the guest, " I planted that rose last year, and see how it's flowering already (it's already flowering to that extent)." 11. I have informed my cousin by letter that my wife was coming out of hospital so that she did not have to come. 12. I wondered if it might not be foggy tomorrow too, but as there's a little wind blowing it may be fine. 13. I tried to stop the train by waving a red handkerchief, but I was not in time. 14. The teacher told him not to read so frivolous a book. 15. Do you think that fellow escaped by crossing the temple garden?

II. 1. Watasi ga sono zinzya e itta no wa mada daigaku ni ita toki desita. 2. Sensyuu no kayoo-bi no sinbun wa doko ni aru ka sitte imasu ka. 3. Kono bara wa daibu mae ni ueta no desu ga kotosi wa sakanain' d'ya nai ka to sinpai site imasu. 4. Konna sabisii mura ni wa mata sumitaku arimasen. 5. Syatyoo wa syoki ni kiri ga aru ka doo ka to kikimasita. 6. "Kanai wa isya ga kita toki ni wa mada ikite imasita," to iimasita. 7. Moo kuzi desu ga mada ii desu ka. E, mada ii desu. 8. Sono kaisya o yameta toki ni wa moo kekkon site itan' desu. 9. O-kyaku wa moo itido denwa o kakete kure to iimasita. 10. Otooto wa kesa yuubin ga atta ka doo ka siranai to henzi simasita. 11. Zyuuzi desu kara moo tera e dekaketan' d'ya nai ka to omoimasu. 12. Ozi wa itoko ni tumaranai hanasi wa sinai yoo ni (to) iimasita. 13. Anna tokoro e ikitai to omoimasen ka. 14. Kisya no mado kara ude o dasite hankati o huru yoo ni ugokasite imasita. 15. Tomodati wa sonna rippa na saru wa mita koto ga nai to iimasita.

Exercise 22 (p. 131)

I. 1. I was given both these oil-paintings by a friend, but I will give you one of them. 2. Grandmother didn't seem able to pull the cork out of the bottle, so I pulled it out for her. 3. I thought that I had put the cupboard key in the drawer, but however much I looked for it, it couldn't be found. 4. My cousin who had been ill in hospital since last year yesterday died, after all. 5. Mr. Tanaka, who came back from America last Saturday, gave me this watch. 6. The waiter brought us some ice, but we didn't want it, so I got him to take it back again. 7. Did someone throw away the big bag that I had put on the table? 8. Mr. Akai took my umbrella by mistake, it seems, and tomorrow I intend to exchange it (for the one he left behind). 9. I should like you, too, to go to the coming exhibition if you have the opportunity. 10. As it is beginning to rain, let us sow the seed some other day. 11. The mathematics teacher went home, saying that he would think of some not too difficult examination questions. 12. Picking up a curious sea-shell, I opened it to look at it, but there was nothing in it. 13. A lot of planes flew over, and the noise was so great that I placed my hands over my ears. 14. The dog heard the voice of my elder brother, who came in saying "Tadaima", and went out wagging its tail. 15. As the day after tomorrow is the birthday of the old man next door, I should like to give him something for a present.

II. 1. Tenrankai e iku mae ni kutu o migaite moraimasita. 2. Watasi wa kondo no doyoo-bi ni nyuuin simasu kara sugu kaette kite kuremasen ka. 3. Obaasan wa todana kara kasi o dasite watasi ni hitotu kuremasita. 4. Inu wa watasi no koe o kiite sippo o hutte haitte kimasita. 5. Mezurasii kai o takusan motte kaette kimasita kara anata ni mi ni kite moraitai to omoimasu. 6. Kodomo no nakigoe ga taihen yakamasikatta no de mimi ni te o atete imasita ga tootoo heya o dete simaimasita. 7. Titi ga kaette konai uti ni torikaete kimasyoo. 8. Kinoo wa tonari no oziisan no tanzyoo-bi desita kara okurimono o agemasita. 9. Tomodati kara moratta tane wa asita maku tumori desu. 10. Suugaku no sensei ga mainiti tukatte iru mannenhitu ga mitukaranakatta no de watasitati mo sagasite agemasita. 11. Matigaete koori o sutete simaimasita kara mukoo no mise e itte sukosi katte kite kudasai. 12. Hikooki ga tonde kuru oto ga kikoeta no de niwa e dete mimasita ga nanimo miemasen desita. 13. Kikai ga areba watasi wa itte mo iin' desu ga, hoka no hito ga iku koto ga dekiru ka doo ka yoku kangaete oite kudasai. 14. Ame ga hutte kimasita kara kasa o kasite kudasai. 15. Muzukasii koto na no de anata ni mo soodan site moraitai to tegami de itte kite imasu.

Exercise 23 (p. 142)

I. 1. As I have only been to that town in Summer, I don't know whether or not it is very cold in Winter. 2. He said that he would without fail be at the right-hand entrance by four o'clock, so let us wait until he comes. 3. On hearing that news my younger sister did nothing but weep. 4. In Autumn the year before last I went only as far as China, but I should like this time to go to India. 5. I only met him, a year ago just at this time, at a cinema exit in Osaka. 6. I dropped my vest on the wet floor and got it wet, so will you dry it for me by three o'clock? 7. That Italian has only recently come to Japan, but he speaks Japanese fairly well. 8. You turn to the left at that corner, and the library is the second building. 9. How far did you walk during the Spring holiday? About 30 *ri*. 10. Mr. Kimura does nothing but make insulting remarks, and the more people get annoyed, the more he seems pleased. 11. If only you promise not to do it again I shall let you off today, just this once. 12. Until we meet him and see, we shall not know whether or not he is just an ordinary scholar. 13. I have sent about five picture-books to my younger brother, who has gone into hospital. 14. When is his third girl getting married? In April next year. 15. It seems that he has drunk some poison and he looks very ill.

II. 1. Otooto wa tada naku bakari de yurusite kure to iimasen desita. 2. Doku no haitte iru no wa hidari kara sanbanme no bin dake desu. 3. Kono mati ni wa dono kurai (nannin gurai) hito ga sunde imasu ka. Rokusennin gurai desyoo. 4. Sanzi made ni matigai naku kaette kuru to itte imasita ga mada kaette (kaette kite) inai yoo desu. 5. Soto de kimono o kawakasu koto ga dekiru no wa natu dake desu. Huyu ni wa kawakimasen. 6. Imooto-san wa itu made Parii ni imasu ka. Aki made iru to omoimasu. 7. Kondo no kai ni wa Nihon no gakusya sika atumarimasen ga, rainen no haru ni wa gaikoku no gakusya mo takusan kuru soo desu. 8. Kotira (Kotiragawa) ni wa iriguti dake atte deguti wa nai yoo desu. 9. Konogoro warui sirase bakari ukeru (ukete iru) no de kaoiro ga yoku arimasen. 10. Ano Itariizin wa watasi ga atta toki ni wa Huransugo sika hanasimasen desita. 11. Kane wa ima otosita bakari desu kara mada dokoka yuka no ue ni aru desyoo. 12. Tada no kippu o moratte uresii desu ga tenrankai wa hiru (hiru no aida) sika aite imasen kara iku koto ga dekinai ka mo siremasen. 13. Kinoo nyuuin site iru tonari no kodomo ni e-hon o gosatu hodo okurimasita kara imagoro wa mite iru desyoo. 14. Ano kado o migi e magatta hito o mireba miru hodo Nihonzin rasiku nai to omoimasu. 15. Hito no warukuti bakari itte ita Tamura-san wa watasi ga okotte kara nisyuukanme ni Oosaka e itte simaimasita.

Exercise 24 (p. 148)

I. 1. What has happened to these scissors? I can't cut anything with them. 2. What sort of goods are imported from the Far East? 3. Please excuse me, I was the one who made the mistake; from now on I shall be very careful. 4. As there is still plenty of time until the departure of the train, shall we go and look at the shops in front of the station or something? 5. The teacher asked whether or not there wasn't anyone who would help Mr. Torii. 6. Provided it doesn't cost any money, I don't mind any sort of plan. 7. He is saying that he wants to give up his present work and do something more easy. 8. Where he spent his Summer holiday was neither in Switzerland nor in Italy. 9. Don't worry about your hat! Look at your face in the mirror—it's disgraceful how dirty it is! Go and wash it at once! 10. What happened to the farm? I sold it because my losses on it were too great. 11. How are you going to England? I am going via America. 12. Please explain to me in detail the meaning of the word *syoogun*. 13. Please do not hesitate to tell me all about it, for I intend to try to do all I can for you. 14. It doesn't have to be today; please come on Thursday if you can. 15. Please excuse me; there was some business that I simply couldn't avoid, and it has made me late.

II. 1. Dooka sitan' desu ka. Ie, doo sitan' de mo arimasen. 2. Kore o kiru ni wa doo yuu hasami ga itiban ii desyoo ka. 3. Doomo sumimasen, kaimono ni itta no de okuremasita. 4. Mada sukosi hayai yoo desu kara sanpo ni de mo ikimasyoo ka. 5. Donna eigo no zibiki de mo ii desu. 6. Dareka issyo ni ongakkai e ikitai hito wa inai ka to itte imasita. 7. Nanika atarasii keikaku de mo kangaete irun' desyoo. 8. Kinoo wa soozi o site isogasii hi o sugosimasita ga kyoo wa raku na sigoto sika site imasen. 9. Kono kotoba no imi wa "kagami" de mo "tokei" de mo arimasen. 10. Yunyuu sita sinamono wa doo sitan' desu ka. Yasuku urana-kereba naranakatta no de son ga ookikatta desu. 11. Tooyoo e wa doo ikimasu ka. Dekiru dake hayaku ikitai no desu ga mada doo iku ka kimete imasen. 12. Asita noozyoo e iku ka doo ka (doozo) kiite kudasai. 13. Nandemo go-enryo naku kiite kudasai; kuwa-siku setumei site agemasu. 14. Watasi no yoo wa doodemo ii desu; issyo ni itte agemasyoo. 15. Doositemo tasukete agetai to omoimasu kara nanika tekitoo na sigoto ga areba sirasete kudasai.

Exercise 25 (p. 154)

I. 1. The robber was not captured, although the policeman tried to catch him. 2. The girl who was playing in the front garden was bitten in the leg by a dog and burst out crying. 3. That officer was robbed of his purse and couldn't pay the bill. 4. The potatoes have all been thoroughly (cleanly) peeled. 5. If you want to find out where that town is look at the map hanging on the wall. 6. The children made such a disturbance that they were scolded by their parents. 7. This doll was made by my younger sister, but it's so well done that the child next door says that she wants it. 8. At first he couldn't write (characters) very well, but he practised hard, and now he's certainly writing superbly. 9. The door that I thought I had closed was not properly shut. 10. My eldest son, who was praised by his headmaster, is very pleased, but my next son, who was kept in school, is looking very sad. 11. That old lady was helped on to the bus by a young woman. 12. As I was some time having my passport examined, I was not able to land at once. 13. A lot of swords that the enemy had left abandoned are laid out in rows. 14. Both the fellows who had had a fight were taken off to the police. 15. The cat kept by the man next door was hit with a stick and died.

II. 1. Nimotu wa itu todokimasu ka. Asita ka asatte todoku to omoimasu. 2. Zinan wa zi ga zyoozu na (zi o zyoozu ni kaku) no de sensei ni homeraremasita. 3. Kyaku ni korarete ongaku no rensyuu ga dekimasen desita. 4. Mon ga simatte iru (simete aru) no de hairemasen. 5. Sono onna no hito ga katte iru neko o tukamaeyoo to sita seinen (wakai otoko) wa ki kara otimasita. 6. Inu ni asi o kamareta kodomo no oya wa zyunsa o turete kaette kimasita. 7. Kirei ni katazukete aru heya de katana o mite imasita. 8. Kinoo teki no syookoo ga sannin tukamarimasita. 9. Otooto wa gakkoo no mae de kenka o site kootyoo ni sikararemasita. 10. Sono oziisan wa ooki na otoko ni boo de utarete kaneire o nusumaremasita. 11. Kabe ni kakete aru tizu wa taihen hurui desu kara teeburu no ue ni aru no o goran nasai. 12. Omote no niwa de asonde ita imooto wa ningyoo o kowasaremasita. 13. Sibaraku kanzyoo ga haraemasen desita kara taihen sinpai simasita. 14. Sono imo no kawa wa taberaremasen yo. 15. Hutaritomo ryokoo-menzyoo o motte inakatta no de zyooriku ga dekimasen desita.

Exercise 26 (p. 162)

I. 1. This watch is no good, for it keeps on gaining and losing. 2. The fish I bought with the intention of eating it last night developed an unpleasant smell and became uneatable. 3. I feel that I have met that musician before. 4. The doctor told him to lie quietly in bed because the illness might become serious. 5. He is not yet used to the life of a blind man. 6. He does drive a car, but it doesn't look as if he has become very skilful yet. 7. Do you think it will rain? No, it's beginning to get a little cloudy, but there won't be any rain, I think. 8. There's some strange noise upstairs,

I tell you ; it sounds as though someone is walking about. 9. Do you believe that there's the possibility of his agreeing? 10. It has been decided that when my younger brother leaves the University next year he will become a government official. 11. He *did* return the money he borrowed, but it was after a long time had passed. 12. As an actor he's a very interesting chap, but as an individual he's quite worthless. 13. A (glass) window broke, and he hurt his face and hands very badly. 14. The children went to the Botanical Gardens, and they say it was a very profitable visit. 15. It was not I who arranged for him to be punished.

II. 1. Ima wa yakunin ni natte seikatu wa raku rasii (na yoo) desu. 2. Matuo-san wa syokubutuen e iki wa simasita ga amari nagaku wa tomaranakatta yoo desu. 3. Karita kane o kaesu to itte imasu ga hontoo desyoo ka. Iya, kaesi wa simasen yo, kane ga nain' desu kara nee. 4. Yakusya dattari ongakka dattari site ite omosiroi hito desu yo. 5. Kono bara wa taihen ii nioi ga simasu ne. 6. Sakuban nikai de mita yoo na ki ga surun' desu. 7. Kega o sita toki ni wa nani mo kan-zinakattan' desu ga ima wa taihen itai desu. 8. Nareru to (narereba) zibun de unten dekiru yoo ni naru desyoo. 9. Amari yakamasikereba dokoka sizuka na tokoro e iku koto ni simasyoo. 10. Kozin to site wa ii desu ga syusyoo to site wa dame desu. 11. Mekura ni natta tomodati to issyo ni ikimasu kara sukosi okureru ka mo siremasen. 12. Kemusi ga ooi no de niwa no sigoto ga iya ni narimasita. 13. Ame ni narimasita ga watasitati wa susumanakereba ikemasen desita. 14. Ano hito ga sansei suru kanoosei wa arimasen. 15. Garasu-mado wa arimasita ga kumotte kita no de heya no naka de hon o yomu koto ga dekinaku narimasita.

Exercise 27 (p. 169)

I. 1. Our boy says that when he grows up he'll become a scientist. 2. If you go out you'll be cold, so you'd better stay indoors all day today. 3. While they were dancing we went out into the garden. 4. On account of the floods people who live beside the river had to flee towards the hills. 5. The watchman's corpse had been dumped in the wood, but nothing is known about why he was killed. 6. The number of members has gone right down, so we ought to do something to increase them again. 7. My intention was to go to the seaside as soon as the holidays began, but I have been disappointed, for it has rained every day. 8. I thought I had a cold and took my temperature ; it was 38° (C.). 9. I was ten when my father went to America. 10. We discussed it while we drank our coffee. 11. My parents are on the ship which is due to reach this port tomorrow. 12. This primary school exists for the purpose of educating blind children. 13. You mustn't go to the hospital like that. 14. The captain should have been back by nine o'clock, but even at ten he had not appeared. 15. I tried to telephone the rice merchant so as to order some rice, but I was quite unable to get through.

II. 1. Kinoo kaette kuru hazu no otooto ga tukanakatta no de ryoosin wa gakkari simasita. 2. Ano onna-no-ko wa uta o utai-nagara odotte imasu. 3. Sanzi ni demasita kara moo byooin ni tuite iru hazu desu. 4. Kono mama de netu o hakatte mo ii desu ka. 5. Zyuuitizi ni naru to minna koohii o nomi ni dekakemasita. 6. Nan no tame ni sonna tokoro de kodomo o kyooiku simasu ka. 7. Nantoka site sono kagakusya ni awanakute wa narimasen. 8. Hune ga minato ni haittara sentyoo wa byooki ni narimasita. 9. Oomizu ga atta tame ni syoogakkoo e kuru kodomo no kazu ga hette imasita. 10. Kinoo (wa) itinitizyuu sizuka na mori no naka de hon o yonde sugosimasita. 11. Tatemono no naka e hairu to bannin ga sitai o misete kuremasita. 12. Kaiin ni naru to kono sinamono ga taihen yasuku kaemasu (kau koto ga dekimasu). 13. Ano hito ga inai aida ni kane o watasite kudasai. 14. Ano komeya wa kome o todokeru kuruma no kazu o huyasu hazu da soo desu. 15. Huku o tyuumon sita hito wa mise no to o aketa mama de dete ikimasita.

Exercise 28 (p. 174)

I. 1. Please do not allow the children to throw a ball in the garden. 2. I thought I would put the bird that I caught yesterday in a cage, but I took pity on it and let it go. 3. He was saying that he had been made to invite even some people that he didn't want to go with him. 4. That patient requested the doctor not to allow anybody to touch his stomach. 5. I let my daughter go to the cinema with that young man. 6. I can't go, so I intend to have my eldest son represent me. 7. I tried to get them to write their names and addresses, but as there were some who couldn't write, I had them get somebody else to do it for them. 8. I wonder if I can get you to have me called so as not to be late for the first train. 9. The teacher had his assistant investigate some dialect differences. 10. I try to get him to save some money, but he says he can't with his present low salary. 11. My younger brother always does things to make people laugh. 12. Please have the maid open some tinned meat and bring it in. 13. For the reason that I know the way best, I was made the guide. 14. A lot of people were standing in front of the house, but when they saw me (my face) they let me through without saying anything. 15. My son is not very strong, so I don't want to make him study unreasonably.

II. 1. Watasi wa sukosi mo ikitaku nakatta no desu ga tootoo ikaserarete simaimasita. 2. Gogo kodomo o tama o nagete aso-basemasita. 3. Musuko wa mainiti byoonin o okoraseru koto o simasu. 4. Kanzume no kudamono o kai ni musume o yarimasita. 5. Kawaisoo datta no de nigasimasita. 6. Kane o sukosi tamesase-tain' desu ga ima no mama de wa dekinai desyoo. 7. Onaka ga taihen itakatta no de zyotyuu ni isya o yobasemasita. 8. Ressya ga tuku made mataseru yoo ni tanomimasita. 9. Kanai ni namae to zyuusyo o kikasemasyoo ka. 10. Kootyoo wa sensei ni kodomotati ni hoogen o tukawasenai yoo ni (to) iimasita. 11. Kyoo wa taihen samui desu kara inu o uti no naka e o-ire nasai. 12. Sukunai kyuu-ryoo de muri ni hatarakasaremasu. 13. Kono gakkoo o daihyoo suru hito mo sasowasete kudasai. 14. Miti-annai o saseyoo to simasita ga syooti simasen desita. 15. Tigai ga amari ookii no de zyosyu ni riyuu o sirabesasemasita.

Exercise 29 (p. 184)

1. It's autumn now; the colour of leaves has begun to change. 2. It's rather a difficult thing to say, so I wonder whether to keep silent about it. 3. These gloves are too small, and I can't get them on. 4. The paint which you went and bought yesterday is very easy to use, isn't it? 5. These fireworks catch fire very easily, so let's put them in a safe place. 6. They started to build it last year, but it is not finished yet. 7. I was the first one to undertake the task of educating the natives here. 8. His hat was caught up in the tree. 9. The red-faced man with a fierce look in his eyes pulled the ugly man's ear. 10. If that child sees that other people are itching, he too exclaims, "I've got an itch". 11. I only tell her to do simple things, but she forgets half of them. 12. The sentences I wrote yesterday are not satisfactory, so I am rewriting them. 13. In this book there are a lot of places where Mr. Hayakawa has written something in in red pencil. 14. Unfortunately the address has not been taken down. 15. The dog bit off the wool with which my younger sister was knitting a sock. 16. At the beginning we were listening seriously to his talk, but during the course of it we burst out laughing. 17. Even a child (Even if one is not an adult one) can put together these bookshelves. 18. He is extremely tall, and I have to look up at him when I talk to him. 19. My elder brother went to the station to see his friend off. 20. I like climbing a mountain and looking down at the scenery below. 21. When my second son came home from school he threw his books on to the table and went out. 22. Be careful not to swallow any bones. 23. The children were afraid of the dog and fled. 24. One of my buttons has come off; will you please sew it on? 25. I remember his face, but I simply can't recall his name. 26. Even now, I am unable to give up the idea of going to America. 27. When you meet him you should talk to him calmly and slowly. 28. Now please don't get so excited, but calm yourself down. 29. It is bad for one's health to inhale tobacco smoke. 30. This blotting-paper doesn't blot very well, does it? 31. When I opened the back door all the birds which were (had settled) on the tree flew up in the air. 32. Shouting, "Fire, fire!" a naked man came running out. 33. The youth who saw a child fall in the river jumped into the water with his trousers on. 34. I am unable to go out because of illness, so please cancel tomorrow's appointment. 35. When I went to get back my gold cigarette-case, contrary to my expectations, I was treated very roughly. 36. The people who have just moved in next door are very unsociable. 37. He bolted his food and rushed out. 38. He said that he crashed into the wall when trying to avoid a child. 39. He resigned from the firm because he was afraid of making himself disliked (of being disliked). 40. He wished to sit on the *tatami*, but I was afraid he'd get a pain in his legs, so I got him to sit in a chair.

GLOSSARY

(*a.*, adjective; *adv.*, adverb; *conj.*, conjunction; *imp.*, imperative; *int.*, interjection; *n.*, noun; *num.*, numeral; *p.*, pronoun; *part.*, particle; *pref.*, prefix; *suf.*, suffix; *u.*, unit; *vi.*, verb intransitive; *vt.*, verb transitive).

a, aa *int.* expression of surprise, admiration, sorrow, pain, dislike, etc.

aa *adv.* in that way, like that

abekobe na *a.* back to front, the other way about
   abekobe ni *adv.*

abunai *a.* dangerous

abura *n.* oil, fat, grease
   abura-e *n.* oil-painting

agaru *vi.* rise, ascend; (polite, 2nd person) eat, drink, smoke
   agatte iru be up

ageru *vt.* raise, give to someone else (*see* Lesson 22)

ago *n.* chin, jaw

ai *n.* love
   ai-suru *vt.*
   aizin *n.* lover

aida *n.* interval, space between

ainoko *n.* half-blood, mixed blood

aisatu *n.* greeting, salutation
   aisatu suru *vi.*

aite *n.* companion

akai *a.* red
   aka *n.*

akari *n.* light

akarui *a.* bright, light

akeru *vt.* open

aki *n.* autumn

aki *n.* gap, space, vacancy

aku *vi.* become open
   aite iru is open

akubi *n.* yawn

amai *a.* sweet (taste), soft

amari (anmari) *adv.* too much, (with neg.) not very

ame *n.* rain

Amerika *n.* America
   Amerikazin *n.* an American

ami *n.* net

amimono *n.* knitting, knitwork

amu *vt.* knit

ana *n.* hole

anata *p.* you

ane *n.* elder sister

ani *n.* elder brother

anna *a,* that sort of, such a . . . as that
   anna ni *adv.* to that extent

annai *n.* guide; invitation
   annai suru *vt.*
   annaizyo *n.* enquiry office, information bureau

ano *a.* that (*see* Lesson 3)

anone *int.* expression of calling attention

anoo *int.* ditto, *but with a certain politeness and hesitation*

ansin *n.* peace of mind
   ansin suru *vi.* be free from anxiety

anzen na *a.* safe
   anzen ni *adv.*

aoi *a.* blue
   ao *n.*

arau *vt.* wash

are *p.* that over there (*see* Lesson 4)

ari *n.* ant

arigatoo *int.* thank you (*see* Lesson 30)

arisama *n.* situation, state

aru *vi.* be (*see* Lessons 1 and 5)

aru *a.* a certain

arukooru *n.* alcohol, spirits

aruku *vi.* walk
  arukihazimeru *vi.* start to walk
  arukituzukeru *vi.* continue to walk
aruminyuumu *n.* aluminium
asa *n.* morning
  asa-gohan *n.* breakfast
asa *n.* flax, hemp, linen
asai *a.* shallow
asatte *n.* and *adv.* the day after tomorrow
asi *n.* leg, foot
  asiato *n.* footprint
  asikubi *n.* ankle
  asiyubi *n.* toe
asita (asu) *n.* and *adv.* tomorrow
asobi *n.* play, game, pastime
  asobiaite *n.* companion in play or game
asobu *vi.* play, amuse oneself
  asonde iru be idle, be playing
asoko *p.* over there (*see* Lesson 1)
atama, *n.* head
atarasii *a.* new
atarimae na *a.* proper, reasonable, natural
ataru *vi.* strike against, hit the mark ; warm oneself
  atatte iru has hit the mark
atatakai (atataka na) *a.* warm
atena *n.* address
ateru *vt.* hit, put, guess ; expose to heat
atira (atti) *p.* over there (*see* Lesson 10)
ato *n.* what is left behind, time after
atui *a.* hot
atui *a.* thick
atumaru *vi.* gather
  atumatte iru be together, have gathered
atumeru *vt.* collect
au *vi.* meet
azi *n.* taste, flavour
Azia *n.* Asia
azukaru *vt.* and *vi.* receive in trust, take charge of ; take part in

azukatte iru have received in trust, have taken charge of
azukeru *vt.* entrust

baai *n.* circumstances, case
bai *n.* double
  -bai *u.* (*see* Appendix II)
baka *n.* fool
  bakabakasii *a.* ridiculous, foolish
  baka na *a.* foolish
  baka ni *adv.* awfully
bakari part (*see* Lesson 23)
baketu *n.* bucket
bakkin *n.* fine, penalty
bakuhatu *n.* explosion
  bakuhatu suru *vi.*
ban *n.* evening
  -ban *u.* (*see* Appendix II)
  ban-gohan *n.* evening meal
ban *n.* watch, duty ; one's turn ; number
bangoo *n.* number
-banme *suf.* (*see* Lesson 23)
bannin *n.* watchman
banti *n.* plot number, house number
  -banti *u.* (*see* Appendix II)
bara *n.* rose
bas-suru *vt.* punish
basu *n.* bus
basya *n.* carriage, coach
bata *n.* butter
batu *n.* punishment
Beikoku *n.* U.S.A.
  Beikokuzin *n.* an American
benkyoo *n.* study, assiduity
  benkyoo suru *vt.* and *vi.*
benri na *a.* convenient
  benri ni *adv.*
bentoo *n.* lunch, packed lunch
  bentoo-bako *n.* lunch-box
benzyo *n.* lavatory
beru *n.* bell
Berurin *n.* Berlin
betu *n.* distinction, exception
  betubetu ni *adv.* separately
  betu na *a.* another, different
  betu ni *adv.* additionally, especially
biiru *n.* beer

bikko *n.* lameness, cripple

bin *n.* bottle
  bin-zume *n.* bottling, bottled goods

binboo *n.* poverty
  binboo na *a.* poor
  binboonin *n.* the poor
  binboo suru *vi.* become poor
  binboo site iru be in poverty

binsen *n.* notepaper

bizyutu (bizitu) *n.* art, the fine arts
  bizyutukan *n.* art museum, art gallery

boku *p.* I (*see* Lesson 30)

bonyari (to) *adv.* dimly, distractedly
  bonyari suru *vi.* be dull, be absent-minded

boo *n.* stick, bar

boosi *n.* hat, cap

botan *n.* button

-bu *u.* (*see* Appendix II)

bubun *n.* section, portion

budoo *n.* grape
  budoosyu *n.* (grape) wine

bukiyoo na *a.* clumsy
  bukiyoo ni *adv.*

bukkyoo *n.* Buddhism

bun *n.* part, segment, fraction
  -bun *u.* (*see* Appendix II)

bunboogu *n.* stationery
  bunbooguya *n.* stationer('s)

bungaku *n.* literature

bunka *n.* culture, civilization

bunpoo *n.* grammar

bunryoo *n.* quantity, measure

bunsyoo *n.* sentence, writing

burasi *n.* brush

buriki *n.* tin-plate

buta *n.* pig

buturi *n.* physical laws, physics
  buturigaku *n.* physics
  buturigakusya *n.* physicist

-byoo *u.* (*see* Appendix II)

byooin *n.* hospital

byooki *n.* illness
  byooki na *a.* ill
  byoonin *n.* person who is ill

da *vi.* be (*see* Lesson 5)

dai *n.* stand, base

K

-dai *u.* (*see* Appendix II)

dai- *pref.* (*see* Lesson 23)
  daiiti *adv.* firstly

daibu *adv.* quite a lot

daibubun *n.* greater part, majority

daidokoro *n.* kitchen

daigaku *n.* university

daihyoo *n.* representative, representation
  daihyoo suru *vt.*
  daihyoosya *n.* representative
  daihyooteki na *a.* representative, typical

daikon *n.* giant radish

daiku *n.* carpenter

daimyoo *n.* *daimyoo*, Japanese feudal lord

daisuu *n.* algebra

daitooryoo *n.* president (U.S.A., etc.)

daizin *n.* minister of state

daizyoobu na *a.* safe, requiring no anxiety

dakara *conj.* so, therefore, accordingly

dake *part.* (*see* Lessons 15 and 23)

damaru *vi.* become silent
  damatte iru is silent

damasu *vt.* deceive, cheat

dame na *a.* no good

dan *n.* step

dandan *adv.* by degrees, gradually

danna(san) *n.* master of a house, husband

dantai *n.* party, group, body, company

dare *p.* who
  daredemo *p.* (*see* Lesson 17)
  dareka *p.* (*see* Lesson 10)
  daremo *p.* (*see* Lesson 10)

dasu *vt.* send out, take out, put out

de *part.* (*see* Lesson 5)

deau *vi.* encounter

deguti *n.* exit

dekakeru *vi.* go out

dekiagaru *vi.* be completed

dekiru *vi.* be possible, be made, be produced
  dekite iru is ready

denki *n.* electricity

denpa *n.* electric wave

denpoo *n.* telegram

densin *n.* telegraph

    densinkyoku *n.* telegraphic office

densya *n.* electric train, tram

dentoo *n.* electric light

denwa *n.* telephone

    denwa-bangoo *n.* telephone number

    denwa-kookankyoku *n.* telephone exchange (office)

    denwasitu *n.* telephone room, telephone kiosk

    denwatyoo *n.* telephone directory

deru *vi.* go out, come out

    dete iru is out

desu *vi.* be (*see* Lesson 5)

-do *u.* (*see* Appendix II)

Doitu *n.* Germany

    Doitugo *n.* German (language)

    Doituzin *n.* a German

doko *p.* where

    dokodemo *p.* (*see* Lesson 17)

    dokoka *p.* (*see* Lesson 10)

    dokomo *p.* (*see* Lesson 10)

doku *n.* poison

donata *p.* who (deferential level)

donna *a.* what sort of, what kind of

    donna ni *adv.* to what extent

dono *a.* which (*see* Lesson 10)

doo *n.* copper

    dooka *n.* copper coin

doo *adv.* in what way, how

    doodemo *adv.* (*see* Lesson 24)

    dooka *adv.* (*see* Lesson 24)

    doomo *adv.* (*see* Lesson 24)

    doosite *adv.* why

    doositemo *adv.* (*see* Lesson 24)

    doozo *adv.* (*see* Lesson 24)

doobutu *n.* animal

    doobutuen *n.* zoo

    doobutugaku *n.* zoology

    doobutugakusya *n.* zoologist

doogu *n.* tool, furniture

    doogu-bako *n.* tool-box

dore *p.* which (*see* Lesson 10)

    doredemo *p.* (*see* Lesson 17)

doreka *p.* (*see* Lesson 10)

doremo *p.* (*see* Lesson 10)

doroboo *n.* robber

dotira (dotti) *p.* which of two (*see* Lesson 10)

    dotirademo *p.* (*see* Lesson 17)

    dotiraka *p.* (*see* Lesson 10)

    dotiramo *p.* (*see* Lesson 10)

doyoo-bi *n.* Saturday

dozin *n.* native

e *n.* picture, drawing, painting

    e-hagaki *n.* picture postcard

    e-hon *n.* picture-book

    e-kaki *n.* artist

e *part.* (*see* Lesson 6)

e (ee) *int.* (*see* Lesson 11)

e *int.* expression of surprise, anger, disgust, contempt, etc.

eda *n.* branch

eeto *int.* 'let me see'

eiga *n.* film

    eigakan *n.* cinema

Eigo *n.* English (language)

Eikoku *n.* Great Britain

    Eikokuzin *n.* an Englishman, the British

eikyoo *n.* influence, effect

    eikyoo suru *vi.*

eki *n.* station

    ekityoo *n.* station-master

-en *u.* (*see* Appendix II)

enpitu *n.* pencil

enryo *n.* reserve, regard for another's feelings

    enryo-naku *adv.* without reserve

    enryo suru *vi.* and *vt.*

entotu *n.* chimney

enzin *n.* engine

erabu *vt.* choose

erai *a.* great, remarkable

fooku *n.* fork

ga *part.* (*see* Lesson 1)

ga *conj.* (*see* Lesson 14)

gaikoku *n.* foreign countries

    gaikokugo *n.* foreign language

    gaikokuzin *n.* foreigner

gaikoo *n.* diplomacy
  gaikookan *n.* diplomatic official
gakkari suru *vi.* be disappointed
gakkoo *n.* school
gakumon *n.* learning, studies
gakusei *n.* student
gakusya *n.* scholar
gannen *n.* first year (of year period)
ganzitu *n.* New Year's Day
garasu *n.* glass (substance)
  garasu-do *n.* glass door
  garasu-mado *n.* glass window
-garu *suf.* (*see* Lesson 29)
  (abuna-, atu-, ita-, iya-, kayu-kitana-, kowa-, mezurasi-, okasi-, osi-, sabisi-, samu-)
gasorin *n.* petrol
gasu *n.* gas
-gawa *suf.* side
  (atira-, dotira-, hidari-, higasi-, kata-, kita-, kotira-, migi-, minami-, mukoo-, nisi-, ryoo-, sotira-)
gei *n.* art, craft
geinin *n.* artiste
geisya *n.* geisya (girl), woman entertainer in Japan
geizyutu (geizitu), *n.* art
  geizyutuka *n.* artist
gendai *n.* our own time, contemporary times
gen-in *n.* cause
genkan *n.* front door, hall
genki na *a.* vigorous, high-spirited
  genki ni *adv.*
genzai *n.* present time
-getu *u.* and *suf.* month
getuyoo-bi *n.* Monday
gimu *n.* duty, obligation
  gimu-kyooiku *n.* compulsory education
gin *n.* silver
  gin-dokei *n.* silver watch
  gin-iro *n.* silver colour
  ginka *n.* silver coin
ginkoo *n.* bank (financial)
  ginkooin *n.* bank clerk (employee)

giron *n.* argument, discussion
gizyutu (gizitu) *n.* technics
go *num.* five
go- *pref.* (*see* Lessons 18 and 30)
gogaku *n.* language study
  gogakusya *n.* linguist
gogatu *n.* May
gogo *n.* and *adv.* afternoon, p.m.
gohan *n.* meal, boiled rice
gomi *n.* dust, rubbish
  gomibako *n.* dust-bin
gomu *n.* gum, India rubber
  gomu-gutu *n.* rubber shoes
  gomu-wa *n.* rubber band
-goo *u.* (*see* Appendix II)
goozyoo *a.* obstinate
goran (*see* Lessons 18 and 30)
-goro (koro) *suf.* time (*see* Lesson 23)
gotisoo *n.* feast, treat
  gotisoo-sama *n.* thanks for another's hospitality
  gotisoo suru *vt.* entertain with food and drinks, give hospitality
gozaimasu *vi.* be (*see* Lesson 30)
gozen *n.* and *adv.* forenoon, a.m.
guai *n.* condition
gun *n.* sub-prefecture (*see* Lesson 23)
gunkan *n.* warship
gunpuku *n.* military uniform
guntai *n.* military, armed forces
gunzin *n.* members of the armed forces
gurai (kurai) *part* (*see* Lessons 15 and 23)
-guramu *u.* (*see* Appendix II)
guuzen ni *adv.* by chance
gyogyoo *n.* fishery
-gyoo *u.* (*see* Appendix II)

ha *int.* (*see* **hai**)
ha *n.* tooth
  ha-isya *n.* dentist
  hamigaki *n.* toothpaste
ha *n.* blade
  hamono *n.* edged tool, cutlery
ha *n.* leaf
haba *n.* width

hadaka *n.* nakedness
hae (hai) *n.* fly (insect)
hagaki *n.* postcard
haha *n.* mother
hai *n.* ashes
  hai-iro *n.* ash colour, grey
  haizara *n.* ash tray
hai *n.* lungs
hai (ha) *int.* (*see* Lesson 11)
-hai *u.* (*see* Appendix II)
haiken suru *vt.* see, look at (depreciatory) (*see* Lesson 30)
hairu *vi.* go in, come in
  haitte iru be in
hakama *n. hakama*, Japanese skirt
hakari *n.* measure, balance, scales
hakaru *vt.* measure
hakken *n.* discovery
  hakken suru *vt.*
  hakkensya *n.* discoverer
hakkiri (to) *adv.* clearly, definitely
  hakkiri suru *vi.* become clear
hako *n.* box
  -hako *u.* (*see* Appendix II)
haku *vi.* wear, put on (trousers, footwear)
hakubutukan *n.* museum
hakuzin *n.* white man
hakuzyoo suru *vt.* and *vi.* confess
hamaru *vi.* get into, become fitted in
  hamatte itu be fitted in
hameru *vt.* fit round, insert
han- *pref.* half
  hanbun *n.* and *adv.* half
  hanniti *n.* and *adv.* half-day
  han-tosi *n.* and *adv.* half-year
  han-tuki *n.* and *adv.* half-month
-han *suf.* half
hana *n.* nose
hana *n.* flower
  hanami *n.* flower-viewing
  hanawa *n.* wreath
  hanaya *n.* florist, flower shop
hanabi *n.* fireworks

hanareru *vi.* separate, come off, depart
  hanarete iru be apart from
hanasi *n.* speech, story, talk
  hanasiaite *n.* someone to talk to
hanasu *vt.* separate, disconnect, let go
hanasu *vt.* speak
hane *n.* feather, wing
hankati *n.* handkerchief
hantai *n.* opposition
  hantai suru *vi.*
haori *n. haori*, Japanese coat
harau *vt.* pay off, wipe off
hareru *vi.* clear up, become clear (weather)
  harete iru be clear
hari *n.* needle
  harisigoto *n.* needlework
harigane *n.* (piece of) wire, wiring
haritukeru *vt.* stick on, paste on
haru *n.* spring (season)
haru *vt.* stick on, stretch over
hasami *n.* scissors
hasi *n.* chopstick
hasi *n.* bridge
hasigo *n.* ladder, stairs
hasira *n.* pillar, column
hasiru *vi.* run
hata *n.* flag
  hatazao *n.* flagpole
hatake *n.* field (cultivated but not rice)
hataraku *vi.* work
hatati *n.* twenty years of age
hati *n.* bee, wasp
hati *num.* eight
hatigatu *n.* August
hatudooki *n.* motor, engine
hatuka *n.* and *adv.* twentieth day, twenty days
hatumei *n.* invention
  hatumeika *n.* inventor
  hatumei suru *vt.*
hayai *a.* early, quick
hayasi *n.* wood, forest
hazi *n.* shame, disgrace
hazimaru *vi.* begin
  hazimatte iru have begun

hazime *n.* beginning
hazimeru *vt.* begin
hazimete *adv.* for the first time
hazu *n.* (*see* Lesson 27)
hebi *n.* snake
hei *n.* wall
heihoo *n.* square
   heihoo-meetoru *n.* square
   metre
heiki na *a.* calm, unmoved
heikin *n.* average, mean
heikoo *n.* parallel
   heikoosen *n.* parallel lines
   heikoo suru *vi.* run parallel to
heitai *n.* soldier, troops
heiwa *n.* peace
hen *n.* region, vicinity
hen na *a.* strange, peculiar, sus-
   picious (looking)
   hen ni *adv.*
henzi *n.* reply
   henzi suru *vi.*
herasu *vt.* cause to diminish
heru *vi.* decrease
   hette iru be less than before
heta na *a.* unskilful, inexpert
heya *n.* room
hi *n.* sun, day
hi *n.* fire, light
hidari *n.* left
hidoi *a.* terrible, awful
higasi *n.* east
hige *n.* moustache, beard
hikari *n.* light, ray, flash
hikaru *vi.* shine
-hiki *u.* (*see* Appendix II)
hikidasi *n.* drawer
hikidasu *vt.* take out, draw out
hikitoru *vt.* take over, take back ;
   expire
hikitukeru *vt.* attract, fascinate
hikiukeru *vt.* undertake (responsibility, etc.)
hikkakaru *vi.* become caught up
   (on wire, etc.)
   hikkakatte iru be caught up
hikoo *n.* flying
   hikooka *n.* aviator
   hikooki *n.* aeroplane
   hikoosen *n.* airship
   hikoo-yuubin *n.* air mail

hikoozyoo *n.* aerodrome
hiku *vt.* pull, play (stringed
   instrument)
hikui *a.* low
hima *n.* time to spare
himitu *n.* secrecy
   himitu na *a.*
himo *n.* string
hinode *n.* sunrise
hinoiri *n.* sunset
hinomaru *n.* sun-flag
hipparu *vt.* drag away, pull
hiragana *n.* one form of Japanese
   syllabary
hiroi *a.* wide, large
hirou *vt.* pick up
hiru *n.* noon, daytime
   hiru-gohan *n.* midday meal
hiruma *n.* day, daytime
hito *n.* person
   hitobito *n.* people
   hitogorosi *n.* manslaughter,
   murder
   hitosasiyubi *n.* forefinger
hito- *pref.* one
   hitotu *num.* one
hitori *n.* one person
   hitorimono *n.* unmarried person, single person
   hitoride ni *adv.* of itself
hitotoori *adv.* in a general way,
   briefly
hituyoo *n.* necessity
   hituyoo na *a.*
hiza *n.* knee
hizi *n.* elbow
hizuke *n.* date, dating
hizyoo *n.* emergency
   hizyoo na *a.* extraordinary
   hizyoo ni *adv.*
ho *n.* sail
   hokakebune *n.* sailing boat
   (or ship)
hodo *part.* (*see* Lessons 15 and
   23)
hoka *n.* otherness (*see* Lesson 19)
hoken *n.* insurance
homeru *vt.* praise
hon *n.* book
   hon-bako *n.* bookcase
   hon-dana *n.* bookshelf

hon-ya *n.* bookshop

-hon *u.* (*see* Appendix II)

hone *n.* bone

hontoo *n.* truth

hontoo ni *adv.* truely

hoo *n.* direction, side

hoo (hoppeta) *n.* cheek

hooboo *n.* and *adv.* every direction, all sides

hoogen *n.* local dialect

hoohoo *n.* method, means

hookoo *n.* direction

hooritu *n.* law

hoosoo *n.* broadcast

hoosookyoku *n.* broadcasting station

hoosoo suru *vt.* and *vi.*

horu *vt.* dig

hosi *n.* star

hosii *a.* desirous

hosoi *a.* thin (of cylindrical things)

hosonagai *a.* slender

hosyu *n.* conservativeness

hosyusyugi *n.* conservatism

hosyusyugisya *n.* conservative (person)

hosyuteki na *a.* conservative

hosyutoo *n.* conservative party

hoteru *n.* hotel

hotoke (hotokesama) *n.* Buddha, the deceased

hotondo *adv.* almost ; (with negative verbs) hardly

hu *n.* urban prefecture (*see* Lesson 23)

hu- *pref.* dis-, un-, etc.

(-hituyoo na, -kanzen na, -keizai, -kenkoo, -kisoku, -mazime na, -manzoku na, -nare na, -sansei, -seikoo, -siawase, -sinsetu, -syooziki na, -tekitoo na, -ziyuu)

huben *n.* inconvenience

huben na *a.*

hude *n.* writing-brush

hueru *vi.* increase

huete iru have increased

huhei *n.* complaint

hukai *a.* deep

huku *n.* suit, dress, clothes

huku *vi.* blow

huku *vt.* wipe

hukuro *n.* bag, packet, sack

-hukuro *u.* (*see* Appendix II)

hukuzatu na *a.* complicated

-hun *u.* (*see* Appendix II)

hune *n.* boat, ship

Huransu *n.* France

Huransugo *n.* French (language)

Huransuzin *n.* a Frenchman, the French

huro *n.* bath

huroba *n.* bathroom

huru *vi.* fall (rain, snow, etc.)

huru *vt.* wave, shake

hurueru *vi.* tremble, shiver

hurui *a.* old

huru-doogu *n.* second-hand article

huru-hon *n.* second-hand book

huta *n.* lid

huta- *pref.* two

hutatu *num.* two

hutari *n.* two persons

hutoi *a.* thick, big

hutoru *vi.* grow fat

hutotte iru be fat

hutuka *n.* and *adv.* second day, two days

hutuu (ni) *adv.* usually, normally

huuhu *n.* husband and wife

huutoo *n.* envelope

huyasu *vt.* increase

huyu *n.* winter

hyaku *num.* and *u.* hundred (*see* Appendix II)

hyoo *n.* list, table, diagram

hyoomen *n.* surface

hyoozyun *n.* standard, norm

hyoozyungo *n.* standard language

i *n.* stomach

ido *n.* well

ie *n.* house

ie (iie) *int.* (*see* Lesson 11)

Igirisu *n.* England, Great Britain

Igirisuzin *n.* an Englishman, the British

ii (yoi) *a.* good
   -ii *suf.* (*see* Lesson 29)
iidasu *vt.* utter, come out with (remark, etc.)
iin *n.* member of committee
   iinkai *n.* committee meeting
iitukeru *vt.* command, tell (someone to do something)
-ika *suf.* below, less than
ikaga *adv.* how, what
ike *n.* pond
ikenai *neg. vi.* won't do
iki *n.* breath
iki *n.* going
   -iki *suf.* bound for
ikiru *vi.* become alive
   ikite iru be alive
iku *vi.* go
   itte iru have gone
ikura *adv.* how much (*see* Lesson 11)
   ikurademo *adv.* (*see* Lesson 17)
   ikuraka *adv.* (*see* Lesson 17)
   ikuramo *adv.* (*see* Lesson 17)
ikutu *adv.* how many (*see* Lesson 11)
   ikutudemo *adv.* (*see* Lesson 17)
   ikutuka *adv.* (*see* Lesson 17)
   ikutumo *adv.* (*see* Lesson 17)
ima *n.* and *adv.* present time
   imagoro *adv.* about this time
imi *n.* meaning
imo *n.* potato, sweet potato, etc.
imooto *n.* younger sister
Indo *n.* India
   Indozin *n.* an Indian
inaka *n.* the country (as opposed to town)
inki *n.* ink
inoti *n.* life
insatu *n.* printing
   insatu suru *vt.* and *vi.*
   insatuzyo *n.* printing office
inu *n.* dog
ippai *adv.* full
ippoo *n.* one side, one hand
irassyaru *vi.* (*see* Lessons 18 and 30)
ireba *n.* artificial tooth

iremono *n.* container
ireru *vt.* put in
iriguti *n.* entrance
iro *n.* colour
iroiro na *a.* various
   iroiro ni *adv.*
iru *vi.* be (*see* Lesson 3)
iru *vi.* be necessary
isi *n.* stone
isiki *n.* consciousness
   isiki suru *vt.*
   isikiteki ni *adv.*
isogasii *a.* busy
isogu *vi.* hurry
isoide *adv.* in a hurry
issyo ni *adv.* together
isu *n.* chair
isya *n.* physician, doctor
ita *n.* board, plank
itai *a.* painful
Itarii *n.* Italy
   Itariigo *n.* Italian (language)
   Itariizin *n.* an Italian
itasu *vt.* and *vi.* do (*see* Lesson 30)
iti *num.* one
itiban *adv.* most
itibubun *n.* one part
itido (ni) *adv.* one time, once
itigatu *n.* January
itigo *n.* strawberry
itiiti *adv.* one by one; without omission
ito *n.* thread
itoko *n.* cousin
itoma *n.* spare time ; leave
   o-itoma suru *vi.* take one's leave
ittai *adv.* (what, etc.) on earth
itu *adv.* when
   itudemo *adv.* (*see* Lesson 17)
   itugoro *adv.* (*see* Lesson 23)
   ituka *adv.* (*see* Lesson 12)
   itumo *adv.* (*see* Lesson 17)
itu- *pref.* five
   itutu *num.* five
ituka *n.* and *adv.* fifth day, five days
iya (iiya) *int.* (*see* Lesson 11)
iya na *a.* repugnant
   iya ni *adv.*
-izyoo *suf.* above, more than

ka *n.* mosquito
ka *part. (see* Lesson 2)
-ka *suf. (see* Lesson 10)
kaado *n.* card
kaban *n.* travelling bag, trunk
kabe *n.* wall
kaburu *vt.* wear, put on (hat, etc.)
kado *n.* corner
kaeri *n.* return
kaeru *vi.* return
　kaette iru be back
kaeru *vt.* change, alter
kaesu *vt.* give back
kaette *adv.* on the contrary
kagaku *n.* science
　kagakusya *n.* scientist
　kagakuteki na *a.* scientific
　kagakuteki ni *adv.*
kagaku *n.* chemistry
　kagakusya *n.* chemist
　kagakuteki na *a.* chemical
kagami *n.* mirror
kage *n.* shadow, shade
-kagetu *u. (see* Appendix II)
kagi *n.* key, lock
　kagiana *n.* key-hole
kagiri *n.* limit
kagiru *vt.* limit
kago *n.* cage, basket
kagu *vt.* smell
kai *n.* shell(-fish)
kai *n.* meeting, association
　kaiin *n.* member of club, etc.
　kaityoo *n.* president, chairman
　kaizyoo *n.* place of meeting
-kai *u. (see* Appendix II)
kaidan *n.* steps, stairs
kaigun *n.* navy
　kaigunsyoo *n.* Navy Ministry
kaii (kayui) *a.* itchy
kaikyuu *n.* class
kaimono *n.* shopping
kaisya *n.* company, firm
　kaisyain *n.* company employee
kakari *n.* charge, expenses
kakaru *vi.* cost, take (time), hang *(see* Lesson 29)
　kakatte iru be suspended, etc.
kakato *n.* heel

kakeru *vt.* hang up, put up, sit down, spend *(see* Lesson 29)
kakiireru *vt.* fill in (form)
kakikata *n.* manner or style of writing, penmanship
kakinaosu *vt.* rewrite
kakitoru *vt.* take down (from dictation)
　kakitori *n.* dictation
kako *n.* past days
kakomu *vt.* enclose, encircle
kaku *vt.* write, draw
kakugo *n.* resolution
　kakugo suru *vi.* be resolved
kakureru *vi.* hide
　kakurete iru be hidden
kakusu *vt.* conceal, hide
kamaeru *vt.* set up (house); put oneself in a posture
kamau *vi.* care (about)
kami (kamisama) *n.* god
kami *n.* paper
　kamiire *n.* wallet
kami *n.* hair of head
　kami-no-ke *n.* ditto
kamikiru *vt.* bite off
kaminari *n.* thunder
kamisori *n.* razor
kamoku *n.* subject or course of study
kamotu *n.* goods, cargo
　kamotusen *n.* cargo-boat
　kamotusya (kasya) *n.* goods van
　kamotu-zidoosya *n.* lorry
kamu *vt.* bite
kan *n.* tin
　kan-kiri *n.* tin opener
　kan-zume *n.* tinned goods
-kan *u. (see* Appendix II)
-kan *suf.* period, duration
kana *n.* Japanese syllabary
　kanamaziri *n.* mixed writing of Chinese characters with the Japanese syllabary
kanai *n.* (one's own) wife
kanari *adv.* considerably
kanasii *a.* sad
kandankei *n.* thermometer
kane *n.* metal, money, bell (church, etc.)

kaneire *n.* purse

kanekasi *n.* money-lending, money-lender

kanemoti *n.* wealthy man

kangae *n.* thinking, thought, idea

kangaekata *n.* one's way of thinking, one's point of view

kangaeru *vt.* consider

kango *n.* Chinese word

kankei *n.* relation, connection
  kankei suru *vi.*
  kankei site iru be connected

kanoosei *n.* possibility

kanpan *n.* deck (ship)

kansetu (ni) *adv.* indirectly

kantan na *a.* simple
  kantan ni *adv.*

kanzen na *a.* perfect
  kanzen ni *adv.*

kanzi *n.* Chinese character

kanzi *n.* feeling, sensation

kan-ziru *vt.* feel

kanzyoo *n.* emotion, sentiment
  kanzyooteki na *a.*

kanzyoo *n.* account, bill
  kanzyoogaki *n.* bill
  kanzyoo suru *vt.* count

kao *n.* face
  kaoiro *n.* complexion

kara *n.* emptiness

kara *part.* (*see* Lesson 6)

karaa *n.* collar

karada *n.* body, health

karai *a.* salty, hot (taste)

kari *n.* borrowing, debt

kari *n.* temporariness
  kari ni *adv.* provisionally, supposing

kariru *vt.* borrow
  karite iru have borrowed

karui *a.* light (weight)

kasa *n.* umbrella, lamp-shade

kasanaru *vi.* become piled
  kasanatte iru be piled up

kasaneru *vt.* pile up

kasi *n.* cake

kasi *n.* lending, loan
  kasiya *n.* house to let

kasikomaru *vi.* assent to with respect ; sit straight

kasu *vt.* lend, let (room, etc.)

kata *n.* shoulder

kata *n.* person (honorific)

kata- *pref.* one of two
  kataasi *n.* one leg
  katahoo (katappoo) *n.* one side
  katame *n.* one eye
  katate *n.* one hand
  kataude *n.* one arm

katai *a.* hard, solid, strict

katakana *n.* one form of Japanese syllabary

katana *n.* sword

katati *n.* form, shape

katazukeru *vt.* tidy up, finish off

katazuku *vi.* be put in order, be tidied
  katazuite iru be tidy

katei *n.* home, family

katoo na *a.* low, inferior

katu *vi.* win
  katte iru have won

kau *vt.* buy
  kaite *n.* buyer

kau *vt.* keep (animals)

kawa *n.* skin, peel, leather, bark

kawa *n.* river

kawairasii *a.* charming, adorable

kawaisoo na *a.* pitiable
  kawaisoo ni *adv.*

kawakasu *vt.* dry

kawaku *vi.* dry
  kawaite iru be dry

kawari *n.* change, alteration

kawaru *vi.* change, become different
  kawatte iru be different

kayoo-bi *n.* Tuesday

kazaguruma *n.* windmill

kazari *n.* ornament

kaze *n.* wind ; a cold

kazi *n.* fire (conflagration)

kazoku *n.* family, members of a family

kazu *n.* number

ke *n.* hair, fur, feather
  keito *n.* wool

kega *n.* injury

keikaku *n.* plan
  keikaku suru *t.*, and *vi.*

keikakuteki na *a.* planned, intentional

keiken *n.* experience
    keiken suru *vt.*

keikoo *n.* tendency

keisatu *n.* police
    keisatusyo *n.* police station

keisiki *n.* form, formality
    keisikiteki na *a.* formal
    keisikiteki ni *adv.*

keizai *n.* economy
    keizaigaku *n.* economics
    keizaigakusya *n.* economist
    keizai-sosiki *n.* economic system
    keizai suru *vt.* economize
    keizaiteki na *a,* economical, economic
    keizai-zyootai *n.* economic condition

kekka *n.* result

kekkon *n.* marriage
    kekkonsiki *n.* wedding
    kekkon suru *vi.* marry
    kekkon site iru be married

kekkoo na *a,* excellent

kekkyoku *adv.* after all

kemuri *n.* smoke

kemusi *n.* caterpillar

ken *n.* prefecture (*see* Lesson 23)

-ken *u.* (*see* Appendix II)

kenbutu *n.* sightseeing
    kenbutunin *n.* sightseer, spectator
    kenbutu suru *vt.*

kenka *n.* quarrel, fight
    kenka suru *vi.*

kenkoo *n.* health
    kenkoo na *a.*

kenri *n.* right, claim

kerai *n.* retainer

keredo(mo) *conj.* but

keru *vt.* kick

kesa *n.* and *adv.* this morning

kesiki *n.* scenery

kessite *adv.* definitely ; never (with neg. verbs)

kesu *vt.* extinguish

ki *n.* tree

ki *n.* yellow (colour)
    ki-iro na (kiiroi) *a.* yellow

ki *n.* feeling, spirit

kibisii *a.* strict, severe

kibun *n.* mood

kieru *vi.* go out, be extinguished
    kiete iru be out

kika *n.* geometry

kika *n.* naturalization
    kika suru *vi.*
    kika site iru be naturalized

kikai *n.* machine
    kikaiteki ni mechanically

kikai *n.* opportunity

kiki *n.* crisis

kikoeru *vi.* be heard
    kikoete iru be heard

kikoo *n.* climate, weather

kiku *vt.* listen, hear, ask

kimaru *vi.* be decided
    kimatte iru be decided

kimeru *vt.* decide

kimi *p.* you (*see* Lesson 30)

kimono *n.* *kimono*, Japanese dress, clothes

kimoti *n.* feeling

kimuzukasii *a.* moody, hard to please

kin *n.* gold
    kin-dokei *n.* gold watch
    kin-iro *n.* gold colour
    kinka *n.* gold coin

kinodoku na *a.* to be pitied

kinoo *n.* and *adv.* yesterday

kinu *n.* silk
    kinuito *n.* silk thread

kinyoo-bi *n.* Friday

kinzyo *n.* neighbourhood

kippu *n.* ticket

kiraku na *a.* carefree

kire *n.* piece (of cloth etc.)

kirei na *a.* pretty, clean, neat

kireru *vi.* be cut, break
    kirete iru be broken

kiri *n.* fog, mist

kiru *vt.* cut

kiru *vt.* put on, wear

kisen *n.* steam ship

kiseru *vt.* put clothes on somebody else

kisoku *n.* regulation
    kisokuteki na *a.* regular

kisya *n.* steam train

kisya *n.* reporter, journalist
kita *n.* north
kitanai *a.* dirty
kitigai *n.* madman
kitte *n.* stamp
kiyoo na *a.* skilful
ko *n.* child
ko- *pref.* little, child
(-inu, -neko, -tori, -uma, -usi, -yama, -yubi)
koboreru *vi.* spill
koborete iru be spilt
kobosu *vt.* spill
kodomo *n.* child
koe *n.* voice
kogitte *n.* cheque
kogitte-tyoo *n.* cheque book
koi *a.* thick (liquid), dark (colour)
koko *p.* here (see Lesson 1)
kokono- *pref.* nine
kokonotu *num.* nine
kokonoka *n.* and *adv.* ninth day, nine days
kokoro *n.* heart, mind
kokuban *n.* blackboard
kokumin *n.* nation
kokunai *n.* within a nation
kokuritu *n.* state ownership
kokusai *n.* internationalness
kokusai-kankei *n.* international relations
kokusai-rengoo *n.* United Nations
kokuzin *n.* black man
komaru *vi.* feel embarrassed, not know what to do
komatte iru be in difficulties
kome *n.* rice
komeya *n.* rice merchant('s)
komu *vi.* crowd in, push in
konde iru be crowded
komugi *n.* wheat
kon- *pref.* this
(-ban, -getu, -niti, -syuu)
kona *n.* powder, flour
kondo *n.* and *adv.* this time, next time
konkuriito *n.* concrete
konna *a.* this sort of, such a —— as that

konna ni *adv.* to this extent
kono *a.* this (see Lesson 3)
konoaida (konaida) *adv.* recently
konogoro *adv.* nowadays
konyaku *n.* betrothal, being engaged
konyaku suru *vi.*
koo *adv.* in this way, like this
kooba *n.* (see koozyoo)
koobutu *n.* mineral
koobutugaku *n.* mineralogy
koobutugakusya *n.* mineralogist
kooen *n.* park
koogoo *n.* empress
koogyoo *n.* engineering industry
koogyoo *n.* mining industry
koohii *n.* coffee
kookan *n.* exchange
kookankyoku *n.* (telephone) exchange
kookan suru *vt.*
kookoku *n.* advertisement
kookoku suru *vi.*
kookoo *n.* filial piety
koori *n.* ice
koosen *n.* (beam of) light
koosi *n.* minister (diplomatic)
koosikan *n.* legation
kootetu *n.* steel
kootoo-gakkoo *n.* high school
kootuu *n.* traffic, communication
kootyoo *n.* headmaster (-mistress)
koozyoo *n.* factory, workshop
kore *p.* this (see Lesson 4)
koro *n.* time (see Lesson 23)
korosu *vt.* kill
koruku *n.* cork, stopper
kosi *n.* waist
kosikakeru *vi.* sit down
koso *emphatic part.*
kosyu *n.* head of family
kotira (kotti) *p.* (see Lesson 10)
koto *n.* (abstract) thing, fact
kotoba *n.* word, language
kotosi *n.* and *adv.* this year
kowai *a.* frightening, frightened
kowareru *vi.* be smashed, break
kowarete iru be broken
kowasu *vt.* break, destroy

kozin *n.* individual
  kozinsyugi *n.* individualism
kozukai *n.* messenger, porter
kozutumi *n.* parcel
  kozutumi-yuubin *n.* parcel post
ku *num.* nine
ku *n.* urban district (*see* Lesson 23)
kubetu *n.* distinction
  kubetu suru *vt.*
kubi *n.* neck
  kubiwa *n.* necklace, collar (dog)
kudamono *n.* fruit (edible)
kudasaru *vt.* (*see* Lessons 18 and 30)
  kudasai *imp.* (*see* Lesson 18)
kugi *n.* nail
kumi *n.* group, class, team
  -kumi *u.* (*see* Appendix II)
kumiai *n.* association, (trade) union
kumitateru *vt.* assemble, fit together
kumo *n.* cloud
kumoru *vi.* cloud over
  kumotte iru be cloudy
-kun *suf.* Mr. (*see* Lesson 30)
kuni *n.* country, one's native place
kuraberu *vt.* compare
kurabu *n.* club
kurai *n.* rank
  kurai *part.* (*see* **gurai**)
kurai *a.* dark
kurasi *n.* living
kurasu *vi.* live
kureru *vt.* give (*see* Lesson 22)
kuroi *a.* black
  kuro *n.*
kuru *vi.* come
  kite iru be here
kuruma *n.* cart, carriage
kurusii *a.* full of suffering, hardship
kurusimeru *vt.* cause suffering
kurusimu *vi.* suffer
kusa *n.* grass, plant (other than trees and crops)
kusari *n.* chain

kuse *n.* habit
kusuri *n.* medicine
  kusuriya *n.* chemist('s)
  kusuriyubi *n.* third finger, ring finger
kusyami (kusame) *n.* sneeze
kuti *n.* mouth
  kutibiru *n.* lip
kutu *n.* shoe, boot
  kutusita *n.* socks, stockings
  kutuya *n.* shoe shop, shoe maker
kuugun *n.* air force
  kuugunsyoo *n.* Air Ministry
kuuki *n.* air
kuwasii *a.* detailed
kuzureru *vi.* collapse
  kuzurete iru have collapsed
kuzusu *vt.* break into small pieces, change (bank-note)
kyaku *n.* guest
  kyakusen *n.* passenger-boat
  kyakusitu *n.* drawing-room
  kyakusya *n.* passenger coach (railway)
kyonen *n.* and *adv.* last year
kyoo *n.* and *adv.* to-day
kyooiku *n.* education
  kyooiku suru *vt.*
kyookai *n.* church
kyoomi *n.* interest (not financial)
kyoosan *n.* common property
  kyoosansyugi *n.* communism
  kyoosansyugisya *n.* communist
  kyoosantoo *n.* communist party
kyoosoo *n.* competition, race
  kyoosoo suru *vi.*
kyori *n.* distance
kyuu- *num.* nine
kyuu na *a.* sudden
  kyuu ni *adv.*
kyuuryoo *n.* salary
kyuuzi *n.* waiter, office boy

ma *n.* interval of time
maa *int.* expression of surprise, admiration, indecision, etc.
mada *adv.* (*see* Lesson 21)
made *part.* (*see* Lesson 23)
mado *n.* window

mado-garasu *n.* window-pane
mae *n.* front part (*see* Lesson 4)
  maeasi *n.* front leg
magaru *vi.* turn, twist
  magatte iru be twisted
mageru *vt.* turn, twist, bend
-mai *u.* (*see* Appendix II)
mai- *pref.* every
  (-asa, -ban, -getu, -nen, -niti, -syuu)
mairu *vi.* (*see* Lesson 30)
makeru *vi.* be defeated
  makete iru have been defeated
maki-tabako *n.* cigarette
makka na *a.* bright red
makkura na *n.* completely dark
makkuro na *a.* completely black
maku *vt.* sow, scatter
makura *n.* pillow
mama *n.* (*see* Lesson 27)
mame *n.* beans, peas, etc.
mamonaku *adv.* shortly
mamoru *vt.* protect, observe
man *num.* and *u.* ten thousand (*see* Appendix II)
maneku *vt.* beckon, invite
manmarui *a.* completely round
mannaka *n.* centre
mannenhitu *n.* fountain-pen
manzoku *n.* satisfaction
  manzoku na *a.* satisfactory
  manzoku suru *vi.* be satisfied
marui *a.* round
massao na *a.* deep blue (sky, etc.), pallid (face)
massiro na *a.* dead white
-masu *suf.* (*see* Lesson 5)
massugu na *a.* straight
  massugu ni *adv.*
mata *adv.* again
mati (tyoo) *n.* town (*see* Lesson 23)
  mati-yakuba *n.* Town Hall
matigaeru *vt.* mistake
matigai *n.* mistake
matigau *vi.* make mistake
  matigatte iru be wrong
matigainaku *adv.* without fail
matti *n.* match
matu *n.* pine
matu *vt.* wait for

mawari *n.* area around
mawaru *vi.* go round
mawasu *vt.* turn round
mazeru *vt.* mix
mazime na *a.* serious
  mazime ni *adv.*
maziru *vi.* mix
  mazitte iru be mixed
mazu *adv.* first of all
mazui *a.* tasteless, distasteful
me *n.* eye
  me-isya *n.* eye specialist
-me *suf.* (*see* Lesson 23)
meate *n.* aim
medatu *vi.* be prominent
  medatte iru ditto
medetai *a.* to be congratulated
-meetoru *u.* (*see* Appendix II)
megane *n.* spectacles
meirei *n.* order, command
  meirei suru *vt.*
Meizi *n.* year period (*see* Appendix)
mekata *n.* weight
mekura *n.* blindness, blind man
mendoo na *a.* troublesome, complicated
menkai *n.* interview
  menkai suru *vi.*
menzyoo *n.* licence, diploma
mesitukai *n.* servant
mesu *n.* female (animal)
mezurasii *a.* rare
mi *n.* fruit (general)
mi- *pref.* three
  mittu *num.* three
miageru *vt.* look up at
midasi *n.* headline
midori *n.* green (colour)
  midoriiro *n.* ditto
mieru *vi.* be visible
migaku *vt.* polish
migi *n.* right (as opposed to left)
mikan *n.* Japanese orange
mikata *n.* friend (as against enemy)
mikka *n.* and *adv.* third day, three days
mimi *n.* ear
mina (minna) *adv.* all

minasan *p.* Ladies and Gentlemen

minami *n.* south

minato *n.* harbour, port

minsyu *n.* democracy

   minsyusyugi *n.* democratism

   minsyusyugisya *n.* democrat

   minsyutoo *n.* democratic party

miokuru *vt.* see off

miorosu *vt.* gaze on from above

miru *vt.* see, look at

miruku *n.* milk

mise *n.* shop

misemono *n.* show, spectacle

miseru *vt.* show

misoka *n.* last day of month

miti *n.* road, street, way

   miti-annai *n.* guide

mitu *n.* honey, nectar

mittomonai *a.* disgraceful

mitukaru *vi.* be found, be discovered

   mitukatte iru be discovered

mitukeru *vt.* find, discover

mizikai *a.* short

mizu *n.* water

   mizuguruma *n.* water-wheel

   mizuire *n.* water-jug

mizuumi *n.* lake

mo *part.* (*see* Lesson 2)

-mo *suf.* (*see* Lesson 10)

modan na *a.* modern

mokuyoo-bi *n.* Thursday

mokuteki *n.* aim, object

   mokutekiti *n.* destination

momen *n.* cotton

   momen-ito *n.* cotton thread

-monme *u.* (*see* Appendix II)

momo *n.* thigh

momo *n.* peach

   momoiro *n.* pink

mon *n.* gate(way)

   monban *n.* gate keeper

monbusyoo *n.* ministry of Education

mondai *n.* question, problem

mono *n.* (concrete) thing

monooki *n.* shed

monosugoi *a.* terrible

moo *adv.* (*see* Lesson 21)

moosu *vt.* say (*see* Lesson 30)

morau *vt.* be given (*see* Lesson 22)

   moraimono *n.* gift one receives

mori *n.* wood, forest

mosi *adv.* (with conditional verbs) if

mosimosi *int.* expression of calling other person's attention, hello

Mosukoo *n.* Moscow

moti *n.* wear, durability

motiron *adv.* of course

moto *n.* origin

motomoto *adv.* from the first

motto *adv.* more

motu *vt.* hold, possess

   motte iru have

mu- *pref.* six

   muttu *num.* six

mugi *n.* corn, barley, wheat

muika *n.* and *adv.* sixth day, six days

mukasi *n.* old times

mukau *vi.* face

   mukatte iru face, be opposite

mukeru *vt.* turn towards

mukoo *n.* opposite side

mune *n.* chest, breast

mura *n.* village

   mura-yakuba *n.* village office

murasaki *n.* purple (colour)

muri *n.* unreasonableness

   muri na *a.*

   muri ni *adv.*

musi *n.* insect

musubu *vt.* tie

   musubime *n.* knot

musubitukeru *vt.* tie on

musuko *n.* son

musume *n.* daughter

muzukasii *a.* difficult

na *n.* (*see* **namae**)

na *part.* (*see* Lesson 7)

na *neg. imp. part.* (*see* Lesson 30)

nabe *n.* pot, pan

nado *part.* (*see* Lesson 10)

nagai *a.* long

   nagagutu *n.* boots

nagame *n.* view

nagameru *vt.* gaze at

-nagara *suf.* (see Lesson 27)
nagareru *vi.* flow
nagasu *vt.* cause to flow, pour
nagedasu *vt.* throw out, throw away
nagekomu *vt.* throw in
nageru *vt.* throw
nai *a.* non-existent
-nai *suf.* (see Lesson 8)
naihu *n.* knife
naiti *n.* Japan proper
naiyoo *n.* contents
naka *n.* middle, interior
nakagoro *n.* middle (time)
nakanaka *adv.* considerably
nakayubi *n.* middle finger
nakidasu *vi.* burst into tears
nakigao *n.* tearful face
nakigoe *n.* cry
naku *vi.* cry
nakunaru *vi.* get lost; pass away (honorific)
   nakunatte iru be lost
nakusu *vt.* lose
namae (na) *n.* name
nami *n.* wave
namida *n.* tear
nan *p.* what (see Lesson 4)
   nandemo *p.* and *adv.* (see Lesson 17)
nan- *pref.* what
   (-gatu, -nen, -niti, -yoo-bi, -zi)
nana- *pref.* seven
   nanatu *num.* seven
nandaka *adv.* somehow or other
nani *p.* what (see Lesson 2)
   nanika *p.* (see Lesson 10)
   nanimo *p.* (see Lesson 10)
nanoka *n.* and *adv.* seventh day, seven days
nantoka *adv.* something or other
   nantoka site *adv.* by some means or another
nantonaku *adv.* for no particular reason
nan-yoo *n.* South Seas
naoru *vi.* get better, be repaired
   naotte iru be better, be repaired
naosu *vt.* cure, mend, repair

nara *part.* (see Lesson 27)
naraberu *vt.* put in line
narabu *vi.* get in line
   narande iru be in line
narasu *vt.* cause to sound, ring
narasu *vt.* tame
narau *vt.* learn
nareru *vi.* become used to
   narete iru be used to
naru *vi.* become (see Lesson 26)
   natte iru (see Lesson 26)
naru *vi.* sound, ring etc.
naruhodo *int.* I see
nasaru *vt.* and *vi.* do (see Lessons 18 and 30)
   nasai *imp.* (see Lesson 18)
nasi *n.* pear
natu *n.* summer
naze *adv.* why
   nazeka *adv.* for some reason or other
ne (nee) *int.* expression used in seeking confirmation of preceding statement, etc.
ne *n.* root
nedan *n.* price
neesan *n.* (other person's) elder sister, etc.
negai *n.* request
negau *vt.* request
nekasu *vt.* put to bed
neko *n.* cat
nemuru *vi.* fall asleep
   nemutte iru be asleep
-nen *u.* (see Appendix II)
nenryoo *n.* fuel
neru *vi.* lie down, go to bed
   nete iru be in bed
nettyuu suru *vi.* get absorbed in
   nettyuu site iru be absorbed in
netu *n.* heat, temperature (of body, etc.)
nezi *n.* spiral
   nezikugi *n.* screw
nezireru *vi.* become twisted
   nezirete iru be twisted
neziru *vt.* twist
nezumi *n.* rat, mouse
   nezumiiro *n.* grey (colour)
ni *part.* (see Lesson 1)
ni *num.* two

nigai *a*. bitter

nigasu *vt*. allow to escape

nigatu *n*. February

nigedasu *vi*. run away

nigeru *vi*. escape
 nigete iru have escaped

nigiru *vt*. grip

nigoru *vi*. (of liquid) become cloudy, become muddy
 nigotte iru be cloudy, be muddy

Nihon *n*. Japan
 Nihongo (Nippongo) *n*. Japanese language
 Nihon-ryoori *n*. Japanese cooking
 Nihon-siki Japanese style

niisan *n*. (other person's) elder brother, etc.

nikai *n*. upstairs, first floor

niku *n*. flesh, meat
 nikuya *n*. butcher('s)

-nikui *suf*. (see Lesson 29)

nikumu *vt*. hate

nimotu *n*. luggage

-nin *u*. (see Appendix II)

ningen *n*. human being

ningyoo *n*. doll

ninpu *n*. workman

nioi *n*. smell, scent

Nippon *n*. Japan
 Nippon-iti *n*. best in Japan
 Nipponzin (Nihonzin) *n*. Japanese people

niramu *vt*. glare at

niru *vt*. cook

niru *vi*. resemble
 nite iru resemble

nisi *n*. west

-niti *u*. and *suf*. day (see Appendix II)

nitiyoo-bi *n*. Sunday

niwa *n*. garden

niwatori *n*. chicken

no *part*. (see Lesson 4)

no *p*. (see Lesson 13)

noboru *vi*. go up
 noborihazimeru *vi*. start to climb
 nobotte iru be up

nodo *n*. throat

nohara *n*. fields (uncultivated)

nokori *n*. remainder

nokoru *vi*. remain
 nokotte iru be left

nokosu *vt*. leave

nomikomu *vt*. swallow

nomu *vt*. drink
 nomimono *n*. drinks

noogyoo *n*. agriculture

nooto *n*. exercise-book

noozyoo *n*. farm

nori *n*. paste

norikae *n*. change (trains, etc.)

norikaeru *vi*. change (trains, etc.)

norikumiin *n*. crew

noru *vi*. ride on, mount, go aboard
 norimono *n*. carriage
 notte iru be on, be riding on

noseru *vt*. put on

nuitukeru *vt*. sew on

nukeru *vi*. come out, be extracted
 nukete iru be out

nuku *vt*. pull out, extract

nurasu *vt*. wet, soak

nureru *vi*. get wet
 nurete iru be wet

nusumi *n*. stealing

nusumu *vt*. steal

nuu *vt*. sew
 nuimono *n*. sewing, sewn garments

nyuuin *n*. entering hospital
 nyuuin suru *vi*.
 nyuuin site iru be in hospital

nyuusu *n*. news

Nyuuyooku *n*. New York

o *part*. (see Lesson 5)

o- *pref*. (see Lessons 18 and 30)

oba *n*. aunt

obaasan *n*. grandmother, old woman

obi *n*. *obi*, Japanese sash

oboeru *vt*. learn, commit to memory
 oboete iru remember

odori *n*. dance

odoroki *n*. surprise

odoroku *vi*. be surprised

odoroite iru be surprised
odoru *vi.* dance
ogawa *n.* stream
oi, ooi *int.* expression used in calling somebody
oide (*see* Lessons 18 and 30)
oisii *a.* tasty, delicious
oka *n.* hill
okaasan *n.* (other person's) mother, etc.
okage *n.* thanks due to another
okasii (okasi na) *a.* funny, odd
-oki ni *suf.* every other
okiru *vi.* arise, get up
  okite iru be up
okoru *vi.* get angry, lose one's temper
  okotte iru be angry
okoru *vi.* happen
  okotte iru have happened
okosu *vt.* wake up, rouse
oku *vt.* put (*see* Lesson 22)
oku *num.* and *u.* hundred million (*see* Appendix II)
okureru *vi.* become late, become backward
  okurete iru be late, be backward
okurimono *n.* gift
okuru *vt.* send
okusan *n.* somebody else's wife
omatidoo-sama *n.* expression used when apologizing for keeping somebody waiting
omae *p.* you (*see* Lesson 30)
omedetoo *int.* congratulations (*see* Lesson 30)
omoi *a.* heavy
omoidasu *vt.* call it to mind, remember
omoide *n.* memory
omoikiru *vt.* give up thoughts of, resign oneself to losing
omosiroi *a.* interesting
omote *n.* front (of house, etc.)
omou *vt.* think
onaka *n.* abdomen, inside, stomach
onazi *a.* same
  onazi ni *adv.*
ongaku *n.* music

ongakka *n.* musician
ongakkai *n.* concert
ongakutai *n.* band
ondo *n.* temperature
onna *n.* woman
onna-no-ko *n.* girl
onsen *n.* hot spring
oo- *pref.* great, large
  (**-ame, -doori, -goe, -kaze, -kazi, -sawagi, -tigai, -warai, -yorokobi, -zisin**)
ooba *n.* overcoat
ooi *a.* numerous
  ooku *adv.* mainly
ookii (ooki na) *a.* big, large
ookisa *n.* size
oomisoka *n.* last day of year
oomizu *n.* flood
oo-sama *n.* king
ore *p.* I (*see* Lesson 30)
orenzi *n.* orange
oreru *vi.* break (bone, stick, etc.)
  orete iru be broken
oriru *vi.* descend
  orite iru be down
orosu *vt.* lower
oru *vt.* weave
  orimono *n.* woven goods
oru *vt.* break (bone, stick, etc.)
oru *vi.* be (*see* Lesson 30)
osaeru *vt.* push down, keep down, repress
osieru *vt.* teach, tell
osii *a.* regrettable
osoi *a.* late, slow
osoreru *vt.* fear
osorosii *a.* frightful
osu *n.* male (animal)
osu *vt.* push
otiru *vi.* fall
  otite iru have fallen
otitukeru *vt.* settle, calm
otituku *vi.* become settled, become calm
  otituite iru be settled, be calm
oto *n.* sound, noise
otoko *n.* male, man
otoko-no-ko *n.* boy
otona *n.* adult
otoosan *n.* (other person's) father, etc.

otooto *n.* younger brother

otosu *vt.* let fall, drop

ototoi *n.* and *adv.* the day before yesterday

ototosi *n.* and *adv.* the year before last

oturi *n.* change (difference between price and money tendered)

otuyu *n.* soup, gravy

owari *n.* end

owaru *vi.* finish
   owatte iru be finished

oya *n.* parent
   oyako *n.* parent(s) and child(ren)
   oyayubi *n.* thumb

oyogi *n.* swimming

oyogu *vi.* swim

ozi *n.* uncle

oziisan *n.* grandfather, old man

paipu *n.* pipe

pan *n.* bread
   pan-ya *n.* baker('s)

Parii *n.* Paris

-peizi *u.* (*see* Appendix II)

pen *n.* pen
   pen-saki *n.* pen nib

penki *n.* paint

piano *n.* piano

pin *n.* pin

poketto *n.* pocket

ponpu *n.* pump

rai- *pref.* next
   (-getu, -nen, -syuu)

raku na *a.* easy, comfortable
   raku ni *adv.*

ranboo na *a.* disorderly

rasii *a.* (*see* Lesson 20)

razio *n.* radio

rei *n.* example

rei *n.* thanks

rei *n.* zero

rekisi *n.* history

rekoodo *n.* record

renga *n.* brick

renraku *n.* communication, connection
   renrakusen *n.* ferry-boat

rensyuu *n.* practice
   rensyuu suru *vt.*

rentyuu (renzyuu) *n.* group, company

ressya *n.* train

-ri *u.* (*see* Appendix II)

rikoo na *a.* clever

riku *n.* land

rikugun *n.* army
   rikugunsyoo *n.* Army Ministry

ringo *n.* apple

rippa na *a.* splendid, fine

rippoo *n.* cube
   rippoo-meetoru *n.* cubic metre

-rittoru *u.* (*see* Appendix II)

riyuu *n.* reason

roku *num.* six

rokugatu *n.* June

ronbun *n.* essay, article

Rondon *n.* London

roo *n.* wax

roodoo *n.* labour
   roodoosya *n.* labourer
   roodootoo *n.* Labour Party

Rooma *n.* Rome

Rosi(y)a *n.* Russia
   Rosi(y)ago *n.* Russian (language)
   Rosi(y)azin *n.* a Russian

rusu *n.* absence from home
   rusuban *n.* person looking after house, etc., in absence of the occupant

ryokan *n.* hotel (Japanese style), inn (ditto)

ryokoo *n.* travel
   ryokoo-menzyoo *n.* passport
   ryokoo suru *vi.*
   ryokoosya *n.* traveller

ryoo- *pref.* both
   (-asi, -gawa, -hoo, -te)

ryoori *n.* cooking
   ryoorinin *n.* cook
   ryoori suru *vi.* cook
   ryooriya *n.* restaurant

ryoosin *n.* parents

ryoozi *n.* consul
   ryoozikan *n.* consulate

ryuukoo *n.* fashion
   ryuukoo suru *vi.*

sa *int.* expression used when one urges some action, etc.

-sa *suf.* (*see* Lesson 7)

saa *int.* expression used when one is making one's mind up, etc.

sabisii *a.* lonely

sae *part.* (*see* Lesson 18)

sagasu *vt.* search for

saguru *vt.* search

saiban *n.* trial

  saibankan *n.* judge

  saiban suru *vi.*

  saibansyo *n.* law court

saka *n.* slope, hill

sakaba *n.* bar (drinking)

sakana *n.* fish

sakan na *a.* flourishing

  sakan ni *adv.*

sakasama na *a.* upside down

sakaya *n.* wine merchant('s)

sake *n.* rice wine

sakeru *vt.* avoid

saki *n.* (pointed) end, tip

saku *vi.* bloom (flower)

sakuban *n.* and *adv.* last evening

sakura *n.* cherry

-sama honorific form of **-san**

samasu *vt.* cool ; wake

samazama na *a.* various

  samazama ni *adv.*

sameru *vi.* become cool ; wake

  samete iru be cool; be awake

samurai *n.* Japanese feudal warrior

samui *a.* cold (weather)

san *num.* three

-san *suf.* Mr. Mrs. Miss (*see* Lesson 3)

sangatu *n.* March

sanpo *n.* stroll, walk

sansei *n.* agreement

  sansei suru *vi.*

sanzyutu (sanzitu) *n.* arithmetic

sao *n.* pole

sara *n.* saucer, plate, dish

sarai- *pref.* one after next (**-getu, -nen, -syuu**)

saru *n.* monkey

sasiageru *vt.* (*see* Lesson 30)

sasou *vt.* induce, invite

sas-siru *vt.* guess

sasu *vt.* point out, at, pierce, sting, put up (umbrella)

satoo *n.* sugar

-satu *u.* (*see* Appendix II)

sawagi *n.* disturbance

sawagu *vi.* make a disturbance

sawaru *vi.* touch

sayonara (sayoonara) *int.* goodbye

se *n.* back (of body), stature

sebone *n.* back-bone

seihu *n.* government

seikatu *n.* life, living

  seikatu suru *vi.*

seikoo *n.* success

  seikoo suru *vi.*

seinen *n.* young man

seiri *n.* putting in order

  seiri suru *vt.*

seiryoku *n.* power, energy

seisin *n.* mind, spirit

seisitu *n.* nature, character

seito *n.* pupil

seitoo *n.* political party

seiyoo *n.* the Occident

  seiyoo-ryoori *n.* Western cooking

  seiyoo-siki Western style

  seiyoozin *n.* Westerner

seizi *n.* politic

  seizika *n.* politician

  seizi-sosiki *n.* political system

  seiziteki na *a.* political

  seizi-undoo *n.* political movement

sekai *n.* world

  sekai-iti *n.* best in the world

seki *n.* cough

seki *n.* seat

sekidoo *n.* equator

sekinin *n.* responsibility

  sekininsya *n.* person responsible

sekitan *n.* coal

sekiyu *n.* oil

sekken *n.* soap

semai *a.* narrow

semento *n.* cement

sen *n.* line

sen *num.* and *u.* thousand (*see* Appendix II)
-sen *u.* (*see* Appendix II)
sen- *pref.* last
  (**-getu, -syuu**)
senaka *n.* back
senmon *n.* speciality
  senmongo *n.* technical term
  senmonka *n.* specialist
sensei *n.* teacher
sensoo *n.* war
sentaku *n.* washing
  sentakumono *n.* laundry
  sentaku suru *vt.*
  sentaku-ya *n.* laundry
sentyoo *n.* ship's captain
senzo *n.* ancestor
setomono *n.* china
setumei *n.* explanation
  setumei suru *vt.*
setto *n.* set
sewa *n.* assistance
  sewagakari *n.* person in charge
  sewa suru *vt.* look after, assist
si *n.* city (*see* Lesson 23)
  sityoo *n.* City Mayor
  siyakusyo *n.* City Hall
si *num.* four
siai *n.* match, game
siawase *n.* good fortune
  siawase na *a.*
sibai *n.* play (theatre)
sigatu *n.* April
sigoto *n.* work
siharai *n.* payment
siharau *vt.* pay
sika *part.* (*see* Lesson 23)
sikaru *vt.* scold, tell off
sikasi *con.* but
sikata *n.* method
siken *n.* examination
  siken-mondai *n.* examination questions
  sikenteki na (ni) *a.* (*adv.*) experimental
siki *n.* ceremony
  -siki *suf.* style
sima *n.* island
simaru *vi.* shut
  simatte iru be shut

simau *vt.* (*see* Lesson 22)
simeppoi *a.* damp
simeru *vt.* shut, close
sina *n.* goods
  sinamono *n.* goods
Sina *n.* China
  Sinago *n.* Chinese (language)
  Sinazin *n.* a Chinese
sinbun *n.* newspaper
  sinbunsya *n.* newspaper office
sindai *n.* bed
sinpai *n.* anxiety
  sinpai na *a.*
  sinpai suru *vi.*
sinpo *n.* progress
  sinpo suru *vi.*
  sinpoteki *a.* progressive
sinri *n.* psychology
  sinrigaku *n.* psychology
  sinrigakusya *n.* psychologist
  sinriteki na *a.* psychological
  sinri-zyootai *n.* psychological condition
sinrui *n.* relative(s)
sinsetu na *a.* kind
sinsitu *n.* bed-room
sinu *vi.* die
  sinde iru be dead
sin-ziru *vt.* believe in
sinzoo *n.* heart (organ)
sio *n.* salt
sippo (o) *n.* tail
siraberu *vt.* investigate, search
sirase *n.* news, information
siraseru *vt.* inform
sireru *vi.* become known
  sirete iru be known
siriai *n.* acquaintance(ship)
siroi *a.* white
  siro *n.*
siru *vt.* get to know
  sitte iru know
sirusi *n.* mark, sign
sita *n.* tongue
sita *n.* lower part (*see* Lesson 4)
sitagi *n.* underwear
sitai *n.* corpse
sitaku *n.* preparation
  sitaku suru *vi.*
sitasii *a.* close, intimate
siti *n.* pawn

sitiya *n.* pawnbroker('s)

siti *num.* seven

sitigatu *n.* July

situmon *n.* question
  situmon suru *vt.*

siturei *n.* lack of politeness
  siturei na *a.* impolite
  siturei suru *vi.* excuse oneself
    from doing something

sizen *n.* nature
  sizen-kagaku *n.* natural science
  sizen (ni) *adv.* naturally
  sizenteki ni *adv.* ditto

sizi *n.* support
  sizisya *n.* supporter
  sizi suru *vt.*

sizuka na *a.* quiet

sizumu *vi.* sink
  sizunde iru be sunk

sizumeru *vt.* sink

soba *n.* side

sode *n.* sleeve

soko *n.* bottom

soko *p.* there (*see* Lesson 1)

-soku *u.* (*see* Appendix II)

sokuryoku *n.* speed

somuku *vi.* betray

son *n.* loss

songai *n.* damage

sonkei *n.* respect
  sonkei suru *vt.*

sonna *a.* that sort of, such a ——
    as that
  sonna ni *adv.* to that extent

sono *a.* that (*see* Lesson 3)

sontyoo *n.* village mayor

soo *n.* (*see* Lesson 20)
  -soo na *suf.* (*see* Lesson 20)

soo *adv.* in that way

-soo *u.* (*see* Appendix II)

soobetukai *n.* farewell party

soodan *n.* consultation
  soodan-aite *n.* adviser
  soodan suru *vi.*

soozi *n.* cleaning (room, etc.)
  soozi suru *vt.*

soozoo *n.* imagination
  soozoo suru *vt.*

sora *n.* sky

sore *p.* that (by you)

sorezore *adv.* each

soru *vt.* shave

sosiki *n.* system, organization
  sosiki suru *vt.*
  sosikiteki na *a.* systematic

sosite *conj.* then, next

sotira (sotti) *p.* (*see* Lesson 10)

soto *n.* outside

suberu *vi.* slide, slip

sugata *n.* shape, form, appear-
    ance

-sugi *suf.* past

sugiru *vi.* pass, be in excess

sugosu *vt.* spend (time), pass
    (time)

sugu (ni) *adv.* immediately

suihei *n.* horizon

suikomu *vt.* inhale

suitoru *vt.* soak up, absorb
  suitorigami *n.* blotting-paper

suiyoo-bi *n.* Wednesday

sukaato *n.* skirt

suki na *a.* fond of
  sukikirai *n.* likes and dis-
    likes

sukii *n.* ski, skiing

sukkari *adv.* completely

sukosi *adv.* a little

sukunai *a.* few

sumanai *a.* regrettable

sumi *n.* charcoal, Indian ink

sumi *n.* corner

sumu *vi.* reside

-sun *u.* (*see* Appendix II)

suna *n.* sand

sunpoo *n.* size, dimension

suppai *a.* sour

supuun *n.* spoon

suru *vt.* and *vi.* do (*see* Lessons 6
    and 26)

susumeru *vt.* advance

susumu *vi.* go forward, progress,
    become fast (clock)
  susunde iru be progressive, be
    fast

sutekki *n.* walking-stick

suteru *vt.* abandon, throw away

sutokkingu *n.* stocking

suugaku *n.* mathematics
  suugakusya *n.* mathematician

suu *vt.* inhale, suck

suupu *n.* soup

suwaru *vi.* sit
  suwatte iru be seated
suzi *n.* sinew, thread
suzusii *a.* cool
syakai *n.* society
  syakaigaku *n.* sociology
  syakai-kagaku *n.* social science
  syakai-sosiki *n.* social system
  syakaisyugi *n.* socialism
  syakaisyugisya *n.* socialist
  syakaitoo *n.* socialist party
  -syaku *u.* (*see* Appendix II)
syasin *n.* photograph
  syasinki *n.* camera
  syasinya *n.* photographer
syatu *n.* vest
syatyoo *n.* president, chairman
  (company)
syoki *n.* secretary
syokubutu *n.* vegetable
  syokubutuen *n.* botanical gar-
    den
  syokubutugaku *n.* botany
  syokubutugakusya *n.* botanist
syokudoo *n.* dining-room
  syokudoosya *n.* dining-car
syokumin *n.* colonization
  syokuminti *n.* colony
syokuzi *n.* meal
-syoo *u.* (*see* Appendix II)
syoobu *n.* victory and defeat,
  result
syoogakkoo *n.* primary school
syoogatu *n.* New Year
syoogun *n.* title of (military)
  ruler of Japan before 1868,
  general
syoogyoo *n.* commerce
syookai *n.* introduction
  syookai suru *vt.*
syookoo *n.* (military) officer
syoonin *n.* tradesman
syoorai *n.* future
syoosen *n.* merchant ship
syoosetu *n.* novel
  syoosetuka *n.* novelist
syooten *n.* shop, store
syooti *n.* consent
  syooti suru *vi.*
syoototu *n.* collision
  syoototu suru *vi.*

Syoowa *n.* year period (*see* Appendix II)
syooziki na *a.* honest
syorui *n.* documents
syurui *n.* kind, sort
  -syurui *u.* (*see* Appendix II)
syugi *n.* principle, idea
syusyoo *n.* prime minister
syuu *n.* week
  -syuukan *u.* (*see* Appendix II)
syuukan *n.* habit, custom
syuukyoo *n.* religion
syuuten *n.* terminus
syuzin *n.* master of house, shop,
  etc., husband
syuzyutu (syuzitu) *n.* surgical
  operation
  syuzutu (syuzitu) suru *vi.*

ta *n.* rice-field
tabako *n.* tobacco, cigarette
  tabakoire *n.* cigarette case
taberu *vt.* eat
  tabemono *n.* food
tabi *n.* tabi, Japanese socks
tabitabi *adv.* often
tabun *adv.* perhaps
tada *adv.* (*see* Lesson 23)
tadaima *adv.* (*see* Lesson 22)
tadasii *a.* correct
tagai ni *adv.* mutually
-tagaru *suf.* (*see* Lesson 29)
-tai *suf.* (*see* Lesson 19)
taido *n.* attitude
taihen na *a.* grave, exceptional
  taihen *adv.* very
taiin *n.* leaving hospital
  taiin suru *vi.*
taipuraitaa *n.* typewriter
taira na *a.* flat, even
tai-sita *a.* important, serious
taisi *n.* ambassador
  taisikan *n.* embassy
Taisyoo *n.* year period (*see* Appendix II)
taitei *adv.* for the most part,
  generally
taiya *n.* tyre
takai *a.* high, dear
take *n.* bamboo
  takenoko *n.* bamboo shoot

takusii *n.* taxi
takoku *n.* other country or land
takusan *adv.* a lot
tama *n.* ball, jewel
tamago *n.* egg
tamaru *vi.* accumulate
  tamatte iru have accumulated
tame *n.* purpose, benefit
tameru *vi.* accumulate
tana *n.* shelf
tane *n.* seed
tan-i *n.* unit
tanin *n.* other people
tanki na *a.* short tempered
tanomu *vt.* request, rely on
tanosimi *n.* enjoyment
tanosimu *vi.* enjoy
tansu *n.* chest of drawers, wardrobe
tansyo *n.* shortcoming
tanzyoo-bi *n.* birthday
taoreru *vi.* collapse
  taorete iru have collapsed
taosu *vt.* knock down
tarai *n.* washing-tub
tariru *vi.* be enough
tasika na *a.* certain
  tasika *adv.* " if my memory is correct "
  tasika ni *adv.* certainly
tassya na *a.* healthy
tasu *vt.* add
tasukaru *vi.* be helped, be rescued, survive
  tasukatte iru ditto
tasukeru *vt.* help, rescue
tasyoo *adv.* more or less
tatami *n.* *tatami*, mat
tate *n.* upright
tatemono *n.* building
tateru *vt.* erect
-tati *suf.* (*see* Lesson 3)
  (**anatatati, bokutati, hitotati, kodomotati, watasitati**)
tatimati *adv.* immediately, suddenly
tatoeba *adv.* for example
tatu *vi.* stand (up), depart, elapse
  tatiba *n.* standpoint
  tatte iru be erect

tayori *n.* news ; trust
te *n.* hand, arm
teasi *n.* arms and legs
teate *n.* allowance, looking after (sick, etc.)
tebukuro *n.* glove
teeburu *n.* table
tegami *n.* letter
teido *n.* degree, extent
teikoku *n.* empire
  teikokusyugi *n.* imperialism
teki *n.* enemy
-teki na (ni) *suf.* forming adjective (adverb)
tekitoo na *a.* suitable
  tekitoo ni *adv.*
tekubi *n.* wrist
ten *n.* spot, dot, mark, point
-ten *u.* (*see* Appendix II)
tenki *n.* weather
  tenkiyohoo *n.* weather forecast
tennoo *n.* emperor
tenrankai *n.* exhibition
tenzyoo *n.* ceiling
tera *n.* temple (Buddhist)
terevizyon *n.* television
tetu *n.* iron
tetudai *n.* help
tetudau *vt.* help
ti *n.* blood
tigai *n.* difference
  tigainai *a.* doubtless
tigau *vi.* differ
tiisai (tiisa na) *a.* small, little
tikai *a.* near
  tikagoro *adv.* recently
  tikaku *n.* neighbourhood
tikara *n.* strength
tikuonki *n.* gramophone
tikyuu *n.* globe
tiri *n.* geography
  tirigaku *n.* geography
  tirigakusya *n.* geographer
tisiki *n.* knowledge
titi *n.* father
tizu *n.* map
to *n.* door
to *n.* metropolis (*see* Lesson 23)
to *part.* (*see* Lesson 10)
to- *pref.* ten
  too *num.* ten

-to *u. (see* Appendix II)

tobiagaru *vi.* jump up, fly up
  tobiagatte iru have jumped up

tobidasu *vt.* jump out, fly out

tobikomu *vi.* jump in

tobioriru *vi.* jump down
  tobiorite iru have jumped down

tobu *vi.* fly, jump

todana *n.* cupboard

todokeru *vt.* deliver, report

todoku *vi.* be delivered, reach
  todoite iru have reached

tokei *n.* clock, watch

tokeru *vi.* melt
  tokete iru have melted

toka *part. (see* Lesson 10)

toki *n.* time

tokidoki *adv.* occasionally

toko *n.* bed

tokonoma *n. tokonoma,* a recess for pictures and ornaments

tokoro *n.* place

tokorode *conj.* thereupon

tokoroga *conj.* however

toku *n.* gain

toku *vt.* untie, explain

toku ni *adv.* especially

tokubetu na *a.* special
  tokubetu ni *adv.*

tomaru *vi.* stay, stop

tomeru *vt.* stop, put up (guest)

-tomo *suf.* both, all; (with neg.) neither, none
  (**huuhutomo, hutaritomo, hutatutomo, mittutomo, ryooasitomo, ryoogawatomo, ryoohootomo, ryootetomo, sannintomo**)

tomodati *n.* friend

tonari *n.* next door

tonikaku *adv.* anyhow

tooge *n.* mountain pass

tooi *a.* far

tooka *n.* and *adv.* tenth day, ten days

toori *n.* street, road
  toori ni (-doori ni) *adv.* according to

toorikakaru *vi.* pass by

tooru *vi.* go through, go along

toosu *vt.* send through, send along

tootoo *adv.* finally, at last

tooyoo *n.* the Orient
  tooyoozin *n.* Orientals

toreru *vi.* come off, be removed
  torete iru be off

tori *n.* bird
  torikago *n.* bird cage

toriageru *vt.* take up

torihiki *n.* transaction
  torihikizyo *n.* exchange (stock, etc.)

torikaeru *vt.* exchange, replace

torikaesu *vt.* recover

torikesu *vt.* cancel

toru *vt.* take

tosi *n.* age
  tosisita *n.* younger person
  tosiue *n.* older person
  tosiyori *n.* elderly person

tosyokan *n.* library

totemo *adv.* very

toti *n.* land, spot

totuzen (ni) *adv.* suddenly

totyuu *n.* midway

-tu *u. (see* Appendix II)

tubomi *n.* bud (flower)

tubu *n.* grain (corn, etc.)

tugi *n.* next one
  tugi ni *adv.* next
  tugitugi ni (to) *adv.* one after another

tugoo *n.* convenience

tui *adv.* unintentionally

tui ni *adv.* finally

tuide ni *adv.* incidentally

tuitati *n.* first day (of month)

tukamaeru *vt.* capture

tukamaru *vi.* be captured
  tukamatte iru ditto

tukamu *vt.* catch, grab

tukareru *vi.* become tired
  tukarete iru be tired

tukai *n.* messenger
  tukaimiti *n.* use

tukau *vt.* use

tukeru *vt.* fix, put on, etc. *(see* Lessons 20 and 29)

tuki *n.* moon

tukiau *vi.* become friendly with
  tukiai *n.* sociability
  tukiatte iru be friendly with
tuku *vi.* reach, arrive, become attached, accompany, etc. (*see* Lessons 9 and 29)
tukuru *vt.* make, cultivate
  tukurikata *n.* method of making
tuma *n.* wife
tumaranai *a.* frivolous, insignificant
tumari *adv.* in short
tume *n.* nail, claw
tumekomu *vt.* cram in, force in
tumeru *vt.* ditto
tumetai *a.* cold (to touch)
tumi *n.* sin, crime
tumori *n.* intention
tunagu *vt.* tie, link
tuno *n.* horn (deer, etc.)
tureru *vt.* take someone with you
turi *n.* fishing, angling
  turizao *n.* fishing-rod
turu *vt.* fish, angle
tutumi *n.* parcel
tutumu *vt.* wrap, pack
tuti *n.* earth, soil
  tutiiro *n.* earth colour
tuu-ziru *vi.* get through (telephone, etc.), be well acquainted with (a subject)
tuusin *n.* communication
  tuusin suru *vi.*
tuyoi *a.* strong
tuyu *n.* dew
tuzukeru *vt.* continue
tuzuku *vi.* continue
  tuzuite iru be continuous
tya *n.* tea
  tya-iro tea colour, brown
tyanto *adv.* properly
tyawan *n.* rice- or tea-bowl
tyokusetu (ni) *adv.* directly
tyoo (mati) *n.* town (*see* Lesson 23)
  tyootyoo *n.* Town Mayor
tyoo (tyootyoo) *n.* butterfly
-tyoo *u.* (*see* Appendix II)
tyoodo *adv.* just, exactly
tyooku *n.* chalk

-tyoome *u.* (*see* Lesson 23 and Appendix II)
tyoonan *n.* eldest son
tyoosi *n.* tune, condition
tyoosyo *n.* good point
tyotto *adv.* a little, just
-tyuu *suf.* in the course of (gozentyuu, hanasi-tyuu, insatutyuu, keikakutyuu, ryokootyuu, saibantyuu, sensootyuu, zikkentyuu)
tyuugakkoo *n.* middle school
tyuui *n.* attention, note
  tyuui suru *vi.*
tyuumon *n.* order (from shop)
  tyuumon suru *vt.*
tyuusin *n.* centre

ude *n.* arm (limb)
  udedokei *n.* wrist-watch
ue *n.* upper part (*see* Lesson 4)
ueru *vt.* plant
ugokasu *vt.* move, set in motion
ugoku *vi.* move
ukabiagaru *vi.* become afloat
  ukabiagatte iru be afloat
ukabu *vi.* float
ukagau *vt.* visit, ask (*see* Lesson 30)
ukeru *vi.* receive, get
  uketori *n.* receipt
  uketoru *vt.* receive
  uketotte iru have received
uma *n.* horse
umi *n.* sea
umu *vt.* give birth
umareru *vi.* be born
  umarete iru be born
undoo *n.* physical exercise; movement
  undooka *n.* athlete; agitator
  undookai *n.* sport meeting
  undoo suru *vi.* take exercise; agitate
  undoozyoo *n.* playground, playing-field
unten *n.* driving (car, etc.)
  unten suru *vt.*
  untensyu *n.* driver
ura *n.* rear, back
uresii *a.* pleased

uru *vt.* sell
  urite *n.* seller
usi *n.* cow, bull, ox
usiro *n.* back part (*see* Lesson 4)
uso *n.* lie
usui *a.* thin (cloth, etc.,) light (colour)
usugurai *a.* dim
uta *n.* song, poem
utagai *n.* doubt
utagau *vt.* doubt
utau *vt.* sing
uti *n.* inside, home, house
utitukeru *vt.* nail on, drive in
utu *vt.* hit, strike
utukusii *a.* beautiful
uturu *vi.* change position, move (house)
  ututte iru have moved
utusu *vt.* move
uttaeru *vi.* appeal
uwagi *n.* outer clothing

wa *n.* wheel, ring
wa *part.* (*see* Lesson 2)
waisyatu *n.* shirt
wakai *a.* young
wakare *n.* separation
wakareru *vi.* separate, say good-bye
  wakarete iru be separated
wakaru *vi.* be clear, be understandable
wakasu *vt.* boil
wake *n.* reason
wakeru *vt.* divide
waku *vi.* boil
  waite iru have boiled, be boiling
warai *n.* laugh
waraidasu *vi.* burst out laughing
waraigoe *n.* laughter
waraigao *n.* smiling face
warau *vt.* and *vi.* laugh
wari *n.* portion
warui *a.* bad
warukuti *n.* insulting remark
Wasinton *n.* Washington
wasureru *vt.* forget
  wasuremono *n.* thing left behind

wasurete iru have forgotten
wata *n.* cotton
wataru *vi.* cross over
watasi *p.* (*see* Lesson 3)
watasu *vt.* hand over, take across

ya, yaa *int.* expression used before formal greeting
ya- *pref.* eight
  yattu eight
yahari (yappari) *adv.* after all
yakamasii *a.* noisy, fault-finding
yakeru *vi.* burn, bake
  yakete iru have burnt, be burning
yaku *vt.* burn, bake
yaku *n.* duty, office
  yakuba *n.* office (local government)
  yakuin *n.* official
  yakunin *n.* government official
  yakusyo *n.* government office
yakusoku *n.* promise, appointment
  yakusoku suru *vi.*
yakusya *n.* actor, actress
yama *n.* mountain
yameru *vt.* cease, resign, refrain
  yamete iru have left off
yamu *vi.* cease
  yande iru have stopped
yane *n.* roof
yaoya *n.* greengrocer('s)
yarinaosu *vt.* re-do
yaru *vt.* and *vi.* do, give (*see* Lesson 26)
yasai *n.* vegetables
yasasii *a.* easy, gentle, kind
yaseru *vi.* become thin
  yasete iru be thin
yasui *a.* cheap
-yasui *suf.* (*see* Lesson 29)
yasumu *vi.* rest
  yasumi *n.* holiday, vacation
yatto *adv.* finally
yawarakai *a.* soft
yo *int.* expression used to emphasize an assertion
yo- *pref.* four
  yottu *num.* four

yoake *n.* dawn
yobu *vt.* call, invite
yohoo *n.* forecast
yokei na *a.* unnecessary, out of place
yokka *n.* and *adv.* fourth day, four days
yoko *n.* side
  yokogao *n.* profile
yoku *n.* greed
yoku *adv.* (*see* ii)
yominaosu *vt.* re-read
yomu *vt.* read
  yomikata *n.* the manner or method of reading, reading
yon- *pref.* four
yoo na (ni) *a.* (*see* Lesson 20)
yoo *n.* business, what one has to do
  yoozi *n.* ditto
yooka *n.* and *adv.* eighth day, eight days
yoohuku *n.* Western clothes
  yoohukuya *n.* tailor('s)
Yooroppa *n.* Europe
yoosu *n.* appearance, state
yoosiki *n.* style, form
yori *part.* (*see* Lesson 150)
yorokobasu *vt.* please
yorokobi *n.* joy
yorokobu *vi.* rejoice
yorosii *int.* very well then
yoru *n.* night
yoru *vi.* depend upon, become advanced (age), call on
yowai *a.* weak
yu *n.* hot water
yuka *n.* floor
yuki *n.* snow
yukkuri (to) gently, slowly
yume *n.* dream
yunyuu *n.* importation
  yunyuu suru *vt.*
yurumeru *vt.* loosen
yurumu *vi.* loosen
  yurunde iru be loose
yurusi *n.* permit, forgiveness
yurusu *vt.* forgive, permit
yusyutu *n.* exportation
  yusyutu suru *vt.*
yuu *vt. vi.* say

yuubin *n.* mail
  yuubin-gitte *n.* postage-stamp
  yuubinkyoku *n.* post office
yuumei na *a.* famous

zaimoku *n.* timber
zaisan *n.* property, fortune
zannen na *a.* regrettable
zassi *n.* magazine, periodical
zei *n.* tax
  zeikin *n.* taxes
zenbu *n.* the whole
zenzen *adv.* completely
zi *n.* character, letter (of alphabet, etc.)
zibiki *n.* dictionary
zibun *n.* self
zidai *n.* period
zidoosya *n.* motor-car
zidoosiki *a.* automatic
zidooteki (ni) automatically
zikan *n.* time, hour
  -zi(kan) *u.* (*see* Appendix II)
  zikanhyoo *n.* timetable
ziken *n.* incident, affair
zikken *n.* experiment
  zikken suru *vt.*
zimusyo *n.* (unofficial) office
zinan *n.* second son
zinkoo *n.* population
zinzya (zinsya) *n.* Shinto shrine
zisatu *n.* suicide
  zisatu suru *vi.*
zisin *n.* earthquake
zissai *n.* fact
  zissai-mondai *n.* practical problem
  zissai ni *adv.* actually
  zissaiteki na (ni) *a.* (*adv.*) practical(ly)
zitensya *n.* bicycle
zitu *n.* truth
ziyuu *n.* freedom
  ziyuu na *a.* free
  ziyuusyugi *n.* liberalism
  ziyuusyugisya *n.* liberal
  ziyuutoo *n.* Liberal Party
zo emphatic part.
zonziru *vi.* (*see* Lesson 30)
zubon *n.* trousers
zunoo *n.* brains

zutto *adv.* far more

zyama *n.* hindrance
  zyama suru *vt.*

-zyoo *u.* (*see* Appendix II)

zyoobu na *a.* strong, healthy
  zyoobu ni *adv.*

zyoodan *n.* joke

zyooken *n.* condition

zyooki *n.* steam

zyooriku *n.* going ashore, landing
  zyooriku suru *vi.*

zyootoo na *a.* high class

zyoozu na *a.* skilful, good at
  zyoozu ni *adv.*

zyosyu *n.* assistant

zyotyuu *n.* maid servant

zyunsa *n.* policeman

zyunzyo *n.* order, sequence

zyuu *num.* ten

-zyuu *suf.* entire
  (aida-zyuu, aki-zyuu, haru-
    zyuu, hitoban-zyuu, huyu-
    zyuu, itinenzyuu, itinitizyuu,
    karada-zyuu, kuni-zyuu,
    natu-zyuu, sekaizyuu, uti-
    zyuu)

zyuugatu *n.* October

zyuuitigatu *n.* November

zyuunigatu *n.* December

zyuusyo *n.* address, residence

zyuuyaku *n.* company director

INDEX

(Additional references for individual particles and other Japanese words will be found in the Glossary.)

ADVERTISING & PUBLICITY   ALGEBRA   AMATEUR ACTING   AN
BOOK-KEEPING   BRICKWORK   BRINGING UP CHILDREN   BUSIN
CHESS   CHINESE   COMMERCIAL ARITHMETIC   COMMERCIAL A
COMPOSE MUSIC   CONSTRUCTIONAL DETAILS   CONTRACT BRIDG
SPEEDWORDS   ECONOMIC GEOGRAPHY   ECONOMICS   ELEC
ENGLISH GRAMMAR   LITERARY APPRECIATION   ENGLISH RENAS
REVIVAL   VICTORIAN AGE   CONTEMPORARY LITERATURE   ETC
FREELANCE WRITING   FRENCH   FRENCH DICTIONARY   FRENC
LIVING THINGS   GEOLOGY   GEOMETRY   GERMAN   GERMA
GOOD CONTROL OF INSECT PESTS   GOOD CONTROL OF PLANT DIS
GOOD FARMING BY MACHINE   GOOD FARM WORKMANSHIP   GO
GOOD MARKET GARDENING   GOOD MILK FARMING   GOOD PIG
GOOD ENGLISH   GREEK   GREGG SHORTHAND   GUIDEBOOK TO
GREAT   BOLIVAR   BOTHA   CATHERINE THE GREAT   CHATHAM   CL
LIBERALISM   HENRY V   JOAN OF ARC   JOHN WYCLIFFE   LENIN   LOU
ROBES

GIVE INSTRUCTION
TO A WISE MAN ···

HOUS
WRIT
MECH
MOTO
PHYSI
ADMI
PHR   OK   SAILING   SALESMANSHIP   SECRETA
DEBAT   SPELLING   STAMP COLLECTING   STUDE
TYPEWRITING   USE OF GEOGRAPHY   WAY TO POETR
COOKERY FOR GIRLS   DOGS AS PETS FOR BOYS AND GIRLS   KN
PHOTOGRAPHY FOR BOYS AND GIRLS   RADIO FOR BOYS   RIDIN
SOCCER FOR BOYS   STAMP COLLECTING FOR BOYS AND GIRLS
ACTING   ANATOMY   ARABIC   ASTRONOMY   BANKING
CHILDREN   BUSINESS ORGANISATION   CALCULUS   CANASTA
COMMERCIAL ART   COMMERCIAL CORRESPONDENCE   COMME
CONTRACT BRIDGE   COOKING   CRICKET   DRAWING   DRE
ECONOMICS   ELECTRICITY   ELECTRICITY IN THE HOUSE   ELO
ENGLISH RENASCENCE   ENGLISH RENASCENCE TO THE ROMANT
LITERATURE   ETCHING   EVERYDAY FRENCH   TO EXPRESS YOU
DICTIONARY   FRENCH PHRASE BOOK   GARDENING   GAS IN
GERMAN   GERMAN DICTIONARY   GERMAN GRAMMAR   GERM
CONTROL OF PLANT DISEASES   GOOD FARM ACCOUNTING
GOOD FARM WORKMANSHIP   GOOD FRUIT FARMING   GOOD G
GOOD MILK FARMING   GOOD PIG KEEPING   GOOD POULTRY K
GREGG SHORTHAND   GUIDEBOOK TO THE BIBLE   HINDUSTANI
CATHERINE THE GREAT   CHATHAM   CLEMENCEAU   CONSTANTINE C
ARC   JOHN WYCLIFFE   LENIN   LOUIS XIV   MILTON   PERICLES   PETER
USE OF HISTORY   WARREN HASTINGS   WOODROW WILSON   HOC
HOUSEHOLD ELECTRICITY   HOUSE REPAIRS   ITALIAN   JOINER
MANAGEMENT   MATHEMATICS   HAND TOOLS   ENGINEERIN
DRAUGHTSMANSHIP   METEOROLOGY   MODELCRAFT   MODERN D
MUSIC   NORWEGIAN   PERSONAL EFFICIENCY   PHILOSOPHY   PH
SHORTHAND   PLANNING AND DESIGN   PLUMBING   POLISH